T0207189

Communications
in Computer and Information Science   **2124**

Rationale

The CCIS series is devoted to the publication of proceedings of computer science conferences. Its aim is to efficiently disseminate original research results in informatics in printed and electronic form. While the focus is on publication of peer-reviewed full papers presenting mature work, inclusion of reviewed short papers reporting on work in progress is welcome, too. Besides globally relevant meetings with internationally representative program committees guaranteeing a strict peer-reviewing and paper selection process, conferences run by societies or of high regional or national relevance are also considered for publication.

Topics

The topical scope of CCIS spans the entire spectrum of informatics ranging from foundational topics in the theory of computing to information and communications science and technology and a broad variety of interdisciplinary application fields.

Information for Volume Editors and Authors

Publication in CCIS is free of charge. No royalties are paid, however, we offer registered conference participants temporary free access to the online version of the conference proceedings on SpringerLink (http://link.springer.com) by means of an http referrer from the conference website and/or a number of complimentary printed copies, as specified in the official acceptance email of the event.

CCIS proceedings can be published in time for distribution at conferences or as post-proceedings, and delivered in the form of printed books and/or electronically as USBs and/or e-content licenses for accessing proceedings at SpringerLink. Furthermore, CCIS proceedings are included in the CCIS electronic book series hosted in the SpringerLink digital library at http://link.springer.com/bookseries/7899. Conferences publishing in CCIS are allowed to use Online Conference Service (OCS) for managing the whole proceedings lifecycle (from submission and reviewing to preparing for publication) free of charge.

Publication process

The language of publication is exclusively English. Authors publishing in CCIS have to sign the Springer CCIS copyright transfer form, however, they are free to use their material published in CCIS for substantially changed, more elaborate subsequent publications elsewhere. For the preparation of the camera-ready papers/files, authors have to strictly adhere to the Springer CCIS Authors' Instructions and are strongly encouraged to use the CCIS LaTeX style files or templates.

Abstracting/Indexing

CCIS is abstracted/indexed in DBLP, Google Scholar, EI-Compendex, Mathematical Reviews, SCImago, Scopus. CCIS volumes are also submitted for the inclusion in ISI Proceedings.

How to start

To start the evaluation of your proposal for inclusion in the CCIS series, please send an e-mail to ccis@springer.com.

Tomislav Volarić · Boris Crnokić · Daniel Vasić
Editors

Digital Transformation in Education and Artificial Intelligence Application

Second International Conference, MoStart 2024
Mostar, Bosnia and Herzegovina, April 24–26, 2024
Proceedings

 Springer

Editors
Tomislav Volarić ⓘⒹ
Faculty of Science and Education
University of Mostar
Mostar, Bosnia and Herzegovina

Daniel Vasić ⓘⒹ
Faculty of Science and Education
University of Mostar
Mostar, Bosnia and Herzegovina

Boris Crnokić ⓘⒹ
Faculty of Mechanical Engineering,
Computing and Electrical Engineering
University of Mostar
Mostar, Bosnia and Herzegovina

ISSN 1865-0929   ISSN 1865-0937 (electronic)
Communications in Computer and Information Science
ISBN 978-3-031-62057-7   ISBN 978-3-031-62058-4 (eBook)
https://doi.org/10.1007/978-3-031-62058-4

This Springer imprint is published by the registered company Springer Nature Switzerland AG
The registered company address is: Gewerbestrasse 11, 6330 Cham, Switzerland

If disposing of this product, please recycle the paper.

Preface

We are proud to present the proceedings of MoStart 2024: the 2nd International Conference on Digital Transformation in Education and Artificial Intelligence Applications, held from April 24–26, 2024, in Mostar. This event, hosted by the University of Mostar, continued to foster international collaboration and showcase innovative research in AI and digital education.

The conference featured a broad range of topics including computer vision, natural language processing, and the latest advancements in the digital transformation of education. Notably, the application of artificial intelligence, the incorporation of gamification and robotics into learning processes, and innovative technologies such as IoT were thoroughly explored. The event attracted 32 submissions, with 17 high-quality papers selected for presentation after a meticulous single-blind peer review process.

The conference was highlighted by a keynote speech from Professor Koiti Hasida, which provided fascinating insights into practical applications of graphical methods in enhancing critical thinking skills. Additionally, a panel discussion on the integration of artificial intelligence in education offered a platform for in-depth discussions on current challenges and future directions in this field.

A workshop also underscored the importance of collaboration between the University of Mostar and the University of Split, reinforcing the conference's emphasis on academic partnerships.

We extend our heartfelt thanks to the program committee members and all contributors for their vital roles in the conference's success. Our sponsors are also gratefully acknowledged for their support.

Reflecting on MoStart 2024's achievements, we are encouraged by the productive discussions and new connections formed. We look forward to advancing these conversations in future editions of the conference.

Thank you for your participation in MoStart 2024.

April 2024

Daniel Vasić
Tomislav Volarić
Boris Crnokić

Organization

General Chairs

Tomislav Volarić   University of Mostar, Bosnia and Herzegovina
Boris Crnokić   University of Mostar, Bosnia and Herzegovina

Program Committee Chair

Daniel Vasić   University of Mostar, Bosnia and Herzegovina

Steering Committee

Boris Crnokić   University of Mostar, Bosnia and Herzegovina
Tomislav Volarić   University of Mostar, Bosnia and Herzegovina
Mirela Kundid Vasić   University of Mostar, Bosnia and Herzegovina
Krešimir Rakić   University of Mostar, Bosnia and Herzegovina
Davorka Topić Stipić University of Mostar, Bosnia and Herzegovina
Daniel Vasić   University of Mostar, Bosnia and Herzegovina
Damir Vasilj   University of Mostar, Bosnia and Herzegovina
Marin Bošnjak   University of Mostar, Bosnia and Herzegovina
Tin Brdar   Ministry of Science, Education, Culture and Sports, The Herzeg-Bosnian Canton, Bosnia and Herzegovina
Emil Brajković   University of Mostar, Bosnia and Herzegovina
Krešimir Čavar   University of Mostar, Bosnia and Herzegovina
Željko Ćorić   Institute of Education, Mostar, Bosnia and Herzegovina
Snježana Damjanović School Center Martin Nedić (OFM), Orašje, Bosnia and Herzegovina
Josip Doko   University of Mostar, Bosnia and Herzegovina
Goran Dujak   Ministry of Education, Science, Culture and Sports, The Posavina Canton, Bosnia and Herzegovina
Ana Kordić   Ministry of Education, Science, Culture and Sports, The West Herzegovina Canton, Bosnia and Herzegovina

Hrvoje Ljubić	University of Mostar, Bosnia and Herzegovina
Maja Marić	University of Mostar, Bosnia and Herzegovina
Anton Martinović	University of Mostar, Bosnia and Herzegovina
Petar Matić	University of Mostar, Bosnia and Herzegovina
Vedran Mihalj	University of Mostar, Bosnia and Herzegovina
Manlio Napoli	University of Mostar, Bosnia and Herzegovina
Ivan Ostojić	University of Mostar, Bosnia and Herzegovina
Tomislav Papac	University of Mostar, Bosnia and Herzegovina
Ana Pinjuh	University of Mostar, Bosnia and Herzegovina
Karlo Popović	University of Mostar, Bosnia and Herzegovina
Robert Rozić	University of Mostar, Bosnia and Herzegovina
Jelena Skoko	Institute for Upbringing and Education, Bosnia and Herzegovina
Robert Slišković	University of Mostar, Bosnia and Herzegovina
Goran Škvarč	Croatian Academic and Research Network – CARNET, Croatia
Valentina Vidović	Ministry of Science, Education, Youth, Culture and Sports, Bosnia and Herzegovina
Franjo Vučić	University of Mostar, Bosnia and Herzegovina
Selena Knežić Buhovac	University of Mostar, Bosnia and Herzegovina
Inja Stojkić	University of Mostar, Bosnia and Herzegovina

Program Committee

Sanja Bijakšić	University of Mostar, Bosnia and Herzegovina
Mirjana Bonković	University of Split, Croatia
Ivo Čolak	University of Mostar, Bosnia and Herzegovina
Juan Manuel Fernández Luna	University of Granada, Spain
Irena Galić	University of Osijek, Croatia
Sven Gotovac	University of Split, Croatia
Tamara Grujić	University of Split, Croatia
Rainer Herpers	Bonn-Rhein-Sieg University of Applied Sciences, Germany
Branko Katalinić	Vienna University of Technology, Austria
Zdenko Klepić	University of Mostar, Bosnia and Herzegovina
Goran Martinović	University of Osijek, Croatia
Pedro Miguel Moreira	Polytechnic Institute of Viana do Castelo, Portugal
Vladan Papić	University of Split, Croatia
Ljiljana Šerić	University of Split, Croatia
Maja Braović	University of Split, Croatia

Marko Rosić	University of Split, Croatia
Slavomir Stankov	University of Split, Croatia
Zoran Tomić	University of Mostar, Bosnia and Herzegovina
Drago Žagar	University of Osijek, Croatia
Boris Crnokić	University of Mostar, Bosnia and Herzegovina
Malik Čabaravdić	University of Zenica, Bosnia and Herzegovina
Ani Grubišić	University of Split, Croatia
Tonćo Marušić	University of Mostar, Bosnia and Herzegovina
Jonathan Schler	Holon Institute of Technology, Israel
Jan Snajder	University of Zagreb, Croatia
Hrvoje Novak	University of Zagreb, Croatia
Danijel Topić	University of Osijek, Croatia
Tomislav Volarić	University of Mostar, Bosnia and Herzegovina
Branko Žitko	University of Split, Croatia
Krunoslav Žubrinić	University of Dubrovnik, Croatia
Elisabete Cunha	Polytechnic Institute of Viana do Castelo, Portugal
Bárbara Cleto	Polytechnic Institute of Porto, Portugal
Angelina Gašpar	University of Split, Croatia
Janez Gotlih	University of Maribor, Slovenia
Miroslav Grubišić	University of Mostar, Bosnia and Herzegovina
Timi Karner	University of Maribor, Slovenia
Mirela Kundid Vasić	University of Mostar, Bosnia and Herzegovina
Nikola Ljubešić	University of Ljubljana, Slovenia
Željko Marušić	University of Mostar, Bosnia and Herzegovina
Mirza Oruč	University of Zenica, Bosnia and Herzegovina
Ivan Peko	University of Split, Croatia
Krešimir Rakić	University of Mostar, Bosnia and Herzegovina
Višnja Simić	University of Kragujevac, Serbia
Suzana Tomaš	University of Split, Croatia
Daniel Vasić	University of Mostar, Bosnia and Herzegovina
Josip Vasilj	University of Split, Croatia
Nikolina Maleta	University of Mostar, Bosnia and Herzegovina
Lada Maleš	University of Mostar, Bosnia and Herzegovina
Iva Klepić	University of Mostar, Bosnia and Herzegovina

Contents

Advanced Technologies in Education

The Exhibition, Games and Virtual Reality - Technologies in Math Education

Bojan Crnković[iD], Vedrana Mikulić Crnković[(✉)][iD], and Ivona Traunkar[iD]

Faculty of Mathematics, University of Rijeka, Radmile Matejčić 2,
51000 Rijeka, Croatia
{bojan.crnkovic,vmikulic,inovak}@math.uniri.hr

Abstract. Integrating math, computer science and technology into the classroom can improve students' understanding and appreciation of these subjects, and using games to illustrate algorithms is particularly effective in making abstract concepts more concrete and accessible to learners.

The idea behind [ai] explore exhibition is to show the application of math and computer science in solving real-world engineering problems. By presenting visualizations created with the HEDAC algorithm, students can see first-hand how mathematical concepts are used in practical contexts.

The development of two games, [ai] explore game using GeoBoard and a game using micro:bits, to explain the algorithm behind the exhibits is a creative way to reinforce learning. Games have the potential to make learning more interactive and fun, thus increasing student engagement and understanding. In this paper, we describe how new math and engineering results can be explained and turned into a playable game that can be used in the classroom. Finally, we present the results of a short survey among students about their attitudes towards the games presented and the results of the activities carried out.

Keywords: game-based learning · math education · [ai] explore! popular scientific exhibition · technology in mathematical education · virtual reality

1 The Motivation

Mathematics education should promote computational thinking and awareness of the connection between mathematics and computer science. Computational and analytical thinking involves breaking down complex problems into smaller, manageable pieces and developing algorithms to solve them. This skill is crucial in various fields such as math, engineering, and science. The use of algorithms and mathematical principles underlies many scientific concepts. By emphasizing these connections, math classes can provide a more holistic understanding of various disciplines [3].

By incorporating computational thinking into math lessons, teachers foster students' creativity and encourage them to think outside the box when solving

T. Volarić et al. (Eds.): MoStart 2024, CCIS 2124, pp. 3–13, 2024.
https://doi.org/10.1007/978-3-031-62058-4_1

math problems. This often leads to a deeper understanding of mathematical concepts and offers different approaches to solving a particular problem.

Many real-world systems are too complex to understand intuitively. Mathematical modelling, an essential part of scientific research in various fields, allows us to reduce complex problems into simpler components and show how they interact and influence each other. This understanding can reveal underlying patterns and mechanisms that are not apparent through observation alone. By creating mathematical models of real systems, we can make predictions and forecasts about future behaviour. Mathematical modelling is important for problem solving because it improves our understanding of a particular problem and helps predict the behaviour of a system.

The [10] report emphasises that teaching literacy, numeracy and problem-solving skills in technology-rich environments has the potential to innovate and improve teaching and student learning outcomes. For this reason, mathematics education should encourage the use of new technologies such as interactive simulations, dynamic geometry software, and graphing calculators to help students grasp mathematical concepts in ways that were not previously possible. Teachers, on the other hand, often lack these digital skills and avoid using technology and cross-curricular teaching in their classrooms (see [6]). Computer tools and software are powerful instruments for analysis and problem solving. By familiarising students with these tools, mathematics education can prepare them to solve more complex problems and promote their self-efficacy through independent research. However, [1,12] report that the effects of using technology in the mathematics classroom are inconclusive. These findings suggest that the use of technology in the classroom needs to be well thought out and the impact reviewed to ensure that the intended goals are being met. To substantiate this, let us give another example. In [11] the activity Does the robot navigate well in the coordinate system? is developed and described for high school students. The activity was carried out in the classroom and used micro:Maqueen and micro:bit to solve the tasks. After the activity, students completed a short evaluation form and 19/20 students indicated that they would like to work with digital tools more often in mathematics lessons.

Many modern mathematical problems and applications require the use of technology for analysis, simulation and modelling. By incorporating technology into math lessons, students gain experience with tools and techniques that are directly relevant to real-world challenges in fields such as engineering, business, biology and computer science. This hands-on experience bridges the gap between theory and application and helps students understand the relevance of math to the world around them. In today's digital world, mastery of technology is essential for success in many fields. By integrating technology into math classes, students gain valuable skills that directly impact their future professional and academic careers.

We should also teach the mathematical background of many technological innovations and the application of mathematical research in everyday life. By making multiple connections between math and current technology, everyday life and business, we can show that our knowledge and awareness of the world around us depends on mathematical research. By harnessing the power of technology, math teachers can create dynamic and engaging learning environments that prepare students for success in an increasingly digital and data-driven world.

By harnessing the power of technology with the analytical tools of mathematics, we can tackle difficult problems in modern education and drive advances in technology and science.

2 Exhibition, Games and Virtual Reality in Math Education

For many years, the authors of this paper have been developing and implementing various activities aimed at strengthening mathematical literacy, developing computational thinking and raising awareness of the importance of mathematics.

As an introduction to the topic, we will briefly describe some of these activities that have used an interdisciplinary approach, game-based learning and digital tools.

Within the Erasmus+ project InAMath - An interdisciplinary approach to mathematical education [5], many interdisciplinary activities have been developed that connect mathematics and other school subjects in the lower primary grades. Let us name some of them: Secrets of Cryptography - introduction to cryptography through a treasure hunt and the use of micro:Maqueen and micro:bit [9], Day in π rhythm - a collection of activities to celebrate π day and the International Day of Mathematics playing with digital tools [2], Escher meets Arhimed - an activity where students explore tessellation in the plane and create exhibition exhibits using mathematics and 3D printing. For more information on mathematical exhibitions and an example of the Taxicab geometry exhibition in [8] (Fig. 1).

Virtual reality and VR headsets are very interesting topics for students, and we have managed to design and run some activities that combine virtual reality and mathematics. One of them is the lecture on the math behind 360° videos and 360° photos, in which we answer the following questions: what a 360° camera sees, what it captures, what a VR headset shows. We answer these questions by explaining different models of the geometry of the Euclidean plane. We also developed and designed Math Escape - a mathematical escape room where students escape from the virtual space using 3D printed props designed for this activity.

We have recently developed new educational games with educational robots. Many more educational games and game-based teaching activities will be developed as part of the activities in the Eramsus+ project SciMaG - Science&Math educational games from preschool to university [13].

Fig. 1. 360 photo of the Taxicab geometry exhibition

2.1   Exhibition [ai] Explore!

In this section we describe in detail an interdisciplinary activity aimed at explaining the results of scientific research and their application to the interested public and students: Exhibition [ai] explore! (Fig. 2).

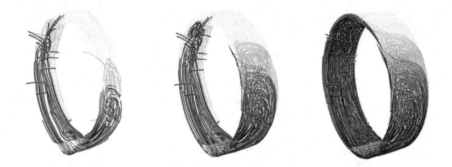

Fig. 2. Example of [ai] explore exhibit

The popular science exhibition [ai] explore! presents visualisations of engineering problems from the field of civil engineering as well as some computationally demanding scientific research examples. The visualisation was created using the mathematical algorithm HEDAC, and the exhibits show the process by which the algorithm learns to recognise objects and explore their shape. The algorithm successfully explores and reproduces real works of art.

The algorithm is based on the scientific work [7]. In the background of the algorithm is a dynamic, autonomous system, i.e. a swarm of agents that moves and explores the given domain. The swarm communicates and coordinates its actions via a changing scalar field, which is obtained as a solution of the heat equation on the given domain. The applications of the algorithm are numerous, and we list only some of them: exploration and search in unknown space, painting, planning of agricultural spraying, scanning of 3D objects, etc.

The popular science exhibition [ai] explore! has been designed to be experienced in different ways: you can walk through the exhibit and enjoy the beautiful paintings, you can walk through the exhibit and try to figure out what engineering problems they show, you can walk through the exhibit and try to figure out how the mathematical algorithm that painted the pictures works, etc. Each exhibit had a QR code behind which the answers to the questions posed above and explanations of the exhibits were hidden.

The exhibits were created in interdisciplinary collaboration between employees of the Faculty of Mathematics and the Faculty of Civil Engineering at the University of Rijeka. The authors of the exhibition are Bojan Crnković, Vedrana Mikulić Crnković, Ivona Traunkar from the Faculty of Mathematics of the University of Rijeka and Nina Čeh, Edita Papa Dukić from the Faculty of Civil Engineering of the University of Rijeka.

The exhibition was presented on the outdoor exhibition panels in the Trsat University Campus in Rijeka (Croatia), on the exhibition panels on the main promenade Korzo in the city centre of Rijeka (Croatia) and in the Moise Palace in Cres (island of Cres, Croatia). You can still experience the exhibition by taking a virtual walk. You can find out more about the exhibition [ai] explore! and the virtual tour prepared for VR headsets at [4]. There you will also find the print-ready exhibits and an explanation of each exhibit, which anyone can use under the Creative Commons Attribution-NonCommercial 4.0 International Licence.

To create an immersive experience, we have also added a 360-degree video showing the application of the HEDAC algorithm on a sphere [14]. We included this video in our activities during the "European Researchers' Night 2023" in Rijeka, and visitors had the opportunity to watch the video using smartphones and VR boxes.

To complement the exhibition, we developed two educational games that illustrate how the mathematical algorithm works: a game using GeoBoard and a game using micro:bits.

2.2 [ai] Explore! Game on GeoBoard

A GeoBoard is a mathematical manipulative board used primarily in elementary and middle school mathematics education to explore concepts in geometry, such as shapes symmetry and the concepts of perimeter and shape area. It consists of a square or rectangular board with a certain number of wooden or metal pegs arranged in an orthogonal grid pattern. The board comes with rubber bands that are stretched around the pegs to create different shapes.

In our version of a board game, we modify the GeoBoard by applying different colours to the pegs (Fig. 3). Each colour is assigned a numerical value. The rules of the game are very simple: connect the starting peg at the top left corner with the bottom right peg by a continuous shortest path with the maximal sum of peg values along the path. We have provided different boards of sizes 8×8 and 11×11 pegs to provide different levels of difficulty for the players. The total number of possible paths is easy to calculate $\binom{2n}{n}$ where n represents the number of pegs in each row or column. We can see that the number of possible paths grows very fast with n, but the number of optimal paths depends on the choice of the board. With our boards, there was only one or possibly two solutions to a given problem, but there were many near-optimal solutions. Several examples of the game and the optimal paths were generated using a computer by adjusting the algorithm used for the [ai] explore! exhibition for this specific purpose.

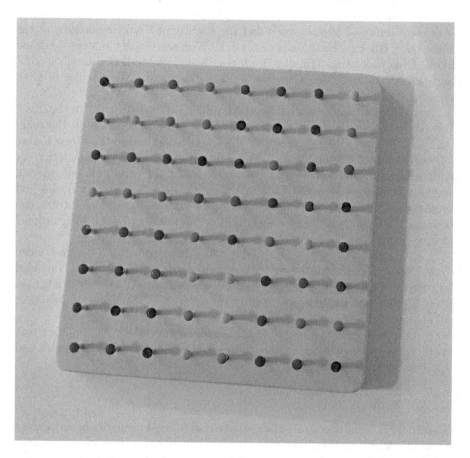

Fig. 3. GeoBoard of size 8×8 prepared for [ai] explore! game

There is also a paper printed version of the same game which is not as practical to use but is very easy to prepare (Fig. 4).

To find optimal solutions for this problem we wrote a Python program in which you can choose the size of the board and the color pallet for the pegs. The program generates all possible shortest paths on the board and calculates the weight of each path by summing up peg values on each path. The program returns a sorted list of weights of all paths from which you can read the optimal solution and the rank of all almost optimal solutions if the player ref Python output (Fig. 4).

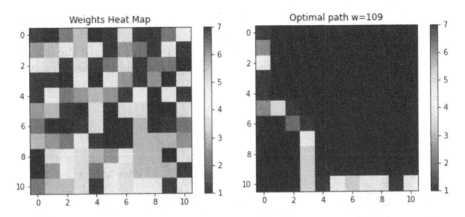

Fig. 4. Geoboard realization on a 11 × 11 grid with 7 colors on the left and optimal path on the right

2.3 [ai] Explore! Game Using Micro:Bits

The micro:bit is a pocket-sized computer that introduces you to the interaction between software and hardware. It has an LED light display with 25 LED lights (arranged in 5 rows and 5 columns), two buttons, sensors and many input/output functions that you can program and physically interact with.

The main goal of this version of the game is to illustrate the algorithm used for the [ai] explore exhibition. We have developed a game that shows the application of the algorithm to catch Pokémons. The playing field is a 5 × 5 board on which the micro:bits are placed at some nodes (see Fig. 6). Each micro:bit on the board indicates the level of heat, which is displayed using LED lights in a level from 1 to 5 (see Fig. 5). The heat levels on the micro:bits indicate the probability that the Pokémonis at that node. The micro:bits are programmed so that the heat rises every 4 s and cools down again by pressing the button on the micro:bit.

The rules of the game are simple: every 4 s (indicated by the sound signal on the main micro:bit (not on the game board) you have to move one step to the next node: to the left, right, up or down, so that you have to move to the nearest hot micro:bit. If there is a micro:bit on the node, you must check whether the Pokémon is there by pressing the button on the micro:bit. The game ends after

Fig. 5. Levels of heat shown on the micro:bit

20 moves (20 beeps). The number of Pokémon collected at the end of the game is displayed on the main micro:bit.

This game can be played with one or more players. Interestingly, the number of Pokémon collected does not need to be increased as the number of players increases.

Fig. 6. [ai] explore! game field

3 Evaluation of the Games

After the presentation of the exhibition and the games, a short survey was conducted among the students about their experiences and attitudes, with each statement being assigned a numerical value depending on how much they agreed with the statement: 1 - strongly disagree; 2 - disagree; 3 - neither agree nor disagree; 4 - agree; 5 - strongly agree. In addition, the students had the opportunity to write down comments in the form of open questions.

On June 13, 2023, after the tour of the exhibition, 23 high school students played [ai] explore! game using micro:bits. The Table 1 shows the results of the survey conducted. There were no negative comments. Several students liked the teamwork and cooperation of the students. A few suggestions were made to make a "bigger" game with more micro:bits and nodes.

Table 1. Results of the conducted survey for [ai] explore! game using micro:bits

Question	1	2	3	4	5	Average
I found the game interesting	0	0	1	7	15	4.61
I would like to play the game again	0	1	5	5	12	4.22
I would recommend the game to friends	0	1	7	4	11	4.09
I understand how the algorithm presented in the game works	0	1	2	3	17	4.57

On September 11, 2023, after visiting the exhibition, 22 high school students played [ai] explore! game using micro:bits and [ai] explore! game on GeoBoard. The Table 2 shows the results of the survey. There were comments, none specific, but all positive.

Table 2. Results of the conducted survey for [ai] explore! game using micro:bits and game on GeoBoard

Question	1	2	3	4	5	Average
I found the game interesting	1	0	5	6	10	4.09
I would like to play the game again	2	3	1	11	5	3.64
I would recommend the game to friends	2	1	4	6	9	3.86
I understand how the algorithm presented in the game works	1	2	2	12	5	3.82

On January 30, 2024, after the short talk about the exhibition, 11 high school students played [ai] explore! game on GeoBoard. The Table 3 shows the results of the survey. There were comments, none specific, but all positive.

Table 3. Results of the conducted survey for [ai] explore! game on GeoBoard

Question	1	2	3	4	5	Average
I found the game interesting	0	0	0	2	9	4.82
I would like to play the game again	0	1	1	3	6	4.27
I would recommend the game to friends	1	0	1	6	3	3.91
I understand how the algorithm presented in the game works	0	0	1	7	3	4.18

[ai] explore! game on GeoBoard was also presented to the visitors of the "European Researchers' Night 2023" in Rijeka. Although they weren't given the possibility to fill out a survey, the reactions and generated interest were truly positive where up to 1000 kids and adults tried the game on their own in five hours of demonstration. We should point out that in this demonstration of the game, we did not explain the connection between the game and the HEDAC algorithm.

4 Conclusions and Plans for Future Work

From the survey results, the general impression is that the students react positively to the games presented.

The results are slightly better when only one game is presented, suggesting that the time allotted for the activities was too short for some students to master both games and both game concepts. This suggests that it is probably better to select one game and develop a few activities that focus on that game rather than switching the game from activity to activity, but this remains to be investigated.

From the reactions of the visitors of the "European Researchers' Night 2023" we conclude that the developed educational game on GeoBoard has good playing characteristics, is very practical and can easily be used in different environments and situations, including classrooms. In addition, we emphasize that most of the students themselves indicate that they have a good understanding of the presented algorithm and how it works. The results of the survey motivate us to continue the development of the [ai] explore! games. Specifically, we will develop teaching scenarios on how the [ai] explore! Game on the GeoBoard can be used as an educational game in mathematics and computer science lessons to teach different content, e.g.: sequences and combinatorics in mathematics, if-else statements, loops and recursion in computer science lessons. In order to evaluate the efficiency of the developed teaching methods using educational games, we plan to develop and conduct research involving the implementation of the teaching scenario in school classrooms.

From the survey results, we conclude that the inclusion of micro:bits and teamwork in the game makes it more interesting for students. On the other hand, implementing a game with digital tools in the classroom can be challenging for teachers in many ways, i.e. they need to have the equipment, the technical knowledge on how to use the equipment, a suitable room for the game, enough space and time in the curriculum, etc. However, the results of the survey motivate us to develop a new, improved version of the game [ai] explore! which includes more digital tools, e.g. micro:bit, micro:Maqueen, HuskyLens - AI Camera, and which we will include in our science outreach activities in the future.

Acknowledgments. The research has been funded by the Erasmus + Programme of the European Union, KA220-SCH - Cooperation partnerships in school education, under the project "Science&Math educational games from preschool to university" (023-1-HR01-KA220-SCH-000165485) and by the University of Rijeka (Croatia) under the project uniri-iskusni-prirod-23-223.

References

1. Cheung, A.C.K., Slavin, R.E.: The effectiveness of educational technology applications for enhancing mathematics achievement in K-12 classrooms: A meta-analysis. Educ. Res. Rev. **9**, 88–113 (2013)
2. Crnković, B.,Mikulić Crnković, V., Rašpolić, L., Traunkar, I.: Međunarodni dan matematike u Pi ritmu, MIŠ: Matematika i škola, 118 (2023)
3. Crnković, B., Mikulić Crnković, V., Traunkar, I.: Development of computational thinking through interdisciplinary activities in mathematics education. In: 9th International Scientific Colloquium Mathematics and Children. Osijek, Croatia (2023)
4. Exhibition [ai] explore - webpage. https://socri.uniri.hr/eng/ai-explore/. Accessed 2 Feb 2024
5. InAMath - An interdisciplinary approach to mathematical education - project webpage. https://inamath.uniri.hr/inamath/. Accessed 2 Feb 2024
6. Istenič, A., Simčič, B., Mikulić Crnković, V., Volk, M.: Croatian elementary school teachers' maths teaching efficacy beliefs: knowledge domains and cross-curricular maths in the post-digital era. SAGE Open, **13(3)** (2023)
7. Ivić, S., Crnković, B., Mezić, I.: Ergodicity-based cooperative multiagent area coverage via a potential field. IEEE Trans. Cybern. **47**(8), 1983–1993 (2017)
8. Mikulić Crnković, V., Mlacović, D., Mrvoš, M.: Kako organizirati matematičku izložbu - izložba Taxi geometrija. Matematika i škola **113** (2022)
9. Mikulić Crnković, V., Traunkar, I., Crnković, B.: Treasure hunt as a method of learning mathematics. In: Proceedings of the 16th European Conference on Games Based Learning, pp. 349–357. Lisbon, Portugal (2022)
10. OECD. (2019). OECD skills outlook 2019: Thriving in a digital world. https://read.oecd-ilibrary.org/education/oecd-skills-outlook-2019_df80bc12-en#page1. Accessed 30 2022
11. Paulić, T.: STEM revolucija u nastavi matematike, finale theses (2023)
12. Reed, H.C., Drijvers, P., Kirschner, P.A.: Effects of attitudes and behaviours on learning mathematics with computer tools. Comput. Educ. **55**, 1–15 (2010)
13. SciMaG - Science&Math educational games from preschool to university - project webpage. https://inamath.uniri.hr/scimag/. Accessed 2 Feb 2024
14. Video HEDAC 360 on YouTube channel of Faculty of Mathematica University of Rijeka. https://www.youtube.com/watch?v=wLpWw_diLIE&t=3s. Accessed 2 Feb 2024

Enhancing Student Discussion Forum Analysis Through Natural Language Processing

Daniel Vasić[1]([✉]) [iD], Slavomir Stankov[2] [iD], and Angelina Gašpar[3] [iD]

[1] Faculty of Science and Education, University of Mostar,
Mostar, Bosnia and Herzegovina
daniel.vasic@fpmoz.sum.ba
[2] Faculty of Science, University of Split, Split, Croatia
slavomir.stankov@pmfst.hr
[3] Catholic Faculty of Theology, University of Split, Split, Croatia
angelina.gaspar@kbf-st.hr

Abstract. Online discussion forums serve as dynamic environments where students and teachers collaboratively generate and utilize a wealth of content for knowledge sharing and assessment. The research involved 18 informatics graduates at the Faculty of Science at the University of Mostar, Bosnia and Herzegovina and two teachers who extracted and analyzed transcripts from an online forum, which was part of the online course "Evaluation of E-Learning Systems (EES)" held on Moodle during the winter semester of the academic year 2022/2023. The paper introduces a novel Natural Language Processing (NLP) approach to evaluating student contributions by contrasting their postings with corresponding instructional materials. Utilizing text similarity measurement, the research addresses key questions: Does the content extracted from individual student postings reflect student knowledge on a given topic? Do similarity scores align with human rankings of contribution relevance? Do students equally benefit from collaborative learning? The research evaluates the efficacy of five multilingual sentence embedding models and integrates human analysis to assess the relevance of students' contributions. Contributions of this study include the evaluation of multilingual sentence embedding models and a thorough examination of the human-perceived relevance of student contributions. The findings aim to enhance the understanding of whether this approach can effectively assess and validate the educational value of student discussions within online forums and contribute to the optimization of collaborative learning experiences.

Keywords: student discussion forum · student contributions · sentence similarity · Sentence Transformer models

The presented results are the outcome of the research project "Enhancing Adaptive Courseware based on Natural Language Processing" undertaken with the support of the United States Office of Naval Research Grant (N00014-20-1-2066).

T. Volarić et al. (Eds.): MoStart 2024, CCIS 2124, pp. 14–26, 2024.
https://doi.org/10.1007/978-3-031-62058-4_2

1   Introduction

Online discussion forum is a unique and dynamic environment where students and teachers both generate and leverage a substantial volume of information. Whereas students find it beneficial for knowledge sharing, peer consultation, problem-solving and trust-building, teachers often use it to assess students, share resources, monitor student progress and engagement, encourage self-directed learning or reuse data in scientific research. Discussion forum is a valuable tool that facilitates active learning, collaboration, and communication in an educational setting. It promotes engagement, critical thinking, and a supportive learning community, benefiting both students and teachers alike. Students can not only absorb information but also construct knowledge collaboratively. Due to the benefits of student discussion forum, it has become an integral component of contemporary online learning environments.

The analysis of student discussion forums can be approached from various perspectives, including both quantitative and qualitative methods. Quantitative analysis quantifies the frequency and consistency of student participation through the number of posts, responses, and the relevance of individual contributions. This approach utilizes content analysis techniques, employing text mining and natural language processing to identify common themes and topics. Qualitative analysis allows for a deeper understanding of the content and context of discussions through identification of recurring themes and patterns. Learning analytics assesses whether active engagement in online discussions correlates with academic performance. It includes time-on-task analysis that examines the time students spend on the discussion forum in relation to their learning outcomes. Sentiment analysis techniques assess the emotional tone of forum posts, i.e. the prevalent sentiments expressed by students, whether positive, negative, or neutral. Technological approach evaluates the usability and accessibility of the discussion forum platform, examining how its features and interface design impact user engagement and satisfaction and how integrated multimedia content (e.g., images, videos) contributes to the overall learning experience.

In our Natural Language Processing (NLP) approach to the discussion forum, the primary goal is to evaluate student contributions. This is achieved by contrasting student-created postings across four discussion boards with instructional material[1] that students were required to master. The research questions addressed include whether the content extracted from individual student postings reflects their knowledge on the given topic, whether obtained similarity scores align with human rankings of the relevance of students' contributions, and whether students equally benefit from collaborative learning. To address these questions, two teachers conducted quantitative and qualitative discussion forum analysis. Subsequently, they employed five Sentence Transformer models to capture semantic similarity between student postings and the instructional materials. Students were explicitly instructed to articulate their opinions and ideas,

---

[1] S. Stankov, D. Vasić: Evaluation of the e-learning system (October 2022 - designed for students enrolled in the EES 22/23 course), Mostar, 2022.

utilizing appropriate terminology from the learning material. The contributions of this paper are as follows: evaluation of five multilingual sentence Transformer models; human analysis of the relevance of students' contributions. After brief Introduction, the review of related work in Sect. 2, followed by Methodology in Sect. 3. Section 4 elaborates on the results and Sect. 5 concludes the paper.

2   Reference Literature

The empirical study on the benefits and difficulties of using online discussion forums from the instructors' point of view [8] revealed strategies and improvements that can be implemented to facilitate their use. An overview of existing NLP methodologies (sentiment annotations, entity annotations, text summarization, and topic modelling) that can be implemented or adopted in education domain indicates their benefits but also challenges in analyzing student feedback in textual format, be it surveys, questionnaires, or a learning management system [3]. An earlier approach to a qualitative analysis of discussion forums was based on text mining technique which used a graph formalism to represent relevant terms and their relationships in a text [5]. In [20] authors used the text and sentiment analysis of university discussion forums to examine the role of meta-cognitive, emotional, and motivational aspects in supporting mentoring process. Another pilot study was conducted to assess students' perception of engagement, higher-order thinking, Bloom's taxonomy, and peer review interaction in utilizing video-based discussion board assignments [4].

In the article [6] authors proposed a new approach to measure the similarity between sentences written in Portuguese using statistical and deep learning features to overcome the meaning problems. A framework proposed by [7] relied on the meaning of a sentence defined by its context, and measured sentence similarity by comparing the probabilities of generating two sentences given the same context. In [2] authors proposed a methodology for estimating pairwise similarities of discussion forum threads. It leveraged their structural information by decomposing them into weighted overlapping components. Linguistic similarity in an algebra discussion forum was analyzed [9] using multi-method approach for feature engineering, the bag-of-words classification model, AI using the local interpretable model-agnostic explanations, and a two-step cluster analysis to extract innate groupings between linguistic similarity and emotion. The results indicated that linguistic similarity within and between the threaded discussions varied significantly and word choice could moderately predict linguistic similarity between posts within threaded discussions. To examine whether the data collected from educational discussion boards can improve the quality of learning and teaching, [10] employed the Latent Semantic Analysis (LSA), a statistical model to establish the relationship between the set of messages published by students and a course content students had to master. The students' opinions about problematic educational issues were analyzed by sentiment analysis techniques.

Another commonly used NLP technique is text similarity measurement, which helps assess the likeness or relatedness between two or more sentences by examining their content and structure. This method is often employed to match or group similar sentences, enabling the extraction of meaningful information from a given text. However, the majority of current sentence embedding models are designed for English or extended English model to other languages, given the limited availability of training data for less-resourced languages such as Croatian. Reimers and Gurevych [12] developed Sentence-BERT (SBERT), a modification of the pretrained BERT network that use siamese and triplet network structures to derive semantically meaningful sentence embeddings that can be compared using cosine-similarity (measuring the angle between two vectors). Reimers and Gurevych [11] also extended the existing monolingual sentence embedding model to 50+ languages. The training was based on the idea that vector spaces are aligned across languages, i.e., identical sentences in different languages are close. So, a translated sentence should be mapped to the same location in the vector space as the original sentence.

To examine whether multilingual sentence Transformer LaBSE could be a strong multilingual word aligner, in the article [13] authors proposed to finetune LaBSE on parallel corpus. Experimental results on seven language pairs showed that their AccAlign, a more accurate multilingual word aligner with the multilingual sentence Transformer LaBSE outperforms previous state-of-the-art models. Nevertheless, recent research has identified inherent constraints in multilingual transformers. In the article [14] note that enhancing a model's cross-lingual performance by pre-training it with an expanding array of languages only yields improvements up to a certain threshold. Beyond this point, observable drops in performance occur—a phenomenon commonly referred to as the curse of multilinguality. In addition to this problem, recent studies have reported significantly lower cross-lingual and monolingual capabilities in models designed for low-resource languages with limited pre-training data such as Croatian [15,16]. Transformers commonly face limitations with long sequences, primarily stemming from their quadratic attention complexity concerning the number of tokens. Typically, only the initial 512 tokens are utilized, and any subsequent ones are discarded. The simplest approach to handling long sequences involves truncating them at the maximum sequence length supported by the model [17]. In the article [19] authors highlight two challenges in existing methods for measuring sentence similarity: limited labeled datasets for training supervised neural models and a training-test gap for unsupervised language modeling (LM) models, which affect semantic score computation between sentences. The proposed framework addresses these challenges by emphasizing that a sentence's meaning is defined by its context. It measures sentence similarity by comparing the probabilities of generating two sentences with the same context. Vasić and Brajković [18] introduced a model designed for the generation of word embeddings in morphologically complex Croatian language. The efficacy of the produced word embeddings was assessed through an evaluation on a word similarity corpus (WordSim353-hr). The model demonstrated inferior performance attributed to the loss of word order.

3   Methodology

Transcripts were extracted from an online forum created by 18 graduates of informatics (Faculty of Science at the University of Mostar, Bosnia and Herzegovina) and two teachers. There were five male and 13 female graduates. The forum was part of the online course "Evaluation of E-Learning Systems (EES)" held on Moodle (moodle.com) during the winter semester of the academic year 2022/2023. The course included 13 online classes and two in-person sessions with the Moodle forum, organized into four boards for peer-to-peer consultations on specific topics. Each board focused on a distinct topic: Board 1 covered the introduction to CMap Tools and Memory platforms, as well as instructional material selection; Board 2 involved collaborative student tentative course design on joint CMap Cloud & Memory platform; Board 3 addressed the introduction to evaluation criteria and sub-criteria), while Board 4 focused on course design evaluation and peer feedback. Students were instructed to ensure their postings were clear and concise, meticulously choosing words that most effectively expressed their thoughts on the assigned topics. Additionally, they were required to divide into three groups of six students and coordinate peer-led discussions. Teaching sessions took place on e-learning platforms, focusing on the utilization of concept maps through tools such as CMap Tools (cmap.ihmc.us) and CMap Cloud (cmapcloud.ihmc.us), along with the integration of digital flashcard technology using Memory (memory.com).

To assess the equality of student benefit from collaborative learning and to investigate the alignment between text similarity scores and human rankings of student contributions, text similarity measurement was employed. Here's the passage rewritten in the passive voice, focusing on clarity and conciseness: Following data preprocessing (lemmatization, tokenization, and removal of stopwords, HTML tags, punctuation, URLs, and emojis), semantic similarity between individual student discussions and instructional materials was measured. Five SentenceTransformer models (distilluse-base-multilingual-cased-v1, distilluse-base-multilingual-cased-v2, paraphrase-multilingual-MiniLM-L12-v2, paraphrase-multilingual-mpnet-base-v2, LaBSE), trained on multilingual parallel data including Croatian, were employed for this analysis. These models identify semantically similar sentences within and across languages. The models convert student-generated sentences into meaningful vector representations, comparing them against the vectors of the reference text to calculate similarity scores for each sentence within its context. Individual student discussions were initially compared with the entire instructional material for each board. Subsequently, the discussions were filtered to ensure data relevance and accuracy, comparing them with instructional material for each board summarized to 20 sentences using ChatGPT 4.0. Models applied to summarized versions of instructional materials bear extensions, such as LaBSE_v2, Dist_v1_2. To improve clarity, irrelevant information such as forum headers, post counts, posting times, and similar metadata was removed through the implementation of a filtering method. This dual approach offered a robust framework for analyzing and comparing student discussions, closely aligning with the educational goals and content of the course. Aggregated scores provided insights into patterns of consistent high performers, students showing improvement, and those potentially in need of additional instructional attention.

4   Results

A combination of quantitative and qualitative analyses was employed to validate the findings and offer a comprehensive understanding of the problem.

4.1   Quantitative Analysis

All postings on the forum were analyzed comprehensively, with no filters applied. As illustrated in Table 1, eleven students demonstrated remarkable engagement by initiating one, two, or three threads, accounting for a total of 15 threads. Collectively, all 18 students contributed to the forum, generating 269 postings, and employing 17,988 words. Students who initiated threads exhibited significantly higher activity levels, contributing 183 postings, compared to their peers who contributed only 86 postings. In contrast, teachers took on the roles of moderators and facilitators by initiating 17 threads and contributing 47 postings, utilizing a total of 3,031 words.

The analysis of discussion forum activity per board, detailed in Table 2, provides insights into the extent of engagement manifested by students and teachers in generating discussion threads. In Board 1, students initiated 36 postings, complemented by 14 contributions from teachers. Student-generated postings comprised a total of 428 words, slightly surpassed by teachers with a word count of 572. In Board 2, students exhibited significantly higher engagement, generating 223 contributions, while teachers contributed only 19 postings. This high engagement is reflected in the substantial word count, with students employing 6117 words compared to the 1107 words used by teachers. Board 3 observed 98 contributions from students and 22 teacher postings, with student-generated content totaling 7068 words and teacher contributions amounting to 1063 words. Board 4 had 71 contributions from students and 11 teacher postings, with students utilizing 4474 words and teachers using 190 words. The highest level of student engagement was observed in Board 2, while Board 1 demonstrated the lowest level of student participation. The varying degrees of student engagement across discussion boards can have implications for instructional strategies and the facilitation of effective online discourse.

4.2   SentenceTransformer Models

To further assess the educational value and relevance of student contributions, we utilized five Sentence Transformer models. These models, through an understanding of the contextual meaning and relationships within words, phrases, and sentences, generate a numerical representation of semantic similarity. Our objective was to ascertain whether the derived similarity scores align with the human

Table 1. Discussion threads per student/teacher

No.	Student	Discussion thread No.	Reply No.	Word count
1	Student1	3	21	1298
2	Student16	2	32	2883
3	Student10	2	20	1273
4	Student2	1	16	1052
5	Student17	1	19	1036
6	Student18	1	16	955
7	Student5	1	13	905
8	Student7	1	19	802
9	Student4	1	9	787
10	Student12	1	7	541
11	Student8	1	11	295
12	Student14	0	8	1578
13	Student6	0	14	1057
14	Student3	0	19	1034
15	Student15	0	12	997
16	Student11	0	13	694
17	Student13	0	8	456
18	Student9	0	12	345
Total		15	269	17988
Teacher1		1	4	278
Teacher2		17	43	2753
Total		18	47	3031
Overall		33	316	21019

ranking of student contributions and whether collaborative learning was beneficial for students. The results presented in Table 3 illustrate the similarity scores computed for each student using Sentence Transformer models. Each row in the table corresponds to a specific student, whose identity remains anonymized, while the columns display the similarity values obtained from the five models. For each model, there are two columns: the first indicates the similarity scores derived by comparing student postings with the entire instructional material for the individual board, and the second relates to the comparison of student postings in the individual board with the summarized version of the instructional material.

The highest similarity score, at 0,66, was computed by the dist_v1 2 model for Student 8, followed by equal scores of 0,56 obtained by LaBSE and dist_v1 models for Student 17 and Student 8, respectively. Slightly lower scores of 0,55 and 0,53 were computed by minlm_v2 2 (Student 8) and mpnet_v2 2 (Student

Table 2. Discussion forum analysis per board

Board	Thread	Contribution per thread		Word count per thread	
		student	teacher	student	teacher
Board 1	Teacher2 - Difficulty working with CMap Tools	0	3	0	62
	Teacher1 - forum discussion dynamic	16	2	65	55
	Teacher2 - Checking on CMap Tools installation	10	4	186	148
	Teacher2 - assignment on Memory - completion	0	2	0	171
	Teacher2 - Memory ongoing activity	2	1	35	41
	Student7 - Question - the completion of the assignment	4	1	43	61
	Student2 - Question-time spent on Moodle	4	1	99	34
	Total	**36**	**14**	**428**	**572**
Board2	Teacher2 - on the use of CMapCloud&Memory platforms	26	2	329	228
	Teacher2 - learning materials, learning objectives, autonomous group formation	44	8	2044	506
	Student1 - Scratch-brief introduction	51	6	1061	95
	Teacher2 - the use of flashcards	2	2	24	169
	Student12 - First steps in computer work-brief introduction	33	0	339	0
	Student16 - Weaving the Web-brief introduction	67	0	2320	0
	Teacher2 - comment on Weaving the Web	0	1	0	109
	Total	**223**	**19**	**6117**	**1107**
Board3	Teacher2 - evaluation criteria, Python programming	0	1	0	79
	Teacher2 - group work	48	9	549	439
	Teacher2 - evaluation criteria and sub-criteria selection and argumentation	42	2	6247	26
	Teacher2 - ongoing group work, assignment deadline	0	2	0	148
	Teacher2 - support, problem solving	6	6	216	290
	Teacher2 - dis16 - ongoing work instruction	2	2	56	81
	Total	**98**	**22**	**7068**	**1063**
Board4	Teacher2 - Application of evaluation criteria - Initial discussion	0	2	0	37
	Student10 - Data files - Initial discussion	9	0	652	0
	Student17 - Data types - Initial discussion	10	0	876	0
	Student1 - Array, function, methods, example - Initial discussion	5	1	144	7
	Student16 - Algorithm - Initial discussion	15	2	1001	68
	Student18 - Procedures and functions - Initial discussion	11	3	822	53
	Student10 - Data files, task correction	4	0	88	0
	Student8 - Operators, expressions, variables - Initial discussion	7	2	169	18
	Student5 - Basic concepts and debugging in the program - Initial discussion	10	1	722	7
	Total	**71**	**11**	**4474**	**190**

4), respectively. LaBSE and LaBSE 2 models showed nuanced differences in similarity values, while overall scores obtained by the dist_v1 2 model outperformed those obtained by dist_v1. Conversely, overall similarity scores obtained by dist_v2 and dist_v2 2 models were the lowest. Figure 1 shows similarity scores per student and model.

Figure 2 illustrates the average similarity score per student. The highest average similarity scores were achieved by Student 8, Student 4, Student 17, Student 14, and Student 15, whereas Student 9 had the lowest average similarity score.

Table 3. Similarity score per student and model

Student	LaBSE	LaBSE _2	Dist _v1	Dist _v1_2	Dist _v2	Dist _v2_2	minlm _v2	minlm _v2_2	mpnet _v2	mpnet _v2_2
1	0.46	0.44	0.37	0.41	0.16	0.13	0.23	0.26	0.19	0.27
2	0.39	0.40	0.37	0.42	0.11	0.08	0.25	0.30	0.28	0.33
3	0.48	0.45	0.33	0.42	0.10	0.10	0.37	0.39	0.27	0.31
4	0.46	0.43	0.52	0.59	0.34	0.29	0.43	0.47	0.46	0.53
5	0.46	0.46	0.45	0.55	0.14	0.19	0.25	0.33	0.23	0.33
6	0.51	0.52	0.43	0.52	0.19	0.27	0.25	0.37	0.24	0.37
7	0.47	0.44	0.34	0.43	0.21	0.14	0.21	0.26	0.21	0.30
8	0.42	0.45	0.56	0.66	0.27	0.35	0.46	0.55	0.39	0.51
9	0.30	0.32	0.39	0.46	0.08	0.06	−0.05	0.01	−0.10	−0.08
10	0.46	0.45	0.36	0.44	0.22	0.19	0.28	0.32	0.28	0.35
11	0.49	0.49	0.37	0.46	0.21	0.19	0.29	0.33	0.28	0.34
12	0.44	0.42	0.37	0.46	0.32	0.25	0.36	0.39	0.22	0.30
13	0.43	0.42	0.32	0.38	0.18	0.17	0.16	0.22	0.20	0.29
14	0.39	0.40	0.36	0.47	0.28	0.25	0.34	0.40	0.37	0.46
15	0.47	0.43	0.40	0.47	0.36	0.26	0.31	0.33	0.30	0.36
16	0.37	0.34	0.37	0.46	0.18	0.19	0.27	0.31	0.22	0.31
17	0.56	0.51	0.40	0.47	0.42	0.31	0.32	0.41	0.45	0.50
18	0.42	0.44	0.30	0.44	0.13	0.19	0.07	0.20	0.21	0.33

Legend: LaBSE, dist_v1 - distilluse-base-multilingual-cased-v1, dist_v2 - distilluse-base-multilingual-cased-v2, minim_v2 - paraphrase-multilingual-MiniLM-L12-v2, mpnet_v2 - paraphrase-multilingual-mpnet-base-v2.

The results indicate that students employed diverse strategies in approaching the discussion forum, as reflected in their similarity scores. Despite this variation, the majority of students demonstrated comparable average similarity scores, suggesting relevance and potential benefits from collaborative learning. Chart 2 displays similarity scores obtained per student and model. Models LaBSE and LaBSE_2 exhibit minimal variations in similarity scores among individual students, followed by models Dist_v1 and Dist_v1_2. In contrast, other models demonstrate more disparate similarity results for individual students. To ensure the reliability of the models in analyzing semantic similarity of student postings with instructional materials, a Pearson coefficient correlation analysis was conducted. High correlations between specific models indicate consistency in sentence analysis, while moderate correlations suggest unique approaches by individual models, providing insights into their distinctiveness. LaBSE shows a moderate to strong correlation with other models, particularly with mpnet_v2 (0.59). Dist_v1 exhibits a moderate correlation with minlm_v2 (0.59). Dist_v2 demonstrates a strong correlation with both minlm_v2 and mpnet_v2 (over 0.70). Minlm_v2 and mpnet_v2 display a very high correlation (0.85), indicating a significant level of consistency in their ratings. LaBSE 2 exhibits a moderate correlation with other models, with the strongest correlation observed with mpnet_v2 2 and minlm_v2 2 (0.50). Dist_v1 2 and Dist_v2 2 display a strong correlation with each other (0.72), signifying similarity in their ratings. Minlm_v2 2 and mpnet_v2 2 reveal a very high correlation (0.90), suggesting remarkably similar similarity scores. The robust correlation between minlm_v2 and mpnet_v2 models implies a shared approach to text analysis, rendering them consistent in their assessment of similarity.

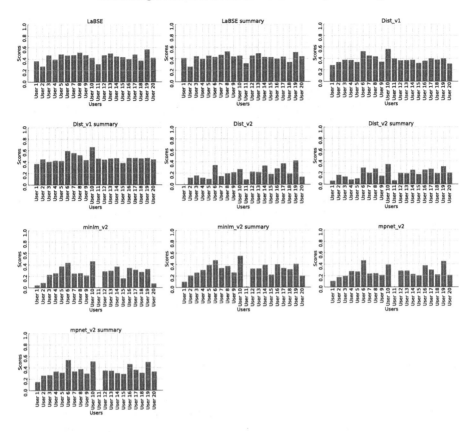

Fig. 1. Similarity scores per student as evaluated by employed models

4.3   Qualitative Analysis

Boards 2, 3, and 4, which exhibited high student engagement, were subsequently analyzed. This analysis yielded a total of 392 student-created contributions. Considering both the quality of initiated discussions and replies, Student1 was the most active and engaged participant, followed by Student 16 and Student 6. The educational value of contributions generated by Student 10, Student 17 and Student 2 was also remarkable as they demonstrated critical thinking, knowledge of the assigned topic and skillful guidance of the discussion. Both students and teachers showed their agreement or disagreement with posted ideas, elaborated on their arguments, or asked questions or clarification, etc. Students that initiated discussions not only provided useful information in the forum but also strong and relevant arguments when commenting on their peers' postings. Their critical thinking skills influence the quality and educational value of their postings. By reading and commenting on their peer's postings, students could also identify their own weaknesses such as deficiencies in clear writing skills, discussion skills, or a reluctance to make mistakes. Some students were hesitant or lacked knowledge to criticize their peers, so they mostly replied to those with

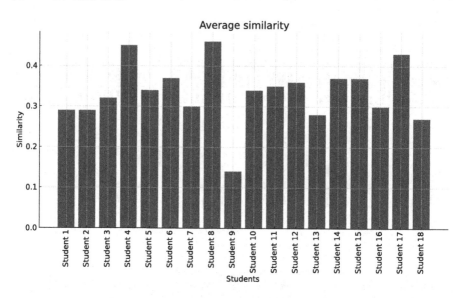

Fig. 2. Average similarity score per student.

whom they agreed. Student 7, Student 8, Student12, Student 13 and Student 14 were rather passive, and their postings were of a lower quality. While Student 8 and Student 14 provided relevant educational content, they failed to address the specific topic. Given that the discussion forum was a non-graded component of the course, students enjoyed complete autonomy in their decision-making processes, self-organization within groups, problem-solving efforts, and the evaluation of the trustworthiness of peer-provided information. The analysis of individual student engagement and contributions can enhance the quality of the online discussion environment. The highest average similarity scores were achieved by Student 8, Student 4, Student 17, Student 14, and Student 15, whereas Student 9 had the lowest average similarity score. However this ranking of students with the highest average similarity scores differs significantly from the rankings provided by the two teachers. Teachers' top ranking students were: Student 1, Student 16, Student 6, Student 10, Student 17 and Student 2. This disparity in perceived teachers' perception on student contributions and their similarity scores obtained by Sentence Transformer models indicate that models do not perform optimally when dealing with the education domain. Undoubtedly, variations in writing style, communication skills, and terminology may impact the accuracy of similarity scores.

5   Conclusion

Quantitative analysis revealed varying levels of engagement among students, with student-led discussion significantly impacting their participation. Overall, student contribution was considerable since they generated 428 postings and used 18,087 words. In contrast to students, teachers played more of a guiding role, focusing on moderating and facilitating discussions rather than actively contributing content. The discussion forum was a non-graded component, granting students autonomy in decision-making, self-organization, problem-solving, and the evaluation of peer-provided information. A slight variation in students' scores suggests that their discussions were relevant and that they likely benefited from collaborative learning. The difference between teachers' perceived views of student contributions and the similarity scores generated by Sentence Transformer models suggests that these models are not ideal for tasks related to the education domain. Neither model produces outcomes that match with human assessments of the similarity between individual student discussions and instructional materials. Developing a multilingual model demands substantial computational resources and data, posing a challenge for researchers working with less resourced languages, such as Croatian. Clearly, variations in writing style, communication abilities, and use of terminology might affect the precision of similarity scores.

Combining these metrics with other natural language processing techniques or considering domain-specific metrics might enhance the overall analysis of student interactions in a discussion forum. Since all students successfully completed the course, it can be inferred that value was derived from peer interactions, support, and information exchange facilitated by the teachers. This research is constrained by a smaller sample size of students. Nonetheless, this limitation also serves as a facilitating factor, making the analysis and manipulation of data from student discussions more manageable. Subsequent efforts will concentrate on refining the online discussion environment and enhancing assessment strategies for greater effectiveness.

Acknowledgments. The presented results are the outcome of the research project "Enhancing Adaptive Courseware based on Natural Language Processing" undertaken with the support of the United States Office of Naval Research Grant (N00014-20-1-2066).

References

1. Koloski, B., Pollak, S., Škrlj, B., Martinc, M.: Extending neural keyword extraction with TF-IDF tagset matching. In: Proceedings of the EACL Hackashop on News Media Content Analysis and Automated Report Generation, Kiev, Ukraine, pp. 22–29 (2021)
2. Singh, A., Deepak, P., Raghu, D.: Retrieving similar discussion forum threads: a structure based approach. In: Annual International ACM SIGIR Conference on Research and Development in Information Retrieval (2012)
3. Shaik, T., et al.: A review of the trends and challenges in adopting natural language processing methods for education feedback analysis, arXiv:2301.08826v1 [cs.CL] (2023)
4. Hamadi, H., Tafili, A., Kates, F.R.: Exploring an innovative approach to enhance discussion board engagement. TechTrends **67**, 741–751 (2023). https://doi.org/10.1007/s11528-023-00850-0

5. Azevedo, B.F.T., Behar, P.A., Reategui, E.: Qualitative Analysis of Discussion Forums (2011)
6. Pinheiro, A., Ferreira, R., Ferreira, M.A.D., Rolim, V.B., Tenório, J.V.S.: Statistical and semantic features to measure sentence similarity in Portuguese. In: Proceedings 2017 Brazilian Conference on Intelligent Systems (BRACIS), Uberlandia, Brazil, pp. 342–347 (2017). https://doi.org/10.1109/BRACIS.2017.40
7. Sun, X., et al.: Sentence similarity based on contexts. Trans. Assoc. Comput. Linguist. **10**, 573–588 (2022). https://doi.org/10.1162/tacl_a_00477
8. De Lima, D.P., Gerosa, M.A., Conte, T.U., et al.: What to expect, and how to improve online discussion forums: the instructors' perspective. J. Internet Serv. Appl. **10**, 1–15 (2019). https://doi.org/10.1186/s13174-019-0120-0
9. Banawan, M.P., Shin, J., Arner, T., Balyan, R., Leite, W.L., McNamara, D.S.: Shared language: linguistic similarity in an algebra discussion forum. Computers **12**(3), 53 (2023). https://doi.org/10.3390/computers12030053
10. Zarra, T., Raddouane, C., Rdouan, F., El Afia, A.: Using textual similarity and sentiment analysis in discussions forums to enhance learning. Int. J. Softw. Eng. Appl. **10**, 191–200 (2016)
11. Reimers, N., Gurevych, I.: Making monolingual sentence embeddings multilingual using knowledge distillation. In: Proceedings of the 2020 Conference on Empirical Methods in Natural Language Processing (2020)
12. Reimers, N., Gurevych, I.: Sentence-BERT: sentence embeddings using Siamese BERT-networks. In: Proceedings of the 2019 Conference on Empirical Methods in Natural Language Processing (2019)
13. Weikang, W., Guanhua, C., Hanqing, W., Yue, H., Yun, C.: Multilingual sentence transformer as a multilingual word aligner *arXiv* (2023)
14. Conneau, A., et al.: Unsupervised cross-lingual representation learning at scale. In: Proceedings of the 58th Conference of the Association for Computational Linguistics, ACL 2020, Virtual Conference, July 6-8, 2020, pp. 8440–8451 (2020)
15. Lauscher, L., Ravishankar, V., Vulic, I., Glavaš, G.: From zero to hero: on the limitations of zero-shot language transfer with multilingual Transformers. In: Proceedings of the 2020 Conference on Empirical Methods in Natural Language Processing (EMNLP), pp. 4483–4499, Online (2020b)
16. Artetxe, M., Ruder, S., Yogatama, D.: On the cross-lingual transferability of monolingual representations. In: Proceedings of the 58th Annual Meeting of the Association for Computational Linguistics, pp. 4623–4637, Online. Association for Computational Linguistics (2020)
17. Abadaoui, A., Dutta, S.: Attention over pre-trained Sentence Embeddings for Long Document Classification, ReNeuIR 2023. In: Workshop on Reaching Efficiency in Neural Information Retrieval, arXiv:2307.09084v1 [cs.CL] (2023)
18. Vasić, D., Brajković, E.: Development and evaluation of word embeddings for morphologically rich languages. In: Proceedings 2018 26th International Conference on Software, Telecommunications and Computer Networks (SoftCOM), Split, Croatia, pp. 1–5 (2018). https://doi.org/10.23919/SOFTCOM.2018.8555822
19. Xiaofei, S., et al.: Sentence similarity based on contexts. Trans. Assoc. Comput. Linguist. **10**, 573–588 (2022). https://doi.org/10.1162/tacl_a_00477
20. Kuzilek, J., Zdrahal, Z., Vaclavek, J., Fuglik, V., Skocilas, J.: Exploring exam strategies of successful first year engineering students. In: Proceedings of the Tenth International Conference on Learning Analytics & Knowledge (LAK 2020), Frankfurt, Germany, pp. 124-128. Association for Computing Machinery, New York, NY, USA (2020). https://doi.org/10.1145/3375462.3375469

Artificial Intelligence in Elementary Math Education: Analyzing Impact on Students Achievements

Ana Bešlić[1]([✉])[iD], Josip Bešlić[2][iD], and Dina Kamber Hamzić[3][iD]

[1] Osnovna škola Ivana Mažuranića, Šimuna Čuture 16,
88240 Posušje, Bosnia and Herzegovina
`annaostojic@gmail.com`
[2] Superclever LLC, 16192 Coastal Highway Lewes, Lewes, DE 19958, USA
`josip.beslic@superclever.com`
[3] Faculty of Science, University of Sarajevo, Zmaja od Bosne 33-35,
71000 Sarajevo, Bosnia and Herzegovina
`dinakamber@pmf.unsa.ba`

Abstract. The study investigates the impact of integrating Artificial Intelligence (AI) in teaching mathematics to seventh-grade students, typically aged 12–13, focusing on the chapter about integer numbers. It explores how AI can revolutionize traditional teaching methods by providing innovative, engaging, and personalized learning experiences. Through an experimental design involving control and experimental groups, the research aims to uncover the benefits and limitations of AI in education, offering insights and practical guidelines for its effective integration into teaching practices. The broader implications for education suggest that AI could be beneficial in various segments of the educational process, not only in terms of improving the understanding of specific subjects but also in preparing students for a job market increasingly reliant on AI. This perspective encourages a comprehensive view of the educational process, beyond singular outcomes, and opens avenues for further research and application of evolving AI models like large language models. The study concludes by highlighting the importance of continuing to explore new paths for education and other segments of human activity through the application of rapidly evolving AI technologies.

Keywords: Artificial Intelligence · Math Education · Integer Numbers

1 Introduction

The increasing integration of Artificial Intelligence (AI) into educational processes is opening new doors in pedagogy, offering innovative approaches to teaching and learning. This research focuses on a specific segment of education-the teaching of mathematics to seventh graders, with special emphasis on the chapter

T. Volarić et al. (Eds.): MoStart 2024, CCIS 2124, pp. 27–40, 2024.
https://doi.org/10.1007/978-3-031-62058-4_3

of Integer Numbers. In a context where traditional teaching methods are increasingly finding their limits, AI, particularly through tools like ChatGPT, represents a promising avenue that could revolutionize how students approach and understand mathematical concepts, but potential negative effects must also be identified [33]. Through an experimental design that involves dividing students into control and experimental groups and conducting pre- and post-tests, we aim to provide insights into the potential benefits and limitations of using AI in an educational setting. This study not only strives to contribute to the academic discourse on the use of AI in education but also aims to offer practical guidelines for teachers and educational policymakers in integrating AI tools into curricula.

In recent times, the education sector is facing a significant challenge due to the dwindling number of teachers in STEM fields, including mathematics, natural sciences, and computer science. This shortage poses a critical threat to the quality and continuity of STEM education, which is pivotal for cultivating future innovators and technologists. AI emerges as a potential solution to bridge this gap by supplementing or, in certain cases, substituting traditional teaching methodologies [12]. However, harnessing AI's full potential in education requires comprehensive research and development to ensure that AI-driven teaching tools can autonomously conduct lessons effectively and empathetically, aligning with pedagogical standards and catering to diverse learning needs.

The methodology of this research is designed to consider every aspect of the student experience, from their initial reaction to ChatGPT to the long-term impact on their understanding of mathematical concepts. Through a detailed analysis and synthesis of the collected data, this study seeks to contribute to the broader debate on the role of technology in education, specifically on how AI can serve as a powerful tool for fostering deeper engagement and motivation among students.

AI has become a staple in our daily lives, and as time progresses, its presence will expand across a broader spectrum of human endeavors. As educators, when we chose this profession, we understood that adapting our methodologies to emerging trends would be essential.

The use of various technologies in teaching has been a fact for a long time [3]. Traditional tools like the blackboard and chalk, while having made a significant impact on many generations, are no longer central to contemporary educational practices. There are now tools whose effects must surpass those of blackboards and chalk, along with other aids that are becoming obsolete. The aim of this study is to explore these modern tools within the educational context and to assess their contributions to the learning process. Our students have changed radically. Today's students are no longer the people our educational system was designed to teach. The aim of our work is to find a better approach than what we currently have [26]. The hypothesis of this study is that the learning process with AI should be more effective than traditional methods, and the auxiliary hypothesis posits that learning with AI tools leads to better outcomes compared to traditional teaching methods. The structure of this paper is as follows: the second chapter presents a review of the literature, the third chapter describes the conducted experiment and the methods used, and the fourth chapter presents and analyzes the results of the research.

2   Theoretical Framework

2.1   Review of Related Works

Given the increasing popularity of using AI in education, this study explores the impact of 10-min sessions with large language models for text generation [2,6,7,10,14,16,18,19,21,23,32,35–37,39,40], integrated with an avatar, on enhancing student achievements in seventh-grade mathematics classes. The goal is to investigate whether regular interaction with this AI tool, both in the classroom and at home, can improve students' understanding of integer numbers, a topic that often poses a challenge for many students. In addition to providing new tools and methods for personalized learning, AI has the potential to enhance student engagement and offer additional support, thereby fundamentally transforming education. Adaptive educational environments enabled by AI can cater to the individual needs and learning styles of each student, personalizing the learning experience and increasing its effectiveness. Moreover, interactive and visually appealing platforms that utilize AI can generate greater student interest in mathematics, making learning not only more effective but also more enjoyable [5,28,33,34]. AI can assist students in gaining a deeper understanding of integer number concepts through visualizations and interactive manipulations [22].

However, it is important to emphasize that AI cannot fully replace the role of the teacher [4,8].Teachers remain crucial in ensuring a deep understanding of mathematical concepts among students, developing critical thinking, and inspiring students. Therefore, effective integration of AI in mathematics education requires careful planning and professional development for teachers, as well as collaboration between educators, researchers, and AI tool designers to ensure that AI tools are beneficial and effective in an educational context.

In his work, Schiff highlights the potential key role of AI tools in personalizing learning [29]. The responsible use of AI can lead to transformative changes in how mathematics is taught and learned, improving learning outcomes for all students and enabling tailored and engaged learning that meets the needs and abilities of each student. Additionally, using such teaching methods can reduce math anxiety and improve efficiency [17]. This research is based on a mixed-methodological approach, integrating quantitative and qualitative methods to enable a comprehensive understanding of the impact of AI on mathematics teaching. Quantitative analysis allowed for an objective evaluation of the effectiveness of AI tools through a comparison of test results between the experimental and control groups, while qualitative analysis provided deeper insights into students' perceptions, experiences, and their interaction with the AI tool.

The importance of this approach lies in its ability to capture nuances in student learning that quantitative data alone may not reveal. Through interviews, surveys, and observations, the research managed to capture subjective aspects of the student experience, such as motivation, engagement, and the perceived utility of AI in the learning process. Implementing AI in the educational process represents a significant shift from traditional teaching methods, so it is crucial to understand how students adapt to and utilize new technologies in their learning. The work of Saha et al. [27] demonstrates the potential of ICT tools in mathematics education, which is relevant for researching the impact of AI on teaching integer and rational numbers in the seventh grade. The development and implementation of AI-based programs in mathematics education can build on the results of these studies and use ICT tools in innovative ways to enhance number learning. Efforts must be made to adequately prepare the AI model for teaching and make it available to students for learning and instruction. Frieder S. et al. [11], authors of a 2023 study, somewhat ironically conclude that if one wishes to pass a math exam using AI tools, it might be better to copy from an average peer. This highlights that the language model is prone to making various mistakes, and as previously mentioned, significant effort and preparation are required to ready the model for use in teaching, rather than becoming a source of ridicule for students. On the other hand, Gattupalli S. et al. [13] state that AI offers useful ideas that can complement and expand the way teachers think about teaching mathematics in the classroom. Thus, thorough preparation and adaptation of the model are prerequisites for establishing a connection between improving math instruction and using such modern methods. Additionally, the work of Zafrullah et al. [38] shows that the AI model can significantly increase student motivation for learning, which can contribute to positive learning outcomes, the primary focus of this work. In general, we can categorize the cited papers under two main themes: AI in general education and AI in mathematics education.

AI in General Education
Papers that discuss the broader implications of AI in the educational landscape, focusing on its capacity to enhance engagement, personalize learning, and support adaptive learning environments, include:

Hatim et al. [14], Li [21], Borbajo et al. [6], Kumar et al. [19], Zhao et al. [40], Baidoo-Anu and Owusu Ansah [2], Boxleitner [7], Kanesci et al. [18], Zhai [39], Yan et al. [36], and Soygazi and Oguz [32].

AI in Mathematics Education
Studies that specifically address the utilization of AI in improving mathematics education, through interactive tools and visualizations, include:

Wardat et al. [34], Salas-Rueda et al. [28], Wardat et al. [33], Bonner et al. [5], and Mukhibin et al. [22].

According to the cited literature, there is no work that demonstrates the application of any form of artificial intelligence in the 7th grade of elementary school among students aged 12 or 13, which makes this work even more valuable. This paper, as a pioneer in the application of artificial intelligence in teaching 7th-grade mathematics, seeks to explore the improvements that could occur with the use of such tools, emphasizing the irreplaceable role of teachers in the educational process and advocating for AI as a supplementary tool rather than a replacement.

3   Methods and Materials

In this study, the main tool used was the popular language model ChatGPT integrated with an avatar for easier understanding and engagement. This model is capable of generating large amounts of text and responding to questions with high accuracy. This model offers a plethora of possibilities that can be applied in teaching. However, it is important to exercise caution throughout the use of this model, especially since it involves students and the educational process. According to Alkaissi et al. [1], it is crucial to be wary of "artificial hallucinations," where the AI tool can generate convincing but inaccurate information. This is particularly challenging in the academic community where accuracy is paramount. Therefore, additional fact-checking and transparency in the use of AI technologies in scholarly work are recommended.

Given this, the AI model used in this study was previously trained using a seventh-grade mathematics textbook, with limitations set to only address questions from that area. This prevented manipulative effects by students and time wastage intended for the educational process. The importance of verification is confirmed by Shakarian et al. [30], who found a 51% accuracy in testing math word problems, while the official data state that the AI model has an accuracy of 59%. However, there are studies indicating high accuracy of AI models in solving tests, over 90% [38].

Considering these results, the instructional units prepared for this teaching format were thoroughly examined to avoid the worst-case scenario in the educational process where a student learns incorrect information from a teacher. According to the Mathematics Curriculum for the seventh grade, integer numbers are part of the syllabus. The instruction was organized in such a way that in the experimental groups, which consisted of two seventh-grade classes, the trained AI model was used for 10 min in each class. Additionally, students in the experimental group had access to the model for homework. This avatar was sourced from d-id.com and implemented into the trained Chat GPT model, which was made available to students on a dedicated website. In the first 5 min, the model introduces the teaching unit, acquaints children with basic concepts and properties, engages them through practical examples from everyday life, and leaves an opportunity for them to ask questions or practice briefly under its guidance after this short presentation. Following that, the next 30+ minutes involve the teacher conducting traditional instruction, after which students have another opportunity to ask any questions they may have to the avatar. Of course, the communication of avatars with students was in their native language, which is Croatian (Fig. 1).

For instance, the model would explain positive and negative integers using examples such as temperature, credit, and similar scenarios. Additionally, it clarified the concept of absolute value in as simple a manner as the students required. The model posed questions that students had to answer with yes or no to ensure their understanding. For aspects that weren't clear, students requested further explanations, which the model provided. The model primarily focused on the conceptual understanding and acquisition of the teaching units, rather than

Fig. 1. Chat GPT with avatar used in this study

solving tasks. This is why the teacher or ChatGPT without an avatar, which could be used for homework and learning assistance, was responsible for this aspect.

Conversely, in the other two seventh-grade classes, this model was not used, and the integer numbers material [24] was covered without any changes to the standard explanation of new math units. Before the intervention with the specified AI model, both the control and experimental groups took a pre-test from the area that typically precedes the unit on integer numbers in mathematics instruction, to facilitate the teaching of these units. The content validity of the test was confirmed by four mathematics teachers and one university professor who reviewed the tasks. The Cronbach's alpha coefficient for this test was 0.688, which is considered an acceptable value for a classroom test.

After completing the training, both groups of participants were subjected to a test on the topic of Integers. Experts, consisting of four teachers and a university professor, thoroughly analyzed every detail of the test to ensure its quality. Their evaluation confirmed the content validity of the test, which means that the test actually measures what it is intended to measure. Additionally, the high Cronbach alpha coefficient value of 0.791, as determined by DeVellis and Thorpe (2022) [9] , emphasizes the consistency of the participants' responses and the internal coherence of the test. These results provide further confidence in the reliability and validity of the conducted testing, which is crucial for ensuring accurate assessment of the participants' knowledge and drawing relevant conclusions.

4   Results

In this study, a total of 95 seventh-grade students from an elementary school participated. They were divided into four classes: 7C, 7D, 7E, and 7F. However, not all students took both the pre-test and the post-test. After excluding students who did not complete both assessments, data from 86 students were analyzed in subsequent phases of the study.

The pre-test comprised 17 tasks, with a maximum achievable score of 16. Within the framework of quantitative achievement evaluation, the scoring of tasks was structured such that each adequately solved problem was valued at one point. However, the last two tasks in the set deviated from this scoring scheme due to their inherent simplicity and lower level of difficulty. These two tasks contributed to the total score with 0.5 points, reflecting an adjusted evaluative scale that mirrors their reduced complexity compared to the preceding tasks. The content of the pre-test did not consist of integer numbers because that is the topic that students need to learn. However, the test therefore covers material from positive integers that precede and are related to the mentioned unit. The pre-test results for each group, as well as the overall results, are presented in Table 1. This table includes descriptive statistics for each group, covering mean values, standard deviations, sample sizes (N), and additionally, the average percentage, specifically the Mean/Total points ratio.

Table 1. Descriptive statistics for pre-test

	N	Mean	Standard Deviation	Mean/Total points
7c	20	10.475	3.1434	0.655
7d	23	11.913	1.8626	0.745
7e	23	12.239	2.4209	0.765
7f	20	11.700	3.1389	0.731
Total	86	11.616	2.6950	0.720

One-way ANOVA revealed no statistically significant difference in the results between the four groups: $F(3, 82) = 1.75$, $p = 0.163$, suggesting comparable pre-test knowledge.

Subsequently, innovative teaching methods using a large language model were introduced in two classes, which we called the experimental groups. In parallel, traditional mathematics instruction continued in the other two classes without any innovations.

The post-test was made up of 27 tasks, with each correctly completed task earning one point, culminating in a total maximum of 27 points. This setup further guaranteed clear grading, as each task equally influenced the final score. The outcomes of the post-test are detailed in Table 2, which supplies descriptive statistics for each group and the aggregate, encompassing mean scores, standard deviations, and the count of students (N).

Analysis of covariance (ANCOVA) conducted on the post-test results of groups 7C, 7D, 7E, and 7F, taking pre-test results as a covariate, did not reveal any statistically significant differences among the groups. The results showed an

Table 2. Descriptive statistics for post-test

	N	Mean	Standard Deviation	Mean/Total points
7c	20	16.575	4.8294	0.614
7d	23	19.283	4.8916	0.714
7e	23	18.848	4.7204	0.698
7f	20	19.300	4.3116	0.715
Total	86	18.541	4.7485	0.686

F value of 0.630 with degrees of freedom 3, 81 and a p-value of 0.598, indicating that there was no significant difference in achievements on post-test between different classes. All groups demonstrated similar outcomes in performance, regardless of differences in initial knowledge levels as determined by the pre-test. It is crucial to highlight that the pre-test material included the chapter on natural numbers, the fundamental understanding of which is essential for effectively engaging with and comprehending the content of the integer numbers chapter, the basis of the post-test. Given that the post-test material was more advanced, it was unrealistic to expect an improvement in the percentage of correctly solved tasks compared to the pre-test. This indicates that, despite the increased difficulty, the various learning experiences or applied strategies had a uniform impact on all class sections, irrespective of their initial readiness for the more complex concepts of integer numbers.

Although the analysis did not reveal statistically significant differences in student achievements, it is important to emphasize the significance of the fact that students exposed to a new learning method, which integrates AI with traditional teaching approaches, managed to maintain a similar level of performance as before the implementation of this model. Furthermore, it would be highly beneficial to explore the impact of such an approach on students' motivation for learning mathematics and their perception of the interestingness of the lessons. The research findings suggest the need for the development of innovative strategies to support students in mastering more complex material, regardless of an unchanged level of basic knowledge compared to groups taught exclusively by traditional methods. These insights are of paramount importance for the creation of future educational programs and pedagogical practices. Continuous monitoring of student progress through different educational stages is essential to ensure that teaching methods are aligned with individual needs and learning capabilities. The primary goal is to enable students not only to master the current curriculum but also to develop the competencies necessary for facing future educational challenges.

Upon examining the box-and-whisker plots showed in Fig. 2 for pre-test and post-test scores across the classes 7C, 7D, 7E, and 7F, we observed a general downward trend in scores, indicative of effective educational strategies. However, the degree of improvement varied across classes, particularly in those integrating ChatGPT (7C and 7E) where the performance gains were less pronounced. How-

Box-and-whisker plots of pre-test and post-test scores grouped by class (colored)

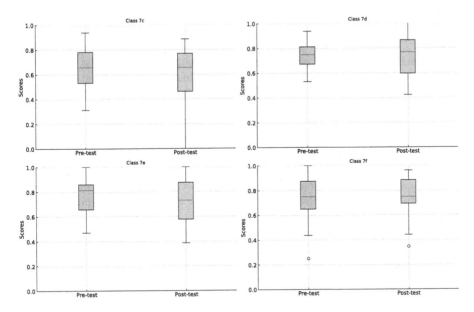

Fig. 2. Distribution of scores for pre-tests and post-tests across different classes, highlighting improvements or changes in student performance.

ever, that difference was not statistically significant. The absence of significant differences between classes, or even the slower progress observed in students who utilized AI tools in their classrooms, might be interpreted as positive news for the educational community. This is particularly relevant in the context of the pervasive concern that AI might supplant human roles across various professions. In the realm of education, such a transition is unlikely to occur rapidly.

- **Class 7C**: The median post-test score slightly increased compared to the pre-test, suggesting modest improvement. The first quartile (Q1) remained relatively stable, indicating that the lower-performing students did not experience significant changes in their scores. However, the third quartile (Q3) showed a slight increase, hinting that higher-performing students saw some improvement. The mean score, while reflecting an overall upward trend, suggested that the distribution of scores widened, indicating variability in how students benefited from the educational interventions.
- **Class 7D**: Demonstrated a more significant increase in both median and mean post-test scores, indicating a robust improvement across the board. The narrowing of the interquartile range from pre-test to post-test suggested that the class became more homogeneous in performance, with fewer students lagging significantly behind.
- **Class 7E**: Similar to Class 7C, Class 7E saw a modest increase in median scores from pre-test to post-test. The interquartile range expanded slightly,

suggesting increased variability in student performance. This could indicate that while some students greatly benefited from the use of ChatGPT, others may not have found it as effective.

- **Class 7F**: Showed notable improvements in both median and mean scores, with a decrease in the interquartile range, suggesting that the class as a whole improved in a more uniform manner. This class did not use ChatGPT, which may imply that traditional methods or other innovations employed were particularly effective for this group.

The less pronounced improvements in classes utilizing ChatGPT (7C and 7E) suggest that the integration of technology into the learning process, while beneficial in certain contexts, requires careful consideration of implementation strategies, student engagement, and content delivery to maximize its potential. The variability in performance, especially noted by the widening of the interquartile range in these classes, underscores the importance of personalized learning approaches to address the diverse needs of students.

Despite expectations that the integration of AI, such as ChatGPT, into mathematics education would contribute to improved student achievements, the results of this research do not support this hypothesis. As Song [31] explores the potential of technological tools in education, the findings of this study suggest that merely introducing AI tools may not be sufficient to achieve significant educational gains without a carefully structured pedagogical approach and integration into the curriculum. This indicates the need for further research to determine the specific conditions under which AI can be most effective in fostering student learning and engagement [20].

4.1 Interpretation in the Context of the Hypothesis

The hypothesis was that students who use AI in class would achieve better results. However, the lack of a significant difference in results between the classes, as shown by ANCOVA, suggests that the use of AI did not lead to better outcomes.

The pre-test showed that students from different classes achieved similar results, so we can conclude that they had similar prior knowledge before we started the experiment. The post-test showed that students achieved similar results, regardless of whether they belonged to the experimental or control group, leading us to conclude that AI had no significant effect on their knowledge.

Therefore, it would be beneficial to continue the research to assess the long-term effectiveness of this method, especially after students become more familiar with the application of AI in learning. This could involve extending the study to other educational segments, such as number theory, where the specific effects of AI on understanding more complex mathematical concepts could be explored. Such an approach could provide additional insights into the potential benefit of integrating AI into various aspects of the curriculum, particularly in light of students' adaptation to this mode of learning and their increased openness to new technologies in education.

5   Conclusion

Huge language model is a powerful AI tool with the potential to transform the educational sector. Its ability to perform tasks requiring knowledge and creative intelligence, such as grading assignments and offering advice to students, could change the way education is delivered. However, challenges associated with integrating AI into education include ensuring the accuracy and reliability of AI-generated responses and concerns about replacing teachers. Education must find a balance between using AI to enhance learning and preserving the human touch and interpersonal communication that are so crucial for knowledge transfer [31]. In this context, it is essential to emphasize the need to develop pedagogical strategies that integrate AI as a support rather than a replacement for teachers, focusing on the synergy between technology and traditional learning methods. Research should also consider how AI can enhance approaches to differentiated instruction, allowing for the customization of pace and learning style for each individual student, thereby fostering greater engagement and understanding of the material.

Future research should evaluate the effectiveness of ChatGPT in improving student learning outcomes and consider the ethical and legal implications of applying AI in education. Furthermore, it is vital to explore how to incorporate ChatGPT and other AI technologies into education in a way that complements rather than replaces teachers, ensuring that learning is enhanced rather than hindered.

This paper becomes one of the pioneers in the use of AI in classrooms within this linguistic region. Given the rapid development of an increasing number of language models that are gaining new capabilities each day, such as more convincing speech and human voice mimicry, creation of video materials and images tailored for various needs in any aspect of human life, there is no doubt that newer research will offer a more significant impact on the quality of the educational process. Although language models are advancing at a galloping pace into the future, one thing is certain: no one can replace a teacher as the leader of the educational process. The spoken word from a human being is best absorbed. Therefore, it is crucial to understand that all future research must focus on enhancing the educational process with the teacher as the main driver.

Ensuring the accuracy and precision of AI-generated responses and developing research strategies to ensure that AI technologies are used in a manner consistent with ethical and legal considerations should also be the focus of future research on the challenges associated with integrating AI into education [25].

As Hwang [15] suggests, AI could be beneficial in various segments of the educational process. On the other hand, the use of AI will be advantageous for students by preparing them for a job market that is increasingly utilizing AI. The educational process is comprehensive and should not be viewed through a single outcome, such as the improvement of mathematical concept understanding in this case. If the stated outcome is not achieved, perhaps the previously mentioned benefits will still materialize, thereby providing room for further research and the application of rapidly evolving models, such as ChatGPT. This opens new avenues for education and many other sectors of human activity.

References

1. Alkaissi, H., McFarlane, S.I.: Artificial hallucinations in chatgpt: implications in scientific writing. Cureus **15**(2), e35179 (2023). https://doi.org/10.7759/cureus.35179, https://www.cureus.com/articles/62046-artificial-hallucinations-in-chatgpt-implications-in-scientific-writing
2. Baidoo-Anu, D., Owusu Ansah, L.: Education in the era of generative artificial intelligence (AI): Understanding the potential benefits of ChatGPT in promoting teaching and learning. Soc. Sci. Res. Netw. (2023). https://doi.org/10.2139/ssrn.4337484
3. Bailey, L.W.: New Technology for the classroom: mobile devices, artificial intelligence, tutoring systems, and robotics, p. 11. IGI Global (2019). https://doi.org/10.4018/978-1-5225-6361-7.ch001
4. Baker, T., Smith, L., Anissa, N.: Educ-AI-tion Rebooted? Exploring the future of artificial intelligence in schools and colleges, Nesta (2019)
5. Bonner, E., Lege, R., Frazier, E.: Large language model-based artificial intelligence in the language classroom: practical ideas for teaching. Teach. English Technol. **23**(1), 23 (2023). https://doi.org/10.46538/teachtech.23.1.2
6. Borbajo, M.N.M., Malbas, M.H., Dacanay, L.R.: Reforming education: the global impact of integrating artificial intelligence in the classroom environment. Am. J. Lang. Literacy Learn. STEM Educ. **1**(5) (2023)
7. Boxleitner, A.: Integrating AI in education: opportunities, challenges and responsible use of ChatGPT. SSRN Electron. J. (2023). https://doi.org/10.2139/ssrn.4566873
8. Cope, B., Kalantzis, M., Searsmith, D.: Artificial intelligence for education: knowledge and its assessment in AI-enabled learning ecologies. Educ. Philos. Theory **53**(12), 1229–1245 (2021). https://doi.org/10.1080/00131857.2020.1728732
9. DeVellis, R., Thorpe, C.: Scale Development: Theory and Applications, 5th edn. SAGE Publications, Thousand Oaks (2022)
10. Frieder, S., Berner, J., Petersen, P., Lukasiewicz, T.: Large language models for mathematicians. arXiv preprint arXiv:2312.04556 (2023). https://doi.org/10.48550/arXiv.2312.04556
11. Frieder, S., et al.: Mathematical capabilities of ChatGPT (2023). https://doi.org/10.48550/arXiv.2301.13867. neurIPS 2023 Datasets and Benchmarks
12. Fuentes, S.Q., Bloom, M.A.: The intricacies of the stem teacher shortage. Electron. J. Res. Sci. Math. Educ. **27**(2), i–vii (2023)
13. Gattupalli, S., Maloy, R.W., Edwards, S.: Comparing teacher-written and AI-generated math problem solving strategies for elementary school students: implications for classroom learning (2023). https://doi.org/10.7275/8sgx-xj08
14. Hatim, M., Jamil, S.I., Khan, S.A.: Exploring the educational potential of ChatGPT. Maulana Azad National Urdu University (2023)
15. Hwang, G.J., Tu, Y.F.: Roles and research trends of artificial intelligence in mathematics education: a bibliometric mapping analysis and systematic review. Mathematics **9**(6), 584 (2021). https://doi.org/10.3390/math9060584
16. Imani, S., Du, L., Shrivastava, H.: Mathprompter: mathematical reasoning using large language models. arXiv preprint arXiv:2303.05398 (2023). https://doi.org/10.48550/arXiv.2303.05398

17. Inoferio, H.V., Espartero, M., Asiri, M., Damin, M., Chavez, J.V.: Coping with math anxiety and lack of confidence through AI-assisted learning. Open J. Syst. **9**(5), 1 (2024). https://doi.org/10.54517/esp.v9i5.2228
18. Kasneci, E., et al.: ChatGPT for good? on opportunities and challenges of large language models for education. Learn. Individ. Differ. **103**, 102274 (2023). https://doi.org/10.1016/j.lindif.2023.102274
19. Kumar, H., Rothschild, D.M., Goldstein, D.G., Hofman, J.: Math education with large language models: Peril or promise? SSRN Electron. J. (2023). https://doi.org/10.2139/ssrn.4641653
20. Li, P.H., Lee, H.Y., Cheng, Y.P., Starčič, A.I., Huang, Y.M.: Solving the self-regulated learning problem: exploring the performance of ChatGPT in mathematics. In: Huang, Y.M., Rocha, T. (eds.) ICITL 2023. LNCS, vol. 14099. Springer, Cham (2023). https://doi.org/10.1007/978-3-031-40113-8_8
21. Li, Y.: The potential application of ChatGPT in higher education management. Lecture Notes Educ. Psychol. Public Media **25**(1), 200–208 (2023). https://doi.org/10.54254/2753-7048/25/20230750
22. Mukhibin, A., Wahyudin, W., Rusyid, H.K., Lutfi, A., Siahaan, E.Y.S.: Review of "Mathematics education in the age of artificial intelligence: how artificial intelligence can serve mathematical human learning. In: Richard, P.R., Pilar Vélez, M., Van Vaerenbergh, S., (eds.) Springer, Cham (2023). https://doi.org/10.1080/03623319.2023.2243688
23. Naveed, H., et al.: A comprehensive overview of large language models. arXiv preprint arXiv:2307.06435 (2024). https://doi.org/10.48550/arXiv.2307.06435
24. Piton, Brkić, K., Boroš, Z., Kvesić: Matematika 7-1: Udžbenik Matematike sa Zbirkom za 2. Polugodište. Školska naklada d.o.o., Mostar (2020)
25. Pradana, M., Elisa, H.P., Syarifuddin: Discussing ChatGPT in education: a literature review and bibliometric analysis. Cogent Educ. **10**(2) (2023). https://doi.org/10.1080/2331186X.2023.2243134
26. Prensky, M.: Digital natives, digital immigrants. On the Horizon **9**(5) (2001)
27. Saha, J., Ahmmed, S., Ali, M., Tamal, M.A., Rezaul, K.M.: ICT based mathematics skill development program: an initiative to overcome mathematics anxiety. Int. J. Emerg. Technol. Learn. (iJET) **15**(14), 252–261 (2020). https://doi.org/10.3991/ijet.v15i14.14149
28. Salas-Rueda, R., Salas-Rueda, E., Salas-Rueda, R.: Analysis and design of the web game on descriptive statistics through the addie model, data science and machine learning. Int. J. Educ. Math. Sci. Technol. **8**(3) (2020). https://doi.org/10.46328/ijemst.v8i3.759
29. Schiff, D.: Out of the laboratory and into the classroom: the future of artificial intelligence in education. AI Soc. **36**, 331–348 (2021). https://doi.org/10.1007/s00146-020-01033-8
30. Shakarian, P., Koyyalamudi, A., Ngu, N., Mareedu, L.: An independent evaluation of chatgpt on mathematical word problems (MWP). In: AAAI Spring Symposium 2023 (MAKE) (2023). https://doi.org/10.48550/arXiv.2302.13814
31. Song, D.: Designing a teachable agent system for mathematics learning. Contemp. Educ. Technol. **8**(2), 176–190 (2017). https://doi.org/10.30935/cedtech/6194
32. Soygazi, F., Oguz, D.: An analysis of large language models and langchain in mathematics education. In: The 7th International Conference on Advances in Artificial Intelligence (ICAAI 2023). İstanbul (2023). https://doi.org/10.1145/3633598.3633614

33. Wardat, Y., Tashtoush, M.A., Alali, R., Jarrah, A.: ChatGPT: a revolutionary tool for teaching and learning mathematics. Eurasia J. Math. Sci. Technol. Educ. **19**(7), 1–18 (2023). https://doi.org/10.29333/ejmste/13272
34. Wardat, Y., Tashtoush, M.A., AlAli, R., Saleh, S.: Artificial intelligence in education: mathematics teachers' perspectives, practices and challenges. Int. J. Contemp. Math. (2024). https://doi.org/10.52866/ijcsm.2024.05.01.004
35. Wei, T., Luan, J., Liu, W., Dong, S., Wang, B.: CMATH: can your language model pass chinese elementary school math test? arXiv preprint arXiv:2306.16636 (2023). https://doi.org/10.48550/arXiv.2306.16636
36. Yan, L., et al.: Practical and ethical challenges of large language models in education: a systematic scoping review. arXiv preprint arXiv:2303.13379 (2023). https://doi.org/10.48550/arXiv.2303.13379
37. Yuan, Z., Yuan, H., Tan, C., Wang, W., Huang, S.: How well do large language models perform in arithmetic tasks? arXiv preprint arXiv:2304.02015 (2023). https://doi.org/10.48550/arXiv.2304.02015
38. Zafrullah, Hakim, M.L., Angga, M.: ChatGPT open AI: analysis of mathematics education students learning interest. J. Technol. Global **V**(1) (2023). https://penaeducentre.com/index.php/JTeG/article/view/35/33
39. Zhai, X.: ChatGPT user experience: implications for education. SSRN Electron. J. (2022). https://doi.org/10.2139/ssrn.4312418
40. Zhao, W.X., Zhou, K., Li, J., et al.: A survey of large language models. arXiv (2023). https://doi.org/10.48550/arXiv.2303.18223

Gamification in Learning Process Enhanced with AI

Ana Šego◉ and Maja Gakić$^{(⊠)}$ ◉

University of Mostar, Mostar, Bosnia and Herzegovina
{ana.sego1,mgakic}@phd.sum.ba

Abstract. The application of gamification in the learning process is developing approach for increasing learners' motivation and engagement by introducing game elements into the educational environment. Gamified learning activities
allow learners to acquire knowledge, improve skills and encourage positive traits
that the game builds specifically for learning purposes. Gamification can enhance
learners' engagement, increase their motivation toward learning, promote collaboration, provide instant feedback, and establish a positive learning environment.
The effects of gamification are mostly positive, but there are also certain challenges or shortcomings, such as the development of such technologies in education is expensive, the question arises of the security of learners' personal data,
the impossibility of determining the long-term effects of gamification, and how to
adapt the elements of gamification to the different personalities of learners. Artificial intelligence (AI) allows gamification to be adapted to a learner in a real-time
environment. AI has become very important for the learning environment, where
the individual needs of each learner take centre stage. One of the most important
goals of Artificial education is to provide individual learners with personalized
learning suggestions on aids depending on their learning status or personal preferences. Tailoring content to unique learning preferences becomes a unique learning
journey and experience for each individual learner.

Keywords: Learning · Gamification · Artificial Intelligence

1 Introduction

The development of information and communication technologies is changing every segment of everyday life, thus setting new ways of learning and teaching in the educational
system. At the very beginning of its application in teaching, information and communication technology served to prepare the teaching process, and with its accelerated development, new innovative techniques, methods and tools in the learning process appeared,
as well as an opportunity for teachers to create interactive teaching methods that increase
learners' motivation and engagement for work and participation in classes. The biggest
challenge for teachers in today's world is how to get learners interested in interactively
participating in classes and thus learning and achieving the set learning outcomes. Thus,
the term "gamification" was introduced into the teaching process as a development approach to increase learner motivation and engagement by including game design elements

T. Volarić et al. (Eds.): MoStart 2024, CCIS 2124, pp. 41–54, 2024.
https://doi.org/10.1007/978-3-031-62058-4_4

in the educational environment [1]. Gamification refers to the application of game design elements to activities that are not games and has been applied to various segments, including education [2]. Learning through gamification enables the personal learning of each individual learner, because learning can be adapted to the individual's abilities in order to successfully master the teaching material. Artificial intelligence enables the adaptation of technologies to the learner in real time. An important goal of artificial intelligence in education is to provide each individual learner with personalized learning suggestions depending on their learning status or personal preferences [3]. The main goal of introducing new teaching methods into the teaching process is a holistic approach to learning that puts the individual in the centre of attention, adapting to his needs and encouraging greater engagement and motivation.

2   Gamification

The first application of gamification was recorded in 1912, when the entrepreneur Jack Cracker put surprise toys in the boxes of his products and thus had a positive effect on increasing the demand for his products. The company Sperry & Hutchinson was among the first to award customers with tokens of loyalty in the form of stamps after each purchase made above a certain amount. This form of customer tracking is widespread even today when there are digital cards that track purchases in certain stores and customers are rewarded with discounts or reward points. An example of gamification are physical badges that are awarded after certain achievements, in the example of scouts who, after completed tasks, win badges as a reward for achieved success.

The use of gamification elements, as a way of encouraging motivation, were not known under the term gamification, the term itself developed only later.

In the 1990s there was a rapid development of technology, and in 1980 Richard Bartle was the first to develop a system for multi-user work - MUD, which many consider to be the first system for massively multiplayer online role-playing games (MMORPG). Players connect to a virtual world where they create their own character that performs tasks in the virtual environment. The year 2002 saw the development of the term Serious games, which represent simulations of real worlds and events. The development of serious games increased the interest of the business world in the application of games in the business sector [4, 5].

The term gamification itself was coined by the British computer game developer Nick Pelling in 2002, was first used in 2003, and began to be actively used in 2011, when it became popular [6]. There are several different definitions of gamification, and the most accepted one is "Gamification is an approach that uses game design elements in non-game contexts" [7–9]. Gamification is used in many areas such as business, production, healthcare, but this paper will deal with its application in education.

Gamification starts from the concept of play, which is considered one of the best ways of developing children at a young age. The game is said to be the easiest to understand. If the game is applied to learning, children will more easily accept learning if it contains elements that are previously known to them as a way of entertainment. To understand the concept of gamification, it is first necessary to clarify how game-based learning works. Game-based learning is the use of games in the learning process. It starts with defining the content and characteristics of the game before the actual game process begins. During the unfolding of the game, the game participant goes through an iterative process during which feedback is obtained from the environment. Certain behaviour takes place and the environment is continuously evaluated and a decision is made when the game process is over or when the desired goal has been achieved. The aim of the game is to stimulate the learner's motivation so that he repeats the game process several times. After the process is completed, the game participant achieves certain results expressed in the form of learned knowledge. The entire process of learning through play is shown in Fig. 1.

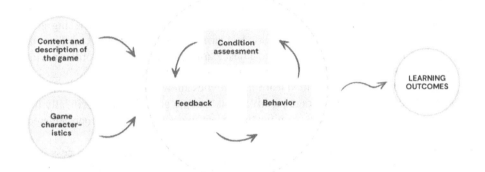

Fig. 1. The process of learning through play. Source: Adapted from Garris et al. (2002)

The game is already used in teaching, but not every use of the game in teaching is gamification. It was created as a result of the emergence of computer games, and it represents the application of mechanics and dynamics taken from computer games that serves to solve problems and achieve certain goals. This would mean that parts of the game are used in certain situations in which the game has not been applied so far.

Often in the literature, certain terms are identified with the term gamification, which leads to problems in determining the true meaning of that word. For this reason, it is necessary to study several sources in order to be able to accurately understand all terms and to notice the differences between them.

Terms that, due to their definitions, are often identified with the term gamification [10–12].

- Free play - represents play in the sense of free and improvised activity without strictly defined rules. An example of free play is a child's play with toys in his own home, this kind of play is not time-limited, does not have a defined goal that must be achieved, nor does it have tasks that need to be done
- Game with rules - represents a structure with rules and a direction of progress, that is, with a given goal. There may be a person who controls the enforcement of the rules of the game. An example of such a game with rules is D&D (Dungeons and Dragons), where there are players, a story, rules of behaviour, a game manager who

designs scenarios and monitors the players' reactions and adjusts the course of the game depending on them.

- Game-inspired design (playful design) – is defined as the application of visual animations or images reminiscent of a game to attract attention. An example is adding graphics to web pages instead of text printing an error. The goal of introducing this kind of design with game elements is to attract attention and achieve a certain impression.
- Serious games - creation of simulations of real events. A large application of so-called serious games is in the army and training academies, where it is of great importance to present the possible situation as accurately as possible so that the participants feel as real as possible a similar situation. An example is a flight simulation for pilots or an operation in medicine.

Teaching in the teaching process changes its form every day by introducing new technologies, so gamification, unlike traditional learning materials, increases motivation, engagement and can provide feedback and adjust learning challenges in accordance with the individual's abilities [13], that is, learning can be personalized.

According to Hoe [14], gamified learning activities allow learners to acquire knowledge, improve skills and encourage positive traits that the game builds specifically for learning purposes. In other words, gamification in learning activities is a learner-centered process [15].

Tools based on gamification have become basic tools in the learning process in a digital environment, and numerous studies highlight the positive effects of using game elements in the acquisition of new knowledge and skills, the use of gamification also strengthens memory, improves cognitive functioning and has a positive effect on teamwork. Gamification must be carefully designed taking into account the psychology of learning and its use as a strategy in the learning process [16]. Within all these contexts, it is expected that gamification can encourage the initiation or continuation of goal-directed behaviour, or motivation [17].

3   Elements of Gamification

One of the very common misconceptions of gamification is it is as simple as the addition of points, badge, or leaderboard-based systems to existing activities. However, by adding these elements to existing processes particular user behaviors will be influenced and modified. This does not necessarily imply that the desired change of behavior will be achieved. The different components and mechanics must be carefully designed and thought through in such a way that they will support the design business dynamics. These dynamics themselves must be clearly linked to key business processes and desired outcomes [15].

From various authors we have statements about different elements of gamification, so Werbach and Hunter (2012) state that the main elements of gamification are dynamics, mechanics and components, while Zichermann and Cunningham (2011) talk about mechanics, dynamics and aesthetics. The authors outline seven basic elements of the mechanics, which are Points, Levels, Leaderboards, Badges, Challenges/Tasks, Engagement, and Engagement Loops. Dynamics imply the interaction of players and mechanics or players with other players, and aesthetics refers to the emotions of players during gameplay and is the result of the interaction of mechanics and dynamics (Fig. 2).

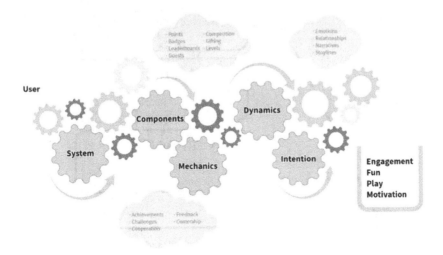

Fig. 2. Gamification process outlined according to Werbach and Hunter

The elements of gamification are defined by Werbach and Hunter (2012) as follows:

Dynamics represent the conceptual structures on which the game is based, such as the narrative and constraints that shape the game itself. In addition, they are the most abstract element of gamification, because players feel their action, but do not directly encounter them. The dynamics are the resulting behaviors and interactions between users that are being incentivized by the components and mechanics described. They depend on the nature and experience of the users [15, 18].

Mechanics are the processes by which the game action is created. Mechanics can also be defined as "processes that drive action and create player engagement". The mechanics are slightly more abstract than the components, and often relate to the ongoing nature of how specific components evolve over time or how users interact within the framework. The mechanics are concepts that define potential actions by and states of the user; especially guidelines that are defining how the game progresses, what are the possible reactions on an occurring event, and what influences the behavior of the user in what kind [15].

Components represent specific game structures that implement mechanics and dynamics Components are related to the intention and purpose of the system, the target user group, and involved (software) tools. However, the intelligent use of these components to successfully meet the designer requirements is more challenging and requires careful thought [15, 19] (Fig. 3).

The Dynamics, Mechanics, and Components comprise a set of items (Table 1). The more integrated these items are, the greater the probability of generating interesting and memorable experiences.

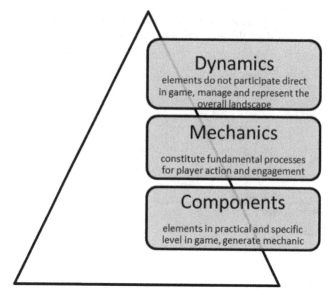

Fig. 3. Pyramid according to Werbach and Hunter

Table 1. Source modified according Werbach and Hunter

Dimension	Game element	Description
Dynamics	Emotions	User experience include curiosity, happiness, frustration, keep users playing
	Relationship	Include the range of interactions
	Narratives and storylines	Gives coherence and purpose to the gaming system, not allowing it to become the sum of random elements. It is the narrative that creates the system's feeling of purpose
Mechanics	Achievements	Reward after completing the activity
	Challenges	The objectives that user must accomplish
	Cooperation	The goal here is to make users experience a feeling of victory or defeat with other people
	Feedback	Allow a user to recognize how they are doing and to initiate further activities. This is provided through leaderboards, messages or other displays
	Ownership	Ownership of resources that can be acquired, used and traded

(continued)

Table 1. (*continued*)

Dimension	Game element	Description
	Progression	Visualizations for the user to see their progress in an activity. Progress can be induced to prevent the user from becoming frustrated when they do not know what to do. This can be facilitated using hints, environment changes, or actively performing the activity for the user
	Transactions	Trading of resources between users
	Avatar	The visual representation of the player in the scope of the game
Components	Points	Type of unit accumulated with successful actions that allow increasing one's levels
	Badges	Visual representations of achievements inside the game
	Leaderboards	Display progression of users and relative success in comparison to opponents
	Quest	Where a user moves through a challenge towards a defined objective, with the intention of being rewarded. Quests are defined by objectives that should be precise, comprehensible, and concise
	Competition/challenge	Provides participants with the feeling of victory or defeat in terms of a contest with other teams or people
	Gifting/sharing	The objectives that users must accomplish The items given by a player to another or the system itself. Sharing of resources between users, allowing users to enjoy the benefits of gifting, helping, and altruism
	Levels	Representation of the players' evolution. The players' level increases as they get better in the game

4 Effects of Gamification on Learners

An effective gamification concept is one that captures and retains learners' attention, engages, entertains and challenges them, and finally teaches them. Learning through games can bring about the development of characteristics, advantages and disadvantages at the same time, some of which are briefly mentioned as following. [20].

Gamification in learning alleviates some current educational difficulties, including decreased learner engagement, motivation and a lack of cooperation among learners. The benefits of gamification lie in its congruence with two psychological theories; the Theory of Flow [21] and the Self-determination theory. Self-determination theory suggested that people are motivated to grow and change by three innate and universal psychological needs. People can become self-determined when their needs for competence, connection and autonomy are fulfilled [19, 22]. Flow as a state of optimal experience characterized by being fully focused and engaged in an activity – has been regarded as one of the most important psychological outcomes of gamification and games [20]. Designers of games and experiences have utilized the flow theory to understand users' activity better. The theory says that when a person is dealing with something challenging that he or she can handle, he or she enters a state of mind, a certain flow, where he or she is captivated, happy and eager, all at once [21].

Many researchers have investigated gamification's effect on learning and found a positive relationship between gamification and learning [23–31]. When teachers use gamification, one of their considerations is whether gamification enhances learners' learning achievements or not. Many researchers [25, 26, 32–34] have shown that gamification of learning can improve learning success.

Gamification makes learning fun and engaging. They make learners feel proud, completing a course after a series of gamified challenges and tasks. When learners feel emotionally connected to the content, their retention increases. Gamification makes learners want to achieve the learning objectives of a course [35–37]. Motivation is the driving force that makes learners want to get to the end of the game and complete the learning. Badges are used as rewards at checkpoints throughout the game. They can be as simple as a sticker or fancier, like a Starbucks gift card for the first 100 learners to complete the game successfully. Badges can be displayed within the game or on the company's website. They are a great technique because they make the user feel important and skilled. Badges give learners a sense of accomplishment [38–40].

The gamification strategy challenges the participants to perform to the best of their abilities. Participants can be challenged to do better in different areas of interest. Thus, ensuring maximized potential [41, 42].

Gamification of learning ensures instant feedback in all scenarios. This makes learning easier by giving them the right solution if they cannot find it themselves, and with the help of instant feedback, it becomes easier to find the domains that need more work. Leaderboards are another way of offering additional feedback. It lets learners see how they are doing compared to their colleagues [20].

Gamification has numerous advantages and creates positive effects for learners, but some research show certain disadvantages. A common opinion is that this type of technology is expensive to use. If not well-designed, learners' attitudes may be adversely affected. Animations, graphics, stock photos and videos, music, and sound effects all cost money. The gamification of learning includes incurrence of additional cost, as it is not cheap to gamify learning scenarios. This includes buying the game and ensuring the system specification suits the game in question for it to run [20].

Assessments in games need to link back to the learning objectives, just like any other learning course. It must be meaningful for the learner [20]. The introduction of gaming in training scenarios propagates competitiveness. While competition is good for gaming scenarios, the organization requires its employees to cooperate [43–46].

Another criticism of gamification in the classroom involves the regulatory and legal issues and, ultimately, the ethics of introducing these concepts to learners. Whenever learners come into play, privacy should always be a concern of educators. Specifically, the amount of personal information learners must share with the gaming program to access the material [20].

Some researchers claim that its recent development has not been sufficiently tested, as there has not been enough time to evaluate the long-term effects of this type of intervention [47, 48].

Some studies point to the varying effects of gamification on different personalities. Learners have benefit from gamification as it will help to enhance learners' motivation. Gamification's effects on different personalities vary. Highly conscientious learners always have their own trigger to motivate them. Behavior of the highly conscientious learners will be the same in the gamified and the non-gamified versions. They revealed that extroverted learners prefer points, badges and social elements such as leaderboards. They are motivated by gamified version. Gamification elements will demotivate neurotic learners, who find these elements boring and annoying [49].

5   Gamification AI

The mention of artificial intelligence brings to mind a supercomputer, a computer with immense processing capabilities, including adaptive behavior, such as inclusion of sensors, and other capabilities, that enable it to have human-like cognition and functional abilities, and indeed, which improve the supercomputers interaction with human beings. Within the education sector, there has been increased application of artificial intelligence, going over and above the conventional understanding of AI as a supercomputer to include embedded computer systems. AI is applied in educational institutions in different ways, including in the form of automation of administrative processes and tasks, curriculum and content development, instruction, and students' learning processes [50].

AI has been increasingly propagated as having strategic value for education [51]. Loeckx [52] suggested that AI could be an effective learning tool that lessens the burdens of both teachers and students and offers effective learning experiences for students. Coupled with current education reforms such as the digitalization of educational resources, gamification, and personalized learning experiences, there are many opportunities for the development of AI applications in education. Examples of AI in education are: board games promote motivation to learn AI; AI challenges learning of the process of creating machine learning models in the form of a game, connecting emerging technology solutions with real-world problems in a playful environment; AI-based gamification platform designed for marketing and consulting fields; Adaptive gamification allow us to provide intelligent adaptive gamification environment in online education to create interactive and engaging learning experiences; digital study assistant based on conversational AI with four application areas communicator, planner, motivator and analyzer [53–55].

Artificial-aided education includes intelligent education, innovative virtual learning and data analysis and prediction. Intelligent education systems provide timely and personalized instruction and feedback for both instructors and learners. They are designed to improve learning value and efficiency by multiple computing technologies [50]. Various techniques are incorporated into AI system for learning analysis, recommendation, knowledge understanding and acquirement, based on machine learning, data mining and knowledge model [56]. AI education system generally consists of teaching contents, data and intelligent algorithm, which can be divided into two parts, i.e., system model (including learner model, teaching model, and knowledge model) and intelligent technologies [57]. Model help to build data map is crucial for improving learning, which establishes structures and association rules for collected education data [58] (Table 2).

Table 2. Techniques for scenarios of AI education according to Chen [50].

Scenarios of AI education	AI related techniques
Assessment of learners and schools	Adaptive learning method and personalized learning approach, academic analytics
Grading and evaluation of paper and exams	Imagine recognition, computer-vision, prediction system
Personalized intelligent teaching	Data mining or Bayes knowledge interference, intelligent teaching systems, learning analytics
Smart school	Face recognition, speech recognition, virtual labs, A/R, V/R, hearing and sensing technologies
Online and mobile remote education	Edge computing, virtual personalized assistants, real-time analysis

Artificial intelligence impact on educational gamification lies the ability to provide personalized learning experiences. Adaptive algorithms, the technological backbone of this personalization, meticulously analyse the strengths and weaknesses of individual learners. Tailoring content to unique learning preferences becomes a unique learning journey and experience for each individual learner. Personalized learning paths, chatbots performance indicators and virtual teaching assistants are examples of deep learning applications in e-learning. One of the most important goals of AI education is to provide individual students with personalized learning suggestions on aids depending on their learning status, preferences, or personal attributes [3]. This holistic approach ensures that education becomes a more immersive and tailored experience for each student.

AI in gamification ensure every learner progress at pace aligned with their abilities fostering a sense of achievement. With AI, feedback becomes instantaneous, allowing students to understand their performance immediately and take proactive steps to improve. When students receive timely recognition for correct answers or commendable efforts, it motivates and encourages them, contributing to a positive learning experience. The impact of real-time feedback extends beyond the individual learner. Educators can use this data to fine-tune their teaching methods, identifying areas where the class may need additional support or challenging material. It fosters a collaborative environment where educators and students actively participate in the learning journey. The future trends of AI in educational gamification are not just about technological advancements but about creating an inclusive and ethical educational ecosystem. Integrating AI into the gamification of education signifies a paradigm shift in learning methodologies. The transformative impact on personalized learning, real-time feedback, and immersive experiences holds the potential to redefine education for the better [59–62].

6   Conclusion

Numerous studies have shown that the conventional learning process is not optimal in all conditions, for all learners, teachers and other aspects and actors that make up the learning process. The information age in which we live brings numerous opportunities for improvement, optimization, and personalization of the learning process. Participants in the learning process in the information age and participants in the learning process in times before general digitization do not have the same opportunities, interests, habits and motives. The UN report from 2017 provides information that young people aged 15–24 represent the most active group in the digital world and 71% of them have access to the Internet compared to 48% of the total population.

Gamification in the learning process has contributed to the digitization of the learning process, while the inclusion of artificial intelligence in the learning process and gamification can be the next significant step forward. Artificial intelligence is a tool of the future and carries great potential for improving education. Research into the application of gamification elements in teaching has shown that the most common advantages are an increase in engagement and motivation for learning, while the most common disadvantage of gamification is how to connect assessment in games with learning outcomes and that long-term effects cannot yet be assessed.

The upgrade of gamification with artificial intelligence has the potential to enable the personalization of the learning process, assist the teaching staff, provide each individual learner with the opportunity to learn and acquire knowledge in an adequate way and thus increase young people's chances of discovering their own possibilities, talents and direction. The analysis of the impact of gamification upgraded with artificial intelligence on the learning process provides numerous opportunities for further research, from the impact on the motivation and acquisition of knowledge of students with different psychological characteristics and orientations, the impact on the acquisition of knowledge and motivation to learn different types of material, to the impact on the work of teaching staff depending on age group. It would be particularly interesting to analyse the impact on students who, from the beginning to the end of their schooling, go through a learning process with elements of gamification, i.e. artificial intelligence.

Applying gamification in the learning process, as well as by introducing AI into learning, which improves gamification in various ways through digital assistants, teaching challenges, games, adaptive learning environments, learners can increase their motivation, adjust and bring learning closer to complex subjects such as AI itself and do it all with elements of fun.

References

1. Dichev, C., Dicheva, D.: Gamifying education: what is known, what is believed and what remains uncertain: a critical review. Int. J. Educ. Technol. High. Educ. **14**, 9 (2017). https://doi.org/10.1186/s41239-017-0042-5
2. Nah, F.F.-H., Telaprolu, V.R., Rallapalli, S., Venkata, P.R.: Gamification of education using computer games. In: Yamamoto, S. (ed.) HIMI 2013. LNCS, vol. 8018, pp. 99–107. Springer, Heidelberg (2013). https://doi.org/10.1007/978-3-642-39226-9_12

3. Bennani, S., Maalel, A., Ben Ghezala, H.: Adaptive gamification in E-learning: a literature review and future challenges. Comput. Appl. Eng. Educ. **30**, 628–642 (2021). https://doi.org/10.1002/cae.22477
4. Christians, G.: The Origins and Future of Gamification, vol. 66 (2018)
5. Fitz-Walter, Z.: A history of gamification - infographic and article (2018)
6. Walter, Z.F.: A brief history of gamification. http://zefcan.com/2013/01/abrief-history-of-gam ification/. Accessed 24 Jan 2013
7. Kim, B.: The popularity of gamification in the mobile and social era. Libr. Technol. Rep. **51**(2), 5–9 (2015). https://doi.org/10.5860/ltr.51n2
8. Lopes A.P., et al.: Gamification in education and active methodologies at higher education. In: Edulearn19 Proceedings, pp. 1633–1640 (2019). https://doi.org/10.21125/edulearn.2019. 0480
9. Barata, G., Gama, S., Jorge, J., Gonçalves, D.: Improving participation and learning with gamification. In: ACM International Conference Proceeding Series, pp. 9–16 (2013). https:// doi.org/10.1145/2583008.2583010
10. Al-Azawi, R., Al-Faliti, F., Al-Blushi, M.: Educational gamification vs. game based learning: comparative study. Int. J. Innov. Manag. Technol. **7**(4), 132–136 (2016)
11. Garris, R., Ahlers, R., Driskell, J.E.: Games, motivation, and learning: a research and practice model. Simul. Gaming **33**(4), 441–467 ((2002))
12. Nikčević-Milković, A., Rukavina, M., Galić, M.: Koristenje i ucinkovitost igre u razrednoj nastavi. Život i škola 25 (2010)
13. Hoe, T.W.: Gamifikasi dalam pendidikan: Pembelajaran berasaskan permainan. Universiti Pendidikan Sultan Idris, Tanjong Malim (2015)
14. Dicheva, D., Dichev, C., Agre, G., Angelova, G.: Gamification in education: a systematic mapping study. J. Educ. Technol. Soc. **18**(3), 9 (2015)
15. Wood, L., Reiners, T.: Gamification (2015). https://doi.org/10.4018/978-1-4666-5888-2. ch297
16. Israel, M.: Game-based learning and Gamification (2017). https://epale.ec.europa.eu/sites/ default/files/game-based-learning-gamification.pdf
17. Schunk, D.H., Pintrich, P.R., Meece, J.L.: Motivation in education: theory, research, and applications (2014)
18. Lovrenčić, S., et al.: Igrifikacija: prema sistematizaciji termina na hrvatskom jeziku. Zbornik radova Računalne igre 2018, stručna konferencija, pp. 1–12. Fakultet organizacije i informatike, str., Varaždin (2018)
19. Werbach, K., Hunter, D.: For the Win: How Game Thinking can Revolutionize your Business. Wharton Digital Press, Philadelphia (2012)
20. Mirzaie Feiz Abadi, B., Khalili Samani, N., Akhlaghi, A., Najibi, S., Bolourian, M.: Pros and cons of tomorrow's learning: a review of literature of gamification in education context. Med. Edu. Bull. **3**(4), 543–554 (2022). https://doi.org/10.22034/meb.2022.350941.1063
21. Csikszentmihalyi, M.: Flow: The Psychology of Optimal Experience, p. 15. Harper and Row, New York (1990). ISBN 0-06-092043-2
22. Ryan, R.M., Deci, E.L.: Intrinsic and extrinsic motivations: classic definitions and new directions. Contemp. Educ. Psychol. **25**, 54–67 (2000)
23. Gee, J.: What Video Games Have to Teach us About Learning and Literacy. Pal grave Macmillan, New York (2003)
24. Gibson, R.: Show gamification some love (2011). http://www.developonline.net
25. Faria, A., Whiteley, T.: An empirical evaluation of the pedagogical value of playing a simula-tion game in a principles of marketing course. Dev. Bus. Simul. Experient. Learn. **17**, 53–57 (1990)

26. Domínguez, A., Saenz-de-Navarrete, J., de-Marcos, L., Fernández-Sanz, L., Pagés, C., Martínez-Herráiz, J. Gamifying learning experiences: practical implications and outcomes. Comput. Educ. **63**, 380–392 (2013)

27. Anderson, J., Rainie, L.: Gamification and the internet: experts expect game layers to expand in the future, with positive and negative results. Games Health **1**(4), 299–302 (2012). https://doi.org/10.1089/g4h.2012.0027. Epub 2012 Jun 25. PMID: 26191633

28. Aldrich, C.: Learning by Doing: A Comprehensive Guide to Simulations, Computer Games, and Pedagogy in e-learning and Other Educational Experiences, 1st edn. Pfeiffer (2005). ISBN-10: 0787977357

29. Kumar, B., Khurana, P.: Gamification in education-learn computer programming with fun. Int. J. Comput. Distrib. Syst. **2**(1), 46–53 (2012)

30. Hakulinen, L., Auvinen, T., Korhonen, A. Empirical study on the effect of achievement badges in TRAKLA2 online learning environment. In: Proceedings of Learning and Teaching in Computing and Engineering (LaTiCE) Conference, pp. 47–54 (2013). https://doi.org/10.1109/LaTiCE.2013.34

31. Su, C., Cheng, C.: A mobile gamification learning system for improving the learning motivation and achievements. J. Comput. Assist. Learn. **31**(3), 268–286 (2015)

32. Smith, A., Baker, L.: Getting a clue: creating student detectives and dragon slayers in your library. Ref. Serv. Rev. **39**(4), 628–642 (2011)

33. Mayo, M.J.: Video games: a route to largescale STEM education? Science **323**(5910), 79–82 (2009). https://doi.org/10.1126/science.1166900. PMID: 19119223

34. Sitzmann, T.: A meta-analytic examination of the instructional effectiveness of computer based simulation games. Pers. Psychol. **64**, 489–528 (2011)

35. Smiderle, R., Rigo, S.J., Marques, L.B., et al.: The impact of gamification on students' learning, engagement and behavior based on their personality traits. Smart Learn. Environ. **7**, 3 (2020). https://doi.org/10.1186/s40561-019-0098-x

36. Rivera, E.S., Garden, C.L.P.: Gamification for student engagement: a framework. J. Further High. Educ. **45**(7), 999–1012 (2021). https://doi.org/10.1080/0309877X.2021.18752

37. Nevin, C., et al.: Gamification as a tool for enhancing graduate medical education. Postgrad. Med. J. **90**(1070), 685–693 (2014)

38. Rivera, E.S., Garden, C.L.P.: Impacts of gamification on intrinsic motivation. J. Further High. Educ. **45**(4), 1–14 (2012)

39. Sailer, M., Hense, J.U., Mayr, S.K., Mandl, H.: How gamification motivates: an experimental study of the effects of specific game design elements on psychological need satisfaction. Comput. Hum. Behav. **69**, 371–380 (2017). https://doi.org/10.1016/j.chb.2016.12.033

40. Motivation through Gamification. https://seppo.io/site/assets/files/2292/motivation-through-gamification-corporate.pdf

41. Shen, Y., Joppe, M.: 4 gamification: practices, benefits and challenges.In: Xu, F., Buhalis, D. (eds.) Gamification for Tourism, Bristol, Blue Ridge Summit: Channel View Publications, pp. 63–80 (2021). https://doi.org/10.21832/9781845418236-006

42. Sabornido, E.B., Garma, V.A., Niepes, G.L., Cabria, F.M.N.: Key challenges and barriers in gamification: a systematic review. Asia Pac. J. Adv. Educ. Technol. **1**(1), 13–19 (2022). SSRN: https://ssrn.com/abstract=4059193

43. Yang, C., Ye, H.J., Feng, Y.: Using gamification elements for competitive crowdsourcing: exploring the underlying mechanism. Behav. Inf. Technol. **40**, 837–854 (2021)

44. Burguillo, J.C.: Using game theory and Competition-based learning to stimulate student motivation and performance. Comput. Educ. **55**(2), 566–575 (2010)

45. Van Grove, J.: Gamification: How Competition Is Reinventing Business, Marketing & Everyday Life. Mashable (2017). Accessed 12 Feb 2013

46. Menezes, C., Bortolli, R.: Potential of gamification as assessment tool. Creat. Educ. **7**, 561–566 (2016). https://doi.org/10.4236/ce.2016.74058

47. Ricciardi, F.F.M.: Gamification and learning: a review of issues and research. J. e-Learn. Knowl. Soc. **11**(3), 13–21 (2015). https://doi.org/10.20368/1971-8829/1072
48. Dremliuga, R., Dremliuga, O., Iakovenko, A.: Virtual reality: general issues of legal regulation. J. Polit. Law **13**(1), 75 (2020). https://doi.org/10.5539/jpl.v13n1p75
49. Ghaban, W., Hendley, R.: Understanding the Effect of gamification on learners with different personalities, pp. 392–400 (2019). https://doi.org/10.5220/0007730703920400
50. Chen, L., Chen, P., Lin, Z.: Artificial intelligence in education: a review. IEEE Access **8**, 75264–75278 (2020). https://doi.org/10.1109/ACCESS.2020.2988510
51. Seldon, A., Abidoye, O.: The Fourth Education Revolution, pp. 1–14, University of Buckingham Press, London (2018)
52. Loeckx, J.: Blurring boundaries in education: context and impact of MOOCs. Int. Rev. Res. Open Distrib. Learn. **17**(3), 92–121 (2016)
53. Choi, E., Park, N.: Demonstration of gamification in education for understanding artificial intelligence principles at elementary school level. İlköğretim Online (2021)
54. Sakulkueakulsuk, B., et al.: Kids making AI: integrating machine learning, gamification, and social context in STEM education. In: 2018 IEEE International Conference on Teaching, Assessment, and Learning for Engineering (TALE), pp. 1005–1010 (2018)
55. Nam, H.W.: Design of AI-based gamification platform for effective educational service using child behavior prediction/change (2021)
56. Chin, D.B., Dohmen, I.M., Schwartz, D.L.: Young children can learn scientific reasoning with teachable agents. IEEE Trans. Learn. Technol. **6**(3), 248–257 (2013)
57. Jones, A.: Philosophical and socio-cognitive foundations for teaching in higher education through collaborative approaches to student learning. Educ. Philos. Theory **43**(9), 997–1011 (2011)
58. Kessler, G.: Technology and the future of language teaching. Foreign Lang. Ann. **51**(1), 205–218 (2018)
59. Tan, D.Y., Cheah, C.W.: Developing a gamified AI-enabled online learning application to improve students' perception of university physics. Comput. Educ. Artif. Intell. **2**, 100032 (2021). https://doi.org/10.1016/j.caeai.2021.100032
60. Babu, S., Moorthy, A.D.: Application of artificial intelligence in adaptation of gamification in education: a literature review. Comput. Appl. Eng. Educ. (2023). https://doi.org/10.1002/cae.22683
61. Yordanova, Z.: Gamification as a tool for supporting artificial intelligence development – state of art. In: Botto-Tobar, M., Zambrano Vizuete, M., Torres-Carrión, P., Montes León, S., Pizarro Vásquez, G., Durakovic, B. (eds.) ICAT 2019. CCIS, vol. 1193, pp. 313–324. Springer, Cham (2020). https://doi.org/10.1007/978-3-030-42517-3_24
62. Koravuna, S., Surepally, U.K.: Educational gamification and artificial intelligence for promoting digital literacy. In: Proceedings of the 2nd International Conference on Intelligent and Innovative Computing Applications (2020). https://doi.org/10.1145/3415088.3415107

Impact of the e-Schools Programme on the Use of the e-Class Register

Ivan Šabić[1]([☒]) [iD], Hrvoje Puljiz[1] [iD], and Ana Smoljo[2] [iD]

[1] University North, Trg dr. Žarka Dolinara 1, Koprivnica, Croatia
{ivsabic,hrpuljiz}@unin.hr
[2] University of Mostar, Trg Hrvatskih Velikana 1, Mostar, Bosnia and Herzegovina
ana.smoljo@sum.ba
https://www.unin.hr/, https://www.sum.ba/

Abstract. The e-Schools Programme is an initiative of the Croatian Academic and Research Network - CARNET- to digitalize the Croatian primary and secondary education system, bridging the gap between traditional methods and modern digital solutions. Earlier solutions should have uniformly integrated digital technology in all schools in Croatia, often due to insufficient infrastructure and education of school staff. Lack of knowledge of new technologies limited digital solutions, such as the e-Class Register, the electronic class register for primary and secondary schools. The e-Schools Programme brought a comprehensive solution, offering not only the necessary equipment and infrastructure but also education and support for teachers in using new technologies, which directly impacted the increase in the use of the e-Class Register. The methodology used in this paper included a quantitative and qualitative analysis of the use of the e-Class Register, evaluating user satisfaction and the efficiency of administrative processes. The key results show a significant increase in using the e-Class Register, greater transparency, and organization in schools, highlighting the e-Schools Programme as a successful model for modernizing education.

Keywords: Digital transformation of education · Education of teachers · Digital technology in schools · Evaluation methodology · Implementation results

1 Introduction

In the past, introducing new technologies in Croatian schools largely depended on the initiative and innovation of individual principals, teachers, and local governments. The "e-Schools: a comprehensive informatization of school operation processes and teaching processes aimed at the Creation of digitally mature schools for the 21st Century" programme, launched in March 2015, represents a crucial step toward the digital transformation of the primary and secondary education system in the Republic of Croatia. Croatian Academic and Research Network - CARENT provides technological infrastructure and support services to educational and research institutions. Through projects such as the e-Schools, it works on digitalizing the Croatian education system, promoting digital tools and resources to improve the quality of education and research.

T. Volarić et al. (Eds.): MoStart 2024, CCIS 2124, pp. 55–68, 2024.
https://doi.org/10.1007/978-3-031-62058-4_5

The e-Schools Programme aimed to strengthen the capacity of primary and secondary schools by increasing their digital maturity level. The goal of the Programme was to prepare students for the labor market, further education, and lifelong learning, providing them with the necessary skills and knowledge to succeed in a digitally oriented world. Specific goals included ensuring a purposeful, reliable, and secure digital environment, improving the efficiency and coherence of processes in the education system, improving digital competencies, and strategic leadership of schools. With 212 million euro in total value, the pilot project covered 151 primary and secondary schools, and the second phase of the project included all schools in the Republic of Croatia financed from the state budget [1].

The impact of the e-Schools Programme on the usage of the e-Class Register is observed through the prism of its infrastructure, equipment, and application solutions that enabled and improved digital communication and administration within the school system. By implementing the elements above, the e-Schools Programme created a favorable environment for the more comprehensive application and functionality of the e-Class Register, thereby contributing to digitalizing the educational process and enabling more efficient use of digital tools in schools. This Programme was also recognized and awarded internationally, confirming its importance and success in creating a more inclusive and digitally equipped educational system.

The e-Class Register is a web application for keeping a class register in an electronic form. The application has all the functionalities of the existing class register, with additional functionalities made possible by digital technologies such as automated notifications, alarms, and reminders. The e-Class Register provides a meaningful overview of all essential data to parents, students, principals, teachers, and other school employees, custom for a particular function [2]. Various reports are available in the application, enabling analysis during pedagogical monitoring and creating reports prepared for the teachers' council sessions. An additional advantage is the prevention of unauthorized entry, as well as theft and inadvertent or intentional destruction of the class register, which sometimes happens in schools.

Student information is downloaded from the e-Schools Register for each class department at the beginning of the school year. During the school year, teachers enter working hours, grades, absences, and other information about classes in the e-Class Registry. At the end of the school year, when the teachers have entered the final grades for the students, the class teacher initiates the process of transferring subjects, grades, exams, absences, pedagogical measures, and management in the e-Schools Register, from which certificates are printed.

2   Introduction

The development of the e-Class Register represented an essential step towards the digitalization of the education system in the Republic of Croatia. The pilot project of introducing this application started in 2011 in three schools, and the e-Class Register has since become the central element for keeping official records, with positive impressions among teachers. The introduction of the Ordinance on Amendments to the Ordinance on the Content and Form of Certificates and Other Public Documents and Pedagogical Documentation and Records in School Institutions in 2012 enabled schools to keep class registers in electronic form, eliminating the need for paper records. With the continuous support of CARNET, including educational courses and technical support, the e-Class Register facilitated administration, improved communication, and encouraged transparency in the Croatian education system [3].

Data obtained from CARNET indicate a constant growth in the number of schools included in the e-Class Register, with only three schools in the 2011/2012 school year up to 200 schools in the 2013/2014 school year. This growth reflects the increased digitization and acceptance of the e-Class Registry as a central tool for managing school teaching and administrative processes. The number of teachers using the e-Class Register has increased from 80 in the 2011/2012 school year to 7,135 in the 2013/2014 school year. The trend indicated that teachers see the value and benefit of using the e-Class Registry in their daily practice, which includes keeping records of grades, absences, and teaching hours.

The research presented by Vrkić Dimić and Vidov in the article "E-Class Register in School Practice - Opinions and Experience of Secondary School Teachers" investigates the attitudes and experience of 127 teachers from nine secondary schools in Zadar about the use of the e-Class Registry. The results suggest a broad acceptance of the e-Class Register among teachers, who consider it a helpful tool for improving the educational process, emphasizing its simplicity and functionality. Despite the generally positive reception, research reveals that teachers do not take advantage of all the possibilities of the e-Class Register but only use selected functions [4]. Furthermore, they note that not a single school that transferred to the e-Class Register has decided to abandon its use and return to classic class registers. The number of schools using the e-Class Register is constantly increasing, as shown in Fig. 1.

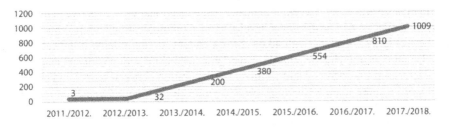

Fig. 1. Graphic representation of the schools using the e-Class Register [4]

The authors conclude that the teachers emphasize the necessity of quality training for older colleagues and teachers who are not inclined to introduce innovations in teaching, as well as the necessity of continuous support within schools as a prerequisite for effective and quality use of the e-Class Register in everyday school life. The research conducted by the Faculty of Philosophy of the University of Rijeka after the end of the e-Schools pilot project showed the frequency with which primary and secondary school teachers participate in various ICT activities after implementing new technologies, as presented in Fig. 2 [5].

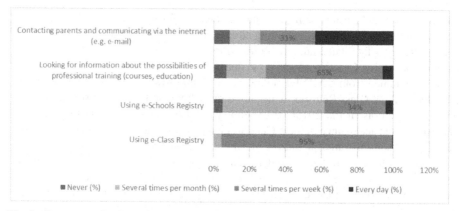

Fig. 2. Data processing from the research of the Faculty of Philosophy from Rijeka, ICT activities related to school and teaching - the percentage of teachers' involvement in certain activities in the final measurement [5]

The use of the e-Class Register stands out, considering that 94.8% of respondents use it several times a week, which indicates that it has become an integral part of the education system. However, since it is used daily by only 0.7% of respondents, the e-Class Register serves specific administrative functions that do not require daily attention. The activity of using the e-Schools Register is relatively low, represented daily by 4.3, and 56.9% of respondents use it several times a month, indicating its use for cyclical or periodic administrative tasks.

Searching for information about professional development opportunities (courses, education) shows high involvement, with 64.9% of respondents actively looking for information several times a week. It indicates that educational workers strive to improve their competencies and professional development. Communication with parents via the Internet is highly prevalent, with 43.6% of respondents doing it daily. It indicates that digital communication has become a standard practice in interaction with parents, which likely increased transparency and facilitated collaboration between school and home.

Based on these data, technology plays a vital role in the modernization and efficiency of the education process, enabling better administrative task management, facilitating professional development, and improving communication between the school and parents. Digital tools such as the e-Class Register and the e-Schools Register have proven crucial in managing school operations, and access to information and digital communication supports development and collaboration.

According to the book "The Road to Digital Maturity: The e-Schools Programme," CARNET aligned its infrastructure strategy with global trends through the implementation of a software-defined data center (SDDC), which is a virtualized cloud storage solution, eliminating the need for physical hardware. This modern solution leads to a reduction of capital and operational costs and simplifies the delivery of services to customers while increasing the security and availability of the infrastructure. The transition to the cloud environment enabled the standardization of administrative processes and security procedures, whereby CARNET centralized its operations and focused on the unification of technological needs and goals, following international directives such as the Directive on measures for a high standard level of cybersecurity across the Union (NIS2 Directives) [6].

By switching to SDDC, CARNET demonstrates a proactive approach to adapting to a rapidly changing technological environment, ensuring the high efficiency and security of its services. However, this approach brings challenges related to cloud data management and security, requiring continuous monitoring and updating security protocols. SDDC implementation also raises questions about the long-term operational costs associated with cloud services and the potential dependence on external service providers. Despite these challenges, the benefits of centralization, simplification of processes, and increased availability of resources make this move strategically essential to maintain CARNET's competitiveness in providing services to the education sector.

Research on the effects of the program "e-Schools: Development of the System of Digitally Mature Schools (Phase II)" carried out on 313 schools and ten educational centers indicates teachers' widespread use of desktop and laptop computers. In contrast, the use of tablets and smart boards was less common. Most teachers use digital technology to prepare lessons, but there is room for increasing its use in teaching. Research has shown that most parents expressed satisfaction with using the e-Class Register, highlighting its usefulness in monitoring their children's grades, absences, and upcoming examinations. This positive perception and satisfaction with the e-Class Register reflects the successful integration of digital technology into the school system and emphasizes the importance of the e-Schools Programme in promoting digital literacy and digital competencies. The recommendations include systematic information and education of parents about the possibilities of the e-Class Register and other digital tools, which indicates the need for continuous improvement and promotion of digital resources in education. Table 1 shows the parents' responses of students from schools from the pilot project and schools included in the second phase of the e-Schools, who showed satisfaction with using the e-Class Register. Half of the parents stated they were completely satisfied with the e-Class Register. However, less than 1% of parents are unfamiliar with the e-Class Register, affecting their ability to express satisfaction with the system. An additional 97% of parents expressed general satisfaction with the e-Class Register [7].

Table 1. Satisfaction of parents of primary and secondary school students from the pilot project and schools involved in II. Phase of the Programme with applications [6]

Parents' satisfaction with applications	School		Not familiar with the application	Not satisfied at all	Mostly unsatisfied	Neither satisfied nor unsatisfied	Mostly satisfied	Completely satisfied
	PS/ SS	Pilot / New						
e-Class Register application	PS	Pilot	0.6	0.3	1.0	3.5	**42.9**	51.8
		New	0.6	0.3	1.6	2.3	**42.9**	52.3
	SS	Pilot	0.6	0.3	1.0	4.9	**46.2**	47.1
		New	0.7	0.2	1.2	3.1	**44.1**	50.7

The results show parents' acceptance of the e-Class Register, highlighting the challenges of using digital technology in the teaching process. It is necessary to further invest in the education of teachers to increase the use of digital tools in teaching, which was especially evident during the pandemic of the COVID-19 virus. The pandemic accelerated the integration of digital technology into the teaching process, but it also emphasized the importance of system preparedness for emergencies. Research has pointed out that before the COVID-19 pandemic, the Croatian education system did not systematically use digital technology, especially at lower levels of education. The pandemic has forced teachers to incorporate technology into their work, and national guidelines and the Action Plan for the Implementation of Distance Learning have provided a framework for action [8].

Continuous teacher education and investment in digital infrastructure are recommended to ensure the resilience of the education system to future challenges and maximize the potential of digital technology in education.

3   Research Methodology

The research methodology for the analysis of the impact of the e-Schools Programme on the use of the e-Class Register service was adapted to include information on the temporal frame and the method of data processing. The analysis covered ten years, from 2014 to 2023, whereby the data was processed monthly to enable a detailed temporal analysis using the e-Class Register. After monthly processing, the data were aggregated into annual groups for each calendar year within ten years to enable better annual comparison and observation of trends.

A descriptive statistical method was used to collect and analyze quantitative data, which included:

- number of classes using the e-Class Register (28,348)
- number of teachers (50,567) and students (451,541) recorded in the system
- number of home schools (1365)
- number of accesses to the system from computers (131,270.131) and mobile devices (5,523.781)
- average number of students (372,557) and parents (10,690) accessing the system annually.

Financial data has also been collected and analyzed for the duration of the e-Schools Programme from 2015 to 2023, including details of investments in education for raising the digital skills of school employees and infrastructure related to the e-Class Register, such as:

- educating school administrators
- organizing workshops
- using equipment
- implementing education
- developing educational content
- education for the development of digital competencies
- creating teaching scenarios.

The research methodology also considered investments in infrastructure components, e.g., equipment for data centers, computer equipment for schools, and upgrading server infrastructure.

The total investment in education for raising the digital skills of teaching and non-teaching staff amounted to 5.8 million euros, while the total investment in infrastructure related to the e-Class Register amounted to 54.6 million euros.

The collected data was then analyzed using advanced data processing tools such as Microsoft Excel and Power BI, which enable data aggregation, synthesis, and visualization for a comprehensive understanding and interpretation of the results. This research enables precise quantification of the e-Class Register usage and related investments, a deep understanding of how trends and usage patterns develop and change over time, and their relation to financial investments.

4 Research Results

Analyzing investments in digital infrastructure and education, Fig. 3 shows that Croatia invests significant resources in the digital transformation of the education sector. The total investments, which include initiatives such as the e-Schools pilot project and its second phase, indicate a strong commitment to developing digitally mature schools that can respond to the demands of the modern age. These projects improve the infrastructure and digital skills of the teaching and non-teaching staff and create an environment where students can acquire the knowledge and skills needed to succeed in the digital economy. Investments of over 218 million euros in these programs demonstrate a clear vision and determination to achieve the goals of digital education and infrastructure, setting Croatia as an example of a country that is actively working to shape the future of education.

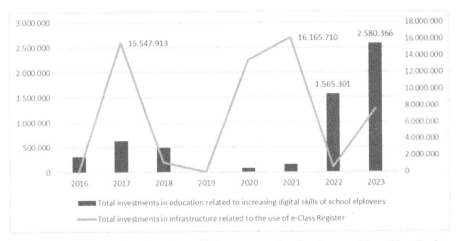

Fig. 3. Total investments in education and infrastructure related to the use of the e-Class Register

Investments in education in the scope of the e-Schools Programme are present during the observed period from 2016 to 2023, with significant fluctuations in annual amounts.

The analysis of total investments in education shows a significant increase in 2022 and 2023, and the investment of 4 million euros is particularly noteworthy, indicating the intensification of activities aimed at various forms of education and the infrastructure related to the e-Class Registry. The increase in investment reflects a strategic approach to improving the quality of education by integrating technological resources and competencies, emphasizing the continued commitment to improving the education system and providing the necessary support and resources for implementing advanced educational technologies in schools.

Investments in infrastructure during 2017, 2020, and 2021 were aimed at modernizing and improving the technological infrastructure essential for developing the e-Class Register and encouraging the use of digital technology in the educational process. Significant investments in 2017, including more than 6 million euros for the data center equipment and over 7 million euros for computer equipment for teachers and classrooms, indicate an intensive approach to the digitalization of schools. Additional investments, such as purchasing computer equipment for internal needs and tokens for teachers, contribute to establishing a robust infrastructure necessary to implement advanced educational technologies efficiently.

Implementing the e-Class Register significantly contributed to the efficient organization of the teaching process, improving communication between teachers, students, and parents. By reducing the administrative burden and simplifying the monitoring of student progress, teachers have recognized and welcomed the benefits of this digital tool.

Analysis of data from the period from 2014 to 2023 indicates an increase in the number of students and teachers using the e-Class Register, which indicates the wide acceptance and integration of this system into school practice. Although the number of classes and students started to stagnate in 2019, the number of teachers using the e-Class Register continued to grow. This trend suggests that training aimed at improving digital skills in education and the distribution of additional equipment for classrooms play a key role in encouraging teachers to use the e-Class Registry more actively. (see Fig. 4.)

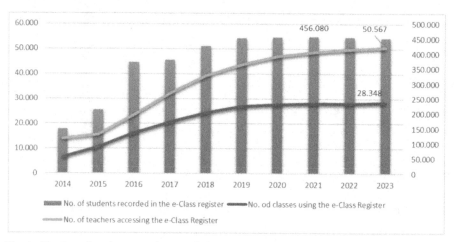

Fig. 4. Number of students, teachers, and classes recorded in the e-Class Register from 2014 to 2023.

The research results emphasize how the e-Class Register facilitates daily administrative tasks related to teaching and promotes transparency and efficiency in monitoring and evaluating student work. The increase in the number of teachers using the e-Class Register indicates the need for continuous support and education in digital technology to ensure that the potential of these tools is fully utilized in the educational context.

Research conducted in the second phase of the Programme "e-Schools: Development of the System of Digitally Mature Schools (II. Phase)" investigated the usefulness of various educational activities in developing digital competencies among teachers. The results show a general tendency towards the high usefulness of video tutorials and the EduBlic platform. Video tutorials are highlighted as the most helpful education format, with almost half of respondents (47%) believing they are mostly helpful, while 85% consider them at least moderately helpful. On the other hand, EduBlic stands out with the highest percentage of respondents who consider it completely useful (13%), suggesting that this format has significant potential for providing effective learning, as highlighted in Fig. 5.

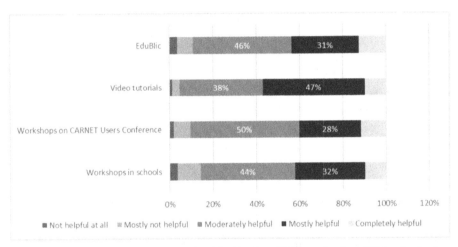

Fig. 5. Processing data from the research of the Faculty of Philosophy from Rijeka, Evaluations of the usefulness of participation in various forms of education for the development of digital competencies - teachers in new schools (% of responses)

Workshops held in schools and at the CARNET Users Conference - CUC proved helpful but with somewhat less enthusiasm among respondents compared to digital education formats. The fact that 90% of respondents consider the workshops at CUC moderately useful implies that personal contact and interaction can play an essential role in perceiving usefulness. However, digital formats lead in terms of comfort and adaptability to the users. These insights point to the need to further integrate digital tools and resources into educational programs to maximize the usefulness and engagement of respondents.

The development of digital maturity within the school system, considering that the number of schools that have reached a medium or high level of digital maturity is increasing, has significantly impacted the use of digital technology in the educational context. This progress has led to greater use of computers in the classroom and broader use of mobile devices among students and teachers. This trend contributed to increased access to the e-Class Register through various platforms, promoting constant interaction among school staff, students, and parents and facilitating the monitoring of educational achievements and administrative obligations.

During the pilot phase of the e-Schools Programme, between 2015 and 2018, a significant increase in the number of schools that implemented the e-Class Register was recorded, with 793 parent schools making up 49.6% of the total number of 1,600 parent institutions, which indicates a wide acceptance and integration of this system, as presented in Fig. 6.

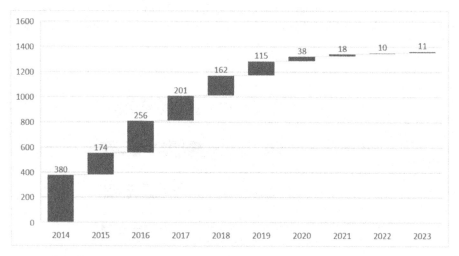

Fig. 6. The trend of including home schools in the e-Class Register system.

This development was not limited to infrastructure improvements but also included improving employees' and students' digital skills, the integration of digital technologies in learning and teaching, optimizing business processes, and improving communication between the school and parents. Such a comprehensive approach to the digitization of education is crucial for preparing students for modern society and the labor market, providing a foundation for the continuous development and adaptation of the school system following technological progress.

Figure 7 shows the analysis of the average number of students and parents who use the e-Class Register. There was a slight decrease in the use of the e-Class Register among students, which is related to the general decrease in the number of students in schools. At the same time, a significant increase in the number of parents accessing the e-Class Register was recorded, with an increase of almost five times compared to previous periods.

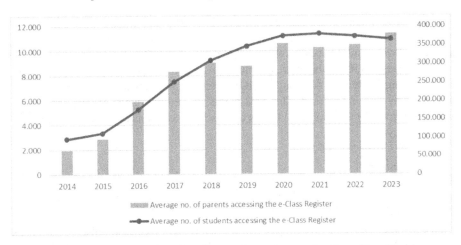

Fig. 7. The average number of students and parents accessing the e-Class Register

This trend indicates a growing acceptance of the e-Class Register among parents as a helpful tool for tracking educational progress and administrative details related to their children despite a general decline in the number of students using the system.

Through the improvement of the digital infrastructure and the development of digital competencies, the e-Schools Programme made it possible to increase access to the e-Class Register from computers and mobile devices, thus improving the accessibility and functionality of this platform in the education system. Such efforts reflect the main goal of the e-Schools Programme, which strives to prepare students for life and work in a digitized environment, promoting the integration of digital tools into the routine of learning and teaching.

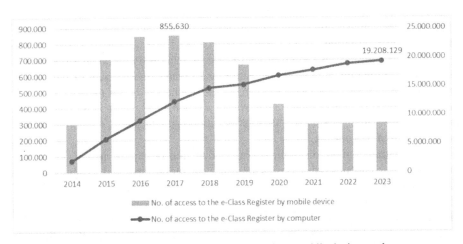

Fig. 8. Number of accesses to the e-Class Register from mobile devices and computers

Figure 8 shows the growing trend of access to the e-Class Register from computers, with more than 19 million accesses recorded in the last year of observation, with a decrease in the number of accesses via mobile devices. The decrease in access via mobile devices can be attributed to the introduction of the e-Class Register application, which is compatible with Android and iOS operating systems and suggests a change in how the system is accessed. This data points to the importance of adapting digital educational tools to technological trends and user needs to ensure maximum usability and efficiency.

5 Discussion

The e-Schools Programme significantly impacted the digital transformation of the Croatian education system. The project aimed to develop digitally mature schools that will prepare students for the modern labor market and lifelong learning. Through this project, schools received the necessary infrastructure, equipment, education, and support to adapt teaching and business processes to the digital age, which resulted in improvements in the learning and teaching process and more efficient organization and transparency of school operations.

The e-Schools Programme particularly emphasized the importance of the e-Class Register as a digital tool. The satisfaction of users, especially parents, confirms the successful implementation of digital technology in the educational process. This program is also recognized internationally, which confirms its importance in creating a more inclusive and digitally equipped educational environment.

Infrastructural changes and raising the level of digital maturity of Croatian schools were achieved through investment in modern infrastructure and equipment. Schools have become able to integrate digital technologies into daily work, including building local computer networks and providing high-performance virtual computers. This improved the availability and efficiency of the e-Class Register for teachers, students, and parents. Progress in the digital maturity of schools, along with teachers' education and professional development, has created a favorable environment for a more comprehensive use of digital tools in teaching.

The use of the e-Class Register during the e-Schools Programme significantly increased, contributing to better organization and greater transparency of the educational process. Positive feedback from parents and teachers indicates the crucial role of the e-Class Register in providing a clear overview of students' obligations and achievements despite challenges such as the need for additional education of school staff and infrastructure improvements.

Implementing digital tools in the Croatian education system through the e-Schools Programme has encountered various challenges, including the need for more infrastructure and technical support in some schools and additional teacher education. These challenges highlight the importance of continuous investment in modern infrastructure, equipment, and professional development of educational workers to maximize the potential of digital technologies in education. Despite these obstacles, the e-Schools Programme has achieved significant success in promoting digital literacy and competencies, also highlighting the need for a systematic approach to solving the mentioned challenges for future progress.

Recommendations for a broader application of digital tools in education include continuous education and professional development of teachers for better use of digital technology, investment in school infrastructure with the necessary technical support, and promotion of more active use of digital technology in teaching to encourage interactive learning. These recommendations aim to overcome existing challenges and maximize the potential of digital technologies in the Croatian education system.

6 Conclusion

This paper demonstrates that the e-Schools Programme represents a fundamental initiative for the digital transformation of the Croatian education system, focusing on infrastructure improvements, digital competencies, and digital tools such as the e-Class Register. The e-Schools enabled a more efficient organization of the teaching process, improving communication between teachers, students, and parents and reducing the administrative burden. The increase in the number of teachers using the e-Class Register and the expansion of the digital infrastructure contributed to the greater integration of digital technologies in learning and teaching, which raised access to the e-Class Register from different devices.

In conclusion, the e-Schools Programme represents a significant step forward in digitalizing the educational process in Croatia. However, the research points to challenges such as teachers' insufficient use of all e-Class Register functionalities and the need for continuous education and support. A critical review of the project and research results suggests the importance of adapting educational programs to the specific needs of teachers and students and emphasizes the need for a systematic approach to solving challenges related to the full use of digital tools in education.

Further development of the e-Class Register system should address these challenges, encouraging more extensive use of digital tools among teachers and students and continuing investments in digital infrastructure and competencies. It is crucial to continuously evaluate the effects of implementing digital tools on the education process to ensure that digitalization contributes to the quality of education and the preparation of students for the demands of a digitally oriented society.

References

1. e-Schools Programme web site. https://www.e-skole.hr/program-e-skole/. Accessed 29 Jan 2024
2. e-Class Register service site. https://www.carnet.hr/usluga/e-dnevnik-za-skole/. Accessed 29 Jan 2024
3. Mišura, I.: e-Class Register (graduation paper). Osijek, Josip Juraj Strossmayer University, Physics Department (2016). https://urn.nsk.hr/urn:nbn:hr:160:397314. Accessed 15 Jan 2024
4. Vrkić Dimić, J., Vidov, S.: e-Class Register in school practice – opinions and experience of secondary school teachers. Acta Iadertina 16(1) (2019). https://hrcak.srce.hr/225576. Accessed 15 Jan 2024
5. Mohorić, T.; Smojver-Ažić, S.; Močibob, M. (2020.) The frequency of ICT use by teachers and students. In: Kolić-Vehovec, S. (ed.) Introduction of Contemporary Technologies in Learning and Teaching: Research on the Effects of the e-Schools Pilot Project, pp. 63–91. Faculty of Philosophy of the University of Rijeka, Rijeka (2020)

6. Smoljo, A., Škvarč, G., Majetić, R. (eds.): The Road to Digital Maturity: the e-Schools Programme (2023). Croatian Academic and Research Network – CARNET, Zagreb. ISBN: 978-953-6802-68-5, NSK: 001197126

7. Kolić-Vehovec, S.: Final research report with conclusions and strategic and operational recommendations. Scientific research on the effects of the project "e-Schools: Development of the system of digitally mature schools (II. phase)". Center for Applied Psychology, Faculty of Philosophy, University of Rijeka (2023)

8. Šabić, I.; Dodig, L.; Luić, L.: COVID-19 impact on the use of ICT tools in the Croatian education system. In: Gómez Chova, L., López Martínez, A., Candel Torres, I. (eds.) ICERI Proceedings, pp. 5781–5786 (2020). https://doi.org/10.21125/iceri.2020.1241

9. Srednja.hr web portal. https://www.srednja.hr/novosti/novi-otuzni-podaci-u-deset-godina-izg ubili-smo-58-570-ucenika-evo-gdje-je-situacija-najgora/. Accessed 2 Feb 2024

Students' Digital Learning Behavior Using the Mandatory and Non-mandatory Platforms in an Online Learning Environment

Slavomir Stankov[1]([✉]) [iD], Suzana Tomaš[2] [iD], and Matea Markić Vučić[3] [iD]

[1] Faculty of Science, University of Split, Split, Croatia
slavomirstankov@gmail.com
[2] Faculty of Humanities and Social Sciences, University of Split, Split, Croatia
suzana@ffst.hr
[3] NSoft, Mostar, Bosnia and Herzegovina

Abstract. Student behavior in the online learning environment encompasses a variety of activities, including learning tasks and knowledge assessments supported by e-learning platforms. In this study, we investigated the behavior of 175 first-year undergraduate students enrolled in the Programming 1 course at the Faculty of Science, University of Split, during the academic year 2021/2022. The course curriculum addressed fundamental programming principles and both theoretical and practical aspects of application development utilizing Python. Instructional materials were delivered through the Moodle and CloudMap&Flash online platforms, consisting of four areas and nine instructional units. The instructional approach followed a hybrid model and was conducted between October 4, 2021, and February 20, 2022, spanning four distinct research phases. Our research aimed to elucidate students' perceptions and engagement levels with online course activities across mandatory and non-mandatory e-learning platforms. To achieve this, we developed an original CAM model incorporating criteria to assess student behavior during learning and knowledge assessment. Our findings indicate a consistent pattern of student engagement with the e-course link, suggesting that activities on the platform are not accessed randomly by students. Moreover, we observed a notable increase in the number of course activities during the mandatory tasks of the initial phase, particularly among students in the Moodle group, compared to the non-mandatory tasks in subsequent phases. Furthermore, a heightened frequency of visits was noted during the formative and summative assessment periods.

Keywords: digital learning behavior · online learning platforms · course activities model · measure student behavior

1 Introduction

An online learning environment is a digital platform or system that facilitates education without requiring physical interaction between teachers and students. It provides teachers with the capability to generate and disseminate instructional materials to students via communication channels. Learning within an online environment broadens

T. Volarić et al. (Eds.): MoStart 2024, CCIS 2124, pp. 69–83, 2024.
https://doi.org/10.1007/978-3-031-62058-4_6

students' horizons, presenting them with an array of opportunities. Furthermore, with internet access, students benefit from an unprecedented wealth of educational resources. However, appropriate conduct in such an environment necessitates adherence to a specialized code of ethics that underscores respect for all participants in both the immediate teaching process and broader social network discussions. Unethical or inappropriate behavior can have severe repercussions, including academic suspension or expulsion. Furthermore, within online teaching supported by digital platforms, behavior is subject to observation and evaluation on a global scale, encompassing the utilization of learning resources, monitoring student progress, and assessing student knowledge. Student behavior within the online teaching process is contingent upon both the nature of the assigned tasks and the platforms employed for their execution. In the context of our research, we examine how students behave themselves in an online learning environment. To delineate this, we introduce the terminological distinction between the learning phase facilitated by a mandatory e-learning platform (prescribed by the teacher) and the learning phase involving a non-mandatory platform (selected by the student from those provided).

Various e-learning platforms aid students in formulating diverse learning strategies and acquainting themselves with a myriad of digital tools. From the teacher's standpoint, this experience is equally advantageous as it allows for the comparison of the efficacy of various platforms to identify the most suitable e-learning environment for a specific field of study. This objective also underpins the research we present herein. The methodology section of this study comprehensively delineates the two phases of e-learning and the chosen online platforms.

During online learning, interactions between students and course content via e-learning platforms generate a substantial volume of data necessitating appropriate collection, measurement, processing, and analysis. This data holds the potential for identifying patterns in student behavior, monitoring their progress, and assessing the effectiveness of teaching strategies and methodologies. Both students and teachers utilize course-related data during online classes: students aim to enhance their learning outcomes, while teachers endeavor to refine instructional content and teaching dynamics. Considering the points above in the introductory context, we have established a comprehensive objective to investigate student behavior concerning online course activities during both mandatory and non-mandatory phases across diverse e-learning platforms.

2 Literature Review

Student behavior is examined from diverse perspectives; however, it is important to monitor the frequency of activities within the online course and their influence on knowledge assessment and evaluation. Nevertheless, establishing a definitive correlation between the number of activities and course success is not always apparent. Several authors argue that this correlation has yet to be sufficiently substantiated [1]. Some studies have identified a positive association between learning time, considered as one metric of learning activity, and course success [2].

The authors of a comprehensive study investigating the influence of online strategies on learning outcomes in academic education [3] propose a redesign of access to instructional content to enhance learning, teaching, knowledge testing, and student-teacher communication.

We facilitate access to instructional content for learning, teaching, knowledge testing, and student-teacher communication through the utilization of a learning management system (specifically, the Moodle platform available at moodle.com), web-based concept mapping software (Cmap Cloud platform accessible at cmapcloud.ihmc.us), and digital flashcard technology (Memory platform, accessible at memory.com).

Moodle serves as an online learning platform that empowers both students and teachers to design and deliver instructional content pertinent to domain knowledge. Employing concept maps [4, 5] effectively organizes and visually represents knowledge while delineating the relationships between elements within the knowledge structure. Memory, a digital flashcard platform, facilitates individual and group-based learning activities through a feature known as Classroom, which is integral to our research. In our approach, the Moodle platform offers comprehensive administrative functionalities alongside tools tailored for the delivery of instructional content to students. Additionally, we have integrated Cmap Cloud and Memory to form a cohesive e-learning experience termed CloudMap&Flash, leveraging their established efficacy in facilitating learning, teaching, and knowledge assessment [6, 7]. This joined platform aligns with the cognitive domain's initial two levels (memory and understanding) of Bloom's taxonomy of knowledge [8]. Concept maps, within the associative network of concepts, elucidate the interconnectedness among ideas, aiding in the comprehension of the broader domain knowledge landscape. Meanwhile, the flashcard algorithm prompts "active recall," engages metacognitive abilities, and facilitates confidence-based repetition [9, 10].

The literature on online learning extensively delves into the factors shaping student behavior and engagement within digital courses. A noteworthy revelation is the mediating role of attitude toward online learning between intrinsic motivation, extrinsic motivation, and student engagement [11]. However, it was also noted that attitude does not act as a mediator in the relationship between intrinsic motivation to accomplish tasks and engagement, suggesting that additional factors may wield a more substantial influence on motivating students in online learning environments [12]. Moreover, self-regulation strategies, such as time management skills and proficiency in implementing learning strategies, emerged as significant factors linked to satisfaction and the perceived usefulness of online classes [13].

The presence of external motivators, such as grades or completion requirements, was found to foster increased engagement and participation in the obligatory phases of online learning. Conversely, non-mandatory phases facilitated more self-regulated behavior driven by intrinsic motivation and individual interest [14]. Students demonstrated heightened activity in mandatory phases when they perceived alignment with their learning objectives or career aspirations. Conversely, non-mandatory phases offered opportunities for autonomy and exploration, enabling students to focus on their specific interests. The degree of instructor support and guidance significantly influenced student behavior, with instructors providing more assistance and feedback in mandatory phases, thereby impacting student motivation and participation [15].

Educational data mining techniques were also utilized to identify students' characteristics, such as academic performance and behavior, enabling a better understanding of their interests and ability to understand educational content [16].

In addition to the factors mentioned above, the selection of a learning platform can exert a notable influence on students' behavior and engagement within online environments. Evaluating the effects of various platforms on student behavior across mandatory and non-mandatory phases can offer valuable insights into the influence of technology on online learning experiences. By comprehending the interplay between platform selection and other determinants, teachers can make informed decisions in selecting and deploying learning platforms to enhance student engagement and academic performance [17].

Furthermore, findings from the research [18] highlight the significance of various factors such as test performance, completion rate, effectiveness, and student participation in enhancing the learning outcomes of college students. This underscores the importance of incorporating strategies such as homework assignments, troubleshooting, supervision, and feedback to optimize teaching activities. Moreover, the study suggests shifting from a 'teacher-centered' to a 'student-centered' approach to encourage active participation and independent learning skills among students. Additionally, attention to the timing of students' logins to the online teaching platform is crucial, as it significantly impacts learning outcomes. Therefore, the design and presentation of teaching resources, as well as homework assignments, should be tailored to suit students' online engagement patterns. Lastly, the provision of replay functions and opportunities for repeated training on the online platform can further enhance students' understanding and retention of course materials.

Additionally, it is noteworthy that studies are scarce specifically comparing student behavior during mandatory and non-mandatory phases within the online learning environment. However, our study endeavors to bridge this gap by concentrating on the comparative analysis of student behavior across these delineated phases. Through scrutinizing disparities and delineating factors influencing student behavior in both mandatory and non-mandatory phases, our research aims to furnish valuable insights for designing efficacious online courses conducive to fostering student engagement and achievement.

3   Research Methodology

3.1   Research Structure

To undertake this research, we are leveraging domain knowledge, encompassing the foundational principles of programming and the theoretical aspects of application development using the Python programming language within the Programming 1 course. Consequently, the teacher must underscore the connection between theoretical understanding and practical application when incorporating program code into the selection of instructional materials and delivering introductory motivational lectures.

The domain knowledge content (Fig. 1) integrated into the CloudMap&Flash platform comprises 941 Memory flashcard blocks and 40 video files. Similarly, the content for 36 components is replicated on the Moodle platform, encompassing lessons, assessments, as well as videos derived from lectures and exercises.

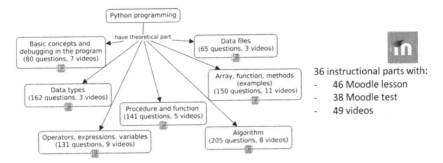

Fig. 1. CloudMap&Flash and Moodle content of domain knowledge

Accessing the instructional content of the integrated CloudMap&Flash platform typically involves three sequential steps through the web links provided within the Moodle
platform (first step). Subsequently, in the second step, students access the concept maps
via the Cmap Cloud platform, followed by the third step, wherein they access the Memory flashcard blocks by selecting the web link associated with the respective concept
map to delve into its details. Nonetheless, students have the option of utilizing direct
access to the Memory platform after their initial registration (Fig. 2).

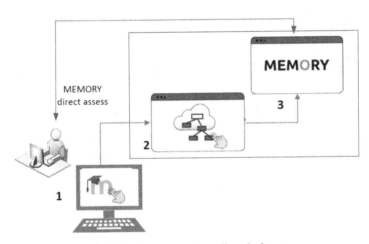

Fig. 2. Student access to online platforms

To structure the instructional content for domain knowledge, we established logical
groupings of the course material within a hierarchical framework, as illustrated in Fig. 3.
The instructional content was categorized into four distinct instructional areas (Area(i)
for i = 1 to 4) and nine instructional units (Unit(i) for i = 1 to 9). Each instructional area
encompasses a course overview and theoretical components, along with two segments
dedicated to Moodle and CloudMap&Flash, respectively, in addition to a section for
knowledge assessment.

Instructional area	Instructional unit		Instructional content files				
	Name and contents of instructional units' elements		First phase		Second phase	Third phase	Fourth phase
			F	M			
Area(1) (Course Overview and Theoretical parts)	Unit(1)	course overview (reports, statistics)	None				
	Unit(2)	instructional content materials for lectures and exercises, teacher messages and notices	9	9	27	29	30
	Unit(3)	video recording of lectures and exercises of traditional instruction for elements of the course	19	19	29	29	29
	Unit(4)	video of instructional contents for elements of the course structure	27	27	51	51	51
Area(2) (Cmap cloud, Memory platform)	Unit(5)	instructional content designed on the Memory platform	15	-	19	19	19
	Unit(6)	concept map web pages for instructional content elements that link to blocks of Flash Memory cards.	14	-	17	17	17
Area(3) (Moodle platform)	Unit(7)	Moodle lessons of instructional content	-	18	38	38	38
	Unit(8)	Moodle tests of instructional content	-	27	49	49	49
Area(4) (Knowledge assessment)	Unit(9)	formative and summative assessment tests	None				
	Total instructional content files		84	100	230	232	233

Note: First phase – (F – Flash group; M – Moodle group)

Fig. 3. Data for instructional areas and instructional units

3.2 Measurement in Online Course Activities

Our research entailed the development of a *Course Activities Model* (CAM) designed to assess student behavior within online learning environments. This multi-layered model relies on tracking the frequency of student engagements on Moodle, serving as indicators for evaluating the efficacy of learning activities and determining the attainment of learning outcomes. The principal objective of gauging online learning activities is to accumulate data conducive to enhancing teaching and learning outcomes within the online environment.

In our approach, online course activities refer to a set of different tasks designed and provided by the teacher through instructional areas and units in the Programming 1 course, particularly within the domain of Python programming (see Fig. 3).

The CAM is based on independent variables in the first layer, which we have described using appropriate physical and mathematical formalism.

Course activities represent the dynamics of the instructional process with learning activities and knowledge assessment including ontology of previously defined instructional units. Mathematically, it is an activity matrix (ACT) $m \times n$ where: $m, n \in N$ and $act_{ij} \in \mathbb{R}$ which can be $! = 0$ or $= 0$ for each $i = 1, 2, ..., m$ and $j = 1, 2, ..., n$. The value of the matrix element $act_{ij} <> 0$ means that the observed student has an activity for the observed day, while $act_{ij} = 0$ has no activity.

The rows of the ACT matrix are the students participating in the activity, while the columns are the dates of the activities Fig. 4.

$$ACT = \begin{bmatrix} act_{11} & act_{12} & act_{13} & ... & ... & ... & act_{1n} \\ act_{21} & act_{22} & act_{23} & ... & ... & ... & act_{2n} \\ act_{31} & act_{32} & act_{33} & ... & ... & ... & act_{3n} \\ ... & ... & ... & ... & ... & ... & ... \\ ... & ... & ... & ... & ... & ... & ... \\ ... & ... & ... & ... & ... & ... & ... \\ act_{m1} & act_{m2} & act_{m3} & ... & ... & ... & act_{mn} \end{bmatrix}$$

Fig. 4. Course activities matrix

Learning Activities

ACT is the primary matrix structure from which the following variables are derived in the second layer of the course activities model:

The number of active students per day – single row ASD matrix $1 \times n$ where is: $n \in N$ and $asd_i \in \mathbb{R}$ the number of ACT elements $! = 0$ for each $j = 1, 2, ..., n$. The ASD matrix is date-oriented and in its elements, it talks about the frequency of active students during the day for the observed phase.

The number of students' activities per day – one column SAD matrix $m \times 1$ where is: $m \in N$ and $sad_i \in \mathbb{R}$ the number of ACT elements $! = 0$ for each $i = 1, 2, ..., m$. The SAD matrix is student-oriented and its elements show an individual student's activity frequency in a day for the observed phase.

Student event context – one column SEC matrix $p \times 1$ where is: $p \in N$ and $sec_p \in \mathbb{R}$ instructional content files numbers on which the student performed learning activities for each $p = 1, 2, ..., nos$, nos is the number of students who access e-learning platforms in the observed phase.

Various methods were employed to assess and evaluate students' knowledge within the third layer. These methods encompassed utilizing the top list feature of the Memory platform, which ranks students based on their knowledge, as well as analyzing the outcomes of summative assessments administered during the second and third phases of the study. Additionally, the final exam in the fourth phase comprised two components, serving as a comprehensive evaluation of students' overall knowledge.

3.3   Research Timetable and Participants

The research comprised four phases spanning from October 4th, 2021, to February 20th, 2022 (refer to Fig. 5). During the first phase, students were divided into two groups: the Flash group and the Moodle group, with course activities primarily conducted through mandatory online e-learning platforms. Subsequently, in the second, third, and fourth phases, students were not assigned mandatory platforms. To facilitate analysis, we subdivided the course activities into a total of 15 periods, allowing for the monitoring of student behavior dynamics across each phase.

Participants are students of the Faculty of Science, University of Split - 1st year of undergraduate study in Programming 1 (2021/2022) (n = 174). Participants contributed to the research voluntarily, anonymously, and free of charge.

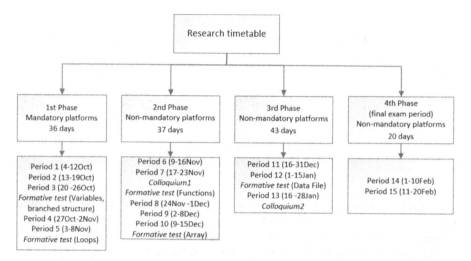

Fig. 5. Research phases and periods

3.4 Research Question and Research Hypotheses

RQ1: How do students behave in an online learning environment during the phase with mandatory platforms?

H1 – There is no difference in the number of active students per day between the Flash and Moodle groups.

H2 – There is no difference in the number of students' activities per day between the Flash and Moodle groups.

H3 – There is no difference in student event context between the Flash and Moodle groups.

RQ2: How do students behave in an online learning environment during the phases with non-mandatory platforms?

H1 – There is no difference in the number of active students per day between the second and third phases.

H2 – There is no difference in the number of students' activities per day between the second and third phases.

H3 – There is no difference in student event context between the second and third phases.

RQ3: How do the students' summative knowledge assessment scores (Colloquium 1 and Colloquium 2) correlate with the final exam?

4   Results with Discussion

The proposed CAM model is tailored to gauge student behavior within applied online platforms, involving several procedural steps such as data collection, preprocessing, processing, and interpretation of research findings. The CAM model is geared towards educators, necessitating proficiency in Moodle online course administration, Microsoft Excel data processing, and statistical spreadsheet software, such as jamovi [19]. The research findings in our study are derived from reports acquired by extracting a Microsoft Excel spreadsheet from the Moodle environment, encompassing data on all students, all days within the research timeframe, and all activities.

Data collection and Preprocessing were executed in the following steps:

1. Obtain Moodle course report with raw data
2. Extract attributes including Date, Name (student name), Event Context, and Event Name

Preprocessing facilitated subsequent processing and presentation of learning activity results, as well as the assessment and evaluation of students' knowledge.

Data processing comprised the subsequent steps:

1. Design a pivot table with Date and students' Name to generate the ACT matrix.
2. Determine:
   a. ASD matrix from the ACT matrix elements - sum act_{ij} non-zero matrix elements
   b. SAD matrix from the ACT matrix elements - count act_{ij} non-zero matrix elements
3. Design a pivot table with Name and Event Context (remove duplicates) for the SEC matrix.
4. Design the pivot table with Date, Name, Context Event, and Event Name for grouping Event Context and Date. Event Context grouping follows the defined instructional unit elements.
5. For both mandatory and non-mandatory phases design the table with students' Name, and values for SAD, and SEC variables.
6. Import data into the jamovi environment for calculations, including descriptive statistics, and t-test analysis for both mandatory and non-mandatory phases.

The total number of activities in student courses diminishes across the research phases (refer to Fig. 6), with the total number of activities in the fourth phase being 16.67 times lower than in the first phase. This reduction signifies a significant decline in student activity within the course.

This observation finds partial validation in the outcomes of prior research [21], which also identified a comparable approach among students engaged in online learning activities. However, researchers have reported similar phenomena in other settings where online instruction is prevalent.

Phases	N	Mean	Sum	SD	Min	Max	Skewness
Phase1 – Flash group – 82 students	36	518	18637	582	83	2468	2.30
Phase1 – Moodle group – 93 students		3209	115552	4048	296	16814	2.51
Phase2 – all – 163 students	37	1319	48795	1180	181	4817	1.59
Phase3 – all – 162 students	44	455	20011	787	10	5177	5.26
Phase4 – all – 153 students	20	403	8050	424	22	1920	2.65

Notes: N – number of days in research phases

Fig. 6. The total number of course activities on e-learning platforms in all research phases

4.1 Results of Learning Activities

Based on the total number of student activities on e-learning platforms by phases and periods of research, we proceeded with analysis according to the number of active students per day (ASD), the number of student activities per day (SAD), the number of files with instructional content used during the learning process (SEC), and the range for instructional unit elements.

Students' Behavior with Mandatory Platforms

In the first phase, we investigate the behavior of students on mandatory platforms in response to the first research question:

How do students behave in an online learning environment during the phase with mandatory platforms? (RQ1)

For all hypotheses, we verified the assumptions of normality of the distribution of variables using the Shapiro-Wilk test and the homogeneity of the variance of the variables using the Levene test. Based on hypothesis checking, we apply the Mann-Whitney statistical U test for hypotheses H1, H2, and H3. Statistical significance for all tests at the $\alpha = 0.05$.

The applied statistical test allows us to conclude the behavior of students with mandatory platforms concerning the set hypotheses:

H1 was accepted because there was not a statistically significant difference in the number of active students per day (ASD) between Flash's students (Mdn = 32.0, N = 36) and Moodle's students (Mdn = 33.0, N = 36), to U = 559, p = 0.319, rpb = 0.137.

H2 was accepted because there was not a statistically significant difference in the number of students' activities per day (SAD) between Flash's students (Mdn = 16.0, n = 82) and Moodle's students (Mdn = 15.0, n = 92), to U = 3663, p = 0.743, rpb = 0.0289.

H3 was rejected because there was a statistically significant difference in student event context (SEC) between Flash's students (Mdn = 51.0, n = 82) and Moodle's students (Mdn = 63.5, n = 92), to U = 2919, p = 0.01, rpb = 0.2263.

Furthermore, we observe student behavior by assessing the completion of course activities (see Fig. 6) based on the designated instructional units on e-learning platforms. This ranking process involved assigning weights to teaching units, corresponding to the number of activities, across a set of seven elements for mandatory platforms and nine for non-mandatory platforms. The reduced count of seven elements for mandatory platforms is due to students in each group lacking access to two instructional units.

The total count of learning activities for the Flash group (18637) markedly contrasts with that of the Moodle group (115521) of students, with the latter exhibiting a ratio slightly exceeding sixfold. This discrepancy primarily stems from the learning environment disparities between Moodle and Memory platforms. Notably, student activities, such as clicks on the Memory platform, remain unrecorded on the Moodle administrative platform. Specifically, the total number of Moodle learning activities, encompassing Moodle Lessons - Unit(7) and Moodle Tests - Unit(8), constitutes 79.1% (or 91,387) of all activities. The indicators for learning activities in the Flash group are notably lower, totaling 15.8% (or 2946) for Unit(5) and Unit(6). These findings were anticipated during the research organization phase, aligning with our expectations, particularly in this mandatory period. Additionally, Unit(1) garners the highest interest among both Flash group students (27.24% or 5076 activities) and Moodle group students (44.07% or 50918 activities). This trend persists throughout all research periods, suggesting a universal interest among students in monitoring platform activities, which serves as a vital information hub.

Students' Behavior with Non-mandatory Platforms

In this section, we unveil the outcomes of students' learning activities on non-mandatory platforms during the second, third, and fourth phases. Instructional content, comprising instructional units, is universally accessible to all students without further division into separate groups. Consequently, the results are presented for the entire population of the online course.

We assess students' behavior on non-mandatory platforms during the second and third phases by addressing the second research question:

How do students behave in an online learning environment during the phases with non-mandatory platforms? (RQ2)

For all hypotheses, we verified the assumptions of normality of the distribution of variables using the Shapiro-Wilk test, and the homogeneity of the variance of the variables using the Levene test. Based on hypothesis checking, we apply the Mann-Whitney statistical U test for hypotheses H1, H2, and H3. Statistical significance for all tests at the $\alpha = 0.05$.

The applied statistical test allows us to conclude the behavior of students with non-mandatory platforms concerning the set hypotheses:

H1 was rejected because there was a statistically significant difference in the number of active students per day (ASD) between second-phase students (Mdn = 60.0, n = 37) and third-phase students (Mdn = 24.0, n = 44), to U = 321, p < 0.01, rpb = 0.606.

H2 was rejected because there was a statistically significant difference in the number of students' activities per day (SAD) between second-phase students (Mdn = 15.0, n = 168) and third-phase students (Mdn = 8.0, n = 162), to U = 7642, p < 0.001, rpb = 0.438.

H3 was rejected because there was a statistically significant difference in student event context (SEC) between second-phase students (Mdn = 29.0, n = 168) and third-phase students (Mdn = 14.0, n = 162), to U = 6373, p < 0.001, rpb = 0.532.

We also observe student behavior in the second and third phases by ranking the number of course activities completed according to the designated instructional units on e-learning platforms. Notably, the number of activities for Unit(7) is nearly half of those for Unit(8), suggesting that students engage in learning activities but may not test the knowledge contained in the lessons. This observation holds true for both the second and third phases. Unit(1) consistently occupies the top ranks during the non-mandatory phases, specifically in the first (Phase 3) and second (Phase 2) positions. This suggests that students access the online course nearly daily to review the situation and, if necessary, complete ongoing tasks assigned by the teacher. Consequently, this frequent engagement is reflected in the second rank for Unit(2). Unit(2) is particularly active in activities related to organizing colloquiums or accessing results for formative and summative tests. The frequency of activities for Unit(9) has also notably risen in both phases, primarily attributed to formative and summative tests. Additionally, it is noteworthy that students are engaging considerably less with activities on the Memory platform, particularly in Unit(5) and Unit(6).

In the fourth phase, which corresponds to the period of the student's final exam, we observe the distribution of instructional content units based on their rank and number of activities. Notably, Unit(2) and Unit(1) are predominant, which we categorize as part of the review activities on the course. Surprisingly, instructional units associated with learning activities experienced a substantial decrease during the preparation period for the final exam. In particular, activities on the Memory platform are nearly nonexistent.

During the research phase, Colloquium 1 and Colloquium 2 served as summative assessments of knowledge conducted at specific intervals (Table 1). Results for Colloquium 1 included both the initial scores on 17 Nov and the scores after correction on 2 Dec. A total of 136 students participated in Colloquium 1, while 71 took part in Colloquium 2. Only the results for students who achieved a score of 50 or higher on these assessments are included.

Table 1. Descriptive statistics for Colloquium 1 (Coll1) and Colloquium 2 (Coll2)

	N	M	Med	Kurt	Skew	SD	V
Coll1	56	59.2	50.0	1.4	1.665	16.4	269
Coll2	43	76.5	75.0	−1.35	−0.097	18.2	332

Note that 56 students, or 41.18%, achieved scores above the threshold (50 points) in Colloquium 1. In Colloquium 2, although the number of students attending the colloquium is lower, success rates are significantly higher, with 43 students, or 60.56%, scoring above 50 points. Descriptive statistics (Table 1) highlight the superior performance of students in Colloquium 2. We specifically focus on analyzing the results of Colloquium 1, as they reflect students' learning activities on both the joined CloudMap&Flash platform and the Moodle platform during the first and second phases of the research (Table 2). These learning activities influenced colloquium outcomes in both the mandatory and non-mandatory platform environments, given the colloquium's timing during the second phase of the research. Due to these circumstances, students who achieved higher rankings on the Top List of the Memory platform tend to perform better in Colloquium 1.

Table 2. Flash and Moodle group students in the Memory Top List

Students' Group	Number of students	Number of Students in Memory Top List	Rang measuring in Memory Top List
Flash	34	29	17
Moodle	22	10	10
Total	54	39	27

In interpretation, it is noteworthy that students in the Flash group had a longer duration for study on the integrated platform compared to students in the Moodle group. Undoubtedly, we believe this significantly influenced the outcome. Moodle students deserve commendation for demonstrating interest in utilizing the Memory platform for learning activities when conditions are allowed during the second phase. Furthermore, the results attained by the Flash group students reaffirm the established value of digital flashcards in learning and teaching [9].

Students ($N = 74$) took the final exam for the *Programming 1* course in February 2022 in two exam periods. This section follows the answer to the research question RQ3:

How do the students' summative knowledge assessment scores (Colloquium 1 and Colloquium 2) correlate with the final exam?

In our study, we investigate multiple correlations involving Colloquium 1, Colloquium 2, and the Final exam, resulting in several correlations to analyze. In this multiple correlation analysis, the objective is to assess the relationship between a dependent variable (Final exam) and independent variables (Colloquium 1 and Colloquium 2). As per the guidelines for interpreting correlations in jamovi, the correlation between Colloquium 1, Colloquium 2, and the Final exam demonstrates a positively moderate relationship. We conclude that the final exam ($M = 71.3$, $SD = 13.8$) positively correlates with Colloquium 1 ($M = 59.2$, $SD = 16.4$) $r = 0.598$, $df = 54$, $p < 0.001$ as well as Colloquium 2 ($M = 76.5$, $SD = 18.2$) $r = 0.590$, $df = 41$, $p < 0.001$.

5   Conclusions

We present the findings of our investigation into student behavior during mandatory and non-mandatory phases within specific e-learning platforms. The results are presented alongside an assessment of accomplishments as well as a critical appraisal:

The study comprised three phases involving learning activities and knowledge assessment spanning 116 days, along with a phase dedicated to evaluating students' knowledge through a final exam, lasting 20 days. We devised original criteria, encapsulated in the CAM model, to measure student behavior during learning activities and knowledge assessments.

Our findings indicate a consistent pattern of student engagement with the e-course link, suggesting that activities on the platform are not accessed randomly by students. Moreover, we observed a notable increase in the number of course activities during the mandatory tasks of the initial phase, particularly among students in the Moodle group, compared to the non-mandatory tasks in subsequent phases. Furthermore, a heightened frequency of visits was noted during the formative and summative assessment periods.

Moodle lessons and tests emerged as the preferred resources among students, followed by visits to the group featuring video lessons and exercises. Conversely, the number of visits to the Memory platform was notably lower. Additionally, our analysis revealed that students did not utilize all available course content files consistently across the phases.

For knowledge assessment, we recommend that students engage more frequently in formative assessment, as it holds significance for both students and teachers alike. Our findings suggest that colloquia were not adequately embraced by students. Additionally, we observed that students who adhered to the ongoing monitoring conditions for the final exam achieved significantly higher grades compared to those who relied solely on the final exam dates.

Finally, we conducted a satisfaction survey with 73 students who participated in the Programming 1 course. The results indicate that students significantly favored the Moodle platform over the joined CloudMap&Flash platform. Additionally, the relationship between concept maps and flashcards is a topic of ongoing research, emphasizing the application of Bloom's taxonomy levels of knowledge for the cognitive domain. Replicating this approach with a more organized scenario of access to teaching content on the concept map and flashcard platform would be beneficial. Our research continues with a focus on understanding how students learn.

We attempted to conduct a focus group discussion with the students, but it was unsuccessful. We believe that engaging in discussions with the students would have provided valuable insights for future organization, and we recommend that this activity be included in future research endeavors.

Acknowledgments. This study was funded by the Office of Naval Research grant, N00014-20-1-2066 "Enhancing Adaptive Courseware based on Natural Language Processing".

References

1. Lu, C., Cutumisu, M.: Online engagement and performance on formative assessments mediate the relationship between attendance and course performance. Int. J. Educ. Technol. High. Educ. **19**(1), 1–23 (2022). https://doi.org/10.1186/s41239-021-00307-5
2. Liu, M.: The relationship between students' study time and academic performance and its practical significance. BCP Educ. Psychol. **7**, 412–415 (2022)

3. Hamdan, K., Amorri, A.: The Impact of Online Learning Strategies on Students' Academic Performance. https://doi.org/10.5772/intechopen.94425. Submitted: September 1st, 2020 Reviewed: October 11th, 2020 Published: May 18th, 2022 Chapter in Mahruf, M., Shohel, C.: E-Learning and Digital Education in the Twenty-First Century, IntechOpen (2022)

4. Novak, J.: Clarify with concept maps: a tool for students and teachers alike. Sci. Teach. **58**(7), 45–49 (1991)

5. Novak, J.D., Cañas, A.J.: The Theory Underlying Concept Maps and How to Construct and Use Them. Technical Report IHMC CmapTools 2006-01 Rev 01-2008, Florida Institute for Human and Machine Cognition (2008)

6. van den Enk, M.C.: Developing a Tool for Learning Concept Maps (final project thesis), Universiteit Twente, 2 July 2017

7. Weiand, A., Ludovico, F.M., da Silva Campelo Costa Barceloss, P.: Virtual learning environments in the light of mind maps and flashcards: a systematic literature review. Int. J. Innov. Educ. Res. **7**(9) (2019)

8. Anderson, L.W., Krathwohl, D.R., et al. (eds.): A Taxonomy for Learning, Teaching, and Assessing: A Revision of Bloom's Taxonomy of Educational Objectives. Allyn & Bacon, Boston. (Pearson Education Group) (2001)

9. Colbran, S., Gilding, A., Colbran, S.: The role of digital flashcards in legal education: theory and potential. Eur. J. Law Technol. **5**(1) (2014)

10. Wadsworth, W.: The Leitner System for flashcards: how to elevate your memory and learning, 10 May 2022. https://examstudyexpert.com/leitner-system/

11. Huang, Y., Wang, S.: How to motivate student engagement in emergency online learning? Evidence from the COVID-19 situation. High. Educ. **85**, 1101–1123 (2023). https://doi.org/10.1007/s10734-022-00880-2

12. Ferrer, J., Ringer, A., Saville, K., Parris, M.A., Kashi, K.: Students' motivation and engagement in higher education: the importance of attitude to online learning. High. Educ. **83**(2), 317+ (2022)

13. Landrum, B.: Examining students' confidence to learn online, self-regulation skills and perceptions of satisfaction and usefulness of online classes. Online Learn. **24**(3), 128146 (2020). https://doi.org/10.24059/olj.v24i3.2066

14. Wang, C.-H., Shannon, D.M., Ross, M.E.: Students' characteristics, self-regulated learning, technology self-efficacy, and course outcomes in online learning. Distance Educ. **34**(3), 302–323 (2013). https://doi.org/10.1080/01587919.2013.835779

15. Cole, A.W., et al.: Student predisposition to instructor feedback and perceptions of teaching presence predict motivation toward online courses. Online Learn. **21**(4), 245–262 (2017)

16. Gushchina, O.M., Ochepovsky, A.V.: Data mining of students' behavior in E-learning system. In: Journal of Physics: Conference Series, vol. 1553, p. 012027 (2020). https://doi.org/10.1088/1742-6596/1553/1/012027

17. Chen, C.H., Chiu, C.H.: Employing intergroup competition in multitouch design-based learning to foster student engagement, learning achievement, and creativity. Comput. Educ. **103**, 99–113 (2016)

18. Lu, X., Qiu, J., Wu, R.: Research on the relationship between online learning behavior and learning effect of college students in the digital learning environment. In: Advances in Social Science, Education and Humanities Research, vol. 543, pp. 377–382 (2021)

19. The jamovi project: jamovi. (Version 2.3), Computer Software (2022). https://www.jamovi.org

20. Grubišić, A., et al.: A common model for tracking student learning and knowledge acquisition in different e-Learning platforms. J. E-learning Knowl. Soc. **16**(3), 10–23 (2022)

21. Navarro, D.J., Foxcroft, D.R.: Learning Statistics with jamovi: a tutorial for psychology students and other beginners. (Version 0.75) (2022)

Assessing the Impact of Large-Scale ICT Investment in Education Through Measuring the Digital Maturity of Schools

Goran Skvarc[✉] and Tihomir Markulin

Croatian Academic and Research Network - CARNET, 10 000 Zagreb, Croatia
{goran.skvarc,tihomir.markulin}@carnet.hr
https://www.carnet.hr

Abstract. Croatian Academic and Research Network (CARNET) conducted a major nine-year EU-funded programme called "e-Schools: A Comprehensive Informatization of School Operation Processes and Teaching Processes Aimed at the Creation of Digitally Mature Schools for the 21st Century." The programme was launched in March 2015 with a pilot project covering 10% of Croatian schools (151 schools). Based on the pilot's experiences and results, CARNET initiated the second phase of the programme in September 2018, which included all elementary and high schools in Croatia funded from the state budget (1321 schools), lasting till end of 2023. With a total value of 212 million euros, the e-Schools programme contributed to boosting the performance of the primary and secondary education system so that Croatian students could prepare for further education and lifelong learning, i.e. for entering the labour market. This paper intends to use the concept of digital maturity of schools as an evaluation tool for assessing the programme's impact. The Framework of Digital Maturity and the corresponding Instrument developed during the programme, provided data for assessing the programme's main benchmark. The aim of the paper is to show how the level of the digital maturity of schools, as measured in the pilot phase and upgraded and measured in the second phase, represents the benchmark for evaluating and assessing the impact of the large-scale horizontal ICT investment in the education. More precisely, it will show how the major investment in digital infrastructure through establishing local computer networks, equipping school staff, classroom upgrades, e-services implementation, and development of digital educational materials, including teaching scenarios and staff training raised the digital maturity level of Croatian Schools. Unlike existing research, this paper will provide unique insights into the importance of the concept of digital maturity for the measurement of the programme impact.

Keywords: e-Schools · Investment in Digital Technologies in Education · Project Evaluation · Project Assessment · Digital Maturity

T. Volarić et al. (Eds.): MoStart 2024, CCIS 2124, pp. 84–96, 2024.
https://doi.org/10.1007/978-3-031-62058-4_7

1   Introduction

1.1   Aims of Research

This paper aims to show how the concept of digital maturity can be employed to assess the impact of a large-scale horizontal investment in the digital transformation of the education system, primarily by investment in digital technology. Croatian Academic and Research Network – CARNET conducted one of the largest horizontal projects for the digital transformation of Croatian primary and secondary education system – the e-Schools programme. Worth a total of 212 million euros, the program, over the nine years, has contributed to strengthening the capacity of the primary and secondary education system, ensuring students are prepared for further education and lifelong learning and are ready to enter the job market. Out of the 212 million euros, 151 million euros (73,5% of the budget) was directly or indirectly spent on equipping schools with digital technology. In this paper we aim to show how such investment can be validated through the concept of digital maturity.

1.2   Research Context

The programme, fully titled "e-Schools: Comprehensive Informatization of School Business and Educational Processes to Create Digitally Mature Schools for the 21st Century," facilitated the adoption of contemporary teaching methodologies. It equipped classrooms with digital technology, empowering educators to utilize digital educational resources, extend interaction beyond the traditional classroom setting, and foster a more engaging and participatory learning experience for students. This initiative ensured that teachers are adept in digital literacy, ready to integrate and employ innovative methods in their teaching, and that school administration operates with efficiency and transparency.

Between March 2015 and September 2018, the "e-Schools: Establishment of a System for Developing Digitally Mature Schools" pilot project took place [1]. The outcomes of this pilot formed the foundation for the programme's subsequent stage, "e-Schools: Development of Digitally Mature Schools (Phase II)." This phase extended to all primary and secondary schools in Croatia that receive state budget funding, encompassing a total of 1,321 schools. This number included 907 primary schools, 364 secondary schools, and 50 art schools and centres for education and training.

The project involved setting up a network across more than 2,400 primary and branch school locations, installing active network equipment, setting up functional Wi-Fi networks, and providing over 85,000 laptops to school staff for educational purposes. Additionally, it supported the creation of new e-services. To help educational staff adapt to new technologies and instructional approaches, approximately 70 diverse workshops, webinars, and e-courses were made available, with nearly 70,000 attendees. Furthermore, the project developed 98 digital educational materials, 1,440 subject-specific teaching scenarios, and 350 teaching scenarios for interdisciplinary themes with 119 corresponding interactive contents.

The e-Schools programme was largely funded by two operational programs, the Operational Programme Competitiveness and Cohesion and the Operational Programme

Efficient Human Resources, which covered 85% of each phase of the programme. The Croatian Central State Budget contributed the remaining 15%.

While writing the e-Schools programme proposal, the challenge was how to measure the impact of such a large-scale horizontal investmentb and subsequently, how to design result indicators. It was decided that the programme will use the concept of Digital Maturity to set up its main result indicators – proportion of primary and secondary schools at e-enabled level of digital maturity and the proportion of schools that will improve their digital maturity for at least one level. Therefore, the measurements of the level of the digital maturity of schools in the e-Schools programme pilot phase and the measurements of the digital maturity of schools in the e-Schools programme second phase represent the main indicator of success of the e-Schools programme. In more narrow terms, the goal of this paper is to describe how the assessment of the one field of digital maturity, namely that of digital infrastructure, proved to be an excellent indicator of the programme impact thus accounting for the general success of the programme.

1.3 Digital Maturity

Digital maturity refers to organization's capability to leverage digital technology to transform its operations, improve customer experiences, and innovate effectively in a rapidly changing digital environment. Although definitions can vary, they generally focus on the organization's ability to adapt and thrive in a digital world. One perspective considers digital maturity as a measure of how well an organization can use digital tools to adapt quickly to technology-driven market needs and consumer preferences. It's about optimizing operations, enhancing customer experiences, and fostering innovation. A digitally mature organization is agile, responsive, and competitive, continuously seeking ways to leverage technology for growth and customer satisfaction.

The concept of digital maturity holds immense significance in the educational context, shaping the effectiveness and efficiency of educational institutions, facilitating the integration of advanced technologies such as interactive learning platforms, virtual classrooms, and multimedia resources. Furthermore, educational institutions play a pivotal role in preparing students for the demands of the future workforce. Digital maturity ensures that students are exposed to cutting-edge technologies, developing digital literacy and skills that are increasingly essential in the modern workplace [2]. Digital maturity enables the creation of flexible learning environments, allowing students to access educational resources and materials anytime, anywhere. This flexibility accommodates diverse learning styles and supports lifelong learning initiatives [3]. Additionally, digital maturity in education involves the effective use of data analytics to inform decision-making processes. Educational institutions can utilize data to assess student performance, tailor teaching methods, and identify areas for improvement in the curriculum. With digital maturity, educational institutions can connect with peers globally, fostering collaboration and cultural exchange. Virtual classrooms and online collaborative tools break down geographical barriers, providing students with a broader perspective on global issues [4]. Digital maturity also allows for the implementation of personalized learning pathways. Adaptive learning platforms and intelligent tutoring systems cater to individual student needs, providing targeted support and addressing learning gap. Educational institutions benefit from digital maturity in terms of administrative efficiency.

Automation of administrative processes, such as enrolment, grading, and resource allocation, streamlines operations, allowing educators to focus more on teaching and student engagement [5]. Digital maturity supports the integration of technology into pedagogical approaches. Teachers can leverage digital tools to create interactive lesson plans, conduct virtual experiments, and engage students in innovative ways, promoting active learning [6].

Broadly speaking, various digital maturity models prove valuable not only for measuring digital proficiency but also for offering support and guidelines to educators in their technology use [7, 8]. Taking a broader perspective, exploring maturity levels entails an examination of technology adoption that combines both - factors linked to teachers and the context of professional practice [9, 10]. Therefore, digital maturity, as defined by Jugo et al. where digitally mature schools are defined as schools with a high level of digital technology integration, and schools which have developed a systematic approach towards using digital technologies in school management and educational processes [11] will be used further on as a conceptual tool in this paper. In order to achieve such comprehensive digital maturity, Croatian e-Schools programme was initiated aiming to digitize and modernize educational practices at individual level while ensuring that schools are well-equipped to prepare students for a digital future at the institutional level.

1.4 Digital Maturity and Public Policy in the Republic of Croatia

The entire e-Schools programme was based on the Strategy of Education, Science and Technology [12] that was adopted in The Croatian Parliament on October 17, 2014. Based on the strategic plans of the Ministry of Science, Education and Sports for the periods 2014–16 [13] and 2015–17 [14] CARNET conducted the Feasibility study [15] of the pilot project e-Schools that showed several challenges regarding the integration of digital technologies in education and the lack of systematic approach towards using digital technologies in school educational and management processes. Prior to this, there had been a notable absence of a coordinated approach to the implementation of digital technologies in educational and other school activities. Furthermore, there were no clear guidelines or systems for the evaluation of digital maturity of schools. Additionally, there was a minimal exploitation of the opportunities that digital technologies offer within the education sector, compounded by the lack of an officially recognized framework and strategy for the development of digitally mature schools [15].

Croatian Framework for the Digitally Mature Schools was developed on the basis of The European Framework for Digitally-Competent Educational Organisations [16] and The e-Learning Roadmap [11]. Additionally, two key reports were created – Report on the implementation and results of the final self-evaluation and final external evaluation of the digital maturity of schools at the end of the Pilot project [17], and Report on the implementation and results of the final self-evaluation and the final external evaluation of the digital maturity of schools [18] in 2023. All further research activities were based on these reports.

It is important to note that within the e-Schools programme a Framework for Digitally Mature Schools [19] was developed as well as the instrument for assessing digital maturity of schools deriving from the Framework. To our knowledge, such framework was unprecedented in European Union, rendering the programme a pioneering effort in

European public policy. The Framework will be described in more detail in the following chapter.

2 Methodology

The methodology of this paper is based on secondary research – analysis of existing frameworks and available data from the e-Schools programme. In order to understand the concept of digital maturity within the programme, it is important to describe the process of its conceptualisation and implantation in which the authors of this paper were also involved.

The concept of digital maturity in schools emerged as an increasingly critical aspect within the modern educational framework, underscored by the growing indispensability of technology. The integration of digital technologies transitioned from being a product of individual initiative to a structured, organization-wide strategy, aligned with regional and national directives. The European Commission acknowledged the significance of digital maturity, fostering its enhancement through policies and strategic measures. Notably, the e-Schools programme played a pivotal role, methodically advancing digital maturity in educational institutions while facilitating continuous monitoring of their progression.

Within the framework of the e-Schools programme, digitally mature schools were characterized by a comprehensive integration of digital technology in all aspects of their functioning. These schools exhibited a structured approach to incorporating digital technology within their planning, management, educational, and operational processes. They benefited from a conducive environment supported by necessary resources, encompassing financial means and essential digital infrastructure for various stakeholders. Digital maturity in these schools also entailed a deliberate focus on enhancing digital competencies among educators and students, leveraging digital technology for pedagogical innovation, content development, and evaluative practices aligned with educational goals. Moreover, they fostered collaborative dynamics through online tools and e-services, engaging actively in digital technology- oriented projects.

The e-Schools programme encompassed the creation of the Framework for the Digital Maturity of Schools, a strategic document delineating the various domains and maturity levels of digital integration within schools. This framework was designed to align with the European Framework for Digitally Competent Educational Organisations. Specifically, the Croatian iteration of this framework identified five distinct domains and associated five levels to assess and categorize the digital maturity of educational institutions.

The full document - "The Framework for Digital Maturity of Primary and Secondary Schools in the Republic of Croatia with the Corresponding Instrument" [19] was published by Croatian Academic and Research Network – CARNET in June 2018. The Framework was created jointly by the experts from Faculty of Organization and Informatics of the University of Zagreb and the Croatian Academic and Research Network – CARNET. The concept was designed and developed by leading e-learning experts from CARNET, notably - Gordana Jugo, Jasna Tingle, Jasminka Maravić, Lucija Dejanović and Marijana Pezelj and the team from the Faculty of Informatics and Organisation, who are also authors of the document – Nina Begičević Ređep, Igor Balaban, Marina Klačmer Čalopa and Bojan Žugec.

The Framework for the Digital Maturity of Schools, established as a foundational component within the e-Schools programme, delineated the initial structure for assessing and enhancing digital maturity in educational settings. Developed in alignment with this framework, the programme integrated a system comprising several key elements: the self-evaluation by schools of their digital maturity, an external evaluation process to validate these assessments, and the provision of targeted support to schools aimed at advancing their digital maturity levels.

The core of the Framework for Digital Maturity of Schools was structured into five areas pertinent to the educational system within primary and secondary schools, each addressing different aspects of digital technology integration and usage. These digital maturity areas include 1. Planning, Management, and Leadership, 2. Digital Technology in Learning and Teaching, 3. Development of Digital Competencies, 4. Digital Culture, and 5. Digital Infrastructure. The areas and their constituent elements were designed to be complementary and interconnected, thereby forming a cohesive whole (Fig. 1).

	Digitally unaware	Digital beginners	Digitally competent	digitally advanced	Digitally mature
Leadership, planning and management					
ICT in learning and teaching					
Development of digital competences					
ICT culture					
ICT infrastructure					

Fig. 1. Framework for Digital Maturity

Within the Framework for Digital Maturity of Schools, maturity levels were established to identify the schools' digital development for each area. Levels were inspired by Love, McKean, and Gathercoal's [20] approach from 2004. (see more in Jugo et al. 2017. [11]). The framework encompasses the following levels - Level 1: Digitally Unaware, Level 2: Digital Beginner, Level 3: Digitally Competent, Level 4: Digitally Advanced and Level 5: Digitally Mature. This spectrum allows schools to identify their current state of digital integration and aspire for continuous improvement towards full digital maturity.

At Level 1, termed 'Digitally Unaware,' schools lack recognition of the potential digital technologies applications in teaching, learning, and administration. Consequently, such institutions do not incorporate digital technologies into their strategic planning for growth and development. There is no utilization of ICT in educational or teaching activities, nor is there an effort from educators to enhance their digital skills. Communication with the school via online platforms is generally not feasible, and the digital infrastructure is inadequate, with computers available only in limited areas.

At Level 2, 'Digital Beginner,' schools are aware of the potential for ICT use in education and administration but have yet to adopt it broadly. A minority of educators employ digital technologies in teaching and learning. While there is an acknowledgment of the need to develop digital competencies among staff and students, systematic training is not yet in place. The school's engagement in the online environment remains minimal, and access to its digital resources is significantly restricted. Typically, the digital infrastructure is underdeveloped, with internet-accessible computers limited to certain areas.

At Level 3, 'Digitally Competent,' the school recognizes and utilizes digital technologies across all business facets, with strategic documents and practices evolving accordingly. Digital technologies support students with special educational needs, and staff develop their digital skills, content, and innovative teaching methods. The institution engages in digital technology-focused projects and offers broad access to ICT resources in most areas. Maintenance and software licensing are managed proactively, and the school actively maintains an online presence for content sharing and communication.

At Level 4, 'Digitally Advanced,' the school prominently recognizes benefits of digital technologies across all its operations, integrating digital technologies into strategic documents, plans, and practices. Staff employ advanced digital methodologies for teaching and assessing, creating copyrighted materials, with a shared repository for staff and student use. Continuous professional development in digital competencies for educators is executed, enhancing student skills. Digital resources access is widespread, with planned procurement and maintenance. The school is active in ICT projects and online engagements, maintaining software licensing and ICT security vigilance.

Finally, at Level 5, 'Digitally Mature,' the school thoroughly recognizes and mandates digital technology use across all its functions, detailed in strategic documents and digitalisation-focused development plans. Management practices rely on integrated data from all the school's information systems. Systematic advancement in digital competencies for staff and students is ensured, alongside advanced use of digital technologies in teaching, content creation, and student evaluation. A shared content repository is available, with comprehensive digital resources access and a developed network infrastructure. Information security aligns with best practices, ensuring varied digital technology project activities and collaborative online engagement.

The Instrument

Following the digital maturity framework, the instrument for measurement of digital maturity in schools was developed to measure the impact of the e-Schools programme, aiming to enhance the schools' digital maturity. This tool included an evaluation rubric with five key areas and 37 elements across five maturity stages, alongside a simplified questionnaire for easier participant engagement. The rubric, completed based on questionnaire responses, employed a taxicab geometry method for calculating a school's digital maturity level. Hosted on a cloud platform, this instrument facilitated both self-evaluation and external evaluations of school digital maturity.

Initial Self-Evaluation of Schools

The initial self-evaluation in schools aimed to determine their digital maturity baseline prior to the project's interventions. This process was instrumental in educating and raising digital maturity awareness among school staff, particularly emphasizing the role of self-assessment in fostering school improvement through reflective practice and identification of action areas. All 151 schools in the pilot engaged in this evaluation, with principals and staff collaboratively completing the questionnaire during the summer of 2016.

Initial External Evaluation of Schools

In October 2016, an external evaluation encompassing 151 schools from the pilot project was conducted by 23 trained evaluators to ensure uniform and objective assessments. Utilizing the same tools from the self-evaluation phase, these evaluators conducted interviews with school staff and examined pertinent documents and infrastructures to validate the responses. Evidence like curricula and plans were reviewed, with schools preparing these materials beforehand. The reliability of the evaluative process was confirmed through a consistency check, using Cronbach's alpha, validating the data's integrity for subsequent analysis.

Unlike existing research, this paper will provide unique insights into the importance of the concept of digital maturity for the measurement of the programme impact.

Research

As shown in previous chapter, the Framework for Digital Maturity of Schools defines areas and levels of digital maturity, serving as a fundamental document for self-assessment and external evaluation. These evaluations enable the determination of digital maturity levels at the beginning and end of the project, tracking progress, and planning support for schools. Subsequent paragraphs, are indented to provide a detailed account of the importance of the date collected within the framework for assessing the impact of the programme.

3   Data

This paper uses research data collected in the initial self-evaluation and external evaluation that was carried out in the summer and fall of 2016, as well as research data collected in the final self-evaluation and external evaluation of the project conducted at the end of the project in the spring and summer of 2023.

Altogether 151 school participated in the initial self-evaluation which accounts for all schools that participated in the e-Schools pilot phase of the project accounting for approximately 10% of all Croatian primary and secondary schools. The questionnaire for self-evaluation was completed by principals of schools with the participation of other school staff members. The self-evaluation was important because it offered an opportunity to schools to reflect on their practises and identify areas of action.

The initial external evaluation of schools participating in the pilot projects was carried out in October 2016 by external evaluators which were trained to conduct objective evaluation based on common criteria.

The data indicated that, following self-assessment, half of the schools were categorized at the initial digital maturity level, as Digital Beginners. A notable 45% reached the Digitally Competent stage, while a mere 3% achieved Digitally advanced status, and only 1% were considered Digitally Mature, with none at the basic level as Digitally Unaware. The external evaluations further determined that a predominant 82% of schools remained at the initial stage, classifying them at Digital Beginners level, with the remaining 18% identified as Digitally Competent. At the end of the external evaluation none of the schools were on the initial or the top level of digital maturity.

In Phase II of the E-Schools programme, a total of 1,323 schools in Croatia participated, accounting for all schools funded from the Central State Budget. During this phase, the Framework for Digital Maturity of Primary and Secondary Schools was revised in partnership with Faculty of Organization and Informatics of the University of Zagreb, and both initial and final self-assessment as well as external assessments of digital maturity were carried out. A System for Assessing Digital Maturity of Schools was also developed, which, in addition to separate questionnaires for principals and teachers, provided schools with feedback on the results of self-assessment, feedback on external evaluation results, recommendations for raising the level of maturity, and a modernized visualization of the results with more options.

These outcomes were compared to the initial self and external evaluations conducted at the beginning of the e-Schools pilot project in 2016, enabling an analysis of the schools' maturity at the project's commencement against the level of maturity realized at the project's conclusion, as shown in Table 1.

Table 1. Results of self-evaluation and external evaluation of schools

Maturity Level / Method		Digitally Unaware		Digital Beginner		Digitally Competent		Digitally Advanced		Digitally Mature		
		no.	%	no.	%	no.	%	no.	%	no.	%	
Pilot Project	Self-evaluation	0	0%	76	50,3%	68	45%	6	3,9%	1	0,8%	N = 151
	External evaluation	0	0%	124	82%	27	18%	0	0%	0	0%	
II Phase	Self-evaluation	3	0,2%	89	6,7%	407	30,8%	728	55,1%	94	7,1%	N = 1321
	External evaluation	0	0%	4	1,6%	45	18%	170	68%	31	12,4%	N = 250

For the purpose of this paper, we will further focus on one specific area of digital maturity of Croatian schools, namely, the digital infrastructure, since these results show major increase in the level of digital maturity as measured in the final external evaluation, compared to the initial measurement.

Although the data from both self-evaluation and external evaluation are available, as shown above, this paper focuses on the more reliable data collected during the external evaluation of schools (Table 2).

Table 2. Results of self-evaluation and external evaluation of schools in the DM area of Infrastructure

	Maturity Level / Method	Digitally Unaware		Digital Beginner		Digitally Competent		Digitally Advanced		Digitally Mature		
		no.	%	no.	%	no.	%	no.	%	no.	%	
Pilot Project	Self-evaluation	0	0%	71	47%	62	41%	14	9,3%	4	2,7%	N = 151
	External evaluation	0	0%	0	0%	62	41%	75	50%	14	9%	
II Phase	Self-evaluation	6	0,4%	30	2,3%	77	5,8%	451	34,1%	757	57,3%	N = 1321
	External evaluation	0	0%	1	0,4%	11	4,4%	56	22,4%	182	72,8%	N = 250

4 Discussion

The evaluations of digital maturity within schools have shown a dynamic progression across different phases of assessment. Initially, schools predominantly found themselves at lower maturity levels, with many making significant strides by the end of subsequent phases. This shift signifies not only an enhancement in the infrastructure and resources available but also a greater emphasis on and adoption of digital practices within the schools' educational and administrative processes. The move from 'Digitally Advanced' to 'Digitally Mature' illustrates a transition to a more integrated and strategic use of technology, which is a reflection of concerted efforts within the e-Schools project to advance digital education. This evolution underscores the project's impact on schools' digital landscapes, marking a developmental trend toward comprehensive digital integration.

Initially, most schools were at the "Digital Beginner" level (82%), with some 'Digitally Competent' (18%), and with no schools at the "Unaware" or "Beginner" or "Mature" levels. By Phase II, there was a remarkable shift, with the majority of schools reaching "Digitally Advanced" status (68%). The research positioned 18% of schools as "Digitally Competent" while placing 12,5% of schools at the top level of digital maturity, assessing them as "Digitally Advanced".

No schools were assessed as "Digitally Unaware" in the final evaluation, with only 1,6% rated as 'digital beginners,' a decrease from 82% at the start. This progress reflects, among other project activities, the procurement of digital equipment and the development of network infrastructure, both wired and wireless, as part of the e-Schools project (Fig. 2).

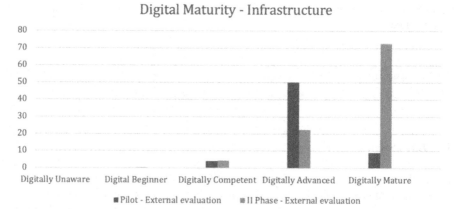

Fig. 2. Comparison of external evaluations of DM in the area of Infrastructure

5 Conclusion

In conclusion, the e-Schools programme, spearheaded by the Croatian Academic and Research Network (CARNET), represents a landmark initiative in elevating the digital maturity of Croatian schools. Spanning nine years and funded by the European Union, this initiative involved a substantial investment in digital technologies across the primary and secondary educational landscape. The programme, which initially focused on 10% of schools and expanded to encompass all state-funded institutions, systematically bolstered the digital capabilities of the Croatian education system.

Throughout the programme, schools underwent a rigorous process of self and external evaluations to measure their digital maturity. The results were illuminating. Initially, many schools demonstrated a preliminary level of digital maturity. By the end of the programme, however, there was a significant increase in the number of schools that reached the 'Digitally Mature' level. This shift was indicative not only of enhanced digital infrastructure but also of a deeper, strategic integration of digital technologies in educational processes.

Furthermore, the implementation of the Framework for Digital Maturity of Schools played a crucial role in guiding this transformation. With clear criteria and structured evaluations, schools could identify their strengths and weaknesses in digital practices, and strategically plan for improvement.

The impact of the e-Schools programme was profound. By increasing digital maturity, it ensured that Croatian students were better equipped for the modern educational environment and future workforce demands. The significant investment in digital technologies was justified, reflected in the tangible advancements in the schools' digital environments. Thus, the e-Schools programme stands as a successful model for large-scale digital transformation in education, setting a benchmark for similar initiatives globally.

References

1. Smoljo, A., Škvarč, G., Majetić, R.: Put prema digitalnoj zrelosti, Hrvatska akademska i istraživačka mreža – CARNET (2023). https://www.e-skole.hr/wp-content/uploads/2023/11/ Carnet_Put-prema-digitalnoj-zrelosti.pdf
2. OECD. Digital Education Strategies: How to Make the Most of ICT for Skills and Equity (2020). https://www.oecd-ilibrary.org/education/digital-education-strategies_221f8525-en
3. UNESCO. UNESCO ICT in Education Policy Review: Belize (2021). https://unesdoc.une sco.org/ark:/48223/pf0000377106
4. Hanushek, E., Woessmann, L.: The Economic Impacts of Learning Losses. OECD Education Working Papers, no. 225 (2020)
5. Picciano, A.G.: The evolution of big data and learning analytics in American higher education. J. Asynchronous Learn. Netw. **16**(3), 9–20 (2012)
6. Nguyen, L.A.T., Habók, A.: Tools for assessing teacher digital literacy: a review. J. Comput. Educ. 1–42 (2023)
7. Lomos, C., Luyten, J.W., Tieck, S.: Implementing ICT in classroom practice: what else matters besides the ICT infrastructure? Large-Scale Assess. Educ. **11**, 1 (2023). https://doi.org/10. 1186/s40536-022-00144-6
8. Kimmons, R., Graham, C.R., West, R.E.: The PICRAT model for technology integration in teacher preparation. Contemp. Issues Technol. Teach. Educ. **20**(1), 176–198 (2020)
9. Harrison, C., Tomás, C., Crook, C.: An e-maturity analysis explains intention–behavior disjunctions in technology adoption in UK schools. Comput. Hum. Behav. **34**, 345–351 (2014)
10. Michel, C., Pierrot, L.: Modelling teachers' digital maturity: literature review and proposal for a unified model. In: 15th International Conference on Computer Supported Education, Prague, Czech Republic, April 2023, pp. 535–542 (2023)
11. Jugo, G., Balaban, I., Pezelj, M., Begicevic Redjep, N.: Development of a model to assess the digitally mature schools in Croatia. In: Tatnall, A., Webb, M. (eds.) WCCE 2017. IAICT, vol. 515, pp. 169–178. Springer, Cham (2017). https://doi.org/10.1007/978-3-319-74310-3_19
12. Strategy of Education, Science and Technology, NN 124/2014 (2014)
13. Strateški plan Ministarstva znanosti, obrazovanja i sporta za razdoblje 2014–2016. Ministry of Science, Educationa and Sports (2014). https://mzo.gov.hr/UserDocsImages//dokumenti/ PristupInformacijama/Strateski//Strate%C5%A1ki%20plan%20Ministarstva%20znanost i,%20obrazovanja%20i%20sporta%20za%20razdoblje%202014.%20-%202016.pdf
14. Strateški plan Ministarstva znanosti, obrazovanja i sporta za razdoblje 2015–2017. Ministry of Science, Educationa and Sports (2015). https://mzo.gov.hr/UserDocsImages//dokumenti/ PristupInformacijama/Strateski//Strate%C5%A1ki%20plan%20Ministarstva%20znanost i,%20obrazovanja%20i%20sporta%202015.%20-%202017.pdf
15. Kupres, D.: Feasibility study of the e-Schools pilot project. Croatian Academic and Research Network – CARNET, Zagreb (2015)
16. Kampylis, P., Punie, Y., Devine, J.: Promoting Effective Digital-Age Learning: A European Framework for Digitally-Competent Educational Organisations, EUR 27599 EN, Publications Office of the European Union, Luxembourg (2015). https://doi.org/10.2760/612227. ISBN 978-92-76-40355-5. JRC98209
17.Ređep, N.B., et al.: Izvješće o provedbi i rezultatima završnog samovrednovanja i završnog vanjskog vrednovanja digitalne zrelosti škola, Zagreb: Hrvatska akademska i istraživačka mreža – CARNET (2018)
18. Među, N.B., et al.: Izvješće o provedbi i rezultatima završnog samovrednovanja i završnog vanjskog vrednovanja digitalne zrelosti škola II faza, Zagreb: Hrvatska akademska i istraživačka mreža – CARNET (2023)

19. Ređep, N.B., et al.: Okvir za digitalnu zrelost osnovnih i srednjih škola u Republici Hrvatskoj s pripadajućim instrumentom Projekt "e-Škole: Uspostava sustava razvoja digitalno zrelih škola (pilot projekt)". Zagreb: Hrvatska akademska i istraživačka mreža – CARNET (2017)
20. Love, D., McKean, G., Gathercoal, P.: Portfolios to webfolios and beyond: levels of maturation. Educ. Q. **27**(2), 24–38 (2004)

Opportunities for the Professional Development of Teachers in Digital Competences Related to the Use of Artificial Intelligence in Education in Croatia

Gordana Jugo[✉] and Andi Bašić

Croatian Academic and Research Network – CARNET, J. Marohnića 5, 10000 Zagreb, Croatia
{gordana.jugo,andi.basic}@carnet.hr

Abstract. Teacher Competence Frameworks were explored from the perspective of the competences needed for teachers to understand and successfully use Artificial Intelligence (AI) in education. A database search for Continuing Professional Development (CPD) programs for Croatian school teachers was conducted to address the following research questions: What topics related to AI in education are represented in informal Continuous Professional Development (CPD) opportunities for Croatian school teachers at the national level? What categories of digital competences, based on DigCompEdu, are represented in these opportunities? How many teachers in Croatia have taken advantage of the available opportunities for CPD related to AI in education? The results and discussions revealed that the proportion of activities specifically related to AI in education is notably low, with certain areas and topics receiving more attention than others. Further research should be conducted to establish the reasons for gaps and inequalities in the offerings of professional development programs for teachers in the field of AI in education. The overall offerings of AI-related professional development programs for teachers should be broadened. The topics should be more diverse, and the DigCompEdu areas should be more equally represented.

Keywords: Teacher Professional Development · Digital Competences · Artificial Intelligence

1 Introduction

In the past few years, remarkable advancements in artificial intelligence (AI) have rapidly integrated into various sectors of industry and government, making it clear that artificial intelligence is certain to influence nearly every aspect of society. As a deeply transformative technology, Artificial intelligence, marks a transition into a new era - the "Age of AI" [1], with profound implications for school education, including personalized learning, radical transformations in formative assessment, reduced teacher workloads, and increased attractiveness of the teaching profession [2].

© The Author(s), under exclusive license to Springer Nature Switzerland AG 2024
T. Volarić et al. (Eds.): MoStart 2024, CCIS 2124, pp. 97–109, 2024.
https://doi.org/10.1007/978-3-031-62058-4_8

According to the European policy foresight report, AI is projected to significantly alter learning, teaching, and education in the coming years. The pace of technological advancement is expected to be rapid, exerting considerable pressure to reform educa-tional practices, institutions, and policies [3]. AI presents teachers with numerous opportunities for enhanced planning (e.g., by identifying students' needs), implementation (e.g., through immediate feedback), and assessment (e.g., through automated essay scoring) of their teaching [4]. Despite the vast potential AI offers to support teaching and learning, its development also introduces new ethical implications and risks, such as concerns regarding privacy, data protection, and potential job displacement for teachers. For instance, during periods of budget reductions, administrators may find it opportune to substitute teaching staff with financially advantageous automated AI solutions, such as intelligent tutors, expert systems, and chatbots. AI holds the promise of enhancing learning analytics capabilities. However, these systems demand vast amounts of data, including sensitive information about students and faculty, which raises significant concerns regarding privacy and data protection [5].

To advance toward the successful integration of AI-based education into classrooms, it is crucial to establish Continuous Professional Development (CPD) opportunities for teachers. This ensures they acquire the necessary knowledge, skills, and attitudes to effectively and ethically integrate AI-based education into the classroom. Even prospective teachers, despite being familiar with digital technology from a young age, cannot be assumed to already possess the knowledge and skills required for effectively integrating technology into their teaching. Thus, training and professional development may be necessary [6].

2 Research Questions

The research questions aimed to be answered in this paper are as follows:

- What topics related to AI in education are represented in informal Continuous Professional Development (CPD) opportunities for Croatian school teachers at the national level?
- What categories of digital competences, based on DigCompEdu, are represented in these opportunities?
- How many teachers in Croatia have taken advantage of the available opportunities for Continuous Professional Development (CPD) related to AI in education?

3 Teacher Competence Frameworks

It is crucial to initially define what are the necessary knowledge, skills, and attitudes for understanding and successfully using AI in education, commonly referred to as AI competences [1, 7]. The paper will examine existing frameworks guiding teachers in acquiring necessary AI competencies. The focus will be on existing European frameworks due to their applicability in the Croatian education system, which is part of the broader European education sector.

The current European Framework for the Digital Competence of Educators: Dig-CompEdu [8] was published in 2017. It describes 22 digital competences specifically tailored for educators, categorised into six areas: Professional Engagement, Digital Resources, Teaching and Learning, Assessment, Empowering Learners and Facilitating Learners' Digital Competence. The Professional Engagement area includes the following competences: Organisational communication, Professional Collaboration, Reflective Practice and Digital Continuous Professional Development. Within the Digital Resources area the following competences are introduced: Selecting digital resources, Creating and modifying digital content, and Managing, protecting and sharing digital resources. The Teaching and Learning area focuses on Teaching, Guidance, Collaborative learning and Self-regulated learning. The Assessment area comprises Assessment strategies, Analysing evidence and Feedback and Planning. The Empowering Learners area is about Accessibility and inclusion, Differentiation and personalisation, and Actively engaging learners. The Facilitating Learners' Digital Competence area consists of the following competences: Information and media literacy, Digital communication and collaboration, Digital content creation, Responsible use and Digital problem solving.

DigCompEdu is applicable to all educational contexts and describes competences for use of digital technology in general, not specifying any particular technology. Specific technologies are mentioned only in the descriptions of Activities and Proficiency statements, e.g. e-mail, digital whiteboards, PCs etc. Although AI competence can be considered a component of digital competence in general, meaning that DigCompEdu can be applicable for AI competence as well, artificial intelligence is not explicitly mentioned in this framework.

However, Kralj [9] argues that artificial intelligence possesses distinctive qualities that differentiate it from traditional information and communication technologies (ICT). Artificial intelligence has the ability to learn and autonomously make decisions, introducing a level of complexity and unpredictability that requires increased focus on human agency and ethical considerations.

The new edition of the DigComp framework, titled "DigComp 2.2: The Digital Competence Framework for Citizens - With new examples of knowledge, skills and attitudes" [10] developed in 2022, includes systems driven by artificial intelligence. However, it is a general framework for citizens and is not specifically aimed at educators.

UNESCO has published the "Draft AI competency frameworks for teachers and for school students" [11], comprising five aspects of competences: Human-centred Mindset, Ethics of AI, AI Foundations & Applications, AI Pedagogy, and AI for Professional Development.

"Ethical guidelines on the use of artificial intelligence (AI) and data in teaching and learning for educators" [12], published by European Commission in 2022, provide some potential indicators of arising educator and school leader competences for ethical use of AI and data in teaching and learning. The potential indicators are matched with the six areas of DigCompEdu:

- Professional Engagement: critically describe the positive and negative impacts of AI and data use in education; understand the basics of AI and learning analytics
- Digital resources: data and AI governance;
- Teaching and Learning: models of learning, objectives of education, human agency, fairness, humanity, and participates in the development of learning practices that use AI and data;

- Assessment: personal differences, algorithmic bias, cognitive focus, new ways to misuse technology;
- Empowering Learners: AI addressing learners' diverse learning needs, Justified choice;
- Facilitating learners' digital competence: AI and Learning Analytics ethics.

The review of Competence Frameworks indicates that DigCompEdu is the most pertinent framework for the Croatian educational context. It is developed specifically for educators and is sufficiently broad to encompass AI competence.

4 Opportunities for Informal Continuing Professional Development for School Teachers in Croatia

Several public institutions operating within the Ministry of Science and Education offer professional development opportunities for school teachers in Croatia. The central computer system EMA [13] enables these institutions to organise and implement professional training programs. On the other hand, the Education Management Application – EMA is a central platform for the registration of teachers from the primary and secondary school systems for professional training programs. It also functions as a database of Continuing Professional Development (CPD) programs for Croatian school teachers and tracks their participation in these programs.

5 Methodology

To address the research question, 'What topics related to AI in education are represented in Continuing Professional Development (CPD) opportunities for Croatian school teachers?' it was essential to define topics relevant to AI in education for teachers. The literature review identified two key sources: the Glossary of AI and Data Terms included in the European Commission [6] and Volaric & Crnokić [14], which formed the foundation for establishing a list of keywords for the database search. The EMA [13] database was then queried for the titles of training activities. The EMA database table for training activities contains 20,166 entries of the titles of training activities.

The initial database search did not yield a sufficient number of relevant results for the research topic. Consequently, the initial list of keywords was revised, and additional sources were explored. Given their novelty and popularity, titles of large language models were incorporated into the keyword list [15]. The final keyword list is as follows:

- AI (Artificial intelligence
- Augmented reality
- Automated decision-making
- Automated feedback
- Automation
- Chatbot
- Character recognition
- Chatbot

- Computer vision
- Deep learning
- Expert system
- Fuzzy logic
- Intelligent agent
- Intelligent computers
- Intelligent tutoring systems
- Learning analytics
- Machine learning
- Machine translation
- Natural language processing
- Neural network
- OCR (Optical Character Recognition)
- Personalized learning systems
- Predictive analytics
- Recommendation systems
- Robotics
- Supervised learning
- Text-to-speech
- Unsupervised learning
- Virtual assistant
- Virtual reality
- Language models
- ChatGPT
- Claude
- Cohere
- Copilot
- Falcon
- Gemini
- Llama
- PaLM

The original keyword list was in the Croatian language.

6 Results

The database search resulted in a dataset of 24 training activities. The learning outcomes of these activities were examined to confirm their relevance to AI in the education field. As a result, one activity was excluded from the table. Additionally, five training activities were removed because they were duplicated. The final list of training activity titles related to AI in education, along with their respective keywords, containing 17 training activities, is presented in Table 1.

The percentage of training activities per keyword is shown in Table 2.

The training activities were then mapped against the areas of digital competences defined in DigCompEdu. The table of training activity titles related to AI in education, along with their respective areas of digital competences, is presented in Table 3.

Table 1. List of training activity titles related to AI in education with keywords

No.	Title of Training Activity	Keywords
1	Learning Analytics in e-Schools	Learning analytics
2	Training for Teachers and School Principals: Learning Analytics in e-Schools	Learning analytics
3	Teacher Training as Part of the Curriculum Reform - Autonomous Database	Autonomous system
4	Creating Chatbots and Artificial Intelligence in eTwinning Projects	Chatbot
5	Web Classroom 4.0: Something New, Something Old - Google Bard and Chat GPT	Chat GPT
6	Science and Personalized Learning Environments in Portugal	Personalized learning systems
7	Robotics in a Virtual Environment	Robotics
8	Robotics in the Erasmus + Program	Robotics
9	Simulation of Robotics in the Operations of Logistic Warehouses	Robotics
10	Creating an Inclusive Environment 2 (Application of Robotics in Working with Children with Disabilities – Blue-Bot)	Robotics
11	Teacher Training as Part of the Curriculum Reform - Artificial Intelligence (AI) and "Digital Assistants"	Artificial Intelligence
12	Artificial Intelligence - Applications in Education (for Beginners)	Artificial Intelligence
13	Artificial Intelligence as Support for Teachers and Educators	Artificial Intelligence
14	Artificial Intelligence in the Classroom	Artificial Intelligence
15	Artificial Intelligence and eTwinning	Artificial Intelligence
16	Artificial Intelligence in Education	Artificial Intelligence
17	Literature and Artificial Intelligence – Let's Talk!	Artificial Intelligence

Table 2. Percentage of training activities per keyword

No.	Keywords	No of training activities	Percentage %
1	Artificial intelligence	7	41.17
2	Robotics	4	23.53
3	Personalized learning systems	1	5.88
4	Chat GPT	1	5.88
5	Language models	1	5.88
6	Autonomous system	1	5.88
7	Learning analytics	2	11.76
	Total	**17**	**~100**

Table 3. List of training activity titles related to AI in education with areas of digital competences

No.	Title of Training Activity	Keywords
1	Learning Analytics in e-Schools	Professional Engagement
2	Training for Teachers and School Principals: Learning Analytics in e-Schools	Professional Engagement
3	Teacher Training as Part of the Curriculum Reform - Autonomous Database	Digital Resources
4	Creating Chatbots and Artificial Intelligence in eTwinning Projects	Digital Resources
5	Web Classroom 4.0: Something New, Something Old - Google Bard and Chat GPT	Digital Resources
6	Science and Personalized Learning Environments in Portugal	Teaching and Learning
7	Robotics in a Virtual Environment	Professional Engagement
8	Robotics in the Erasmus+ Program	Professional Engagement
9	Simulation of Robotics in the Operations of Logistic Warehouses	Professional Engagement
10	Creating an Inclusive Environment 2 (Application of Robotics in Working with Children with Disabilities – Blue-Bot)	Teaching and Learning
11	Teacher Training as Part of the Curriculum Reform - Artificial Intelligence (AI) and "Digital Assistants"	Teaching and Learning

(continued)

Table 3. (*continued*)

No.	Title of Training Activity	Keywords
12	Artificial Intelligence - Applications in Education (for Beginners)	Professional Engagement
13	Artificial Intelligence as Support for Teachers and Educators	Professional Engagement
14	Artificial Intelligence in the Classroom	Professional Engagement
15	Artificial Intelligence and eTwinning	Professional Engagement
16	Artificial Intelligence in Education	Facilitating Learners' Digital Competence
17	Literature and Artificial Intelligence – Let's Talk!	Professional Engagement

Table 4. Percentage of training activities per DigCompEdu area

No.	DigCompEdu Area	No of training activities	Percentage %
1	Professional Engagement	10	58.82
2	Digital Resources	3	17.64
3	Teaching and Learning	3	17.64
4	Facilitating Learners' Digital Competence	1	5.88
	Total	**17**	**~100**

The percentage of training activities per DigCompEdu area of competence is displayed in Table 4.

The table illustrating AI-related training activities, along with their respective keywords and the distribution of the number of enrolled users and certificates awarded, is shown in Table 5. This table displays a total of 8720 enrolled users and 6108 certificates awarded.

The distribution of enrolled users and certificates awarded against the keywords is depicted in Fig. 1.

Table 5. Distribution of the number of enrolled users and certificates awarded

No.	Title of training activity	Enrolled users	Certificates awarded	Keywords
1	Learning Analytics in e-Schools	48	37	Learning analytics
2	Training for Teachers and School Principals: Learning Analytics in e-Schools	121	89	Learning analytics
3	Teacher Training as Part of the Curriculum Reform - Autonomous Database	533	358	Autonomous system
4	Creating Chatbots and Artificial Intelligence in eTwinning Projects	103	40	Chatbot
5	Web Classroom 4.0: Something New, Something Old - Google Bard and Chat GPT	93	88	Chat GPT
6	Science and Personalized Learning Environments in Portugal	220	220	Personalized learning systems
7	Robotics in a Virtual Environment	11	11	Robotics
8	Robotics in the Erasmus+ Program	59	41	Robotics
9	Simulation of Robotics in the Operations of Logistic Warehouses	23	21	Robotics
10	Creating an Inclusive Environment 2 (Application of Robotics in Working with Children with Disabilities – Blue-Bot)	52	38	Robotics
11	Teacher Training as Part of the Curriculum Reform - Artificial Intelligence (AI) and "Digital Assistants"	385	281	Artificial intelligence

(*continued*)

Table 5. (*continued*)

No.	Title of training activity	Enrolled users	Certificates awarded	Keywords
12	Artificial Intelligence - Applications in Education (for Beginners)	3623	2354	Artificial intelligence
13	Artificial Intelligence as Support for Teachers and Educators	1507	1008	Artificial intelligence
14	Artificial Intelligence in the Classroom	1710	1295	Artificial intelligence
15	Artificial Intelligence and eTwinning	107	107	Artificial intelligence
16	Artificial Intelligence in Education	31	27	Artificial intelligence
17	Literature and Artificial Intelligence – Let's Talk!	94	93	Artificial intelligence
	Total	**8720**	**6108**	

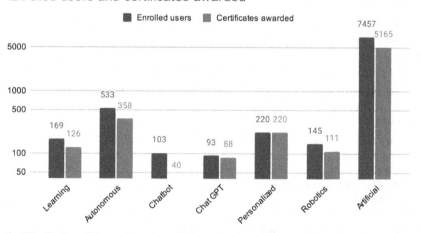

Enrolled users and certificates awarded

Fig. 1. Distribution of the number of enrolled users and certificates awarded against the keywords

7 Discussion

The database search for keywords related to AI in education resulted in a list of 17 different training activities. Considering that there are a total of 20,166 training activities listed in EMA from 18.1.2016 until 1.3.2024, this comprises only 0.084% of all training activities. If we narrow the period to include only the time since the first training activity related to AI in education on 04.04.2017, there have been a total of 19,530 training activities, with the AI-related training activity accounting for 0.087% of all training activities during this time span. Both percentages are extremely low.

The percentage distribution of training activities per keyword (See Table 2) is as follows: Artificial Intelligence is the most prominent topic, accounting for 41.17%. The second most represented topic is Robotics with 23.53%, while Learning Analytics holds the third position with 11.76%.

The distribution of the number of enrolled users and certificates awarded against the keywords (see Fig. 1) reveals that Artificial Intelligence is the most popular topic, with 7,457 enrolled participating teachers. The second-best represented topic is Autonomous Systems, with 533 enrolled participants, while Personalized Learning Systems hold the third position with 220 participants.

The percentage distribution of training activities per DigCompEdu area (See Table 4) indicates that Professional Engagement is the most represented area, accounting for 58.82%. Digital Resources and Teaching and Learning are equally represented at 17.64%. Facilitating Learners' Digital Competence is represented with only 5.88%, while Assessment and Empowering Learners are not included at all.

To summarize, despite the significant number of training activities recorded in the database, the proportion of activities specifically related to AI in education is notably low. Even when considering a more focused time span starting from the first AI-related training activity in 2017, the percentage remains quite modest. Additionally, the distribution of training activities per keyword and per DigCompEdu area reveals specific concentrations, such as Artificial Intelligence being the most prominent keyword and Professional Engagement being the most represented DigCompEdu area.

8 Conclusions and Recommendations

As evident from the results and discussion, within the broader landscape of professional development for teachers in Croatia, there is a very limited emphasis on AI in education, with certain areas and topics receiving more attention than others.

Further research should be conducted to refine the search criteria and to understand the reasons for gaps and inequalities in the offerings of professional development programs for teachers in the field of AI in education. It is also necessary to include learning outcomes of professional development programs for teachers in the database search, since the titles of training activities may not be indicative of the topics they relate to.

The recommendations for providers of professional development programs for teachers in Croatia are as follows: The overall offerings of professional development programs for teachers in the field of AI in education should be broadened, and efforts should be made to attract more teachers to participate. The topics should be more diverse, and the DigCompEdu areas should be more equally represented, with a special emphasis on Assessment and Empowering Learners. In doing so, providers of teacher professional development opportunities should closely monitor advancements in the field of Artificial Intelligence, as well as accompanying policies at the European and global levels. More specific recommendations for expanding CPD opportunities for teachers in the field of AI in education could be developed only after exploring the reasons for gaps and inequalities in the offerings of relevant professional development programs for teachers.

Moreover, as advancements in artificial intelligence continue to shape educational landscapes, it is predictable that specific frameworks aimed at teachers' AI competences will emerge. Consequently, future research should consider these evolving frameworks. Such frameworks would play an important role in equipping educators with the skills and knowledge to effectively harness AI technologies in the classroom. By acknowledging and incorporating these emerging frameworks into research initiatives, we can better understand and address the evolving needs and challenges faced by educators in the age of AI.

Acknowledgments. This paper was funded by Croatian Academic and Research Network – CARNET. It is written as a contribution within the Postgraduate University Doctoral Study in Application of Information and Communication Technologies at the University of Mostar.

References

1. Wang, N., Lester, J.: K-12 education in the age of AI: a call to action for K-12 AI literacy. Int. J. Artif. Intell. Educ. **33**, 228–232 (2023)
2. Tuomi, I., Cachia, R., Villar-Onrubia, D.: On the futures of technology in education: emerging trends and policy implications. Publications Office of the European Union, Luxembourg (2023)
3. Tuomi, I.: The impact of artificial intelligence on learning, teaching, and education. In: Cabrera, M., Vuorikari, R., Punie, Y. (eds.) Policies for the future, EUR 29442 EN. Publications Office of the European Union, Luxembourg (2018)
4. Celik, I., Dindar, M., Muukkonen, H., et al.: The promises and challenges of artificial intelligence for teachers: a systematic review of research. TechTrends **66**, 616–630 (2022)
5. Zawacki-Richter, O., Marín, V.I., Bond, M., et al.: Systematic review of research on artificial intelligence applications in higher education – where are the educators? Int. J. Educ. Technol. High. Educ. **16**, 39 (2019)
6. Seufert, S., Guggemos, J., Sailer, M.: Technology-related knowledge, skills, and attitudes of pre- and in-service teachers: the current situation and emerging trends. Comput. Hum. Behav. **115**, 106552 (2020)
7. Baldoni, M., et al.: Empowering AI competences in children: the first turning point. In: Kubincová, Z., Melonio, A., Durães, D., Rua Carneiro, D., Rizvi, M., Lancia, L. (eds.) MIS4TEL 2022. LNNS, vol. 538, pp. 171–181. Springer, Cham (2023). https://doi.org/10.1007/978-3-031-20257-5_18
8. Punie, Y., Redecker, C. (eds.): European Framework for the Digital Competence of Educators: DigCompEdu, EUR 28775 EN. Publications Office of the European Union, Luxembourg (2017)
9. Cukurova, M., Kralj, L., Hertz, B., Saltidou, E.: Professional development for teachers in the age of AI. European Schoolnet. Brussels (2024)
10. Vuorikari, R., Kluzer, S., Punie, Y.: DigComp 2.2: the digital competence framework for citizens - with new examples of knowledge, skills and attitudes, EUR 31006 EN. Publications Office of the European Union, Luxembourg (2022)
11. UNESCO: AI Competency Frameworks for Teachers (2023)

12. European Commission, Directorate-General for Education, Youth, Sport and Culture: Ethical guidelines on the use of artificial intelligence (AI) and data in teaching and learning for educators. Publications Office of the European Union (2022)

13. EMA Homepage. https://ema.carnet.hr/. Accessed 1 Mar 2024

14. Volaric, T., Crnokić, B.: Umjetna inteligencija u obrazovanju i robotici. Sveučilišna tiskara PRESSUM, Mostar (2022)

15. Best Large Language Models for 2024 and How to Choose the Right One for Your Site. https://www.hostinger.com/tutorials/large-language-models. Accessed March 2024

Artificial Intelligence Application

Crop-Guided Neural Network Segmentation of High-Resolution Skin Lesion Images

Marin Benčević[1,2]([✉]) [iD], Marija Habijan[1] [iD], and Irena Galić[1] [iD]

[1] Faculty of Electrical Engineering, Computer Science and Information Technology Osijek, Josip Juraj Strossmayer University of Osijek, Osijek, Croatia
`marin.bencevic@ferit.hr`
[2] Department of Telecommunications and Information Processing, TELIN-GAIM, Ghent University, Ghent, Belgium

Abstract. Medical images are often exceedingly large in width and height, limiting the maximum batch size when training convolutional neural networks and requiring models with a large number of parameters. Typically, images are uniformly downsampled, leading to losing fine-detailed information. Instead of uniformly downsampling images, we introduce a two-stage end-to-end segmentation network utilizing image crops to reduce network input size. Initially, a uniformly downscaled image is first segmented with a rough segmentation module, and the rough segmentation is used as a saliency map to crop the original high-resolution image to a region of interest. This crop is then re-segmented with a fine segmentation module. Our method's effectiveness is demonstrated in segmenting lesion boundaries in clinical images across two datasets. We establish that this technique maintains comparable segmentation quality to a baseline model while reducing the network input size. Furthermore, our approach enhances the robustness of segmentation outcomes with smaller input sizes, outperforming uniformly downscaled images and baseline models. This improvement is consistent in both in-sample and out-of-sample evaluations.

Keywords: medical image segmentation · data efficiency · skin lesion segmentation · convolutional neural networks

1 Introduction

High-resolution skin lesion images often have dimensions spanning thousands of pixels. It has been shown that convolutional neural networks benefit from proportionally scaling the number of network parameters and the image resolution [21]. However, in medical imaging, there is often an insufficient sample size to train high-capacity networks without overfitting. In addition, large input sizes limit

This work has been supported in part by the Croatian Science Foundation under Project UIP-2017-05-4968, as well as the Faculty of Electrical Engineering, Computer Science and Information Technology Osijek grant "IZIP 2023".

T. Volarić et al. (Eds.): MoStart 2024, CCIS 2124, pp. 113–123, 2024.
https://doi.org/10.1007/978-3-031-62058-4_9

the batch size during training, resulting in slower learning rates and less accurate gradient approximations. Overcoming this issue by uniformly downscaling the images during pre-processing, a standard practice in lesion segmentation, can lead to a loss of fine details critical for accurate segmentation. The downsampling may adversely affect the precision of segmentation results [19], highlighting the need for new strategies to effectively handle high-resolution images for reliable lesion analysis in medical research, diagnostics, and treatment planning.

An additional significant challenge in deep learning for biomedical image segmentation is domain shift [18], where models trained on images from one domain underperform when applied to another due to variations in image acquisition protocols, equipment used, or biases in the training dataset.

In this paper, we address the challenges of large input sizes and domain shift in image segmentation by employing a two-stage segmentation neural network, where each stage processes a smaller image relative to the original resolution. The first stage conducts a rough segmentation of the entire image, identifying a region of interest. A crop of the original-resolution image is then extracted from this region for re-segmentation in the second stage, with the initial segmentation mask also provided as input. Both stages are initially pre-trained using a standard segmentation network and subsequently fine-tuned in an end-to-end manner. Thus, instead of performing the segmentation with one large neural network, we simplify the task by using two smaller neural networks.

This method offers three primary advantages:

1. It reduces the total input size for the networks while preserving access to high-resolution information, enabling the use of larger batch sizes without compromising accuracy.
2. It facilitates the use of networks with fewer parameters, offering a beneficial regularization, especially valuable for small datasets.
3. By cropping each image to a region of interest, we effectively transform images of skin lesions into a virtual domain where each lesion is centered and uniformly scaled. This standardization reduces variance within and across datasets, enhancing the network's robustness to novel datasets. Our experimental results demonstrate superior segmentation performance on unseen datasets compared to standard baseline models.

While our experiments utilize a U-Net-based network, our approach is designed as a general framework, adaptable to various segmentation architectures and backbones. Additionally, this method can be used as a general preprocessing step to enhance the robustness of segmentation models across different image modalities and datasets. All of the code and experiment results for this paper are available at github.com/marinbenc/seg-then-seg-e2e.

2   Related Work

This study builds upon the work of [6], where a rough segmentation network is used to produce a salient region to crop images, and the crops are re-segmented by a separate fine segmentation network. We enhance this method by enabling end-to-end training of the coarse and fine segmentation networks. We achieve this through specific pretraining strategies and incorporating the initial segmentation as an input to the fine segmentation network.

Traditional segmentation models like Mask R-CNN [13] employ a *detect-then-segment* approach involving cropping, but this does not facilitate the utilization of high-resolution data with small input sizes. Some models adopt a process where the image is first segmented, followed by cropping and re-segmenting the segmented region, as seen in [24] and [25]. These models use separate course and fine networks and require multiple segmentation iterations per image. Our method employs one end-to-end network, allowing a single prediction per input image.

Another way to achieve spatial standardization is through Spatial Transformer Networks, typically used in pair-wise registration [3,11,17]. These methods, optimized for registration rather than segmentation, can perform segmentation by deforming a template atlas to fit a new input image [20]. Our approach differs by directly transforming each image based on a rough segmentation, thus bypassing the complexity of training registration-focused neural networks. In addition, our approach allows the use of small input sizes while sampling parts of a high-resolution image.

A similar approach to ours is presented by [15], where an object detection network is used to crop a region of interest, which is then segmented by a separate segmentation network. Our approach differs in that we use the same segmentation-based architecture for both networks and fine-tune them end-to-end. This allows transfer learning between the networks and a more robust segmentation pipeline. Similarly, [14] first pre-train a preprocessing network that learns beneficial image filters. That network is then connected to a segmentation network and the two are trained end-to-end. Our approach offers more flexibility since we use similar architectures for both networks, and as such the output of the preprocessing state can vary drastically from both the original image and the final segmentation mask.

2.1   Skin Lesion Boundary Segmentation

Various deep-learning methods have been developed for skin lesion segmentation. Double-U-Net [16] links two U-Net-like networks, allowing features to transfer between them. In our prior research, we explored various preprocessing techniques for lesion segmentation neural networks such as the polar transform [5] and image cropping [6]. [17] utilize boundary key points to create residual attention within the network, preserving edge information. [23] employ a transformer-based model with a boundary-focused attention gate for enhanced detail capture. Other recent advancements in this area also use transformer-based models such as [22] and [9], as well as diffusion-based models [7].

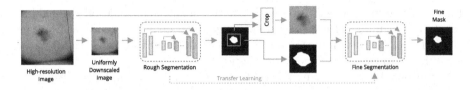

Fig. 1. This figure illustrates our method, comprising two interconnected modules: a coarse and a fine segmentation module, linked via a cropping layer. Both modules are designed to handle images of small, fixed input sizes. The first module processes a downscaled version of the input image. Its segmentation output determines the region of interest in the high-resolution image, which, along with the cropped initial segmentation, is fed into the fine segmentation module. Before being fine-tuned together, both networks are pre-trained as standard segmentation networks.

3   Methodology

A visual summary of our method is shown in Fig. 1. The network consists of two stages, a coarse and fine segmentation stage, connected by a cropping layer. Both stages use the same U-Net-based segmentation architecture. The input size of each stage is fixed and smaller than the original image resolution.

Assuming the input size of the network is $w \times h$, given a high-resolution input image I' of size $W \times H$, the inference process can be described as a series of several steps:

1. First, we uniformly downscale the image into I of size $w \times h$ using linear interpolation.
2. This downscaled image is then input into the coarse segmentation module producing a segmentation mask $M_{coarse}(I)$.
3. The segmentation mask M_{coarse} is then upscaled to M'_{coarse} of size $W \times H$ and thus matches the high-resolution image.
4. Then, a bounding box is calculated such that it encompasses all non-zero regions of M'_{coarse} and expanded by 20 pixels in each direction, clipped to the bounds of the image. In cases where M_{coarse} has no non-zero pixels, the bounding box is set to the whole image, i.e. $I_{crop} = I$. From our experiments, such cases are exceedingly rare.
5. The bounding box is used to crop I' and the crop is then scaled to $w \times h$, producing a high-resolution input region of interest I_{crop}. Note that scaling the crop region to $w \times h$ results in a much lower total scaling than it does when scaling down the whole image. Then, an input vector is constructed for the fine segmentation network as $x_{fine} = [I_{crop}, M_{coarse}]$. In other words, the first channel is the high-resolution crop, while the second channel is the coarse segmentation mask.
6. The fine segmentation network then produces a final segmentation mask $M(x_{fine})$ which is used as the output of the whole model.

We use pre-training to allow the two networks to reliably converge. First, we train a regular segmentation network on uniformly downscaled images I. Once trained, the weights of this model are transferred both to the rough and fine segmentation modules of our proposed network architecture.

3.1 Implementation Details

We use PyTorch 1.10 for all experiments. All models are trained on an Nvidia GeForce RTX 3080. Wherever possible, we fix a random seed value of "2022". We use the Adam optimizer for all training while reducing the learning rate on plateaus by a factor of 0.1. The best model is selected and saved during training based on validation loss. We use a learning rate of 10^{-4} for both pre-training and fine-tuning. We set the batch size to 16 for all input sizes except 512×512, where the batch size was set to 4. For ease of implementation, all high-resolution input images are resized to 1024×1024 pixels, but this is not a required step for our method, which can work with any high-resolution input image size.

3.2 Dataset Description

For the experiments in this paper, we use the University of Waterloo skin cancer database [12] (available at [2]) of clinical skin lesion images. The dataset consists of manual segmentation labels of two publicly available skin lesion databases, DermIS [1] and DermQuest (no longer available). We treat these two collections as two different centers to evaluate out-of-sample performance. The images are of various sizes from 300 to 550 pixels in height and width. As a preprocessing step, each image of each dataset is normalized to $[-0.5, 0.5]$.

We use the following online randomized augmentation steps:

1. A 50% chance of a random horizontal and/or vertical flip.
2. A 50% chance of a 90° rotation.
3. A 50% chance of a random affine transform including rotation up to 45°, scaling up to 10%, and a shift up to 6.25% of the input image size.

4 Results and Discussion

To evaluate our method, we train a baseline U-Net model and our end-to-end image-cropping approach for input sizes 64×64, 128×128, 256×256, and 512×512. The same architecture was used for the baseline U-Net model as well as for the rough and fine segmentation modules in our method. We employed 5-fold cross-validation to evaluate in-sample performance, resulting in five distinct models for each dataset. For out-of-sample performance evaluation, each image in one dataset was segmented using the five models trained on the other dataset. Segmentation metrics were calculated for each prediction and then averaged, ensuring that all reported out-of-sample metrics represent an average from models trained across five different data folds.

The two segmentation metrics we use for the evaluation are the Dice Similarity Coefficient (DSC) as well as the Thresholded Jaccard Index. DSC takes into

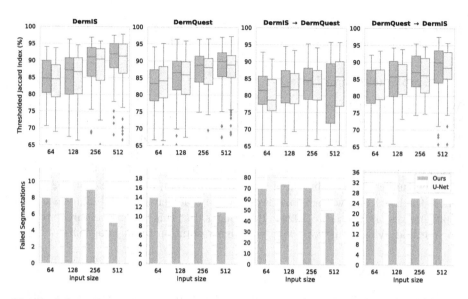

Fig. 2. A box plot of Jaccard indices above or equal to 0.65 (above) and the number of Jaccard indices below 0.65 (below). The first two columns show in-sample results, while the last two columns show out-of-sample results for models trained on DermIS and tested on DermQuest and vice-versa.

account both the accuracy and recall of the method and is thus a good general segmentation metric. The Thresholded Jaccard Index was proposed for lesion segmentation in the ISIC 2018 challenge [10] to account for specific needs in skin lesion segmentation. Low-accuracy segmentations (in this case defined as those with a Jaccard Index less than 0.65) are not useful for further lesion analysis. Therefore, instead of a simple mean result calculation, all results with a Jaccard Index below 0.65 are set to zero. This has been shown to better represent true segmentation performance in the context of lesion segmentation.

Visually, our approach demonstrates enhanced performance in delineating lesion boundaries, as evident in Fig. 3. The segmentation results more accurately adhere to the ground truth contours and exhibit fewer false-positive regions compared to those generated by the baseline models.

Quantitatively, in-sample and out-of-sample results of our model compared to a baseline U-Net are shown in Table 1. When comparing our method and a baseline U-Net using the same input size, we note an increase in DSC in almost all experiments. We see similar results for the Thresholded Jaccard Index. These increases can give us an estimate of how much we can reduce the input size of an image while still retaining the same segmentation quality. For instance, using our approach, we can go from 256×256 to 64×64 images while achieving the same in-sample as well as out-of-sample Thresholded Jaccard Index for DermIS.

The thresholded Jaccard index assumes that any segmentation with a Jaccard index below 0.65 is a failed segmentation, i.e. it cannot be used for further

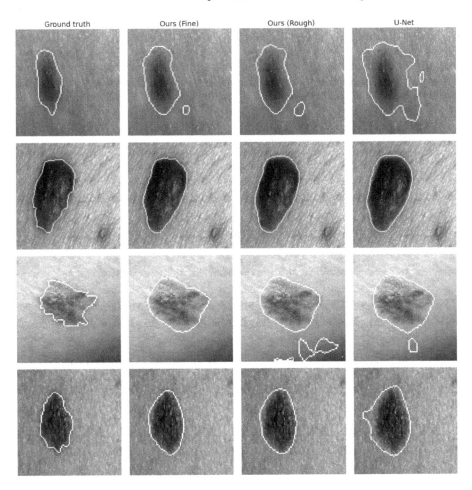

Fig. 3. Randomly chosen examples of out-of-sample segmentation results. The columns, from left to right, show the input image with the ground truth segmentation mask, the final output segmentation mask of our approach, the rough segmentation of our approach, and the output of a baseline U-Net model. The images are zoomed in on the lesion region.

downstream analysis of the legion due to its insufficient accuracy. Consequently, we examined the frequency of these failed segmentations across various input sizes, as depicted in Fig. 2. The findings indicate a general improvement in the mean Jaccard Index (exceeding 0.65) when utilizing our model, particularly for smaller input sizes, and this trend persists even in out-of-sample evaluations. Additionally, there is a noticeable decrease in the incidence of failed segmentations (Jaccard Index < 0.65) in all but two experiments. This decline is most pronounced with smaller input sizes, suggesting that our method significantly enhances the robustness of segmentations derived from images with small input sizes.

Table 1. Results of our approach and the baseline model in terms of the Dice Coefficient (DSC) as well as the thresholded Jaccard index (Th. Jacc.) for various experiments. Results are shown in the form of mean ± standard deviation. The top two groups show in-sample performance within the DermIS and DermQuest datasets, while the bottom two groups show out-of-sample performance when trained on DermIS and tested on DermQuest, and vice-versa.

Size	U-Net		Ours	
	DSC	Th. Jacc.	DSC	Th. Jacc.
	DermIS			
64	85.51 ± 15.50	70.31 ± 31.38	87.01 ± 15.06	74.57 ± 27.97
128	86.53 ± 15.71	72.21 ± 30.78	88.82 ± 11.93	75.84 ± 28.41
256	88.09 ± 14.58	73.58 ± 33.01	89.88 ± 12.49	77.04 ± 30.77
512	89.85 ± 16.90	81.32 ± 26.32	90.35 ± 17.07	83.40 ± 24.35
	DermQuest			
64	87.75 ± 9.07	71.61 ± 29.56	87.83 ± 8.97	73.96 ± 25.84
128	88.83 ± 10.19	76.59 ± 25.76	89.45 ± 10.09	77.93 ± 25.00
256	89.61 ± 11.20	77.34 ± 27.73	90.10 ± 11.22	78.99 ± 26.18
512	91.14 ± 9.18	81.31 ± 23.69	90.52 ± 12.98	81.16 ± 24.76
	DermIS → DermQuest			
64	77.11 ± 13.58	43.40 ± 34.37	80.94 ± 12.85	54.56 ± 31.45
128	80.20 ± 12.92	50.81 ± 33.87	79.61 ± 14.15	52.46 ± 32.36
256	78.67 ± 15.32	51.10 ± 33.30	80.07 ± 14.55	55.18 ± 31.51
512	80.96 ± 14.38	60.73 ± 26.96	83.34 ± 13.29	66.72 ± 24.61
	DermQuest → DermIS			
64	78.94 ± 18.81	54.98 ± 34.36	81.85 ± 17.24	60.87 ± 32.66
128	78.31 ± 19.36	51.57 ± 37.63	81.51 ± 18.23	60.10 ± 35.86
256	81.10 ± 19.54	60.81 ± 35.41	81.97 ± 19.46	63.12 ± 34.89
512	83.60 ± 18.73	65.59 ± 32.99	82.82 ± 19.70	64.50 ± 33.35

5　Conclusion

We have presented a way to incorporate image cropping into an end-to-end lesion segmentation model to reduce network input size as well as the impact of domain shift. By utilizing transfer learning, we successfully addressed issues related to network convergence. We have shown that our approach improves inter-domain and intra-domain lesion segmentation performance and produces more reliable results when compared to baseline segmentation models that do not use image crops. Using our approach, we were able to reduce input sizes by at least half while retaining the same segmentation quality.

A significant advantage of our approach is the reduced requirement for detailed segmentation labels in the rough segmentation stage. This stage only necessitates approximate object localization, achievable through simpler, potentially unsupervised methods like heuristic-based and traditional image processing techniques. Moreover, one could use weakly supervised training using pseudo-labels, instead of segmentation.

However, our approach has certain limitations. Notably, from our experiments in datasets with large sample sizes, our method did not substantially improve segmentation quality when there was a large amount of data. We speculate that our approach acts as a form of regularization, beneficial in scenarios where overfitting is a concern due to small sample sizes and high-capacity networks. This regularization may be redundant in cases with ample sample sizes. Nonetheless, the primary aim of our approach is to improve data efficiency in terms of both input size and sample size. Thus, our evaluation targets are datasets with small sample sizes.

A potential improvement of this approach would be to make the gradient flow more explicit. To achieve this, one could use an approach similar to [8], where a key point is predicted by the first subnetwork in the form of a heatmap. This allows preserving the gradient flow by taking the centroid of the heatmap. Similarly, the approach could be extended to support multiple objects by taking multiple crops as a result of a predicted initial heatmap as in [4].

Although this paper focused on skin lesion segmentation, our previous research has explored the advantages of reducing spatial variation in training medical image segmentation models across various datasets in [5] and [6]. Based on these insights, we believe our method can be broadly applied to enhance segmentation performance and robustness in a variety of image segmentation tasks, particularly where object scale and location variance are significant and the sample size is small.

References

1. DermIS—dermis.net, Department of Clinical Social Medicine (Univ. of Heidelberg) and the Department of Dermatology (Univ. of Erlangen) (2012). https://www.dermis.net/

2. Skin Cancer Detection | Vision and Image Processing Lab—uwaterloo.ca, University of Waterloo (2012). https://uwaterloo.ca/vision-image-processing-lab/research-demos/skin-cancer-detection

3. Balakrishnan, G., Zhao, A., Sabuncu, M.R., Guttag, J., Dalca, A.V.: Voxelmorph: a learning framework for deformable medical image registration. IEEE Trans. Med. Imaging **38**(8), 1788–1800 (2019)

4. Angles, B., Jin, Y., Kornblith, S., Tagliasacchi, A., Yi, K. M.: MIST: multiple instance spatial transformer networks. In: Proceedings of the IEEE Conference on Computer Vision and Pattern Recognition (2021)

5. Benčević, M., Galic, I., Habijan, M., Babin, D.: Training on polar image transformations improves biomedical image segmentation. IEEE Access **9**, 133365–133375 (2021). https://doi.org/10.1109/ACCESS.2021.3116265

6. Benčević, M., Qiu, Y., Galić, I., Pizurica, A.: Segment-then-segment: context-preserving crop-based segmentation for large biomedical images. Sensors **23**(2), 633 (2023). https://doi.org/10.3390/s23020633

7. Bozorgpour, A., Sadegheih, Y., Kazerouni, A., Azad, R., Merhof, D.: DermoSegDiff: a boundary-aware segmentation diffusion model for skin lesion delineation. In: Rekik, I., Adeli, E., Park, S.H., Cintas, C., Zamzmi, G. (eds.) PRIME 2023. LNCS, vol. 14277, pp. 146–158. Springer, Cham (2023). https://doi.org/10.1007/978-3-031-46005-0_13

8. Esteves, C., Allen-Blanchette, C., Kostas Daniilidis, Zhou, X.: Polar transformer networks. In: International Conference on Learning Representations (2018)

9. Chen, B., Liu, Y., Zhang, Z., Lu, G., Kong, A.W.K.: TransAttUnet: multi-level attention-guided U-net with transformer for medical image segmentation. IEEE Trans. Emerg. Top. Comput. Intell. **8**(1), 55–68 (2024). https://doi.org/10.1109/TETCI.2023.3309626

10. Codella, N., et al.: Skin lesion analysis toward melanoma detection 2018: a challenge hosted by the international skin imaging collaboration (ISIC) (2019)

11. de Vos, B.D., Berendsen, F.F., Viergever, M.A., Staring, M., Išgum, I.: End-to-end unsupervised deformable image registration with a convolutional neural network. In: Cardoso, M.J., et al. (eds.) DLMIA/ML-CDS -2017. LNCS, vol. 10553, pp. 204–212. Springer, Cham (2017). https://doi.org/10.1007/978-3-319-67558-9_24

12. Glaister, J., Wong, A., Clausi, D.A.: Automatic segmentation of skin lesions from dermatological photographs using a joint probabilistic texture distinctiveness approach. IEEE Trans. Biomed. Eng. (2014)

13. He, K., Gkioxari, G., Dollár, P., Girshick, R.: Mask R-CNN. In: 2017 IEEE International Conference on Computer Vision (ICCV), pp. 2980–2988 (2017). https://doi.org/10.1109/ICCV.2017.322

14. Iyer, K., et al.: AngioNet: a convolutional neural network for vessel segmentation in X-ray angiography. Sci. Rep. **11**(1), 18066 (2021). https://doi.org/10.1038/s41598-021-97355-8

15. Jha, A., Yang, H., Deng, R., Kapp, M.E., Fogo, A.B., Huo, Y.: Instance segmentation for whole slide imaging: end-to-end or detect-then-segment. J. Med. Imaging **8**(01) (2021). https://doi.org/10.1117/1.JMI.8.1.014001

16. Jha, D., Riegler, M.A., Johansen, D., Halvorsen, P., Johansen, H.D.: DoubleU-net: a deep convolutional neural network for medical image segmentation. In: 2020 IEEE 33rd International Symposium on Computer-Based Medical Systems (CBMS), pp. 558–564 (2020)

17. Lee, M.C.H., Oktay, O., Schuh, A., Schaap, M., Glocker, B.: Image-and-spatial transformer networks for structure-guided image registration. In: Shen, D., et al. (eds.) MICCAI 2019. LNCS, vol. 11765, pp. 337–345. Springer, Cham (2019). https://doi.org/10.1007/978-3-030-32245-8_38

18. Pooch, E.H.P., Ballester, P., Barros, R.C.: Can we trust deep learning based diagnosis? The impact of domain shift in chest radiograph classification. In: Petersen, J., et al. (eds.) TIA 2020. LNCS, vol. 12502, pp. 74–83. Springer, Cham (2020). https://doi.org/10.1007/978-3-030-62469-9_7

19. Sabottke, C.F., Spieler, B.M.: The effect of image resolution on deep learning in radiography. Radiol.: Artif. Intell. **2**(1), e190015 (2020). https://doi.org/10.1148/ryai.2019190015

20. Sinclair, M., et al.: Atlas-ISTN: joint segmentation, registration and atlas construction with image-and-spatial transformer networks. Med. Image Anal. **78**, 102383 (2022https://doi.org/10.1016/j.media.2022.102383

21. Tan, M., Le, Q.V.: EfficientNet: rethinking model scaling for convolutional neural networks. ArXiv abs/1905.11946 (2019)

22. Tang, F., Huang, Q., Wang, J., Hou, X., Su, J., Liu, J.: DuAT: dual-aggregation transformer network for medical image segmentation. arXiv preprint arXiv:2212.11677 (2022)
23. Wang, J., Wei, L., Wang, L., Zhou, Q., Zhu, L., Qin, J.: Boundary-aware transformers for skin lesion segmentation. In: de Bruijne, M., et al. (eds.) MICCAI 2021. LNCS, vol. 12901, pp. 206–216. Springer, Cham (2021). https://doi.org/10.1007/978-3-030-87193-2_20
24. Zhou, Y., Xie, L., Shen, W., Wang, Y., Fishman, E.K., Yuille, A.L.: A fixed-point model for pancreas segmentation in abdominal CT scans. In: Descoteaux, M., Maier-Hein, L., Franz, A., Jannin, P., Collins, D.L., Duchesne, S. (eds.) MICCAI 2017. LNCS, vol. 10433, pp. 693–701. Springer, Cham (2017). https://doi.org/10.1007/978-3-319-66182-7_79
25. Zhu, Z., Xia, Y., Shen, W., Fishman, E., Yuille, A.: A 3D coarse-to-fine framework for volumetric medical image segmentation. In: 2018 International Conference on 3D Vision (3DV), pp. 682–690. IEEE, Verona (2018). https://doi.org/10.1109/3DV.2018.00083

Artificial Intelligence-Based Control of Autonomous Vehicles in Simulation: A CNN vs. RL Case Study

Ive Vasiljević[1] , Josip Musić[1(✉)] , and José Lima[2]

[1] Faculty of Electrical Engineering, Mechanical Engineering and Naval Architecture, University of Split, 21000 Split, Croatia
{ive.vasiljevic.00,jmusic}@fesb.hr
[2] Research Centre of Digitalization and Intelligent Robotics, Instituto Politécnico de Bragança, 5300-253 Bragança, Portugal
jllima@ipb.pt

Abstract. The article provides a comparison of Convolutional Neural Network (CNN) and Reinforcement Learning (RL) applied to the field of autonomous driving within the CARLA (CAr Learning to Act) simulator for training and evaluation. The analysis of results revealed CNNs better overall performance, as it demonstrated a more refined driving experience, shorter training durations, and a more straightforward learning curve and optimization process. However, it required data labelling. In contrast, RL relayed on an exhaustive (unsupervised) exploration of different models, ultimately selecting the model at timestep 600,000, which had the highest mean reward. Nevertheless, RL's approach revealed its susceptibility to excessive oscillations and inconsistencies, necessitating additional optimization and tuning of hyperparameters and reward functions. This conclusion is further substantiated by a range of used performance metrics (objective and subjective), designed to assess the performance of each approach.

Keywords: reinforcement learning · CNN · CARLA simulator

1 Introduction

The autonomous driving phenomenon has significantly advanced over the years of its development [1]. The automotive tech industry has made momentous enhancements to the capability and reliability of sensors, cameras, and vehicle-to-everything (V2X) communication [2]. Collectively, these features generate many consumer benefits, but they also may produce additional value for the auto industry [3,4]. To ensure that automotive companies are following a well-established standard, whilst announcing their progress on the state of their autonomous driving systems, the Society of Automotive Engineers (SAE), a standards-developing organization, has defined six levels of driving automation. Each level puts fewer constraints on the human driver, meaning less attention to the road and actions

T. Volarić et al. (Eds.): MoStart 2024, CCIS 2124, pp. 124–151, 2024.
https://doi.org/10.1007/978-3-031-62058-4_10

are needed. Additionally, each level provides more features, like line centering and adaptive cruise control, automatic emergency break, etc.

The current state of the autonomous driving industry is monopolized by larger companies including Tesla, Ford, Mercedes, General Motors, and Kia/Hyundai [5]. Notably, these companies are considered to have the most reliable systems in place, however, they seem to differ in what SAE level they fall into. The best level most companies have to commercially offer, including Tesla, is only Level 2, as defined by the SAE standard [5]. As of today, Mercedes has rolled out a self-certified Level 3 system (Drive Pilot). However, this standard needs very specific conditions to work, including the feature requests, where a human driver needs to take over the control of the vehicle. The Drive Pilot, doesn't exceed speeds of 45 mph (cca. 72 km/h), in conditions of clear weather during the day, and only on roads mapped by the system [5].

These autonomous driving systems are made possible using numerous sensors attached to a car, giving meaningful information about the environment. Even with all the information available, research suggests that perhaps creating autonomous driving systems was more difficult than first predicted [6,7]. In [7], it is stated that 80% of self-driving is relatively simple - making the car follow the line of the road, sticking to a certain side, and avoiding collisions. The next 10% involve more difficult situations such as roundabouts and complex junctions. The last 10% has proven to be arduous, which covers the problem of "edge cases". They are rare cases that can occur on the road, such as an animal being in the middle of the road, or a child running across the street. This final 20% is why the autonomous driving industry is still not making any significant progress.

While developing autonomous driving systems, there are numerous questions to be explored, including how many sensors to use, what information to use from those sensors, for what purpose to use them, and which algorithms to use alongside these sensors [8]. Sensors like Light Detection and Ranging (LiDAR), radar, and cameras are among a few that are routinely used to sense the world around vehicles. The hardware used in autonomous vehicles has remained relatively stable in recent years, while the software has undergone constant updates and changes. This dynamic nature of software development makes it crucial to demonstrate the capabilities of various learning algorithms especially in the domain of self-teaching cars where vehicles are equipped with advanced artificial intelligence systems that enable them to learn from experiences and adapt their behavior to improve their driving skills autonomously. Furthermore, with the rising popularity of end-to-end (E2E) learning [9], which is a method where a system learns to perform a task directly from input to output, without relying on many intermediate steps, Convolutional Neural Network (CNN) has proven to be an efficient tool for processing various types of raw data and generating meaningful predictions [10]. While CNNs are well-known for their proficiency in handling image and video data (e.g., for tasks like object detection [11], lane recognition [12], and traffic sign classification [13] in autonomous driving systems), they are also applicable and effective in other domains. For instance, they excel in tasks like speech recognition (audio data) [14], natural language processing (text data) [15], and even certain medical diagnoses, where patterns and features can be automatically learned from the data [16]. Another approach that has shown remarkable success in autonomous driving is Reinforcement Learning (RL) [17–19]. Through RL, autonomous vehicles can learn complex driving behaviors and decision-making skills, such as handling various traffic scenarios, obeying traffic rules, and adapting to different road conditions. By iteratively improving through trial and error, RL algorithms can achieve acceptable levels of autonomy in driving tasks.

Obviously, due to safety concerns and ease of implementation (i.e. testing different scenarios, including low probability ones), it is not possible to initially test/develop new software for autonomous vehicles (including various artificial intelligence algorithms) in the real-world scenario [20]. Realistic computer simulations have thus emerged as a viable and practical solution to the problem. Much research [10,18,19] has been focused on it in recent years, with some interesting results. For example, in [19] end-to-end driving policies were developed in CARLA (CAr Learning to Act) simulator [21], and later deployed on a full-sized car (over 9 driving scenarios and more than 400 test drives). RL was used as a basis for developing different driving policies with the vehicle being controlled via throttle and steering variables and an RGB camera used as a main sensor. During testing, authors noted a simulation-to-reality gap which resulted in degraded performance in real-world scenarios. They also noted the positive influence on the performance of regularization and augmentation.

The lack of detail and information richness of computer-generated images compared to real-world images has also been noted in [22] in which increased usage of computer game engines for simulation has been described. For example, the LGSVL simulator (whose active development has now been stopped) is based on the Unity game engine [23], while AirSim uses Unreal Engine [24]. Research [25] has also gone into determining the deterministic level of simulators, namely the CARLA simulator. It was shown that it was non-deterministic, with actor collisions and system resource utilization being identified as the main sources of it. Authors suggest that these parameters need to be monitored for improved performance and that some commercially available simulators could be considered for more consistent performance. Extensive overviews of modeling and simulation approaches used in autonomous vehicles can be found in [26,27].

AI-based algorithms can be found in many tasks associated with autonomous vehicles (in a simulation and real-world scenarios) [28], with (deep) neural networks usually used for perception tasks, decision-making and control, and RL for optimizing driving behavior (control). In [29], a CNN was used in an end-to-end fashion for inference of vehicle steering angle and throttle position within the simulation environment (Udacity open-source simulation platform). Data augmentation was used for generating training data, which resulted in collision-free driving within the tested examples. In [10] CNN-based end-to-end approach (using RBG road images) was also used, but with architecture (and thus computational complexity) optimization in mind. The approach was tested/implemented in the CARLA simulator and compared with nVIDIA's PilotNet. Obtained performance results were comparable (with the difference in Mean Square Error - MSE - of 0.00004), but the resulting network was approximately 40x lighter than PilotNet i.e. it had 4x fewer parameters resulting in somewhat lower inference time. However, it should be noted that PilotNet was tested in real-world scenarios with good results [30], while the proposed architecture was tested in simulation only.

Two additional examples in which the CARLA simulator was used, but with a different artificial intelligence algorithm, RL, are [18,31]. In [18] Deep-Q-Network (DQN) and Deep Deterministic Policy Gradient (DDPG) algorithms were implemented and compared within the simulator. Archived control was compared with traditional controllers like Linear Quadratic Regulator (LQR) with DDPG achieving better results (than DQN) scoring Root Mean Square Error (RMSE) of about 0.1 m (on tracks up to 700 m long). However, the authors used inserted waypoints (employing a path planning algorithm) to achieve desired results, and not, more standard, sensor output like an RGB camera or a LiDAR. The model-free RL algorithms were also used in [31] for controlling an autonomous vehicle in a complex urban scenario like a busy roundabout (with about 50 vehicles in its vicinity in the used map). Algorithms were given a raw bird-eye view of the map as their input (which is not a realistic scenario). All tested algorithms successfully entered the roundabout in 80% of cases but only the Soft Actor-Critic (SAC) algorithm managed to reach the desired goal point in 58% of test cases. It was found that almost all failure cases came from rear-ending the front vehicle.

Based on the presented brief literature review it can be seen that CNNs and RL are among the most widely used AI-based algorithms for autonomous vehicle control. However, comparative analysis of the two in the same scenario is largely missing from the available literature. Thus, this paper aims to develop and implement CNN and RL (with varying implementation hyperparameters) within the CARLA simulator to analyze and compare their results (on the same track) alongside observed implementation details.

2   Materials and Methods

This section focuses on the implementation of CNN and RL in the CARLA simulator. Each method is explained clearly and concisely, highlighting the differences in their implementation.

2.1   Artificial Intelligence-Based Algorithms

Artificial Neural Networks. An Artificial Neural Network (ANN), also known simply as a NN, is a learning system that uses a network of interconnected neurons (nodes) to process inputs and generate desired outputs. The NN itself may be used as a part of other machine learning algorithms, to process complex data inputs into a space that computers can understand [32]. Additionally, it's important to note that there exist numerous types of ANNs, each tailored for specific purposes and accommodating different types of input data. For instance,

CNN excels in image analysis, making it ideal for processing two-dimensional grid-like data, such as images, while Recurrent Neural Network (RNN) is well-suited for sequential data processing, which includes time series data, natural language text, and speech.

NNs have a wide variety of applications, but recently they also faced some limitations that make them not universally applicable to every problem. First and foremost, NNs are hardware-dependent, requiring additional efforts to handle more complex problems. Also, due to their "black box" nature, it becomes challenging to determine the exact degree to which each independent variable affects the dependent variables [33]. Additionally, training data plays a crucial role in NNs, leading to issues like over-fitting and generalization problems, where the model may become too tailored to the specific training data. To perform effectively, NN demands a colossal volume of data, which can be particularly problematic in situations where data collection and labeling are arduous and expensive (of which autonomous driving is a good example). Gathering and annotating such extensive datasets can be resource-intensive, often necessitating substantial human effort and expertise. Despite their limitations, NNs offer numerous advantages that make them versatile [32]. For instance, their adaptability allows them to be applied to both regression and classification problems. Being mathematical models with approximation functions, they can handle any data that can be converted into a numeric format. Moreover, NNs excel at modeling nonlinear data with multiple inputs, such as images. Once trained, they provide fast predictions, and they can be designed with any number of inputs and layers.

When considering the processing of images, a fundamental distinction arises between ANNs and CNNs [32]. ANNs tend to employ a comprehensive network of neurons and connections, resulting in a vast number of parameters that can lead to computational inefficiencies, particularly for larger images. In contrast, CNNs adopt a more efficient approach, leveraging local parameter sharing within convolutional layers to efficiently extract hierarchical features from images. As an example, in [34] comparison between ANN-based and CNN-based image classification was performed. In terms of the number of used parameters for particular networks, the deep ANN network (with five dense layers) had about 31.4 million trainable parameters, while the CNN network (with three convolutional layers and two dense layers) had about 0.4 million trainable parameters, which is a reduction of about 78x. In terms of achieved accuracy for the proposed networks, ANN achieved 90% while CNN achieved 97%.

Reinforcement Learning. In contrast to conventional NNs reliant on labeled datasets for supervised learning, in RL, agents acquire knowledge through dynamic interactions (in unsupirvised manner) with an environment, optimizing actions to maximize cumulative rewards. Unlike supervised learning's dependency on curated and labeled datasets, RL offers a framework where agents autonomously adapt and learn in intricate real-world settings, showcasing its potential for autonomous learning in complex scenarios. Therefore, RL consists of four main parts [17]:

- **Agent** - entity that perceives the environment and acts upon it.
- **Environment** - agent's world in which it interacts.
- **Policy** - a strategy used by the agent for the next action based on the current state.
- **Reward** - signal that the agent observes upon taking actions.

To formalize RL issues, the Markov Decision Process (MDP) is utilized. The agent in MDP continually interacts with the environment and performs actions; the environment responds to each action and develops a new state.

RL offers a range of learning algorithms. Broadly, they are categorized as model-free and model-based algorithms [35], with a simple differentiation: if an agent can predict the next state and reward before taking its next action after learning, it's a model-based RL algorithm; otherwise, it's model-free. Within the model-free category, there is a further division into on-policy and off-policy techniques. On-policy methods focus on improving the policy used to make decisions, while off-policy techniques employ a separate behavioral policy to explore the environment and gather samples. These samples influence both the agent's behavior and the learning of a refined policy called the target policy. In practice, model-free algorithms are more prevalent than model-based ones [35]. It's worth noting that the applicability of each algorithm depends on the agent's action space, whether deterministic or stochastic.

One of the key advantages of RL is its ability to tackle complex and challenging problems that are often beyond the reach of traditional methods. These traditional methods, such as rule-based systems or supervised learning, may struggle when confronted with tasks involving long-term planning, sequential decision-making, and intricate interactions with an environment. RL, on the other hand, excels in achieving long-term objectives and navigating intricate problem spaces. Furthermore, the learning paradigm is very comparable to human learning. But naturally, as with everything, there are limitations to RL, that make it unusable in some situations. For basic problems, RL is not the best option, it needs a large amount of data and processing, and last but not least for genuine physical systems, the curse of dimensionality limits RL. Most of the limitations are very specific and generally, its many advantages make it more desirable and hence this widely used [17,35].

2.2 CARLA Simulator

The CARLA Simulator [21] is a powerful open-source tool for autonomous driving research and development. It provides a realistic virtual environment where machine-learning models can be trained, tested, and evaluated without the need for real-world cars or physical environments. CARLA offers a range of functionalities to create immersive and challenging scenarios. CARLA simulates a variety of real-world elements, such as urban environments, roads, traffic, pedestrians, and dynamic objects as illustrated in Fig. 1. By accurately modeling these components, CARLA provides a sense of realism that is essential for training and

Fig. 1. Examples of default CARLA maps [21]

testing autonomous driving algorithms. The simulator allows users to manipulate various parameters, such as weather conditions, lighting, and traffic density.

One of the key advantages of CARLA is its ability to generate annotated data for training machine learning models. By integrating with the simulator, researchers can collect vast amounts of labeled data, including sensor data (such as camera images, LiDAR point clouds, and radar readings) and ground truth information (such as object positions and semantic segmentation). This data can then be used to train and validate the performance of machine learning models in a controlled and reproducible manner. It provides an Application Programming Interface (API) and libraries, including Python and C++, for customization and integration with external tools and frameworks. Furthermore, CARLA supports the implementation of RL algorithms, where agents learn to navigate and make decisions in the simulated environment through trial and error. However, a persistent challenge is the simulation-reality gap [36], where simulations may not perfectly mirror real-world complexities.

CARLA simulator operates using a client-server architecture, where the server generates and maintains the simulation environment, and the client interacts with the server to control vehicles, access sensor data, and receive simulation updates. Clients connect to the server, which runs simulations using Unreal Engine 4 and CARLA Plugins. The server manages physics and rendering, whereas clients can retrieve data and issue commands via the Python or C++ CARLA API, with Python offering ease of use and C++ providing performance.

During the experiments, CARLA version 0.9.13 was utilized as the foundation for developing and testing the AI-based learning methods. Building CARLA from source allowed for the incorporation of additional features and capabilities, as well as the utilization of the Unreal Editor for asset creation and map manipulation. For creating custom roads and scenarios, a software called RoadRunner was used, courtesy of MathWorks [37]. RoadRunner is an interactive editor that enables designing 3D scenes for simulating and testing automated driving systems.

2.3   Experimental Setup

All the training, testing, and overall development was made on a machine with an NVIDIA GeForce GTX 1070 with 8 GB GDDR5 memory graphics card, 16 GB of DDR4-3200 MHz RAM, a 512 GB NVMe SSD, and Intel Core i5-11600K with 6 cores and 12 threads.

Convolutional Neural Network (CNN). The main emphasis of the CNN implementation lies in five fundamental elements: the setup of the environment, data collection, data preprocessing, data splitting, and an overview of the network architecture.

Environment Setup. To achieve diversity and data generalization, five distinct maps were generated and exported using RoadRunner. These maps shared a consistent environment and road style, differing primarily in their road layouts. Urban features such as houses, trees, bins, and hydrants were intentionally kept minimal to streamline image collection and reduce map size. Each map included both clockwise and anti-clockwise variants to capture data from both driving directions. Furthermore, these maps feature level road surfaces without significant inclines or declines. Four out of the five maps were allocated for training and validation, while the remaining map was dedicated to testing the trained model. Figure 2 depicts all five maps, and how each of them had a different road shape. Upon the completion of map creation in RoadRunner, the maps were exported, and the final enhancements were applied within the Unreal Editor. These enhancements included the addition of imperceptible features, such as specific spawn points on the map and autopilot waypoints.

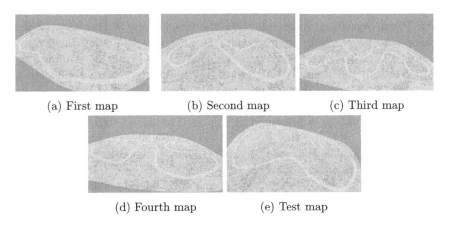

(a) First map   (b) Second map   (c) Third map

(d) Fourth map   (e) Test map

Fig. 2. Training and testing maps used during the experiments

Data Collection. To collect data for training, first, a single camera sensor was attached to the vehicle, designed for collecting RGB images. The camera was placed at the front of the car, a bit below the vehicle's hood. The vehicle that was used during training and testing was a Tesla Model 3. The images were saved to a specific folder using the built-in static function, which saves an image after every frame of the simulation running. Using a specific property in CARLA's world settings, the FPS during the data collection process was fixed at 33.33.

One lap was made around the map in each direction, providing a thorough exploration of the entire road, and making a closing loop. On average, each lap took 4 min and 36 s to complete, therefore for each map around eight to nine minutes, depending on the size of the map and the intensity of the curvatures. The size of the saved images was $300 \times 300 \times 3$. Along with the images, steering angle and throttle values were also recorded. Steering values went from -1 to $+1$, and throttle values go from 0 to $+1$. Since CARLA functions in a client-server principle, the simulator was running in synchronous mode, which means that the client and server were running at the same time.

For the best possible quality of the data collected, a Tesla Model 3 with CARLA autopilot was used. The autopilot followed carefully positioned way-points, and in doing so, it collected steering angle values that contribute to the feature of lane centering. Additionally, by adding invisible features, such as speed limiters, the vehicle knew to maintain a reasonable speed before a curve. The entire behavior replicates human-like driving patterns. This choice was made to address the issue of not controlling a vehicle with a basic keyboard or joystick, which tends to generate noisy data, leading to model instability.

Furthermore, the data collection process was fully automated, eliminating the need for human supervision and reducing the demands on human attention. After collecting data from training maps, in total 29,606 instances of data were saved and consequentially used for training. The captured images took just under 6 GB of disk memory.

Data Preprocessing. After collecting the images, one of the essential parts of the whole process was preprocessing the images before using them for the training. Figure 3 shows the progressive changes made to an example image by applying all the preprocessing steps. The same steps were applied to the whole dataset of images during training and testing. Note that the images were captured with a specific Field-Of-View (FOV) attribute set at 130°.

The original image is presented in Fig. 3a. The initial step in data preprocessing involved cropping the images to extract the Region of Interest (ROI) focused on the road ahead, resulting in new image dimensions of $90 \times 300 \times 3$, as demonstrated in Fig. 3b. This step primarily reduced the image's height to exclude the sky. Subsequently, the images were resized to $224 \times 224 \times 3$ to maintain a square aspect ratio, as depicted in Fig. 3c. Following resizing, the images were converted to grayscale, reducing the color channels to a single channel, as shown in Fig. 3d. Additionally, Gaussian blur was applied to minimize image noise and enhance overall smoothness. Although this step is not visually apparent, it holds practical significance. Lastly, the images underwent normalization using the mean and the standard deviation of the training dataset, which contributes to stabilizing the gradient descent process. This stabilization enables

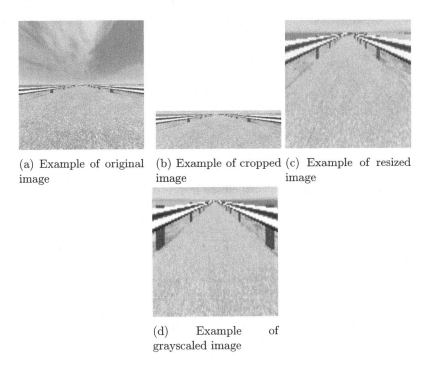

(a) Example of original image

(b) Example of cropped image

(c) Example of resized image

(d)   Example   of grayscaled image

Fig. 3. Examples of image during various stages of the data preprocessing stage

the utilization of larger learning rates and expedites model convergence, as discussed in [38,39]. Figure 4 illustrates the final image appearance after applying all augmentation techniques, which serves as the basis for training.

The images were normalized by subtracting the mean (μ) of each feature and a division by the standard deviation (σ). This way, each feature has a mean of 0 and a standard deviation of 1 [40]. The normalization follows the Eq. 1.

$$x = \frac{x - \mu}{\sigma} \tag{1}$$

Before normalization, the mean and standard deviation of the entire image dataset were calculated. The mean was calculated by summing the pixel values divided by the total number of pixel values. After that, the standard deviation was calculated with the Eq. 2.

$$\sigma = \sqrt{E[X^2] - (E[X])^2} \tag{2}$$

where $E[X^2]$ represents the expectation of the mean of the squared data, while $(E[X])^2$ represents the expectation of the square of the mean of the data [40].

Data Splitting. When the data was collected, the first four maps were used. Furthermore, that data was then split into data for training and data for validation with the ratio of 80:20, thus out of a total number of 29,606 instances of

Fig. 4. Example image after applying all the preprocessing techniques including normalization

data, for training, 23,685 instances of data were used, and 5,921 instances for validation.

Additionally, every time the data was split, the images were shuffled when choosing which images would be used for training and which for validation. Notably, the usage of shuffling distorts the temporal order of the dataset. In some cases where a dataset suffers from sequential dependencies, such as trajectory prediction in the context of complex traffic situations, maintaining that order can be important. However, in situations where temporal order is less critical, such as object detection in individual frames, shuffling can be advantageous to prevent the model from learning unintended patterns. Assuming the dataset used in this work is simple enough to not be affected by the distortion of the temporal order (in part enabled by choosing simple maps, as described previously), the option of not shuffling the dataset was not explored, as the results were already satisfactory.

Network Architecture. The proposed architecture draws inspiration from a well-established architecture developed by Lee, as documented in the GitHub repository [41]. The network uses a lightweight approach in the sense of how many convolutional layers were used, while at the same time maintaining high accuracy. During the implementation of the network, there were additional experiments performed regarding some parameters, such as the dimensions of the images, batch sizes, color model for the images, and number of features for some layers. After experiments, the following architecture was chosen, as depicted in Fig. 5.

The network was divided into two distinct sections. The initial segment focuses on convolution and comprises two convolutional layers, one max-pooling layer, a dropout layer with a 25% dropout rate, and employing the Exponential Linear Unit (ELU) activation function. The first convolutional layer employs a 3 × 3 kernel with a stride of 2, followed by ELU activation. Subsequently, the second convolutional layer utilizes a similar 3 × 3 kernel with a stride of 2. A max-pooling layer with a 4 × 4 kernel and a stride of 4 follows these convolutional layers.

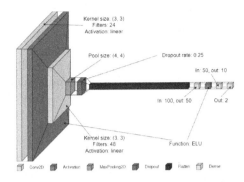

Fig. 5. Simplified architecture of the used CNN

The second section marks the transition from the convolutional layers to the linear NN by flattening the pooled feature map. This transformation retains spatial information while converting it into a format suitable for fully connected layers. The first linear layer, which follows, consists of 8,112 input neurons and 50 output neurons, a direct consequence of the preceding convolutional layers and their operations on the input image. Specifically, the initial $48 \times 13 \times 13$ dimension resulting from the convolutional layers transforms into 8,112 neurons after the flattening process. An additional ELU activation function enhances convergence before the second linear layer, which has 50 input neurons and 10 output neurons. The final linear layer comprises 10 input neurons and concludes with 2 output neurons responsible for predicting steering angles and throttle values (i.e. regression-type output). The transition from a $48 \times 13 \times 13$ dimension in the convolutional layers to a single vector of 8,112 neurons enables seamless progression to the fully connected layers. Model training employed the Adam optimization algorithm with a learning rate set at 0.0001. To monitor network performance during training, MSE loss serves as the criterion.

In the end, the model ended up with 416,838 trainable parameters, with the first part containing 10,656 parameters and the second (flattened) part 406,182 parameters.

Reinforcement Learning (RL). RL implementation involves several key steps. Firstly, setting up the RL environment is crucial, providing a platform for the agent to interact and learn. Next, defining the action and observation spaces allows the agent to explore and perceive the environment effectively. Establishing a reward function guides the agent toward its objectives. Lastly, choosing the appropriate RL algorithm enables the agent to iteratively learn and improve its decision-making process.

Environment Setup. As the basis for the implementation of the RL, a package called Stable-Baseline3 (SB3) was used. It was introduced in [42] as a collection of dependable RL algorithms implemented in PyTorch. To use these RL algorithms, a custom environment had to be implemented to work seamlessly with

SB3. Custom environment in this case is a simple class that inherits from an OpenAI Gym Class [43], which means it has to implement five basic methods: *init, step, reset, render*, and *close*. The rendered screen obtained using Pygame (as an output from the render step) is illustrated in Fig. 6. Please note the upper left corner of the figure in which important RL and vehicle-related data was presented.

Fig. 6. Rendered screen during RL exploration with all the relevant information

Action and Observation Spaces. In the context of vehicle control, values for steering angle and throttle belong in the continuous space. Whilst dealing with such continuous control variables, it is more natural and efficient to represent the action space as a continuous domain. This allows the agent to learn policies that can handle different values within the specified ranges. Moreover, it enables the agent to explore a wide range of actions during training, making it more adaptable to various driving scenarios and ensuring it can handle subtle variations in steering and throttle requirements. Space domain for the steering angle and throttle are defined as shown in Table 1.

Table 1. Action space minimum and maximum values

	Min	Max
Steering ang	−1	1
Throttle	0	1

Furthermore, the observation space consists of an image and speed component. By combining the processed image and the speed value, the observation space provides the necessary information to the agent so that it can make informed decisions about how to control the vehicle based on what it "sees" and how fast it's moving. Please note that the images were processed the same way as for CNN-based implementation.

Reward Function. The reward function is crucial as it serves as the guiding signal for the agent's learning process. When the agent takes an action that leads to a positive outcome or brings the agent closer to achieving its goal, it receives a higher reward. Conversely, if the action results in a negative consequence or moves the agent away from its objective, it receives a negative reward. Therefore, it was essential to design a well-structured reward function that encourages optimal behavior. In this context, the principles for reward assignment were as follows:

If the car has collided with the road barrier

$$R = -200 \tag{3}$$

If the car has not collided and speed is 0

$$R = -5 \tag{4}$$

If the car has not collided and speed is s

$$R = \min\left(r, \frac{s'}{s} \times r\right) \tag{5}$$

The Eq. 3 describes a scenario in which the vehicle collides with the road barrier, resulting in a penalty of -200. In contrast, Eq. 4 addresses a scenario in which the vehicle remains stationary, attempting to exploit the fact that by remaining stationary it will avoid the higher penalty of colliding and forcing it to move around the environment, incurring a smaller penalty of -5. The Eq. 5 employed in the scenario where the vehicle neither collides nor remains stationary relies on three variables. The current speed, denoted as s', is compared to the minimum desirable speed, denoted as s. As s' approaches s, the function increases linearly towards the maximum reward, r. Once the current speed equals or exceeds s, the function consistently returns the maximum reward. This design choice effectively encourages the model to strive for the highest possible speed without imposing an artificial upper limit on the speed itself. The decision was made to omit the imposition of a maximum speed threshold in the reward function, as it did not present a significant concern or challenge in the context of this thesis. In this instance, the reward r can vary between 0.033 and 5, with the minimal desired speed s set at $15\,km/h$.

Algorithm and Parameters. In the process of selecting a suitable RL algorithm, a thorough evaluation was crucial. Several established algorithms, including Proximal Policy Optimization (PPO), DDPG, Twin Delayed DDPG (TD3), and SAC, were tested. The SAC algorithm ultimately emerged as the preferred choice due to its consistent utility during testing. This is in line with observations of other, similar research [31]. To expedite experimentation and given the constraints, certain hyperparameters such as the number of timesteps (set to two million), learning rate (0.0001), and buffer size (1000) were chosen, reflecting a pragmatic approach rather than exhaustive fine-tuning effort.

Model Training. In the RL approach, computational efficiency in model training was aimed for. It deviated from the CNN-based approach by exclusively employing data from a single training map and restricting training to a single driving direction (due to high computational cost and required time). While the streamlined training methodology may initially appear restrictive, its outcomes were satisfactory. The RL model not only demonstrated the capability to learn collision avoidance but also exhibited adaptability to different environments. This adaptability was substantiated through evaluation on an entirely unseen (testing) map. The model's ability to perform effectively on the test map underscored its capacity to generalize knowledge effectively, even when trained solely on a single map.

3   Results and Discussion

3.1   CNN

The proposed CNN architecture was built, trained, and tested using Python programming language (v. 3.8.10), PyTorch (v. 1.13.0+cu117) and PyGame (v. 2.1.2), along with some additional PyTorch utilities (Dataset, DataLoader, SubsetRandomSampler and Torchvision), as well as other Python libraries, such as NumPy (v. 1.23.5) and Pandas (v. 1.5.2).

The training was conducted over 30 epochs using a batch size of 64, leveraging both training and validation data. The training time was three hours and five minutes. It's worth noting that the choice of 30 epochs was determined to be sufficient through repeated training sessions. This approach aimed to strike a balance between training efficiency and model generalization. Throughout the training process, the model exhibited substantial progress in minimizing the MSE loss. As seen in Fig. 7 the MSE loss consistently decreased during each epoch, indicating the model's ability to capture intricate patterns and relationships within the dataset.

Batch size is a crucial NN training parameter that defines the number of training examples in each iteration. During training, data was grouped into batches, and model parameters were updated using the average gradient from batch loss values. Batch size impacts training speed, generalization, and resource use. Selecting an optimal size depends on the dataset, model complexity, and resources. Past research suggests smaller batch sizes may better avoid local minima and uncover global minima [44–46]. Therefore, the model underwent training and testing with a range of batch sizes, spanning from an initial 16 and incrementing successively to 32, 64, 128, and up to 1024 [47]. Table 2 shows the result over each batch size. The results were taken from an epoch that gave the best validation loss. The number in the brackets represents the epoch at which the results were measured.

After evaluating various models trained with different batch sizes, the model utilizing a batch size of 64 stands out. Its strong test performance, along with solid training and validation results, make it a promising choice. These factors highlight its effectiveness for real-world applications. Comparing two different

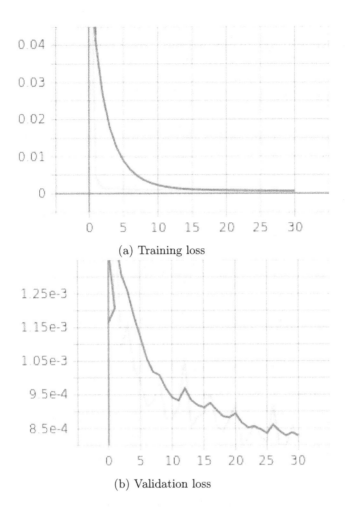

(a) Training loss

(b) Validation loss

Fig. 7. Training and validation loss - Smoothed line is visible and unsmoothed is presented with a higher level of transparency

Table 2. Model MSE results in respect to used training batch size

Batch size (Epoch)	Training Loss	Validation Loss	Testing Loss
16 (16)	0.000604	0.000789	0.000568
32 (24)	0.000569	0.000799	0.000578
64 (27)	**0.000690**	**0.000798**	**0.000554**
128 (29)	0.000856	0.000879	0.000630
256 (27)	0.000926	0.000886	0.000623
512 (28)	0.001158	0.000970	0.000663
1024 (30)	0.001586	0.001130	0.000788

batch sizes, as seen in Fig. 8, 64 and 1024, during the training process reveals a notable observation: the smaller batch size of 64 demonstrates a faster rate of convergence compared to the larger batch size of 1024.

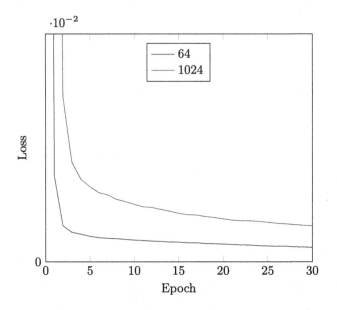

Fig. 8. CNN training MSE difference between two batch sizes – 64 and 1024

When the selected model was tested on an unseen road, the model exhibited challenges in reacting to significant road curves. This raised questions about the impact of vehicle speed on the model's response accuracy. Therefore, an investigation to isolate the variable of vehicle speed was conducted. The vehicle's speed was held at a constant 8 km/h and examined the model's predictions under this controlled setting. However, an unexpected observation emerged over time: the model's inference time, i.e., the time it required to generate predictions from a single image, became apparent. By measuring how much time a model needs to output a prediction for a single image, it averaged 0.025 s for each prediction. This insight held significance as it enabled the determination of an optimal FPS value, indicating the rate at which the model could function seamlessly. Notably, before this discovery, the FPS was at 80. The inference time translated to an effective FPS of approximately 40, meaning the model could process up to 40 images per second. This understanding not only addressed the model's earlier struggles with road curves but also set the stage for a fluid and real-time performance. As a result, the simulation was restricted to 30 FPS to ensure both timely model reactions and the smooth operation of the simulation.

The vehicle followed the road (without collisions), whilst keeping the throttle and speed according to the curvature of the road. The bigger the curvature, the lower the vehicle's speed, and the smaller the curvature, the bigger the speed. The model also recognized how to keep the vehicle in the center of the road, enabling a smooth ride. The maximum speed was set to 30 km/h, and the minimum speed depended on the curvature. On straight sections of the road, the model achieved a maximum speed of 30 km/h, while on curves, the minimum speed depended on the curvature, typically around 21 km/h. While a model's ability to control the vehicle and follow the road is crucial, achieving a smooth ride involves a higher level of finesse and attention to detail. It encompasses factors such as minimizing unnecessary steering corrections, avoiding sudden accelerations or decelerations, maintaining a consistent trajectory, and overall providing a comfortable experience for passengers or users.

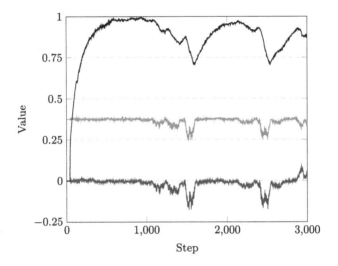

Fig. 9. Values of steering angle (blue), throttle (red), and speed (brown) during testing of the CNN model (Color figure online)

This behavior is illustrated in Fig. 9, where all three values of interest are adjusted according to the curvature of the road. When comparing the three plots, it becomes evident that as the steering angle increases, the throttle decreases, resulting in lower speed. Conversely, when the steering angle decreases, the throttle increases, leading to higher speed. A smooth ride showcases the model's proficiency in not just basic control but also in creating coherent, natural, and safe driving behavior. In the case of starting a vehicle from an unnatural position, or making a mistake during the predictions, the model was still able to correct the vehicle onto a correct trajectory.

3.2 RL

The RL model was built, trained and tested using Python programming language (v. 3.8.10), PyTorch (v. 1.13.0+cu117), Stable-Baselines3 (v. 2.0.0), Gymnasium

(0.28.1), Baselines3 Zoo (2.0.0) and PyGame (v. 2.1.2), along with an additional PyTorch utility Torchvision (v. 0.15.1+cu118), as well as other Python libraries, such as NumPy (v. 1.23.5) and Pandas (v. 1.5.2).

To leverage SAC's capabilities, an extensive training regimen was pursued. Utilizing two million timesteps, the model's learning trajectory was carefully shaped. This process spanned about 7 days (on used hardware), with each iteration enhancing the model's competence. Over these two million timesteps, a special callback class was implemented that saved the model every 100,000 timesteps.

After the training finished, the next step was to figure out which one of the models was the right one. In off-policy RL algorithms like SAC, the primary metric for assessing the quality of learning is often the critic loss. The critic loss represents how well the value function (critic network) is approximating the true value of states or state-action pairs. A lower critic loss indicates that the value function is improving its estimation accuracy, leading to more effective learning and decision-making by the agent. While the actor loss is also important as it reflects how well the policy (actor-network) is improving, the critic loss provides a more direct measure of the algorithm's ability to estimate the value of different states and actions.

Figure 10 depicts how the critic and actor losses range throughout the training process. Both critic and actor loss values are desirable in lower values. During training, the critic loss remains stable at around 50, reflecting progress in approximating state-action values. However, the actor loss, averaging around 150, suggests an ongoing refinement of the policy's action-selection strategy. This divergence between critic and actor losses could be due to task complexity, the balance between exploration and exploitation, or the interaction between value estimation and policy improvement.

Moreover, what is also interesting is the entropy coefficient and its corresponding loss. Figure 11 shows both of these values throughout the training process. Tuning the entropy coefficient helps balance exploration and exploitation during learning. A higher value promotes more exploration, while a lower value prioritizes exploiting the learned policy. The entropy coefficient loss is part of the optimization process in SAC. It is the loss associated with the entropy coefficient and is optimized alongside the actor and critic losses. Optimizing the entropy coefficient helps in dynamically adjusting the exploration level throughout training. The changing entropy coefficient during training is interesting. It starts variable but becomes steadier by the end, indicating an improved balance between exploration and exploitation as the model learns. From this brief discussion, it can be seen that within the RL framework, several (hyper)parameters need to be chosen and adjusted (optimized). This in turn increases the complexity of developing RL-based algorithms compared to CNN-based ones.

Each of the saved models, from 100,000 to 2,000,000, was evaluated to obtain a mean reward and a standard deviation of the mean reward. A high mean reward coupled with a low standard deviation signifies that the agent is consistently achieving high rewards and maintaining stability in its behavior. Across

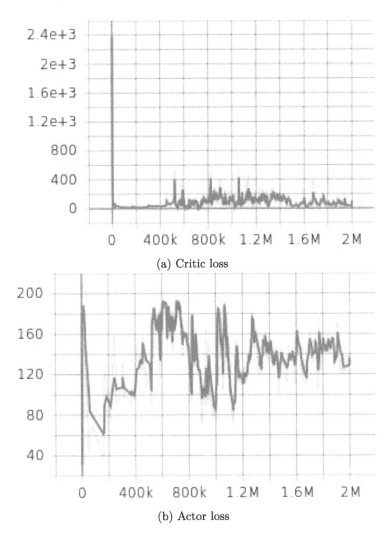

(a) Critic loss

(b) Actor loss

Fig. 10. Critic and actor loss during RL training - Smoothed line is visible and unsmoothed is presented with a higher level of transparency

all models, initial steps (100,000–500,000) exhibited lower speeds, often resulting in collisions with road barriers. Consequently, steering angle and throttle predictions during this phase tend to be inaccurate. Around step 600,000, the vehicle experiences a sudden acceleration to approximately 16 km/h, maximizing speed-based rewards. However, this acceleration introduces oscillations in steering angles, affecting ride smoothness. Between steps 700,000 and 1,300,000, the vehicle gradually reduces speed while stabilizing steering angles. From step 1,300,000 to 2,000,000, the vehicle maintains a slow pace but encounters road barrier collisions once more. Figure 12 shows how the mean reward and stan-

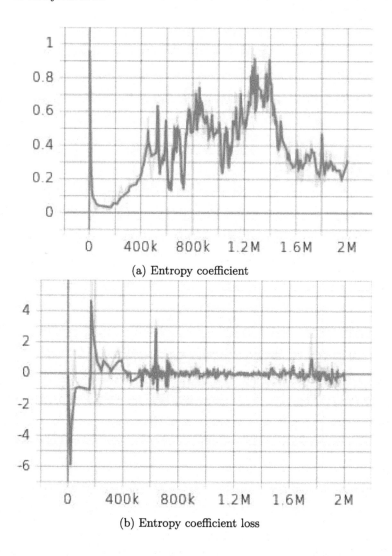

(a) Entropy coefficient

(b) Entropy coefficient loss

Fig. 11. Entropy coefficient and its loss during training - Smoothed line is visible and unsmoothed is presented with a higher level of transparency

dard deviation of the reward move throughout timesteps, while Fig. 13 depicts steering angle and throttle values for the selected/best step.

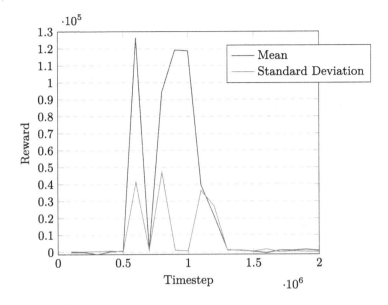

Fig. 12. Mean and standard deviation of rewards

3.3   CNN vs. RL Comparison

As it may be obvious, CNN and RL are two distinct approaches within the realm of artificial intelligence, each serving unique roles in addressing diverse problems. CNNs excel in extracting and understanding visual patterns from data, particularly images, while RL empowers agents to make informed decisions through interactions with their environments (through user-defined reward function). Several general insights can be obtained from the comparison of these two methodologies within this specific context.

Environment. In the CNN approach, this environment setup serves as the foundation for data collection. The focus revolves around gathering pertinent data from the established environment. Conversely, the RL approach mandates an additional layer of complexity. In this case, the establishment of the environment marked only the initial phase. A subsequent step entailed the implementation of a specialized interface, extending the capabilities of the CARLA simulator environment. This augmentation was necessary to accommodate the unique requirements of the RL approach. Notably, the integration demanded the formulation of specialized callback functions. The inclusion of these functions underscores an augmented level of preparatory work requisite for the successful deployment of the RL methodology.

Data. Within the CNN approach, the workflow entails processes of data acquisition, preprocessing, and subsequent partitioning into distinct subsets designated for training, validation, and testing purposes. This method necessitates meticulous manual intervention to scrutinize and manipulate the collected data, a

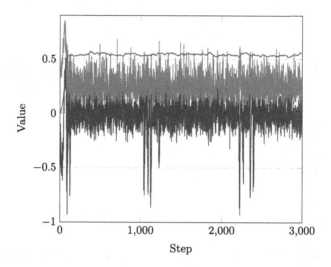

Fig. 13. Values of steering angle (blue), throttle (red), and speed (brown) during testing of the RL model (Color figure online)

critical step that significantly influences CNN's efficacy. Notably, the degree of refinement in data tailoring bears a direct correlation with the model's training quality and ensuing performance. Conversely, the RL approach presents a more streamlined trajectory. It involves the seamless integration of the methodology within a predefined environment, characterized by carefully delineated action and observation spaces. This approach distinctly diverges from the CNN process, as it obviates the need for prior data collection. Instead, RL engages directly with the environment, iteratively interacting to learn optimal strategies. Important to note is that, RL deep in its implementation uses a CNN architecture to leverage the images used to learn. In this way, RL can extract important visual features from the images, and make a connection between the image and the actions needed to be applied for an accurate prediction.

Training and Loss. The CNN training, primarily oriented towards predictive accuracy, employed the MSE loss metric. This metric illuminates the model's capability to forecast values within the given dataset. Additional insights are gained from variations such as the utilization of a validation set, which gauges the presence of overfitting, as well as test loss, which conveys how well a model deals with new unseen data. On contrary, central to RL's training process are metrics encompassing the critic and actor loss. These metrics gauge the convergence of the value estimation and policy networks, integral to RL's decision-making process. Additionally, the entropy coefficient and entropy coefficient loss measurements further accentuate RL's exploration-exploitation balance. The entropy coefficient regulates the level of exploration, influencing the policy's stochasticity. The corresponding loss metric evaluates the alignment of the policy's entropy with the desired exploration strategy. The temporal dimension further underscores the divergence.

CNN training exhibits a notable contrast in time expenditure, typically spanning hours. Empirical analysis, encompassing varied batch sizes, resulted in an average training duration of just over three hours. Conversely, the RL training horizon unfolds across multiple days, marked by considerable temporal investment. It's worth noting that variations exist within the RL domain, with algorithms like PPO showcasing notably reduced training periods, on the order of hours, typically around 12 h. This temporal variation can be attributed to the inherent disparity in the learning dynamics. RL's iterative, trial-and-error-driven learning mechanism inherently demands longer exposure to the environment to discern optimal strategies. Conversely, CNN's supervised learning structure can achieve substantial progress within shorter timeframes due to the availability of labeled data (in simulation). In essence, we can say that CNN reduces computational complexity (in the form of required computational time for training) for the computer/machine by mitigating it to human operators or simulation (through data labeling and image processing). RL on the other hand frees the human operator or simulation of that burden by increasing computational time for the computer/machine in the form of environmental interaction.

Model Selection. In the CNN paradigm, model selection revolved around an exhaustive exploration of varying batch sizes and their corresponding loss outcomes. By assessing the interplay between validation and testing losses, a judicious choice emerged—namely, a batch size of 64. Conversely, the RL methodology undertook a comprehensive model selection approach. This entailed evaluating the mean and standard deviation rewards across all timesteps, in addition to scrutinizing the vehicle's velocity and its propensity for collisions during evaluation. This holistic evaluation framework captures not only the model's reward attainment capabilities but also its proficiency in maintaining optimal speed and navigating the environment without collisions - a fundamental attribute for successful track completion.

Performance. The CNN approach, although resilient, exhibited sensitivity to the simulation's FPS parameter, necessitating careful calibration. Notwithstanding this, its overall performance was commendable, marked by noteworthy attributes. In the CNN paradigm, the vehicle adeptly modulated its throttle and speed according to the road's curvature. It demonstrated a commendable aversion to collisions, showcased an ability to rectify its course in case of errors, and consistently maintained its position at the road's center. This amalgamation of actions facilitated a seamless journey characterized by stability and precision.

Contrastingly, the RL approach, while not achieving the full spectrum of accomplishments exhibited by CNN, garnered satisfactory results. It consistently adhered to a minimum speed threshold of 15 km/h, with minimal fluctuations hovering around 16 km/h, ensuring steadfast performance. Negotiating curves with finesse, it adeptly avoided collisions, reaffirming its competence. However, in comparison to CNN, a notable discrepancy emerged. The RL-driven vehicle displayed pronounced steering angle oscillations, manifesting as significant lateral deviations. This manifested in a somewhat erratic trajectory, characterized by continuous lateral shifts. Additionally, when considering real-world data collection in autonomous driving scenarios, RL is not easily implementable due to safety issues related to its trial-and-error approach.

4   Conclusion

Both the CNN and RL approaches need comprehensive optimizations. The forthcoming paths for enhancement hold distinct focal points, as articulated in the previous section. Within the CNN methodology, a crucial avenue for refinement involves paring down the number of trainable parameters embedded within the model's architecture (decreasing inference time and increasing possible simulation FPS). This strategic streamlining not only alleviates computational overhead but augments the model's adaptability to varying data distributions. Furthermore, architectural enhancements beckon, necessitating the exploration of configurations that harmonize with the task's intricacies. Hyperparameter optimization emerged as another pivotal domain, encompassing quintessential variables like learning rate, optimization algorithm, and batch size. Concurrently, considerations about data preprocessing-ranging from greyscale transformations to cropping strategies and image dimensions-imprint a substantial footprint on performance.

The terrain of RL optimization unfurls as a multidimensional landscape, heavily punctuated by hyperparameters. This emphasis stems from RL's intrinsic reliance on these tunable variables. Among the critical determinants are batch size, action noise, learning rate, and the count of sequential steps, forming a fraction of the parameters meriting meticulous calibration (SB3 has 22 parameters at its disposal to tune). In the same trajectory, the evolution of the reward function constitutes an indispensable facet. The future improvements beckon the construction of a more intricate and nuanced reward function, capably encapsulating the complex dynamics of the environment. Augmenting the sensor suite by introducing additional sensors to monitor the vehicle's relative position concerning the road's orientation emerges as a strategy to inculcate the vehicle with the skill to self-centered on the road.

Additionally, the "Optuna" hyperparameter optimization framework [48] emerges as a potent resource. This tool holds the potential to systematically guide the complex process of parameter optimization, significantly expediting the exploration of optimal configurations. Finally, extensions of RL, like curiosity-driven exploration [49] could be explored, and their performance analyzed and compared to the standard approach.

References

1. Parekh, D., et al.: A review on autonomous vehicles: progress, methods and challenges. Electronics **11**(14), 2162 (2022)
2. Wang, J., Shao, Y., Ge, Y., Yu, R.: A survey of vehicle to everything (V2X) testing. Sensors **19**(2), 334 (2019)
3. Brenner, W., Herrmann, A.: An overview of technology, benefits and impact of automated and autonomous driving on the automotive industry. In: Linnhoff-Popien, C., Schneider, R., Zaddach, M. (eds.) Digital Marketplaces Unleashed, pp. 427–442. Springer, Heidelberg (2018). https://doi.org/10.1007/978-3-662-49275-8_39
4. SAE J3016:2021 standard: Taxonomy and Definitions for Terms Related to On-Road Motor Vehicle Automated Driving Systems. The Society of Automotive Engineers (2021). https://www.sae.org/standards/content/j3016_202104/
5. Croutch, D.: The State of Self-Driving Cars: Autonomous Advances. https://www.techspot.com/article/2644-the-state-of-self-driving-cars/. Accessed 4 June 2023
6. Baldwin, R.: Self-Driving Cars Are Taking Longer to Build Than Everyone Thought. Car and Driver (2020). https://www.caranddriver.com/features/a32266303/self-driving-cars-are-taking-longer-to-build-than-everyone-thought/. Accessed 15 Jan 2023
7. Clarke, L.: How Self-Driving Cars got Stuck in the Slow Lane. The Guardian (2022). https://www.theguardian.com/technology/2022/mar/27/how-self-driving-cars-got-stuck-in-the-slow-lane. Accessed 15 Jan 2023
8. Yeong, D.J., Velasco-Hernandez, G., Barry, J., Walsh, J.: Sensor and sensor fusion technology in autonomous vehicles: a review. Sensors **21**(6), 2140 (2021)
9. Antoniadis, P.: What is end-to-end deep learning? Baeldung on Computer Science. https://www.baeldung.com/cs/end-to-end-deep-learning. Accessed 8 Sept 2023
10. Hassan, I.U., Zia, H., Fatima, H.S., Yusuf, S.A., Khurram, M.: A lightweight convolutional neural network to predict steering angle for autonomous driving using CARLA simulator. Model. Simul. Eng. **2022**, 5716820 (2022)
11. Song, J.G., Lee, J.W.: CNN-based object detection and distance prediction for autonomous driving using stereo images. Int. J. Automot. Technol. **24**, 773–786 (2023)
12. Al Mamun, A., Ping, E.P., Hossen, J., Tahabilder, A., Jahan, B.: A comprehensive review on lane marking detection using deep neural networks. Sensors **22**(19), 7682 (2022)
13. Youssouf, N.: Traffic sign classification using CNN and detection using faster-RCNN and YOLOV4. Heliyon **8**(12) (2022)
14. Mehrish, A., Majumder, N., Bharadwaj, R., Mihalcea, R., Poria, S.: A review of deep learning techniques for speech processing. Inf. Fusion **99**, 101869 (2023)
15. Alshemali, B., Kalita, J.: Improving the reliability of deep neural networks in NLP: a review. Knowl.-Based Syst. **191**, 105210 (2020)
16. Yu, H., Yang, L.T., Zhang, Q., Armstrong, D., Deen, M.J.: Convolutional neural networks for medical image analysis: state-of-the-art, comparisons, improvement and perspectives. Neurocomputing **444**, 92–110 (2021)
17. Sutton, R.S., Barto, A.G.: Reinforcement Learning: An Introduction, 2nd edn. The MIT Press, Cambridge (2018)
18. Pérez-Gil, Ó., et al.: Deep reinforcement learning based control for autonomous vehicles in CARLA. Multimedia Tools Appl. **81**, 3553–3576 (2022)

19. Osiński, B., Jakubowski, A., Ziecina, P., Miloš, P., Galias, C., Homoceanu, S., Michalewski, H.: Simulation-based reinforcement learning for real-world autonomous driving. In: Proceedings of 2020 IEEE International Conference on Robotics and Automation (ICRA), pp. 6411–6418 (2020)
20. Schöner, H.P.: Simulation in development and testing of autonomous vehicles. In: Proceedings of 18. Internationales Stuttgarter Symposium, pp. 1083–1095 (2018)
21. Dosovitskiy, A., Ros, G., Codevilla, F., López, A., Koltun, V.: CARLA: an open urban driving simulator. In: Proceedings of the 1st Annual Conference on Robot Learning, pp. 1–16 (2017)
22. Li, W., et al.: AADS: augmented autonomous driving simulation using data-driven algorithms. Sci. Robot. **4**, eaaw0863 (2019)
23. Rong, G., et al.: LGSVL simulator: a high fidelity simulator for autonomous driving. In: Proceedings of 2020 IEEE 23rd International Conference on Intelligent Transportation Systems (ITSC), pp. 1–6 (2020)
24. Shah, S., Dey, D., Lovett, C., Kapoor, A.: AirSim: high-fidelity visual and physical simulation for autonomous vehicles. In: Hutter, M., Siegwart, R. (eds.) Field and Service Robotics. Springer Proceedings in Advanced Robotics, vol. 5 (2018)
25. Chance, G., Ghobrial, A., McAreavey, K., Lemaignan, S., Pipe, T., Eder, K.: On determinism of game engines used for simulation-based autonomous vehicle verification. IEEE Trans. Intell. Transp. Syst. **23**(11), 20538–20552 (2022)
26. Chao, Q., et al.: A survey on visual traffic simulation: models, evaluations, and applications in autonomous driving. Comput. Graph. Forum **39**(1), 287–308 (2020)
27. Alghodhaifi, H., Lakshmanan, S.: Autonomous vehicle evaluation: a comprehensive survey on modeling and simulation approaches. IEEE Access **9**, 151531–151566 (2021)
28. Yurtsever, E., Lambert, J., Carballo, A., Takeda, K.: A survey of autonomous driving: common practices and emerging technologies. IEEE Access **8**, 58443–58469 (2020)
29. Zhang, J., Huang, H., Zhang, Y.: A convolutional neural network method for self-driving cars. In: Proceedings of 2020 Australian and New Zealand Control Conference (ANZCC), pp. 184–187 (2020)
30. Bojarski, M., et al.: The NVIDIA PilotNet Experiments. arXiv:2010.08776 (2020)
31. Chen, J., Yuan, B., Tomizuka, M.: Model-free deep reinforcement learning for urban autonomous driving. In: Proceedings of 2019 IEEE Intelligent Transportation Systems Conference (ITSC), pp. 2765–2771 (2019)
32. Aggarwal, C.C.: Neural Networks and Deep Learning: A Textbook. Springer, Cham (2018). https://doi.org/10.1007/978-3-031-29642-0
33. Baeldung: Advantages and disadvantages of Neural Networks. Baeldung on Computer Science. https://www.baeldung.com/cs/neural-net-advantages-disadvantages. Accessed 19 Apr 2023
34. Pratama, M.A.: Comparing Image Classification with Dense Neural Network and Convolutional Neural Network. Medium. https://medium.com/analytics-vidhya/comparing-image-classification-with-dense-neural-network-and-convolutional-neural-network-5f376582a695. Accessed 25 Jan 2024
35. Zhang, H., Yu, T.: Taxonomy of reinforcement learning algorithms. In: Dong, H., Ding, Z., Zhang, S. (eds.) Deep Reinforcement Learning, pp. 125–133. Springer, Singapore (2020). https://doi.org/10.1007/978-981-15-4095-0_3
36. Muratore, F., Ramos, F., Turk, G., Yu, W., Gienger, M., Peters, J.: Robot learning from randomized simulations: a review. Front. Robot. AI **11**(9), 799893 (2022)
37. MatWorks: RoadRunner - Design 3D scenes for automated driving simulation. https://www.mathworks.com/products/roadrunner.html. Accessed 18 July 2023

38. Ioffe, S., Szegedy, C.: Batch Normalization: Accelerating Deep Network Training by Reducing Internal Covariate Shift. arXiv: 1502.03167 (2015)
39. Garbin, C., Zhu, X., Marques, O.: Dropout vs. batch normalization: an empirical study of their impact to deep learning. Multimedia Tools Appl. **79**, 12777–12815 (2020)
40. Willaert, J.: How To Calculate the Mean and Standard Deviation - Normalizing Datasets in Pytorch. Towards Data Science. https://towardsdatascience.com/how-to-calculate-the-mean-and-standard-deviation-normalizing-datasets-in-pytorch-704bd7d05f4c. Accessed 18 July 2023
41. Le, H.M.: Car behavioral cloning using Pytorch. Github. https://github.com/hminle/car-behavioral-cloning-withpytorch/. Accessed 15 Mar 2023
42. Raffin, A., Hill, A., Gleave, A., Kanervisto, A., Ernestus, M., Dormann, N.: Stable-baselines3: reliable reinforcement learning implementations. J. Mach. Learn. Res. **22**(268), 1–8 (2021)
43. Brockman, G., et al.: OpenAI Gym. arXiv:1606.01540 (2016)
44. Keksar, N.S., Mudigere, D., Nocedal, J., Smelyanskiy, M., Tang, P.T.P.: On Large-Batch Training for Deep Learning: Generalization Gap and Sharp Minima. arXiv:1609.04836 (2016)
45. Dinh, L., Pascanu, R., Bengio, S., Bengio, Y.: Sharp minima can generalize for deep nets. In: Proceedings of the 34th International Conference on Machine Learning (2017)
46. Kandel, I., Castelli, M.: The effect of batch size on the generalizability of the convolutional neural networks on a histopathology dataset. ICT Express **6**(4), 312–315 (2020)
47. Vasiljević, I., Musić, J., Mendes, J., Lima, J.: Adaptive convolutional neural network for predicting steering angle and acceleration on autonomous driving scenario. In: Optimization, Learning Algorithms and Applications, Third International Conference, OL2A 2023 (2023)
48. Akiba, T., Sano, S., Yanase, T., Ohta, T., Koyama, M.: Optuna: a next-generation hyperparameter optimization framework. In: Proceedings of the 25th ACM SIGKDD International Conference on Knowledge Discovery and Data Mining (2019)
49. Pathak, D., Agrawal, P., Efros, A.A., Darrell, T.: Curiosity-driven exploration by self-supervised prediction. In: Proceedings of the 34th International Conference on Machine Learning (2017)

Fuzzy-Based Knowledge Design and Delivery Model for Personalised Learning

Tomislav Volarić$^{(\boxtimes)}$ ⓘ, Hrvoje Ljubić ⓘ, and Robert Rozić ⓘ

University of Mostar, Trg hrvatskih velikana 1, Mostar, Bosnia and Herzegovina
{tomislav.volaric,hrvoje.ljubic,robert.rozic}@fpmoz.sum.ba
https://www.sum.ba/

Abstract. Adaptation to the level of knowledge of each student remains one of the key challenges of e-learning and education in general. E-learning systems provide opportunity for systematic data collection about learning activities offering valuable insights into the students' knowledge. In order to achieve the personalised learning, this study introduces a Knowledge Design and Delivery Model (KDDM) for intelligent tutoring systems. This model uses a hybrid approach that combines traditional overlay student models with fuzzy logic and multi-criteria decision-making methods. Unlike popular machine learning approaches, these methods do not require existing datasets and they allow direct teacher involvement in knowledge delivery. The KDDM associates student stereotypes with Bloom's revised taxonomy levels, providing a reference point for the cybernetic model. KDDM has been successfully implemented and examined in a two-year experiment which confirmed its effectiveness on 370 participants from two universities in two countries.

Keywords: Personalised learning · Student modeling · Cybernetic model · Multi-critera decision · Intelligent tutoring system

1 Introduction

Traditional e-learning systems simplify delivery and display of static content, but in general do not provide the opportunity for adaptive learning. A special type of systems used not only for the delivery of teaching content, but also for the delivery of knowledge are called the intelligent tutoring systems (ITS). Intelligent tutoring systems are a generation of computer systems aimed to support and improve learning and teaching process in certain domain knowledge, taking into account the individuality of a student as it is done in a traditional one-to-one instruction. The goal of ITS is to provide a learning experience for each student that is similar to the standard of learning that learner would receive in one-to-one instruction from a human teacher.

Considering students learning capabilities, intelligent tutoring systems take into account the knowledge about what to teach, the way to teach, as well as

T. Volarić et al. (Eds.): MoStart 2024, CCIS 2124, pp. 152–163, 2024.
https://doi.org/10.1007/978-3-031-62058-4_11

the relevant information about what student has been taught. In this manner, there are three main components of the ITS conceptual model, namely the (i) domain knowledge, (ii) the teacher, and (iii) the student(s). The most complete discussion is the one initiated and proposed by Shute and Psotka [9] in order to determine the meaning of the sign I in the intelligent tutoring system slogan. Conclusion of the debate highlights two determinants of intelligence: (i) diagnostics of the students' knowledge and (ii) real time help in getting rid of misconceptions and ignorance of concepts of the domain knowledge.

In this paper, the Knowledge Design and Delivery model (KDDM), a novel approach for the Intelligent Tutoring Systems (ITS), has been introduced. The model, utilized for transferring propositions tailored to the student's level of knowledge. Additionally, the cybernetic-based system that effectively implemented this model is showcased. The major contributions of our research are the following (i) cybernetic knowledge design and delivery model for adaptive learning and (ii) a novel hybrid student model based on multi-criteria decision methods. The paper is substantially divided into 7 sections including Introduction. Section 2 includes and analyzes similar and related research; Sect. 3 describes the structure of the cybernetic model of KDDM. In the fourth section, we describe how KDDM is modeling students. Furthermore, Sect. 5 introduces KDDM prototype implementation inside the CMTutor system while Sect. 6 includes experiments and results. Finally, the last section combines conclusion and future work.

2   Related Work

In this section, we analyzed papers that are connected to this research area. We listed 22 systems developed in more than last two decades that share common ground with the approaches which CM Tutor use. The level of research was, in descriptive view, based on structural attributes of the KDDM according to: (i) domain knowledge of the system; (ii) student modeling in the system; (iii) adaptive knowledge acquisition. We conducted a systematic overview of literature based on recommendations appropriate to research within program engineering [22]. As basis of research, we used scientific databases[1] to locate relevant publications as well as an array of keywords as following: (i) Intelligent Tutoring System, (ii) Student modeling, (iii) Adaptive learning, (iv) Adaptive learning with learning analytics. Besides that, we set the research questions as following: (i) How we model a student? and (ii) On what basis the system adapts?.

After detailed analysis and processing of the field, the scientific publications which are focused on more narrow fields which pertain to our research and mostly the ones that are connected to student modeling and student adaptive learning were taken into consideration. The result of our analysis and processing is shown in Table 1. Although not shown in the table, it is important to emphasize that some of these systems use other approaches in system modeling, mostly machine learning and constraint-based approach.

---

[1] Digital libraries ACM and IEEE, Scopus, SpringerLink, Elsevier i Google Scholar.

In the last ten years, many researchers have combined different methods of student modeling and ways of adaptive knowledge acquisition to construct a hybrid student model that represents student attributes. In this manner, the student model can show different individual characteristics and preferences of every student [29]. The authors [40] have encompassed the publications related to the application of artificial intelligence on student modeling during the five year period and concluded that there are eight different student modeling approaches, which are: (i) Bayesian Knowledge Tracing, (ii) Fuzzy logic (FL), (iii) Overlay (OL), (iv) Differential Model, (v) Perturbation Model (PT), (vi) Constraint-Based Model, (vii) Machine Learning, (viii) Stereotype Model (ST).

Table 1. Review of comparable systems/approaches of student modeling and adaptive tutoring with CMTutor

	System/approach name	Year	Student modeling				Adaptive
			OL	ST	PT	FL	
1	INSPIRE [10]	2001	X			X	X
2	Intelligent Learning System [13]	2002				X	
3	Why2-Atlas [12]	2002	X		X		
4	F-CBR-DHTC [16]	2003				X	X
5	TADV [14]	2003	X			X	
6	Multitutor [15]	2003					
7	InterMediActor [17]	2004	X			X	X
8	Vectors in Physics and Mathematics [19]	2005				X	
9	MBTI [20]	2006				X	
10	ADAPTAPlan [21]	2007				X	
11	ADOPTA [23]	2009		X			
12	CoLaB Tutor [25]	2010	X		X		
13	AcWare Tutor [27]	2012	X	X			X
14	ELaC [28]	2013	X	X		X	X
15	BioWorld [31]	2014	X				
16	Java Sensei [34]	2015	X			X	X
17	OSCAR-CITS [41]	2017				X	X
18	CaFAE [43]	2018				X	
19	SLA [44]	2019				X	X
20	POLYGLOT [45]	2020	X	X			X
21	Quiz Time! [46]	2020		X		X	X
22	PARSAT [47]	2022		X		X	X

The system presented in this paper uses a hybrid model of students which combines overlay and stereotype with fuzzy logic, and also falls into the category of adaptive learning system. The authors [30, 32, 39, 42] consider that it is evident that ITS represents a powerful educational tool with a strong foundation and a bright future. On the one hand, it means that the field is well explored. Conversely, a great number of questions still remain unanswered [37]. We want to emphasize that, a decade ago, intelligent systems, despite certain limitations, have shown results comparable to those of a human (one-on-one) tutor in terms of teaching STEM topics [26].

3   Cybernetic Model

Design and delivery of teaching is prerequisite for acquiring the knowledge and testing the students' knowledge. Theoretical framework of KDDM is determined by the basic functionalities of the same model and it is based on instructional design, student modeling and adaption to the current level of student's knowledge. Instructional design is a very complex process which includes set of methods, techniques and tools for designing learning content. We will pay special attention to development of a reliable component for instructional design. To achieve this, we will use conceptual maps [7] as one of the main tools for delivering knowledge. Evaluation of students' knowledge is the foundation for the realization of the idea of student modeling and adapting the knowledge delivery in accordance with the current level of student's knowledge. This achieves the basic premise of intelligent behavior of our system. The adaptation is achieved in the environment of the cybernetic model [8] in which a student is guided, according to a defined reference model, through the process of learning, teaching and testing the knowledge. The current level of the student's knowledge is presented by a manageable input size and observed by the output size of the this process [6]. Elements of the cybernetic model are described in the following subsections.

3.1   The Process of KDDM

The process of KDDM is related to the learning, teaching and testing of the students' knowledge which is conducted as part of the intelligent tutoring system based on the designed and delivered educational content over the defined domain knowledge ontology. To execute the process of determining the level of the students' knowledge the most important question is how to assess it. To achieve that, it is necessary to link the question templates (according to the objective type questions model) with the expected outcomes that questions must achieve. With regard to the definition of student knowledge level, trace attributes are used. This allows the system to determine and adapt to the level of students' knowledge based on the propositions or even concepts from domain knowledge. The adaptation in this system is done with respect to the reference value.

3.2   The Reference Value in KDDM

The reference value of the KDDM has two structural determinants, the first one is related to the syntactic and semantic structure of the concepts and the relation of the domain knowledge over the ontology and the second is associated with attributes for describing the student's stereotype. The idea of the KDDM is basically oriented towards fulfilling the fundamental objective of the educational process - to determine the current level of knowledge with defined reference model over the domain knowledge. We want to discern which concepts of the domain knowledge the student has learned (knows the propositions) and which concepts the student has not learned (does not know the propositions). However, the measure of the learned domain knowledge does not follow a plain binary logic, which justifies the introduction of a fuzzy logic. In order to determine the level of student knowledge, we grouped users with similar knowledge level. In this manner, we are able to define a set of all stereotypes that are directly associated with different levels of Bloom's revised taxonomy of cognitive goals. For this, we define the stereotype and a list of all trace attributes as the reference value on which the process and the control implement the process of teaching and testing.

3.3   The Control in KDDM

The control in the original cybernetic model includes the measurement, control and operation of the executive device [6]. Measurement from KDDM is now transformed into student modeling, while the control is an adaption to the current level of the student's knowledge with the help of the question generation for the given domain knowledge. Trace attributes that are considered by this model are the following: (i) the time spent on the test, (ii) learned propositions, (iii) propositions that student has not learned, (iv) hints used during the test and (v) test results. Evaluation is conducted according to the adapted protocol with a mathematical model based on the principles of multi-criteria approach Analytic Hierarchy Process (AHP) [11] as well as its fuzzy variant Fuzzy AHP (FAHP) [18]. Implementation and definition of student model includes: (i) collecting and editing data from the track records of learning and testing students, (ii) evaluation of the attributes from the point of view of their relative connection, which is written in the matrix form with triangular numbers, (iii) applying a FAHP method to determine the attribute weights and (iv) the result of the FAHP method calculation which is a single column weighting attribute matrix.

The student's knowledge diagnostics was achieved through the multi-criteria TOPSIS method [4] and the modified Bloom's taxonomy of cognitive domain knowledge. In a mathematical view, mapping current trace attributes to the relevant student stereotype is realized by the TOPSIS method. The element of the stereotype vector with maximum value indicates the achieved level of student's knowledge.

4   Student Model

Student modeling is a fundamental part of this model because it encompasses the most important processes expressed with learning, teaching, testing and evaluating of the student's knowledge. Student modeling is, by its nature, a process composed of two phases: (i) student model shaping and (ii) diagnostics of the student knowledge. Student model is described by an array of data - we call them trace attributes trace, while diagnostics of the student knowledge is a process led by these attributes. In the idea of this model we implement hybrid modeling overlay model with the mathematical formalisms FAHP and TOPSIS method of multi-criteria decision making during student stereotype determination. With regard to what was already written, we base this part of the theoretical frame on two approaches of student modeling. One is connected to VanLehn classification [5], and the other with literature overview and Chrysafiadi and Virvou classification [29]. The former approach is traditionally accepted in referent literature, and the second is based on other modeling method - fuzzy modeling of the students as well as the ontological model.

In literature, we have noticed numerous approaches to student modeling, and the reason why we opted for the combination of FAHP and TOPSIS methods is because the knowledge of students cannot be expressed by traditional logic. Hence, the reason we needed fuzzy logic. We consider that the combination of these methods is the best choice for student modeling because we included multiple domain knowledge experts (three in our case) in the process of attribute evaluation. Based on mathematical calculations by FAHP method set the difficulty of every attribute was set. Furthermore, TOPSIS method helps to set student stereotype based on weight value of the trace attributes. The approach we use for development and setting of the process of monitoring student stereotype is not based on the assumption that all members of a certain group of students behave in the same way. Indeed, it is important to emphasize that in this regard we do not neglect the individual differences of the students. Within our approach, two students with the same stereotype can have different paths during learning, teaching and testing of their knowledge. This is done to display an integral image of the application of the modified Bloom taxonomy of student knowledge for a cognitive area in KDDM. The taxonomy was derived according to the categories of student's knowledge as shown in Table 2.

5   Prototype System and Model Implementation

Conceptual maps are used as the knowledge representation for testing and learning. Conceptual maps are introduced from the point of view of the e-learning paradigm and implementation in the environment and the space of the e-learning system. From the aspect of information and communication technology (ICT), it is obvious that concept mapping is a suitable technique for representing knowledge in intelligent tutoring systems. However, the Moodle, in its original distribution, cannot provide knowledge representation of the domain knowledge

Table 2. Relationship of stereotypes with question templates and knowledge levels

Question template (T)	Expected outcomes (i)	Stereotype (S)
Template 1 (t_1)	Knowledge (i_1)	Stereotype_Z (s_1)
Template 2 (t_2)	Understanding (i_2)	Stereotype_R (s_2)
Template 3 (t_3)	Understanding (i_2)	Stereotype_R (s_2)
Template 4 (t_4)	Understanding (i_2)	Stereotype_R (s_2)
Template 5 (t_5)	Analyzing (i_3)	Stereotype_A (s_3)
Template 6 (t_6)	Evaluating (i_4)	Stereotype_V (s_4)
Template 7 (t_7)	Creating (i_5)	Stereotype_S (s_5)

based on the concepts and relationships. A prototype of the Content Modeling Tutor (CM Tutor) software [33] was developed, implemented and installed as an integral part of the KDDM architecture. CM Tutor is set up as an activity in Moodle and can be used in the same manner as all other Moodle activities (e.g. lessons, quizzes, forum and chat). It can also be run as a standalone application, but for testing purposes it is integrated as an activity in Moodle system. The CM Tutor consists of four components described in Fig. 1 which implements following functionalities (i) Interaction module - textual and graphical interface for the delivery of teaching content; (ii) Testing module - knowledge testing is done after the generation of a series of questions (by the model of objective type questions); (iii) Teaching module - learning and teaching using interaction modules according to the concepts that the student did not learn at the test phase and (iv) Stereotype module - determining student's stereotypes in accordance with the current level of student's knowledge and the reference model.

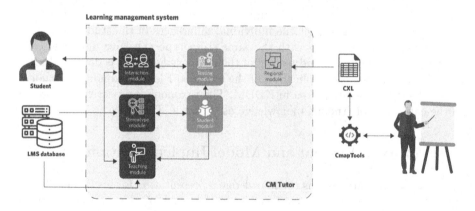

Fig. 1. Structural components of the CM Tutor system.

Determining the level of knowledge of the domain knowledge concepts is carried out by the objective type questions [2,3]. Objective type questions are non-calibrated knowledge tests and an instrument that determines the student's knowledge which is the reference value of the cybernetic model. Diversity of objective question types allows the measurement of knowledge at all levels of the Bloom's knowledge taxonomy for cognitive domain [1]. The revised Bloom's taxonomy for the cognitive domain has been opted for this research [24].

6   Experiments and Results

The ultimate goal of the experiments was to resolve the performance and quality of the presented system as well as the participants satisfaction during learning, teaching and testing of knowledge, but also to provide comparative analysis of CM Tutor and other applied e-learning platforms. The experiments were carried out in two periods with a gap of one year.

6.1   First Experiment Period

The purpose of the first experiment period was to obtain qualitative indicators of CMTutor compared to CoLaB Tutor [25], AcWare Tutor [27] and Moodle. Common for all four platforms was that the domain knowledge was defined over the ontology of concepts and relations between them. In addition to the CM Tutor platform, the remaining three platforms were available and well known as the examples of good practice in previous research in this area. This experiment period was carried out in three time periods lasting two weeks each (six weeks in total for online learning). In each period, students used one e-learning system and one area of knowledge in the learning and teaching area, while in the remaining 9 weeks, traditional classes were conducted in the classroom. In general, at the level of the entire educational period, we organized and conducted the teaching process according to the sub-model of the mirrored classroom of the rotating model of hybrid learning.

A total of 370 students from two countries (Bosnia and Herzegovina and Croatia) participated in these three cycles on the 4 mentioned platforms. The sample in the research is students from the University of Mostar and the University of Split. The students from Mostar are students from the Faculty of Science and Education, from undergraduate and graduate studies at the teacher's course. The students from Split are students of the Faculty of Science and the Faculty of Philosophy (specifically students of the fourth and fifth year of teacher studies). They studied from three topics, (i) "Computer as a system", (ii) "Environment and space of e-learning and e-learning systems" and (iii) "Introductory teaching of programming". The results of the experiment were analyzed in two categories, performance on test and user experience. In terms of performance, the best of the four mentioned platforms was CMTutor with 22 students with a rating of 5 (highest grade), and in terms of satisfaction (user experience), the best was Moodle (which was expected considering that students have been using that platform for years), followed by CMTutor.

6.2   Second Experiment Period

The purpose of the second experiment period was to determine the effect of learning, teaching and testing of the knowledge on CM Tutor with initial and final testing. We conducted the experiment with one group of students over a period of two weeks. The instruments for carrying out the research are objective-type tasks (remembering tasks, completion tasks, alternative tasks, multiple choice tasks, correction tasks, arrangement tasks, connection tasks and essay-type tasks). We introduced the students to the content of the teaching unit "Environment and space of e-learning and e-learning systems". The research was conducted on a sample of 38 students, 28 of whom took both the initial and final test. All students were from the University of Mostar (Faculty of Science and Education), specifically the graduate study of Computer science and Computer science with combinations (Mathematics, Geography, Chemistry).

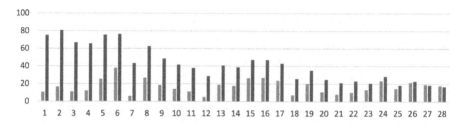

Fig. 2. Comparison of students' performance on initial and final test

The initial test was carried out because the experiment involved students with different skills and backgrounds. It was necessary to identify the initial state of their understanding of the domain knowledge in order to quantify the student knowledge change. A comparison of the results from the initial test and the final test, after learning through CMTutor, is shown in Fig. 2 (blue bar is initial test). ANOVA has confirmed that there is no statistically significant difference between the control and experimental group, mean values concerning pre-test results ($F = 0.842, p - value = 0.474$). The large effect size for CMTutor was $d = 1.791$ so we can say that the resulting effect sizes are statistically significant.

7   Conclusions and Future Work

This paper presented the fuzzy-based cybernetic model for designing and delivering the knowledge in an intelligent tutoring system. CMTutor demonstrated superiority in student performance and user satisfaction compared to compared learning systems. The results of empirical evaluation presented in this paper have shown that the observed intelligent tutoring systems based on ontological domain knowledge representation are effective when compared with traditional learning and teaching process and could be used in addition to traditional methods. Finally, it is shown that this modeling approach adapts to the student's level of knowledge. However, there are certain limitations and opportunities for improvement. Based on the insights from the satisfaction survey, we concluded that it is necessary to improve the user experience for the production version of CMTutor. The ultimate goal is to enable automatic conceptual maps creation from text which has been shown to be possible [35, 36]. Also, we plan to create a deep learning model that will detect at-risk students in the early stages of learning and implement data augmentation techniques, since it has been shown that it is possible to improve such models [38]. These features would greatly facilitate the use of this system for teachers and students.

References

1. Bloom, B.S., et al.: Taxonomy of educational objectives: the classification of educational goals. In: Handbook 1: Cognitive Domain. McKay, New York (1956)
2. Gronlund, N.E.: Measurement and evaluation in teaching. In: Measurement and Evaluation in Teaching, pp. xv–540 (1985)
3. Mužić, V.: Testovi znanja. Školska knjiga (1968)
4. Hwang, C.-L., et al.: Methods for multiple attribute decision making. In: Multiple Attribute Decision Making: Methods and Applications a State-of-the-Art Survey, pp. 58–191 (1981)
5. VanLehn, K.: Student modeling. In: Polson, M., Richardson, J. (eds.) Foundations of Intelligent Tutoring Systems, pp. 55–78 (1988)
6. Božičević, J.: Temelji automatike: I. knjiga: sustavno gledište i automatika, automatsko reguliranje. Školska knjiga (1990)
7. Novak, J.D.: Concept mapping: a useful tool for science education. J. Res. Sci. Teach. **27**(10), 937–949 (1990)
8. Božičević, J.: Od kibernetike do znanosti o sustavima. Sustavsko mišljenje, Hrvat. društvo za sustave, pp. 9–14 (1992)
9. Shute, V.J., Psotka, J.: Intelligent tutoring systems: past, present, and future. Armstrong Laboratory, Air Force Materiel Command (1994)
10. Papanikolaou, K.A., Grigoriadou, M., Kornilakis, H., Magoulas, G.D.: INSPIRE: an INtelligent system for personalized instruction in a remote environment. In: Reich, S., Tzagarakis, M.M., De Bra, P.M.E. (eds.) AH 2001. LNCS, vol. 2266, pp. 215–225. Springer, Heidelberg (2002). https://doi.org/10.1007/3-540-45844-1_21
11. Saaty, T.L.: Fundamentals of the analytic hierarchy process. In: The Analytic Hierarchy Process in Natural Resource and Environmental Decision Making (2001)
12. VanLehn, K., et al.: The architecture of why2-atlas: a coach for qualitative physics essay writing. In: Cerri, S.A., Gouardères, G., Paraguaçu, F. (eds.) ITS 2002. LNCS, vol. 2363, pp. 158–167. Springer, Heidelberg (2002). https://doi.org/10.1007/3-540-47987-2_20
13. Xu, D., Wang, H., Su, K.: Intelligent student profiling with fuzzy models. In: Proceedings of the 35th Annual Hawaii International Conference on System Sciences. IEEE (2002)
14. Kosba, E., Dimitrova, V., Boyle, R.: Fuzzy student modeling to advise teachers in web-based distance courses. Int. J. Artif. Intell. Tools Spec. Issue AI Tech. Web-Based Educ. Syst. **13**(2), 279–297 (2003)
15. Šimić, G., Devedžić, V.: Building an intelligent system using modern internet technologies. Expert Syst. Appl. **25**(2), 231–246 (2003)

16. Tsaganou, G., et al.: Evaluating an intelligent diagnosis system of historical text comprehension. Expert Syst. Appl. **25**(4), 493–502 (2003)
17. Kavcic, A.: Fuzzy student model in InterMediActor platform. In: 26th International Conference on Information Technology Interfaces. IEEE (2004)
18. Greco, S., Figueira, J., Ehrgott, M.: Multiple Criteria Decision Analysis, vol. 37. Springer, New York (2016). https://doi.org/10.1007/978-1-4939-3094-4
19. Stathacopoulou, R., et al.: Neuro-fuzzy knowledge processing in intelligent learning environments for improved student diagnosis. Inf. Sci. **170**(2–4), 273–307 (2005)
20. Salim, N., Haron, N.: The construction of fuzzy set and fuzzy rule for mixed approach in adaptive hypermedia learning system. In: Pan, Z., Aylett, R., Diener, H., Jin, X., Göbel, S., Li, L. (eds.) Edutainment 2006. LNCS, vol. 3942, pp. 183–187. Springer, Heidelberg (2006). https://doi.org/10.1007/11736639_26
21. CP, IP UNED. Adaptation based on machine learning, user modelling and planning for complex user-oriented tasks
22. Kitchenham, B., Charters, S.: Guidelines for performing systematic literature reviews in software engineering, p. 1051 (2007)
23. Bontchev, B., et al.: Architectural design of a software engine for adaptation control in the adopta e-learning platform. In: Proceedings of the International Conference on Computer Systems and Technologies and Workshop for PhD Students in Computing (2009)
24. Anderson, L.W., Krathwohl, D.R.: A Taxonomy for Learning, Teaching, and Assessing: A Revision of Bloom's Taxonomy of Educational Objectives: Complete Edition. Addison Wesley Longman, Inc. (2001)
25. žitko, B.: Model inteligentnog tutorskog sustava zasnovan na obradi kontroliranog jezika nad ontologijom. Diss. Fakultet elektrotehnike i računarstva (2010)
26. VanLehn, K.: The relative effectiveness of human tutoring, intelligent tutoring systems, and other tutoring systems. Educ. Psychol. **46**(4), 197–221 (2011)
27. Grubišić, A.: Model prilagodljivoga stjecanja znanja učenika u sustavima e-učenja. Diss. University of Zagreb. Faculty of Electrical Engineering and Computing. Department of Electronics, Microelectronics, Computer and Intelligent Systems. University of Split. University of Split, Faculty of Science (2012)
28. Chrysafiadi, K., Virvou, M.: PeRSIVA: an empirical evaluation method of a student model of an intelligent e-learning environment for computer programming. Comput. Educ. **68**, 322–333 (2013)
29. Chrysafiadi, K., Virvou, M.: Student modeling approaches: a literature review for the last decade. Expert Syst. Appl. **40**(11), 4715–4729 (2013)
30. Steenbergen-Hu, S., Cooper, H.: A meta-analysis of the effectiveness of intelligent tutoring systems on K-12 students' mathematical learning. J. Educ. Psychol. **105**(4), 970 (2013)
31. Doleck, T., et al.: Augmenting the novice-expert overlay model in an intelligent tutoring system: Using confidence-weighted linear classifiers. In: International Conference on Computational Intelligence and Computing Research. IEEE (2014)
32. Steenbergen-Hu, S., Cooper, H.: A meta-analysis of the effectiveness of intelligent tutoring systems on college students' academic learning. J. Educ. Psychol. **106**(2), 331 (2014)
33. Volarić, T., Vasić, D., Brajković, E.: Adaptive tool for teaching programming using conceptual maps. In: Hadžikadić, M., Avdaković, S. (eds.) Advanced Technologies, Systems, and Applications. LNNS, vol. 3, pp. 335–347. Springer, Cham (2017). https://doi.org/10.1007/978-3-319-47295-9_27

34. Barrón-Estrada, M.L., Zatarain-Cabada, R., Hernández, F.G., Bustillos, R.O., Reyes-García, C.A.: An affective and cognitive tutoring system for learning programming. In: Lagunas, O.P., Alcántara, O.H., Figueroa, G.A. (eds.) MICAI 2015. LNCS (LNAI), vol. 9414, pp. 171–182. Springer, Cham (2015). https://doi.org/10.1007/978-3-319-27101-9_12

35. Zubrinic, K., Kalpic, D., Milicevic, M.: The automatic creation of concept maps from documents written using morphologically rich languages. Expert Syst. Appl. **39**(16), 12709–12718 (2012)

36. Nugumanova, A., et al.: Automatic generation of concept maps based on collection of teaching materials. In: International Conference on Data Management Technologies and Applications, vol. 2. SCITEPRESS (2015)

37. Aleven, V., et al.: Help helps, but only so much: research on help seeking with intelligent tutoring systems. Int. J. Artif. Intell. Educ. **26**, 205–223 (2016)

38. Volarić, T., et al.: Data augmentation with GAN to improve the prediction of at-risk students in a virtual learning environment. In: Wang, N., Rebolledo-Mendez, G., Dimitrova, V., Matsuda, N., Santos, O.C. (eds.) AIED 2023. CCIS, vol. 1831. Springer, Cham (2023). https://doi.org/10.1007/978-3-031-36336-8_40

39. Kulik, J.A., Fletcher, J.D.: Effectiveness of intelligent tutoring systems: a meta-analytic review. Rev. Educ. Res. **86**(1), 42–78 (2016)

40. Sani, S.M., Bichi, A.B., Ayuba, S.: Artificial intelligence approaches in student modeling: half decade review (2010-2015). IJCSN-Int. J. Comput. Sci. Netw. **5**(5) (2016)

41. Crockett, K., Latham, A., Whitton, N.: On predicting learning styles in conversational intelligent tutoring systems using fuzzy decision trees. Int. J. Hum. Comput. Stud. **97**, 98–115 (2017)

42. Wilson, C., Scott, B.: Adaptive systems in education: a review and conceptual unification. Int. J. Inf. Learn. Technol. **34**(1), 2–19 (2017)

43. Al Duhayyim, M., Newbury, P.: Adaptive e-learning system using fuzzy logic and concept map. Int. J. Educ. Pedagogical Sci. **12**(8), 1105–1112 (2018)

44. Troussas, C., Chrysafiadi, K., Virvou, M.: An intelligent adaptive fuzzy-based inference system for computer-assisted language learning. Expert Syst. Appl. **127**, 85–96 (2019)

45. Kumar, A., Ahuja, N.J.: An adaptive framework of learner model using learner characteristics for intelligent tutoring systems. In: Choudhury, S., Mishra, R., Mishra, R.G., Kumar, A. (eds.) Intelligent Communication, Control and Devices. AISC, vol. 989, pp. 425–433. Springer, Singapore (2020). https://doi.org/10.1007/978-981-13-8618-3_45

46. Troussas, C., Krouska, A., Sgouropoulou, C.: Collaboration and fuzzy-modeled personalization for mobile game-based learning in higher education. Comput. Educ. **144**, 103698 (2020)

47. Papakostas, C., et al.: Modeling the knowledge of users in an augmented reality-based learning environment using fuzzy logic. In: Krouska, A., Troussas, C., Caro, J. (eds.) NiDS 2022. Springer, Cham (2022). https://doi.org/10.1007/978-3-031-17601-2_12

The Development of Assistive Robotics: A Comprehensive Analysis Integrating Machine Learning, Robotic Vision, and Collaborative Human Assistive Robots

Boris Crnokić[1]([✉]) [ID], Ivan Peko[2] [ID], and Janez Gotlih[3] [ID]

[1] Faculty of Mechanical Engineering, Computing and Electrical Engineering, University of Mostar, Matice Hrvatske b.b., 8800 Mostar, Bosnia and Herzegovina
`boris.crnokic@fsre.sum.ba`
[2] Faculty of Science, University of Split, Ruđera Boškovića 33, 21000 Split, Croatia
`ipeko@pmfst.hr`
[3] Faculty of Mechanical Engineering, University of Maribor, Smetanova ul. 17, 2000 Maribor, Slovenia
`janez.gotlih@um.si`

Abstract. With integration of collaborative robotics, robotic vision, and machine learning, the high-end frontier reached in assistive robotics is likely to help develop promising solutions to the challenges associated with the needs of aging populations and persons with disabilities. This paper examines recent developments, challenges, and opportunities that relate to the application of these technologies for human assistance. The paper will begin with an explanation of the basic concepts and the rationales driving assistive robotics, and then move on to the technological ground with basic collaborative robots, robotic vision, and machine learning, stressing how they can make human assistance better. Case studies and real-world applications will help to present the potential of integrated assistive robotics not only in healthcare and rehabilitation, but also in domains such as elder care and living on one's own. This paper also highlights some of the critical challenges inclusive of robustness, reliability, human-robot interaction, safety, and ethical considerations along with some of the emerging trends and future research directions related to it. The paper sets up a visionary outlook, where integrated assistive robotics—realized fully through human-centered design, interdisciplinary collaboration, and innovation in technology development—could revolutionize care and support toward fostering the inclusivity, dignity, and independence of those with diverse needs.

Keywords: Assistive Robotics · Collaborative Robots · Robotic Vision · Machine Learning

1 Introduction

In recent years, the interplay of robotics, computer vision, and machine learning has accelerated incredible progress of assistive technologies for an improved human way of life. It is most important for all these needs to be satisfied for new support solutions

© The Author(s), under exclusive license to Springer Nature Switzerland AG 2024
T. Volarić et al. (Eds.): MoStart 2024, CCIS 2124, pp. 164–214, 2024.
https://doi.org/10.1007/978-3-031-62058-4_12

for people in their daily life, since the societies are meeting challenges with the aging population and increased prevalence of disabilities. Assistive robotics is hence one of the major constituents, which in this technological revolution empowers and promotes independence and well-being amongst human beings, employing collaborative robots, robotic vision, and machine learning.

1.1 Background

The recent development of science and technology has opened up new prospects in the development of assistive technologies to assist humans in performing different tasks, including robotics, computer vision, and machine learning. With the continuous increment in the aging population around the world, the increasing demand is for assistive technologies to help the elderly and impaired people to carry on with their lives. This is an assistive robotics that could be done for mobility assistance, household chores, and health care monitoring. The focus of research within this paper encompasses areas including robotics, computer vision, machine learning, and human-computer interaction, as well as healthcare. Interdisciplinary collaborative research efforts by the researchers from those fields are important for the progress of the robotic system. Recently, much attention has been paid to the so-called "real-world" applications of robotics outside of industrial purposes. The use of assistive robots has the great potential for quality of life improvement in persons with diverse needs and is, therefore, an equally promising area for research and development. Integrating collaborative robotics, robotic vision, and machine learning into devices for human assistance throws up technical challenges and opportunities. Addressing these challenges and leveraging the opportunities can lead to significant advancements in the field. This paper is a review of recent developments, challenges, and opportunities in the integration of collaborative robots, robotic vision, and machine learning for the application of assistive robotics, especially that of how these technologies may well enhance human assistance within varied contexts. It may also discuss potential future directions and implications for research, industry, and society.

1.2 Motivation

There is a growing demand for assistive technologies. This, therefore, implies that there is already a growing need for assistive technologies in aiding the people with disabilities and the elderly population in view of the demographic changes to aging populations that societies around the world are witnessing. The main aim of the paper is to show review of solutions relevant to the social needs identified through the exploitation of new results in the domain of robotics, computer vision, and machine learning. Integration of robots through collaboration, vision, and learning is in the frontier of innovation technology with the profoundest impact in the field of assistive robotics. In a nutshell, the paper tries to mirror, by synthesizing and analyzing the most recent breakthroughs in these fields, the transformational potential of an integration of these technologies for enhancing human assistance. With regard to the support in daily activities, independence and social integration, assistive robotics offers promising potential to support quality of life of people with disabilities and the elderly. This paper identifies the capabilities and benefits of integrated assistive robotics systems with the goal of motivating future research and development efforts aimed at realizing their full potential. The paper provides an interdisciplinary platform for collaboration and exchange of knowledge between researchers, engineers, health professionals, policy-makers, and stakeholders, among whom are the target user categories, in the development and deployment of assistive robotics technologies. The paper synthesizes a variety of insights offered by different fields that together create a synthesized insight into the opportunities and challenges within this fast-growing domain.

The primary reason for preparing this paper lays in the promising opportunity to contribute further in the domain of assistive robotics as a transformative domain to enable people with diverse abilities to enhance their lives, foster inclusion, and accessibility in a further compassionate and fairer society.

1.3 Objectives

The main objectives of this paper will focus on:

- To critically review recent developments in the field of collaborative robotics, robotic vision, and machine learning as they find application in assistive robotics, which consolidates research findings, technological advances, and practical applications that enable findings on the state of the art.
- To explore integration of collaborative robots, robotic vision systems, and machine learning algorithms for human assistance. Look at how these technologies can be synergistically combined in order to extend the capabilities of assistive robotic systems and thus improve user interactions and experiences, through addressing the specific needs and challenges mentioned.
- To identify the critical challenges and opportunities in integrating collaborative robots, robotic vision, and machine learning into human assistance, including challenges relating to safety, reliability, and adaptability, and other considerations such as ethical considerations, regulatory requirements, and acceptance by society.
- To show applications and case studies that succeed in proving the potential of changing lives through assistive robotics are showcased: real-life implementations across a whole host of domains, ranging from healthcare and rehabilitation to eldercare and independent living, underline the diversity of what is feasible and beneficial.
- To propose future research directions and development pathways of the assistive robots and intelligent interfaces used by healthcare, the technologies, and approaches that have been developed for them. The paper is further a proposal for those research and development paths to be followed in the future to further the field of assistive robotics. Some of the promising areas for further investigation include novel sensor technologies, human-robot interaction techniques, adaptive learning algorithms, and personalized assistive solutions to the emerging needs.

1.4 Related Surveys and Systematic Reviews

The recent years in this assistive robotics age have been an amazing surge, driven by the confluence of collaborative robots, robotic vision, and machine-learning techniques [1]. This convergence of technologies promises the most when it comes to how the revolution of human assistance can occur in various aspects, including health care, rehabilitation, elderly life, and independent living. With such deploying collaborative robots in operations, which work in the vicinity of humans, robotic vision systems provide perception and interpretation of the environment, and machine learning algorithms that are adaptive, assistive robotics is set to change the lives of humans and other subjects with different needs [2, 3]. The most significant conclusion of studies in this field has been around the advancement of human-robot interaction. According to the article, scientists had been working on new ways that might allow humans and robots to collaborate and live together, using machine learning to help robots understand people better and make movements according to their gestures, expressions, and even their commands [4]. Such an advance provided for more intuitive and effective cooperation, where the assistive robot can provide the right type of help, according to the user's needs and abilities [5].

Further advances in the field of robotic vision have significantly increased the environmental perception capabilities of assistive robots [6]. State-of-the-art sensors and algorithms are integrated into robots that can perceive and interpret their surroundings with unmatched accuracy and reliability [7]. This increased situational awareness shall assist more accurately and effectively navigated complex environments of assistive robots, identifying obstacles, while interacting with objects and people, and thus more usefully and effectively applying in real-world situations [8]. Furthermore, some of the recent researches have expressed that the assistance should be given by personalization, and adaptability is achievable in these systems with the help of machine learning algorithms [9, 10]. In such a sense, analysis of user behavior, preferences, and feedback allows elaborating personalized assistance strategies best fitting every user's needs, thus assuring effective support and a rise in user satisfaction. This people-centered approach makes the overall experience better in addition to granting more autonomy and independence to people who need the assistive robot in order to fulfill some everyday tasks [11–13]. In addition to the technological innovations, there has also been recent research in how to develop integration frameworks and architectures that are robust and enable simple coupling of collaborative robots with the robotic vision and machine learning algorithms. These frameworks will help to address some of the most important challenges in interoperability, scalability, and modularity that allow the development and deployment of integrated assistive robotics solutions in diverse settings [14, 15]. These architectures base the strength of integration of systems for accelerated innovations and translations from advanced technologies to practical applications serving society by researchers and practitioners [16].

Real-world applications and case studies further suggest the future potential of assistive robotics integrated. From assisting in healthcare activities to supporting rehabilitation initiatives and enhancing the quality of elder care services, assistive robots have shown the role they play in enhancing the quality of life and independence in disabilities and the aged [17–20]. These case studies are therefore helpful not only as practical examples of the assistive robotics but also in raising concerns and considering deployment of such technology in the real-world environment [3, 21, 22]. However, in the face of recent advances, several challenges are still present in the design and deployment of integrated assistive robotics systems [23, 24]. Next come the critical factors of safety, ethics, privacy, and societal acceptance, which the research and the practical user are to uphold when using assistive robotics technology in a responsible and ethical manner [25–28]. It is only through such understanding of the natural difficultness and working together at varied levels that the true potential of the field in affecting the lives of human would be realized [23, 29]. Then, the dawn of inclusivity and accessibility will sound like the total revolution of human assistance when all the latest improvements in assistive robotics combine with advances in collaborative robotics, robotic vision, and machine learning [1, 30]. Through its use, the future of assistive robotics may bring about a quantum leap in care and support for those with diverse needs, where strong integration frameworks, personalized approaches, and innovative technologies offer a different landscape of care and support [31–34].

1.5 Scope and Structure of the Paper

The paper will be structured to give a coherent narrative that will guide the reader through the exploration of integrated assistive robotics. This contribution will comprise sections that detail assistive robotics in fundamentals, single components, examples on how to integrate assistive robotic strategies, the exemplary applications, challenges, considerations, and future directions as well as the concluding summary that highlights the transforming potential of assistive robotics in an integrated manner for the positive development of human lives. The respective section shall be further elaborated with relevant literature, research findings, and case studies to discuss the matter in context.

2 Technological Foundations of Assistive Robotics

The convergence point of collaborative robots, robotic vision, and machine learning within the domain of assistive robotics is truly transformational. When these technological pillars join forces, highly sophisticated systems are delivered, which further offer invaluable aid and assistance to people with disabilities, the elderly, and any person in need of physical aid. With regard to assistive robotics, safety is also at the forefront, and collaborative robots are designed to work effectively and safely alongside humans. These robots have features that enhance their safety and, therefore, they will not cause any harm when working closely with humans. The robotic vision acts as the eye for the assistive robotic system so as it can understand and interpret its environment. The visual intelligence permits robots to understand and respond to human cues. This can help in forming a seamless collaboration and assistance. Machine learning is the cognitive engine for adaptability and autonomy in assistive robotics. This capability achieves personalized assistance related to individual users, heightening user satisfaction and effectiveness in totality. The combination of these technological components unfolds a plethora of applications in human assistance. Assistive robots used in healthcare settings can help in daily life activities such as dressing, feeding, and medication management in patients, hence reducing the burden on caregivers and, concurrently, promoting independence among the patients. Personal therapy through these systems is guided, with exercises to be carried out by individuals and the progress made monitored in real time in the process of rehabilitation. As the technology further develops, the potential applications of assistive robotics continue to be exponentially wide in their impact on lives.

Nonetheless, issues like robustness, reliability, and ethical considerations need to be resolved for the innovations to be able to have a full impact on society. By synergizing collaboration of robots, robotic vision and machine learning, a new path would be created for a future where assistive robotics transforms completely how assistance fosters people into independence, dignity, and inclusiveness.

2.1 Collaborative Robots in Assistive Operations

Collaborative robots are being employed in the assistive operations in the various industries. The robots are being designed to work with the humans in assisting them to carry out some of the tasks that may require some form of physical assistance or repetitive action. The implementation of the cobots in the assistive operations maintains a safety focus. Developments in safety technologies, such as force-limiting sensors, vision systems, and better algorithms, all help cobots operate more closely and safely with humans than in the past, when safety cages and barriers were necessary. There is an increasing interest to work on interaction between people and robots. This may involve the ease of interfacing with intuitive interfaces, gesture recognition, and natural language processing to aid the harmony and seamless communication and collaboration between humans and cobots in the assistive tasks. Development of cobots is taking the direction yielding higher levels of customization and adaptability in diverse assistive operations, leading to better overall operational efficiencies. The manufacturers are one step ahead in this by creating modular designs of cobots that are flexibly programmed so as to enable them to be reconfigured or repurposed to perform different tasks in assistive environments. It has an AI and machine learning algorithmic building, where it can learn from human behavior and also adapt to the actions in this respect. This offers the cobot being predictive in relation to human needs and preferences, further amplifying its efficiency and effectiveness in assistive operations. Cobots will integrate the remote operation and monitoring capability so that a supervisor or caretaker can be able to conduct remote operations and monitoring of cobots in assistive tasks. This would be much helpful to the needy or disabled people, in particular, or to care for elderly persons, who require constant support. These cobots, on the other hand, are starting to be used in support operations—health support, rehabilitation, support for the elderly, and support for the home—lifting, moving, and transferring patients, doing exercises for therapy support, support for housework, and even reminding them to take medicine. With the increasing use of cobots in assistive operations, there is greater scope to deal with the consideration of ethics towards issues such as privacy, autonomy, and human employment. The possibilities for developments and continuous development of collaboration robots, which in the future will further the quality of life for people who need support, are outlined by various authors whose works are part of the review in this paper. This trend reflects potential cobots as an enabling technology towards greater independence and access for people who may be disabled or have other limitations.

Definition and Characteristics of Collaborative Robots. Collaborative robots, in a general form, represent a sort of revolution in the traditional sense of robots, enabling closer interaction between humans and robots in a good number of industrial and non-industrial settings. Their attributes of safety, flexibility, ease of use, and adaptability allow for applications not only in manufacturing and logistics but extending into healthcare and beyond as well. The rise of technology and the ever-increasing role of collaborative robots are likely to come into the spotlight as redefining the human way of work and its relationship with machines. In the assistive operations, collaborative robots, therefore, may refer to robotic systems that are designed to help human beings in carrying out a number of tasks that may basically need physical assistance, support, or even augmentation. Often, this may involve activities related to health and rehabilitation care, elderly care, and activities of daily living. Although collaborative robots in industry applications share common issues with those applied in assistive operations, the latter are unique and feature characteristics that are directed towards different issues and challenges in assisting people in the different areas such as medicine, rehabilitation, and care for the elderly [35–38]. Table 1 shows a summary of the most significant characteristics of collaborative robots in general and those in assistive operations.

Table 1. Most significant characteristics of collaborative robots in general and those in assistive operations

Collaborative robots for general purposes (mostly industrial)	
Safety	Enabled with advanced safety features like force and torque sensors, systems for collision detection, and monitoring of speed for safe interaction of human-robotics. Compliance mechanisms and soft materials are employed often to mitigate injury risks in case of contact with humans
Flexibility	Designed so that reprogramming can be easily performed, such as reconfiguration to a variety of tasks and environments Lightweight and compact to facilitate easy deployment and reconfiguration to workspaces
Ease of Use	User interfaces are user-friendly, and programming approaches are intuitive to enable even a non-expert to teach, program, and interact with the robots. Minimal training for operators, contributing to ease of adoption and deployment
Compatibility with Existing Infrastructure	Designed to integrate seamlessly with existing production lines, work cells, and workflows. Can be easily retrofitted into existing facilities with only minor modifications, so that downtime and disruption are minimized

(continued)

Table 1. (*continued*)

Collaborative robots for general purposes (mostly industrial)	
Adaptability	Capable of allowing the robot to dynamically adjust its behavior and performance in function of a change of environment or change of task requirements. Uses learning algorithms, sensor feedback, and autonomous decision-making capabilities
Task Sharing	Ability to work hand in hand with humans on tasks, including automating repetitive and physically demanding tasks, at the same time allowing humans to concentrate on the more complex or cognitive aspects of the work
Collaborative robots in assistive operations	
Safety and Reliability	Stringent safety standards and mechanisms to warrant safe interaction with users, most importantly in facilities such as health facilities or homes Dependable and robust in performance to meet the requirements and conditions of its users and environment
Sensitivity and Empathy	Focus on developing robots that are able to recognize and respond to human emotions, gestures, and intentions Affective integrated computing and emotion recognition technologies for augmented human-robot interaction and engagement
Assistance and Support	Developed to enable the physical assistive and supportive role with the user in functions of mobility assistance, personal care, and home tasks Personalised in task planning for the individual and adaptable to specific personal user requirements and preferences

(*continued*)

Table 1. (*continued*)

Collaborative robots for general purposes (mostly industrial)	
Human-Centered Design	Focused in designing robots centred on the needs, capabilities, and preferences of the users, amongst these being the people with disabilities or limitations. Incorporation of universal design principles ensures accessibility and promotes inclusivity of diverse user population
Adaptability and Learning	Learns from the users' interactions and feedback in order to improve performance of tasks and adapt its way to change in user needs over time. Involves algorithms based on machine learning and adaptive control strategies for better autonomy and responsivity
Collaborative Decision-Making	Collaboration in different decision processes between the robot and the user entailing shared control and autonomy. Empowerment of the user for commanding and monitoring robotic actions, which has been connected to feelings of empowerment and control
Comparison	
Safety	Both general collaborative robots and assistive ones regard their users' safety to be important, but the latter type usually needs extra sensitivity and empathy in order to interact safely with a vulnerable user
Flexibility	While both groups emphasize flexibility, assistive robots may need an extra level of adaptability to respond to different user needs and preferences
Assistance and Support	Assistive collaborative robots, unlike general collaborative robots, are uniquely designed to physically assist and support users—usually under sensitive and personal contexts
Human-Centered Design	Collaborative robots for assistive operations will call for keen adherence to human-centered design principles but with a better focus on accessibility, inclusivity, and eventual acceptance by the user

(*continued*)

Table 1. (*continued*)

Collaborative robots for general purposes (mostly industrial)	
Adaptability and Learning	Although the two classes incorporate adaptability and learning capabilities, assistive robots may need to incorporate more sophisticated algorithms, among them learning from the interaction with the user, and adaptability in the altered user needs over time
Task Sharing	General collaborative robots often focus on automation of the industrial tasks, while assistive operations significantly are geared toward assistance and support of the human users during performing activities of daily living

Benefits and Challenges in Assistive Operations. Benefits of collaborative robots within assistive operations include improved independence, quality of life for the patient or supportee, and improved safety and efficiency. However, the robots also face challenges among which include ethical considerations, technical complexities, and user acceptance. Meeting such challenges will, therefore, require taking a balanced approach that places a premium on the safety of these devices, user-centered design, and interdisciplinary collaboration in a bid to realize the maximum benefits of assistive robots while suppressing risks [39–45]. The following table summarizes the benefits and challenges pertaining to the basic features and application possibilities of collaborative robots in assistive operations (Table 2).

2.2 Robotic Vision for Human Assistance

Role of Robotic Vision in Assistive Operations. This is an area involving technology development, implementing visual perception, for robots to perceive and interpret their surroundings as well as have effective interaction with human beings. This encompasses a wide number of applications in this field, to assist the betterment of life for many people who might need it because of disabilities, due to aging, or by any other limiting condition. Some of the important aspects of robotic vision for human assistance are detailed below:

- **Object Recognition and Manipulation:** The robotic vision technology enables robots to recognize objects from their environment, then to manipulate them at will. It is by virtue of such a capability that the technology is seen as helpful for people with mobility disorders and physically challenged ones, for it assists in functions like picking stuff, pouring drinks, or initiating kitchen appliances [46–48].
- **Navigation and Mobility Assistance:** Vision-based navigation is the process by which robots can autonomously navigate through some indoor environment, thereby assisting people with mobility challenges to move around places of their choice, like

Table 2. Benefits and challenges pertaining to the basic features and application possibilities of collaborative robots in assistive operations

Features and applications	Benefits	Challenges
Enhanced Independence	The assistive robots improve the quality of life by helping people in performing their daily activities and enhancing well-being	While the robots improve independency, there is a danger of dependence which might limit and reduce the quality of lifestyle in the future
Improved Quality of Life	Assistive robots enhance one's quality of life through support in daily living activities, ensuring one's well-being	Dependence on robots in the society may reduce interaction and participation in common social wealth, hence compromising the quality of life
Increased Safety	Safety provision features in collaborative robots help in preventing accidents, ensuring safety	Complex interaction between humans and robots may eventually pose safety hazards, which may require proper design and monitoring in order to avoid possible risk
Efficiency and Productivity	Robots are able to perform tasks systematically, hence reducing the total volume of work to be covered by the caregivers and thus increasing overall productivity	Technical limitations of the robot and operational errors mean that it can be inefficient and have interruptions in task execution
Personalized Assistance	Assistive robots can be customized according to the specific need and preferences of a user, offering personalized support	Design and development of asked for customized help may relatively need resources and skills, hence less scalable and accessible
Social Interaction	Collaborative robots can behave as the user's companions and thus help fight loneliness and isolation among the elderly, as it were	Robots may lack emotions and friendliness, and they have weak attachment to the users, hence low emotional satisfaction from users
24/7 Availability	Robots offer 24/7 support, ensuring service and monitoring that are constant to the users	The running and reliability of the robot for a long time may demand constant maintenance and checking by the support team

(continued)

Table 2. (*continued*)

Features and applications	Benefits	Challenges
Relief for Caregivers	Robots take the burden off the human caregivers, hence permitting them to focus more on rendering emotional support as well as supervision	If there is a reduction in human control over robotic caregiving, the quality of care the caregiver provides will decline hence creating a disconnected or alienated feel for caregivers about users
Skill Augmentation	Collaborative robots enhance both the physical and cognitive abilities of users, hence enabling them to undertake tasks that may be otherwise burdensome	Reinforcing dependence on robot assistance maybe result in a decline in independence because of diminished abilities and skills
Learning and Adaptation	Some robots include machine learning algorithms to adapt to the needs of users, therefore improving task performance and user satisfaction	Machine learning depends on massive data volumes and tends to bias or even complain if not adjusted, thus impacting reliability and effectiveness

homes or any other indoors safely. This system uses cameras and sensors for detection and obstacle identification, such understanding as well, including landmarks that it helps even plan proper paths in a given environment [49–51].

- **Human Detection and Tracking:** The robotic vision system can detect and track human users within its environment in order to be able to further interact with them or provide assistance where necessary. Especially for being able to follow a person around, guide the person, and react on demand if help is required, such human detection and tracking are important features [52–56].
- **Gesture and expression recognition:** They belong to the category of technologies that enable robots to understand human gestures, expressions on faces, or postures. It allows robot-human communication to take place in an intuitive manner, hence improving the user experience and easing provision of help [7, 57, 58].
- **Fall Detection and Emergency Response:** The vision-based systems can be adopted in order to determine the case of a fall or any other emergencies, perceptions of which could be left without having been observed under other conditions, parallel to instigation of an appropriate response in the form of either alerting a caretaker or activating emergency call. It comprises cameras with image processing algorithms that monitor human activities and identify deviations that indicate a potential emergency situation [59, 60].
- **Assistive Healthcare and Rehabilitation:** Robotics vision is not only an aid to the industrial aspect but also in healthcare and rehabilitation. It helps guide the health-beneficiary through physical therapy exercises, keeps track of what progress was made, and provides feedback to help optimise the process. Vision-based systems are

meant to track body motions, monitor posture, offer better form, and tune the exercise regimens to be more conducive towards recovery and rehabilitation [61–65].

- **User Interface and Interaction Design:** Vision-based interfaces to user friendly robots provide intuitive ways of interacting with them, letting a user control and communicate to the robots in gesture, voice commands or other natural modalities of input. The interfaces are designed so that they are usable by anybody regardless of limitation in ability [66–70].

Overall, then, robotic vision enables assistive robots for perceiving, understanding, and action execution within the environments and of the users of them. With advanced vision technologies, an assistive robot will give great support and help to the users across different contexts toward further improved independence, security, and quality of life.

Overview of Robotic Vision Systems. Robotic vision systems incorporate a wide range of technologies and methodologies for enabling a robot to gain visual understanding and meaning from its environment. The robot vision system is an essential part of this scheme, to afford robots a mode of perception and understanding of the environment and communications in a safe way with human beings, hence the accomplishment of the functions is highly effective. Below are shown various types of robotic vision systems together with the technologies to implement them:

- **2D Vision Systems:** Systems that work with 2D vision are generally based on various types of cameras capturing 2-dimensional images of the environment and then having the ability to process them. They are usually used for object detection examples of preprocessing the images for the extraction of meaningful information include concepts, such as filtering, edge detection, image segmentation, and feature extraction. Techniques of thresholding, morphological operations, and contour detection applied would help identify objects and their boundaries in the images [71, 72]. Object detection refers to the process of finding objects that are present in an image or even a scene. Object recognition is the process that identifies as well as recognizes certain objects or patterns within the detected regions. Techniques involved include template matching, machine learning-based classification, and deep learning methods (e.g., convolutional neural networks) for accurate detection and recognition of objects [73–76]. Localization is the act of determining the robot location within its environment. Mapping is creating a representation of the robot environment. Some of these techniques include feature-based localization, simultaneous localization and mapping (SLAM), as well as occupancy grid mapping with 2D vision systems data to guide robots to be self-sufficient in moving and performing tasks [77–80]. Planning algorithms base their work on information that is provided by 2D vision systems to establish optimum paths in a changing surrounding for a robot to follow. Methods used to make plans for the robot include potential fields, A* algorithm, and probabilistic roadmaps (PRMs) [81–84]. Object tracking refers to the process of monitoring the movement of objects with time, whereas motion estimation techniques go on analyzing the motion of objects within a scene. Such tasks as object tracking and motion estimation, usually necessary for robots during robot-human interaction or in dynamic obstacle avoidance, are simplified thanks to the help of Kalman filters, particle filters, and optical flow methods. [85, 86] Seeing humans, observing their mimics, facial expressions, and gestures is feasible in 2D vision systems for a robot as well. With this, features such as gesture recognition, facial recognition, and pose estimation are applied in order to make human-robot interaction natural and intuitive [7, 87]. The 2D vision systems take part in quality control and inspection tasks in manufacturing environments. Product quality is ensured and anomalies in manufacturing processes can be found out by different techniques that span from defect detection, measurement, and pattern recognition [88, 89].

- **3D Vision Systems:** They capture not only the 2D images but also the depth information associated with them; in other words, robots are able to perceive the three-dimensional structure of objects present in the environment. Incorporation of 3D vision systems along with robotic vision systems certainly enhances the capability of robots in a host of application domains like industrial automation, autonomous vehicles, healthcare, agriculture, among others. Stereo vision is a perception of the world based on the consideration of the small differences in images taken from two or more cameras. This has been employed in human binocular vision, and its application is for robots to perceive the 3D structure of the surrounding [90–92]. Robots that could measure distances of the different objects within their environment with precision and accuracy were ToF measures time light takes in getting to and back from stuff, while structured light measures depth by getting a pattern on stuff projected on it and then measuring depth by how the deformation of that pattern happens [93–95]. Point cloud is a set of the points of data in space, which represents the external surfaces of objects. The point cloud is able to be derived by the robot from the 3D sensors, and processing of this data makes it possible to identify the objects and make estimations on their shapes and the motion planning to be made for them [96, 97]. Robots with 3D vision systems can be able to recognize and localize objects in the environment using the 3D shape and features of the object. Localization, object detection, recognition, and estimation of pose are techniques like feature extraction or object segmentation or machine learning algorithms (e.g., convolutional neural networks) [98–100]. On the other hand, SLAM algorithms describe a robot's capability to form a map of a previously unknown environment at the same time that the robot is being localized on the map. The 3D vision systems enable acquiring the needed depth information with the aim of improving the accuracy and reliability of the operation of SLAM algorithms in such a way that robots can act as independent agents in unstructured environments [101]. 3D vision systems provide a great role in robotic grasping and manipulation with respect to giving correct information on depth of objects. A robot can therefore exploit such information for planning its best grasping strategy, for the manipulation of objects with different shapes and sizes, and even for reacting to changes in the environment during manipulation [102]. Systems such as these 3D vision systems, for manufacturing or quality control applications, actually allow robots to review the dimensions, surface defect, and alignment of parts in an amazingly accurate way. The 3D data captured can be compared against predefined specifications or CAD models so that defects can be identified to safeguard quality in the product [95, 103]. 3D vision systems may enable robots to perceive and understand human gestures, poses, and expressions in natural and casual interaction human-robot. Possible applications include collaboration in robotics, robotics assistance to human health care, and installations of interaction in public spaces [4, 87, 104]. Another key integration is that of 3D vision systems with the navigation algorithms, aiding the robots in understanding complex indoor and outdoor environments much effectively. Depth information guides in obstacle detection, planning the path to avoid collision, and ultimately safe navigation in such dynamic environments [105, 106]. This way, 3D vision systems would be one of the core critical sets of AR and VR applications, where they either augment the real world by the virtual world overlaid or would create immersive virtuality. The 3D vision allows these robots to handle objects and environments in a way that, to all intents and purposes, appears life-like and to get into activities like teleoperation, training simulations, and entertainment experiences [107–109].

- **Infrared Vision Systems:** These utilize infrared sensors to detect heat that is emitted by objects, hence making the robots fitted with these capable of sensing their surroundings even in darkness or in situations when the obstacles are invisible to a human eye. It is especially useful in cases of bad visibility such as darkness, smoke, fog, or dust. Infrared radiation is located further from the visible spectrum, and a part of this radiation is emitted by all bodies whose temperature is above absolute zero. Infrared vision systems sense and use such radiation for several objectives like object detection, tracking, and navigation. This is done by capturing the heat that issues from things in general, by use of what is referred to as thermal imaging. Its input is a temperature representation of the scene, due to which robots can detect objects by thermal characteristics of the objects rather than visible appearance [110–113]. Infrared vision systems can detect objects based on their unique thermal signatures. A robot is thus able to find the obstacles, targets, or specific objects of interest by analysing the temperature distribution of the environment. The operation of a robot in a poorly visible environment, such as in a complex space, is enabled by infrared vision systems [114]. This can enable robotic systems to preplan the optimal paths in order to avoid collisions and safely reach their destinations, based on the detected heat from the objects and obstacles [115–117]. Infrared data can be used to enhance localization techniques in indoor or outdoor areas with simultaneous localization and mapping [101]. A lot of applications make use of the infrared vision systems, such as in surveillance and security [112, 118]. The infrared vision systems are core to industrial automation processes, mostly in the field of manufacturing and quality control. The systems can pick up defects in products, monitor the temperatures of equipment, or even inspect machinery for break down. By using infrared sensors coupled with either robotic arms or automatic systems, efficiency and reliability in production lines are increased [119, 120]. Infrared vision systems are invaluable in search and rescue missions, especially in disaster scenarios where the situations become further visibility limited. Thermal imaging cameras mounted on drones or robotic platforms can pick up heat signatures from survivors who are trapped under rubble, leading to the guiding of rescue teams to such locations [111, 121, 122]. Infrared vision systems are used in applications that seek to target environmental monitoring, and some of the advanced uses include wild forest fire detection, pollution control, and wildlife conservation. They can detect temperature anomalies, monitor vegetation health, or even track animal movements within natural habitats—useful data for environmental research and management [123–125].

- **Multi-Sensor Fusion Systems:** Multi-sensor fusion can significantly improve the capabilities of the robot vision system toward being more general, robust, and accurate in perceiving the environment so that the robots can more autonomously and effectively perform their tasks in many practical cases [126]. Multi-sensor fusion combines information from many sensors that have different inputs, such as cameras, LIDAR, radar, or depth sensors, in order to ensure more accurate perception from the robot [127]. Another limitation the vision system might have is where the images captured in certain lighting conditions are not very visible or may have occlusions. Integration of other sensors helps in overcoming these limitations and providing a more comprehensive understanding of the environment [128]. Different sensors have different strengths and weaknesses. For example, while cameras can provide detailed visual information, they can experience problems in low light or with distant objects. On the other hand, LIDAR measures distances well but might have difficulties resulting from material properties or transparent surfaces [129, 130]. The robot's perception is of higher quality via multisensory data fusion, and the choice of the most appropriate sensor modality for a specific situation can be made. The different sensors complement the information of the environment. For instance, a camera provides color and texture information, while a LIDAR sensor provides accurate 3D spatial data. Upon fusion of such inputs, the robot will therefore have a holistic view of its environment, hence make more informed decisions and maneuver complicated environments [131, 132]. Integration of such data from several sensors can enable a robot to better perceive and track objects in the environment. For example, the fusion of visual data and depth information from LIDAR is able to get accurate object recognition and tracking, even in highly cluttered or occluded environments [133, 134]. Robotic vision is one of the most significant components, since it allows the cars and other autonomous types of vehicles to define and identify the objects on the road, lane markings, signs, and people. The multi-sensor fusion integrates the data from sensors to achieve an all-rounded situation awareness which thus allows making safe navigation decisions [135–137]. In agriculture, it is vision systems used for robots in tasks like crop monitoring, estimation of yield, and weed identification. Multi-sensor fusion allows a robot to gather data from different sources like cameras, GPS, and environmental sensors to assist in the optimization of farming processes and therefore improve productivity [138, 139]. The robotics system used in medical procedures such as robot-assisted surgery calls for exact imaging and navigation through vision in robotics. Multi-sensor fusion integrates data on imaging devices such as MRI, CT scans, and ultrasound together with robot vision in the same operating space to boost diagnostic precision and success rates of surgery [140–143].

- **Advanced Vision Systems:** Embedded vision systems are supposed to be compact and power-efficient in such a way that they are ready for deployment on mobile robots or drones. Capable of analyzing aerial images, to integrated with production lines, to do lane detection, traffic sign recognition, pedestrian detection, and obstacle avoidance, etc. [144–149]. Deep learning techniques, particularly convolutional neural networks (CNNs), revolutionized robotic vision to advanced object recognition, segmentation, and scene understanding. [150, 151] Deep learning-based systems find wide applications in autonomous vehicles for tasks like object detection, lane detection, traffic sign recognition, pedestrian detection, and gesture recognition [152, 153]. In a manufacturing setting, robots are made that have vision systems powered by deep learning, which can include functions such as line inspection for quality, sorting of objects, optimization of assembly lines, and control of robotic arms [154, 155]. Precision agriculture uses robot vision combined with deep learning for varied tasks as crop monitoring, weed detection, fruit picking, and yield estimation [156–158]. A vision-enabled drone that operates through vision systems and deep learning algorithms is capable of tasks like aerial mapping, object tracking, environmental monitoring, and search and rescue operations [159–162]. Robots having deep learning vision systems will be able to work on areas like site survey, progress tracking, safety inspection, and material transportation [163, 164]. Active vision systems in robotics are described as the vision system functionality in which it is fused with the ability to control actively the viewpoint or the focus of the camera or sensor. These systems are inspired from the biological vision systems and are aimed towards enhancing the perception and interplay of robots with the environment [165–167]. Motivated by the biological vision which is the way animals shift their gaze quickly to focus on different regions of interest, saccadic eye movements are used in active vision systems to quickly relocate the camera or the sensor. This allows the robots to effectively explore and collect information from the environment [168–170]. It is possible for the active vision system to use this fixation to stabilize the camera or sensor and collect detailed information in respect of objects or features [171, 172]. Visual attention mechanisms guide a robot to focus perception resources on specific, important regions within a visual scene [173]. Visual attention is employed in active vision systems to focus the selection of regions for further analysis or action [174]. In active vision systems, perception motivates action and action motivates perception [175]. For instance, the robot could move his camera to better visualize or get another sample of some object or scene in the environment [176, 177]. The active vision system facilitates human-robot interaction to be better, because the system enables a robot to actively perceive and respond to human gesturing, expression, or actions. Through integrated visual attention and action planning, robots can consequently interact more intuitively and effectively with humans in diversities of tasks and scenarios [178, 179].

2.3 Machine Learning in Robotics

Main Theories and Concepts. In robotics, machine learning plays an important part in enabling robots to perceive, learn, and adapt to their environment. [8] In supervised learning, it is said that the robots are trained on the labeled data such that for each training example, the input-output pair is provided. In the case of robotics, this could be object recognition, whereby the robot is trained with labeled images or sensor data to recognize objects [180, 181]. Unsupervised learning involves training models on unlabeled data by which the robot uncovers patterns and structures in the data. [182] Reinforcement learning is the art of learning to take a sequence of decisions to reach the desired goals in an unknown environment by trial and error while at the same time maximizing a cumulative reward [183]. This could be useful for doing tasks like object recognition, or probably characterizing an environment with similarities that would allow robots to be able to find their way about in an environment without human help. Robotics commonly use reinforcement learning for tasks such as robot navigation, grasping objects, or manipulation of objects in a complex environment [184]. Deep learning, a subset of machine learning, is a part that utilizes neural networks which have many layers, especially to extract hierarchical representations from the given data [185]. On the other hand, applications in robotics include tasks like image recognition, natural language processing (used to interact between humans and robots), control of robotic systems, using deep learning methods [8, 186, 187]. Transferring learning in general refers to the ability to take advantage of experience gained from a certain task or from one domain to enhance learning and related performance in a different task or domain. [188] Transfer learning can be made between a robotic task to another, from simulations to the real world, from one robot to another [189, 190]. SLAM is a robotics method for developing a map of an unknown environment while keeping the path of the robot that works in this environment in mind. With the power of modern machine learning, the accuracy and robustness of SLAM systems are able to be taken to a much higher level than before [191–193]. Inverse reinforcement learning is learning a reward function from demonstrations or expert behavior to explain learning toward hidden objectives of a task, useful to infer latent goals within collaborative tasks or to learn from human demonstrations [194, 195]. Probabilistic robotics is a part of robotics that uses probability to formulate with technological advantage problems related to perception, cognition, and control [196]. Probabilistic robotics uses machine learning techniques such as Bayesian inference and probabilistic graphical models in solving a wide range of tasks including localization, mapping, and object tracking [197, 198]. Learning algorithms that can be done online allow the robot to keep updating its models on the go, adjusting to the changes in the environment at hand. This feature is especially important in robotics applications that have dynamic or uncertain environments [181, 199]. These are only a few of the major theories and concepts related to machine learning in robotics, and ongoing research and development in the area is being done to further advance capabilities in robotic systems.

Applications of Machine Learning in Human Assistance. Machine learning in combination with collaborative robots, robotic vision as well as assistive robotics can shape the subject of human assistance in infinite ways. There is, therefore, vast potential for improving the quality of life for the people with disability using assistive robotics and technologies through combined application of collaborative robots, robotic vision and machine learning to give them more control, support, and help in different areas of living [200]. The robots which may help move around people in an environment can be equipped with sensors and cameras. The machine learning flow will train the robot so that it learns how best to navigate through the environments with safety [201]. The robot will thus learn to avoid obstacles in the environment and move towards the required place in great caution [202, 203]. Robotic vision assisted with learning algorithms can help the robots in object recognition and assisting people in fetching objects, organizing things maybe even other simpler tasks like cooking or cleaning [204–208]. Machine learning can further be used to enable assistive technology to, facial expressions, or where people with communication disabilities are able to interact more effectively with robots in making phone calls, sending messages, or even smart home control [209–212]. By applying machine learning, assistive robots may learn from cycles of user's interaction and preferences so as to be in a position to provide personalized assistance [213, 214]. Applying the above technique will enable the robot to adapt its behavior based on the particular needs of the user, his preferences, as well as soliciting for feedback in case of incorrect tasks or operations making it more friendly to interact with [215–217]. Collaborative robots are equipped with the vision sensors and machine learning algorithms to recognize falls or abnormal motions and in time alert a caregiver, or if possible provide necessary assistance to allow the person to stand by himself/herself not executing any care of others autonomously [218–220]. This means that the cognitive assistance systems enable the development of machine learning algorithms to prompt, remind, and guide in a way that enables the persons to perform the daily tasks independently and efficiently [221–223]. Machine learning algorithms could be of help to train assistive robots to recognize the human emotions and show reactions accordingly. Such robots could offer social interaction, companionship as well as emotional support for the disabled people especially with those who are suffering from loneliness or isolation [224, 225]. Machine learning applications incorporated with robotic systems in patient therapy provide adaptive rehabilitation and treatment to patients with physical disabilities [226–228]. The case where such systems adjust prescribed therapy programs based on monitoring and adjustment of therapy session outcomes towards the achievement of desired goals is evident in this respect [229–231]. The sensor-based and machine learning-based collaborative robots assist the visually impaired persons in navigation by sensing and providing the real-time environment relevant information, locating and avoiding the obstacles as well as guiding the persons safely through the indoor and outdoor environments [232–234]. In this sense, machine learning algorithms would be appropriate for the task, since such algorithms may collect on user experiences and interactions with assistive robots to make the robot more reliable in its functionalities over time [235, 236]. Today, new generations of prostheses and exoskeletons are being developed where machine learning techniques adapt their implementation to the movements and inclinations of the users themselves [237, 238]. The sensor data from the user and feedback awarded by the device, therefore, can be looked into and its judgment through the use of a machine learning algorithm helps to establish optimum control strategies which supply good comfort, stability as well as smooth mobility of the persons with limb disabilities [239–241].

2.4   Integration of Collaborative Robots, Robotic Vision, and Machine Learning

Synergies and integration of cobots, robotic vision, and machine learning for human assistance robots represent the modern approach to robot development in the areas where humans live, work, and rest, such as homes, hospitals, and factories. Hybrid systems combine different technologies and approaches to address complex problems more effectively. Within the paradigm of collaborative robotics, robotic vision, and machine learning, such integration of the hybrid systems enables the robots to perform a plurality of tasks in complex environments, while at the same time effectively collaborating with human operators. This involves creating robots that are truly capable of performing the tasks they are assigned to do, whether in a home or in the workplace, across all forms of operations and more or less the spectrum of human activity. Integrating collaborative robots, with robotic vision, and machine learning usually involves a multi-disciplinary effort that requires expertise from the areas of robotics, computer vision, machine learning, and human factors. For the collaborative robots, the robotic vision improves the understanding of its environment and human and objects around it so that to interact with them safely and effectively. For instance, robotic vision can be included in the robot system for the detection of humans through which the robot adapts to the surrounding behavior differences so as to avoid any kind of collision. Machine learning algorithms would boost the adaptiveness and performance of robots in collaboration. For instance, machine learning models can be trained to improve the recognition of objects or even perfect the planning and execution of tasks with regard to the feedback from human operators and sensors. All these would have to be integrated, meaning very carefully designed and engineered in a manner such that there is smooth communication and coordination among all the different components of the robotic system. This could be everything from custom software interfaces and hardware controllers to fusion algorithms for real-time decision-making and action.

Sensor fusion is a technique that allows integrated understanding by robots operating in various environments with different sensing functionalities, such as cameras and force sensors [242]. Model-based control methodologies allow robots to foresee and adjust human actions or human interaction, which ensures that human interaction with the robot is safe and smooth in collaboration settings [243, 244]. Human-centric design principles support the development of human-robot interaction modalities and user interfaces that make communication and collaboration intuitively used [245–247]. User-centric design principles lay more emphasis on the making of natural and user-friendly interfaces through iterative prototyping, gathering user feedback, and using usability tests [248, 249]. Collaboration effectiveness in human-robot teams calls for appropriate task allocation and coordination mechanisms [250, 251]. Natural language processing is what is believed to enable robots to understand and produce human language commands in order to provide a more intuitive style of communication and collaboration with human users. This would involve not only the division of labor between men and machines on the basis of their abilities and inclinations but also the orchestration of their activities to accomplish jointly efficiently the common goals [19, 252]. Adaptive systems can be a set of behaviors that change dynamically according to needs, either because task requirements change or because the user prefers them [253]. A robot operating in dynamic and unpredictable environments will naturally have new situations and challenges continually presented, hence the need for continuous adaptation [254–256]. Safety to human operators and bystanders shall be of the highest consideration position in the design, control, and execution of collaborative robotic systems. This includes proper safety considerations through collision detection and avoidance and is compliant with major ethical values such as transparency, accountability, and respecting the autonomy and dignity of a human [36, 257–259].

Integrating collaborative robots, robotic vision, and machine learning for better assistive operations with humans, hence, results in several challenges, indicated by the above facts:

- **Safety (prime factor):** It has to be observed in relation to the equipment operation and human safety who would be working in collaboration with the robots. High-sensitivity sensors and algorithms are required that would easily detect and respond to human movements, hence avoiding collisions and, most importantly, injuries [257].
- **Human-Robot Interaction (HRI):** Intuitive interfaces and interaction modalities should be designed for an effective teamwork environment of a human with a robot, like enabling its natural language processing, recognizing gestures, or providing any other means for smooth coordination and collaboration [260].
- **Robotic Vision:** The integration of vision systems within robots to allow them to perceive and understand the environment, thus supporting tasks like object recognition, localization, and navigation. Some of the common challenges are occlusions, variable lighting, and real-time processing requirements [87].
- **Machine Learning for Task Adaptation:** Using the machine learning algorithms to adapt the robot to dynamic environments and tasks under key dimensions of versatility and effectiveness is the most demanding topic. Most challenges relate to data acquisition and annotation, algorithm robustness, and real-time learning and adaptation [8].
- **Integration and Interoperability:** Integration involves putting together different elements of a system such as robots, vision systems, and machine learning algorithms while ensuring compatibility and interoperability. This can be highly involving, but efforts at standardization in coordination with modular design principles can help relieve this challenge [261, 262].
- **Ethical and social concerns:** The integration of robots into human environments will give rise to the question of whether robots raise ethical concerns of privacy, job displacement, and the impacts of automation on society. It is also of prime importance that assistive operations should ensure an increase in human capability but not replace human workers [3].
- **Reliability and Fault Tolerance:** Dependability is one highly desirable quality of execution of the assistive operations, particularly in safety-critical environments such as healthcare and manufacturing. Building a system which is robust against unexpected conditions and tolerates errors while it continuously maintains the safe operations is one of the major challenges [263].
- **Cost and Scalability:** Whereas the use of integration hybrid systems might cost companies, especially those that are categorized under small and medium enterprises, ensuring cost-effective solutions without harming performance is a paramount challenge. Besides, scalability—ensuring the system can handle several workloads and environments—results in added complexity.

2.5   Ethical and Social Implications

As the assistive robotics technologies mature, due attention is required to proactively address the ethical and social implications with maximal benefit to people while minimizing potential risks and harms to them and society. It is here where effective collaboration between researchers, policymakers, industry stakeholders, and end-users could ensure that assistive robots are developed and deployed in a responsible and ethical manner. Ethical considerations will assure that the cobots are programmed with overriding emphasis on human safety and concern for well-being; it respects human autonomy and decision-making authority. Ethical implications are in ensuring that vision algorithms be reliable and accurate in their operations, especially during critical tasks like navigation or manipulation of objects, and respect the privacy by capturing only relevant visual information. It should be based on clear regulatory frameworks, which are to govern development and deployment based on the safety, privacy, and ethical considerations of assistive robotics. Today, there is an increasing role of ethical guidelines and standards with regard to the design, development, and deployment of assistive robotics. This goes as far even into such matters as privacy, safety, transparency, accountability, and fairness in the machine learning algorithms applicable to these systems [264]. There is a growing recognition of the importance of human-centered design principles in creating assistive robots. This will involve the understanding of needs, preferences, and capabilities of end-users (including people with disabilities or elderly persons) and taking their feedback on board at every step of the design process, in order to render technology meeting its requirements as well as ensuring respect for dignity and autonomy [3, 28, 265]. There is an increasing importance for transparent and explainable machine learning algorithms, for various reasons—one such reason is their pivotal roles in assistive robotics. Trust is a highly important issue to assure the user that the robot within acceptable safety and security bounds will exercise its capacities and make proper decisions, according to the design of the system [266, 267]. Privacy issues and data security still seem to loom up front in relation to assistive robots collecting and using personal data. Strong privacy-preserving techniques and security measures to safeguard sensitive information from unauthorized access or misuse of data are in development [268–271]. In regard to bias and fairness in machine learning algorithms implemented by assistive robotics, this is an emerging need in the field. As such, researchers are looking into how these can be designed in ways that understand and help them mitigate biases in data and algorithms so that such assistive robots may provide equal assistance to anyone regardless of their background or characteristics [272–274].

In conclusion to all of the above, the application of Assistive Robotics is guided by several key ethical and social implications and principles:

- **Privacy Issues:** Most of the datasets contain potentially sensitive information about individuals, and access privacy would be useful in helping to decrease risks in violation of privacy that may result from misuse of the data or any access for its unintended use. Observance of the individual's rights in regards to their privacy and confidentiality when in contact with assistive robots, encompasses the effective application of measures for protection of data at risk of being leaked by robotic systems in service delivery and provides for user control in regard to personal data [271, 275].
- **Bias in Data and Fairness:** Machine learning algorithms can perpetuate or even exacerbate biases within the data on which they are trained. This will lead to unfair treatment or discrimination of certain people or groups, especially if services are personalized [273].
- **Dependence and Autonomy:** As human beings continue to look up to assistive robots in executing different activities, the risk exists for an erosion of people's autonomy and the nurturing of dependency. This might bring up ethical considerations such as that of human dignity and loss of self-sufficiency. Ensuring that individuals maintain

autonomy and control over their actions and decisions even when assisted by robots is very important. The crucial principle here is that the human being has to remain the ultimate decision-maker about everything that concerns his or her life, while robots are rather tools to help than to substitute [276, 277].

- **Job Displacement and Economic Impact:** Assistive robotics, being extensively deployed, may compel job displacement in different sectors or even occupations, especially those that entail work with a repetitive or routine nature. This has implications on the moral or ethical issues of the mentioned technological unemployment and the need for retraining programs [278–280].
- **Equity of Access:** Surely, the access of assistive robotics devices may be linked with the disparities on the basis of the socioeconomic status, geographical location, or disability status of the person. Accordingly, equal access to the devices may serve to ensure the prevention from widening social inequalities [281].
- **Safety and Reliability:** Cobot systems operating in close collaboration with humans must comply with the highest level of safety regulations that would prevent accidents or injuries. Reliability of the systems is also another highly wanted feature, since errors and malfunctions could cause serious risk to human users [282, 283].
- **Ethical Decision Making:** Robots based on machine learning algorithms may encounter the necessity to make an ethical decision in real time; for instance, task prioritization or reaction to unforeseen situations. It is a difficult problem to ensure that these systems make ethical decisions aligned with societal values [284].
- **Beneficence and Nonmaleficence:** Care must be given in the design of robots and systems that will fully meet the effective need of the user with a view to benefiting and not causing harm to such a user. Harm should not be inflicted on individuals via assistive robotics. This involves reducing the risks of injury, pain or any other injury that may result from the interaction with robots or mistakes in robotic systems [285, 286].
- **Human-Robot Interaction:** The design of the human-robot interaction interfaces indeed plays a big role in designing the user experience and defining the ethical consequences of the assistive robotics. It involves designing transparency in the capabilities and limitations of the robot, obtaining consent from the user, and control of the robot [287].
- **Inclusivity and Diversity:** The assistive robotics systems designed should hence be able to consider the various needs, preferences, and capabilities of the users. It may therefore involve looking into such considerations as cultural diversity, language diversity, as well as the range in potential levels of physical or cognitive abilities in order to achieve the general use of assistive technologies to as wide a circle of people as possible [288, 289].

3   Case Studies and Applications

The past few years have seen great strides in the application of assistive robotics to many aspects of human assistance. Assisted robotics incorporating collaborative robots, robotic vision, and machine learning in giving human support and assistance actually emerge from different application scenarios in the case studies brought out in this paper. Continued research and development in this area have tremendous potential to improve the quality of life of users and independence in the whole world. As is going to be seen in the forthcoming chapters, there are a very large number of different assistive robotics solutions, such as: Autonomous wheelchair navigation; Smart home assistance; Prosthetic limb control; Assistive exoskeletons; Vision-based object recognition for the visually impaired; Personal care assistance; Autonomous rehabilitation systems; Assistive telepresence robots; Social companion robots; Cognitive assistance systems; Assistive robotic arms; Assistive robots for education; and many others. In this chapter, only a few current case studies will be presented.

3.1 Smart Prosthetics and Exoskeletons

A Semiautonomous Control Strategy Based on Computer Vision for a Hand–Wrist Prosthesis [237]

This paper presents a novel semiautonomous control system (SCS) for hand–wrist prostheses with the use of a Computer Vision System (CVS) integrated in the prosthesis. The SCS is a combination of exteroceptive sensing with the intention of the user obtained from simulated EMG signals to enable reliable prosthesis control. The system is based on three sequential processing steps: Object Detection, Grasp Selection, and Orientation Estimation. Figure 1 shows the Block scheme on the proposed approach.

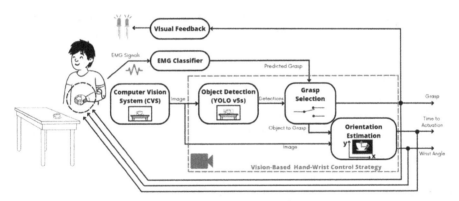

Fig. 1. Block scheme of the proposed approach for Computer Vision based Hand–Wrist Prosthesis [237]

The CVS identifies the objects in the scene and maps them with the grasp configurations based on the user intention, using the YOLOv5 for real-time object detection. The Grasp Selection module ensures coherence between user intention and the detected objects, while the Orientation Estimation module estimates wrist orientation using Principal Component Analysis (PCA) on the segmented regions of interest. Visual feedback using LEDs to alert coherence with the intention and object detection, too. High accuracy ($>97\%$) in object classification and grasping validated experimentally, average angular estimation error $\leq 18°$, stability $\leq 0.8°$. The system achieved a frame analysis frequency of 2.07 FPS. Performance was influenced by camera resolution in which, nonetheless,

240p resolution has better performance in comparison to 480p. The system also showed robustness in complex scenarios, which of a 100% successful phase in recognizing object approaching phases. Future work is expected to follow through with the CVS integration into the prosthetic hand for user testing and further characterization regarding usability aspects and performance metrics. The proposed SCS based on CVS looks promising to enhance prosthesis control performance because of its accuracy, speed, and robustness toward handling complex scenarios. The system is thus portable and has a high level of interoperability, which allows it to be applied to various prosthetic hands and robotic grippers. Future research will focus on user testing and system refinement to optimize usability and performance metrics.

3.2 Autonomous Wheelchairs and Mobility Aids

Autonomous Movement of Wheelchair by Cameras and YOLOv7 [290]

This case study introduces the development of a smart wheelchair focusing on the customization of an octascopic vision of a manually controlled wheelchair. The low-cost autonomous wheelchair integrates two monochromatic camera arrays with 4 cameras each to achieve a 360-degree view. The aim was to design a wheelchair controlled by an embedded processor for indoor autonomous navigation of the physically challenged people with limited mobility because of financial constraints. In the conducted research, extensive testing was executed, and a big set of octascopic images was collected and a YOLOv7-based object detection model was developed to facilitate obstacle avoidance and autonomous movement. This makes an important point in the study that autonomic movement for wheelchairs can be realized by an approach using neural networks and robotic vision. The running real-time object detection system is YOLOv7, in which converged faster and highly precise compared to traditional LiDAR-based systems. The paper details the camera installation process using custom parts to mount the cameras on the wheelchair and connects them through Arducam quadrascopic monochrome camera arrays. The YOLOv7 model was trained with custom classes and annotated using the Labelimg library, where a maximum of 92% mean average precision (mAP) was achieved after 200 epochs of training. The potential of vision sensor arrays and deep learning models in revolutionizing wheelchair technology is therefore highlighted. Object detection models optimized for low power consumption and an ROS-based wheelchair operating system could be some of the possible research directions in the future. The work presented in this paper should be considered as an attempt to design a new system to transfer to an electric car, taking into account current and future electric cars. Thus, the paper has highlighted the promising future of autonomous wheelchairs with the aid of octoscopic vision and state-of-the-art neural network algorithms. The openness of the project design files encourages collaboration and innovation on wheelchair technology toward the improvement of the lives of people with disabilities, both in personal mobility and independence.

3.3 Home Assistance Robots

CHARMIE: A Collaborative Healthcare and Home Service and Assistant Robot for Elderly Care [291]

CHARMIE is an acronym for Collaborative Healthcare and Home Service Assistant Robot for Elderly Care, which brings needed support to aged people who are getting more vulnerable due to global aging, cognitive and physical challenges, and increased single-person households. The robotic system that uses the neural network is easily able to perform map building, safe navigation, human-robot interaction, and also carry out object manipulation activities over any kind of environment. Design in hardware development turns anthropomorphic, which underlines the enhancement of user interaction and adaptability with the human environment. The use of omnidirectional wheels is seen to offer stability and security which is critically needed in a dynamic environment. A lifting mechanism and torso that provides multi-axial movement for object manipulation in order to meet the varied needs of the users. The multi-degrees-of-freedom robotic arm is adopted to let the manipulator function like a human arm. The effective work requires certain components like the multi-degrees-of-freedom robotic manipulator, electrical and mechanical designing, microcontroller, multiplexer, control circuit, and the display. Figure 2 shows CHARMIE different variations.

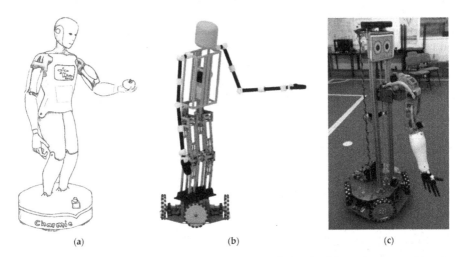

(a)   (b)   (c)

Fig. 2. CHARMIE in different variations: (a) Conceptual sketch of the anthropomorphic robot (b) Developed anthropomorphic design (c) Primary prototype assembled [291]

In its mapping and SLAM module, CHARMIE performs data fusion of the available sensors: 2D LiDAR and the RGB-D camera for complete maps of the entire environment and thus maps for self-localization. The sensors are used for detecting obstacles for safe navigation of the environment. Human-robot interactions are allowed by recognizing gestures and poses with an RGB-D data camera, allowing greater interaction between the user and tasks. With the use of YOLOv3 algorithm to detect objects, it can carry out real-time detection and manipulation of household items and health-related items. CHARMIE is designed to be capable of assisting a broad array of applications from groceries, retrieval of items, checking the fall of patients, and tracking a user from one point to the other. These functionalities are designed to better the life of the elderly people and assist the healthcare workers in difficult environments. Moreover, CHARMIE is a novel tool in tackling offered challenges by COVID-19 in safe alternatives concerning healthcare aid and risk reduction related to person-to-person contact. Future work will be directed towards improvement in terms of mobility support and range of tasks, after thorough real-life testing at homes and care facilities. This is in order to ensure the realization of a socially assistive robot that will have an impact on the quality of life of people who come into contact with it.

3.4 Assistive Robotic Arms

Safely and Autonomously Cutting Meat with a Collaborative Robot Arm [292]

The paper assesses the use of a robot arm for meat processing tasks with respect to its collaborative characteristics aimed at curbing labour shortages facing the meat processing industry. Technologies so far in use in automation in this sector lack collaboration potential, flexibility, and cost effectivity. The study is aimed at providing for human safety and automation betterment with the help of machine learning and robotic vision. Figure 3 shows A multi-purpose collaborative robot arm for meat processing: (Left) A human collaborator places meat in front of the robot. The robot detects the location of the meat using an attached camera. Under proposed framework, the robot might plan and take action to perform desired cuts processing the meat on its own, or the robot could collaborate with the human to plan the cuts to perform. (Right) In the context of experiments, this frame is used to process the pork loin by cutting it into several pieces, removing the fat from these cuts and finally cutting the meat into cubes.

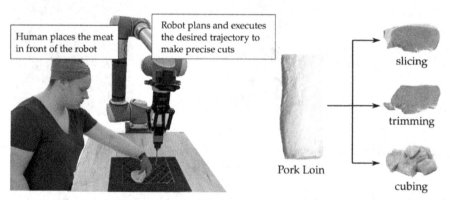

Fig. 3. A multi-purpose collaborative robot arm for meat processing [292]

In terms of safety, the robot arm motion is limited around the cutting board according to ISO/TS 15066 guidelines governing collaboration with robots. The constraint in motion, together with an instrumented knife fitted with proximity and IMU sensors for close contact with meat, is used to lower collision risks. Machine learning algorithms are trained to sense slicing, trimming, and cubing contacts properly. Vision and control algorithms enable the arm of a robot to have a clear procedure of working with meat both independently and interactively. There is a camera attached on the arm to provide images of a cutting board and the meat, processed for identification of meat and fat. It plans cuts trajectories according to the detected meat, and a controller guarantees exact following the planned cut. Experiments prove the effectiveness of the system on slicing pork loins into chops, trimming fat, cubing. The results show that around 70% of the autonomous fat removing cuts by the robot are rated fair or good by the industry experts in respect to the meat product dimensions and meet with the acceptable standard in the industry. Marker guides cuts with human collaboration. The study develops a new collaborative meat-processing approach with machine learning and robotic vision technologies to enhance automation with high safety and precision. The results pointed towards some potential improvements in terms of job satisfaction across the supply chain as well as product availability within the meat industry. The latter would be extended to performance improvement research and the generalization of safety protocols on more diverse cutting tasks and objects.

3.5 Vision-Based Navigation and Autonomous Robotic Guides for the Blind and Visually Impaired Individuals

Assistive Navigation Using Deep Reinforcement Learning Guiding Robot With UWB/Voice Beacons and Semantic Feedbacks for Blind and Visually Impaired People [234]

This study presents an assistive navigation aid for the blind and visually impaired individuals (BVI) using Deep Reinforcement Learning (DRL) aided by robotic vision technology. Ultrawide-bandwidth (UWB) beacons accompany a guiding robot along with a handle device for interaction integrated into the system. Indeed, some common navigation approaches such as SLAM tend to suffer from problems in such dynamic environments. In this respect, the DRL-based method introduced in this work allows for efficient navigation of the robot through specially marked waypoints avoiding obstacles, especially if assisted by UWB beacons considering their use in dynamic pedestrian environments. The handle device provides point-of-interest and turn-by-turn verbal command along with intuitive feedback for BVI users. The guiding robot, similar to the Clearpath Jackal UGV, is outfitted with perceptual sensors LiDAR, depth cameras, as well as mmWave modules. The computation units of the setup consist of an Intel NUC computer and an NVIDIA Jetson TX2 embedded system for carrying out various processing tasks. The system is equipped with a Pozyx UWB module and UniFi WiFi access point that enable localizing and communication functionalities. The UWB/voice beacons, self-sustained with Raspberry Pi computers communicate verbal feedback and are facilitated for real-time monitoring. The DRL algorithm has been designed to navigate waypoints and pick up goal data with the use of either SLAM or UWB localization, in addition to having the requirement of environmental data coming from LiDAR point clouds. This algorithm enables the navigation and collision avoidance tasks by a guiding robot for BVI users. Ranges are estimated by UWB/Voice beacons which act as the thresholds for switching waypoints, and the handle provides semantic feedback. Figure 4 shows key components of the proposed system.

A DRL-based navigation approach has been proposed that trains a model using Distributed Distributional Deep Deterministic Policy Gradient (D4PG), extracts information from LiDAR data and goal points with respect to the robot. The network architectures of critic and actor are similar, which extract features from the LiDAR data. The trained

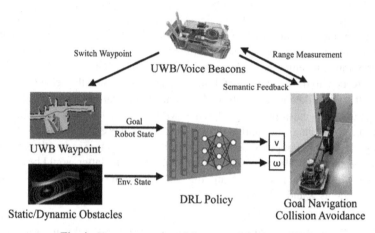

Fig. 4. Key components of the proposed system [234]

agent directly selects optimal control commands without path planning, thereby enhancing the navigation efficiency. The experimental results show us that both DRL and UWB localization are better than the existing SLAM-based methods, especially in dynamic obstacle environments. The user studies show us that the BVI will feel that the application is useful for helping them navigate through unfamiliar environments. Further mentions of the research directions include increasing comfort levels, increase in the number of UWB beacons to cut down effects by dynamic obstacles, betterment in audio cues for user-friendly navigation.

3.6   Assistive Robots for Autism Therapy

Augmenting Mobile App with NAO Robot for Autism Education [293]
The study focuses on the integration of humanoid robots, specifically the NAO robot, with the mobile application to improve education for children with the autism spectrum disorder (ASD). The NAO robot, by a mobile application, was applied as a socially assistive robotic (SAR) tool in classrooms. The children at the age of three to six with mild to moderate symptoms of ASD composed the experiment and were divided into two groups. Results suggest more interaction with and more eye contact towards the NAO robot in the experimental group in comparison to the control group. Some limitations were in the robot's ability to conduct concurrent interactions, language barriers, and restrictions in battery and internet access. Proposed system capabilities should include the ability to communicate with children, repeating commands endlessly, portability, dialogues with the robot to understand a child with autism spectrum disorder, facial recognition execution properly, children's answers taken by the system, organizing lessons, individual tracking of progress, simple and reliable usability, high-performance, accuracy, availability, and usability Fig. 5 shows NAO robot performing at the preschool with autistic children during lesson sessions.

Flexibility, mobility, facial and environmental recognition, and voice capabilities are the intrinsic characteristics of Softbank Robotics' NAO robot that makes it a very

(a) Movement lesson

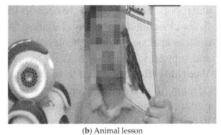
(b) Animal lesson

Fig. 5. NAO robot performing at the preschool with autistic children during lesson sessions [293]

competitive candidate in this application. The whole architecture of the system: from the Python and C++ and programming of the NAO robot in Choregraphe to the Java programming of the smartphone app, and finally, to the data management part utilizing Firebase. The lessons cover different themes depending on the interests of children, and are done in a safe and guided setting. Results indicate significant improvements in eye contact, specifically across autism levels. The frequency of eye contact does not increase much with age. Challenges are in engaging children, technical constraints such as level of interaction concurrently, language barriers, battery life, and internet problems. These limitations need to be addressed in future research so that the use of these educational aids is optimized for autistic children. The integration of robots and AI holds out promising opportunities to reach the educational needs of autistic children effectively, thus promoting more inclusive and personalized learning.

4 Future Directions and Challenges

Recapping the overview of the field as given in this paper along with the case studies available, this chapter will give a brief outline of future directions and challenges in assistive robotics considering the integration of collaborative robots, robot vision and machine learning.

4.1 Emerging Trends in Assistive Robotics

A series of developmental trends has been going on within the assistive robotics domain, shaping it towards evolving trends and developments giving it more opportunity to innovate and take capabilities forward towards better response in the area of disability and aging populations. Such growing trends and developments denote the evolvement of assistive robotics toward more advanced, user-centric, and socially impactful solutions. Ongoing research, collaboration, and innovation in these domains have the potential to contribute toward further independence, autonomy, and improved quality of life of persons with different sorts of disabilities and the elderly populations as well. The emerging key trends are as follows:

- **Soft Robotics for Comfort and Safety:** Soft Robotics is a newly growing and emerging field which promises more compliant and flexible structures in the assistive devices and robots. Soft robotics have benefits including comfort, safety, and adaptability to be fit for close interaction with humans. Soft robotic exosuits, prosthetics, and assistive devices are continuing to be suitable for giving assistance in mobility, rehabilitation, and support in activities of daily living [294–296].

- **Wearable Robotics and Exoskeletons:** Wearable robotics and exoskeletons are developing as assistive technologies of augmentation in mobility and physical rehabilitation. The idea is to augment human natural movements with robotic structures in order to multiply the strength and endurance of the user for the purpose of letting him or her realize activities that would be hard or impossible to accomplish without support. Advanced materials, lightweight, and ergonomic designs with control algorithms are, thus, some of the continuous developments that are being made in the wearable robot in its quest for enhanced practicality and accessibility to a broader range of users [9, 297–299].

- **Brain-Computer Interface (BCI) for Direct Neural Control:** BCIs are now allowing direct communication between the human brain and assistive robots, such that even if a person is severely motor-disabled, he or she can still use thought to control a robotic device. New emerging developments in non-invasive and implantable BCI technologies will ensure new ways of moving, with enhanced speed, accuracy, and reliability of controlling the neural system [300–303].

- **Socially Assistive Robots for Emotional Support:** These are normally designed to offer the much-needed emotional support, companionship, and social interaction among the users, especially the aged and other persons with either cognitive or mental health conditions. It is based on psychology and human-computer interaction skills, where it uses the acquired information to engage in conversation with others, mental exercises, and fun games among each other to bring about well-being and reduce feelings of loneliness and isolation [304, 305].

- **Personalized and Adaptable AI and Machine Learning-based Assistance:** As the pool of available AI and machine learning algorithms keeps on growing and diversifying, assistive robots continue to get better in the way they adapt to the needs and preferences of a person while supporting. Not only can they learn from their interactions with users and adjust their behavior in the course of time, but also anticipate the needs of the user based on context cues and history. Personalized assistance augments user satisfaction and user engagement and, at the same time, enhances general efficiency of assistive robotics systems [8, 39, 306].

- **Mobile Apps and Cloud Connectivity for Remote Monitoring and Assistance:** Integrating an assistive robotics platform with mobile applications and cloud connectivity enabled the patient to interact with assistance robots, view information in real time, and even seek assistance from a remote carer through their mobiles or other connected gadgets. This means remote connectivity to the above deals more with accessibilities and convenience in a place not accessible or getting care from remote carer [307–311].

- **Human-Centered Design and Co-Creation:** Increasing importance is attributed to human-centered design and co-creation in helping assistive robotics solutions to be realized. Close collaboration among the researchers, engineers and the end-users will be facilitated in a way that the assistive robots with the dimension of usability, acceptance, and inclusiveness are designed in such a way that they conform to the needs and preference of the user. Co-creation, therefore, encapsulates a certain process by which the users have been included in the design process—right from ideation and prototyping up to testing and refinement—making the results more intuitive, effective, and empowering assistive robotics solutions for the users [312–315].

4.2 Addressing Remaining Challenges

Integrating collaborative robots, robot vision, and machine learning into assistive robotics is one sure way to take us to the future, but this way has its sets of challenges too. Meeting these challenges will require a concerted effort by researchers, developers, policy makers, and users in order to invent new solutions that will be able to meet the diverse needs of people who need assistive support, and which will also be safe, reliable, and sensitive to any related ethical issues. Some of the yet to be addressed challenges include:

- **Robustness and Reliability:** Perhaps more critical will be that these assistive robots can carry out all the real-world tasks reliably; that is, error-free and without failure. Perception functions need to be robust under variant lighting, cluttered environments, and scenarios with unpredictable human behaviors [9, 316].
- **Human-Robot Interaction (HRI):** Regarding the human-robot interaction, the design has to be intuitive and natural mainly for this kind of robot in assistive robotics, primarily thinking of the kind of user who in general terms can be termed as non-expert in technical. The challenge is to get interfaces that are user-friendly and can be adaptable to a variety of users, communicating information and instructions effectively [185, 287, 317].
- **Safety:** Safety of the users and all concerned is to be paramount in assistive robotics. Collaborative robots are expected to have the potential to sense people, recognize their location and movement, and thus bring in the corrective or preventive action in order to thwart any collision or mishap, particularly when a robot is in play within a dynamic surrounding and the safety of vulnerable individuals at hand is in question [24, 36].
- **Adaptability and flexibility:** It is an enormous challenge how functionalities of assistive robots may apply to a broad spectrum of tasks and environments. Enabling the robots to adapt and learn new environments or tasks, independently or semi-independently, is, in itself, a challenge. That involves developing flexible algorithms that can effectively generalize from past experiences to new situations [9, 24, 318, 319].
- **Ethical and Social Issues:** Bringing assistive robots into society imposes ethical concerns regarding privacy, autonomy, and a possible shift of human workers. Dealing with these concerns will, in turn, presuppose responsible deployment and usage, connoting a wide-ranging discussion of the social ramifications of assistive robotics and consequently the formulation of pertinent policies and regulations [3, 36].
- **Data Privacy and Security:** An assistive robot could collect information about sensitive features of its users, for instance personal health issues, or the routine activities. Secure data related to the above will serve as the key to trustworthiness of users.

Ensure that the data of the user is properly protected from being accessed and misused by unauthorized persons by securing it with good methods of encryption and strictly enforced access controls [27, 320].

- **Integration and scalability:** Are not easily achievable when putting together the robots for collaboration, robot vision, and machine learning algorithms in one integrated system. It denotes that all such integrate smoothly among them while being scalable and interoperable across different hardware platforms and software frameworks and this is a hard challenge required to be faced for going into any wide deployment [261, 321].
- **Costs and access:** Thus, robotic solutions should be quite low in costs to the majority of people, having some portion of impoverished or low-technological populations able to purchase the technology. This is a point that is really very hard to reach—the cost-effectiveness without the quality and performance getting compromised—especially when the high development and production costs are concerned for the advanced robotics technologies [322, 323].

4.3 Opportunities for Future Research and Development

The potential future domains of research and development in the assistive robotics domain are very large, and in particular, the growing demand in these domains for collaborative robots, robot vision, and machine learning technologies is focused in the same area. Therefore, to concentrate on these areas of research and development in the assistive robotics area will mean that this is an area of work that will continue to make leaps and bounds in solving the ever-growing requirement of people needing help in living their daily lives. Here are some of the areas where advancements have the potential of creating a huge impact on assistive robotics:

- **Human-Robot Interaction (HRI):** Make interfaces more intuitive and natural in interacting with the intended users and assistive robots, for example, including speech recognition, gesture recognition, and haptic interfaces. Embrace ways through which robots can understand and answer in a manner similar to a human towards his or her emotions, intentions, and preferences, so that collaboration and communication are more easily supported [324–326].
- **Collaborative Robotics:** Development of advanced control algorithms and safety mechanisms enabling safe physical interaction between the robots and humans to let them work together and help each other closely. Development of advanced designs of shared-autonomy techniques, by which the robots modulate their level of autonomy according to the capabilities and preferences of a user [39, 327–329].
- **Robot Vision:** Enhancing the robot's abilities for object recognition and scene understanding, so that the robot can better assist the user in the manipulation of objects or in moving around in complex environments, or even give contextual information to the user. Enhancing the depth perception and awareness of spatial perception for better and more exhaustive grasping of dynamic environments by the robots to assist the users in doing spatial reasoning [46, 120, 179, 330].
- **Machine Learning:** Developing deep learning, reinforced learning, and transfer learning in machine intelligence that would let robots adjust and learn from interaction and feedback of users. Enhancing the assistive systems that will adjust to

the idiosyncratic preferences of individual users, their levels of abilities, and their changing needs over time. Exploring human-in-the-loop learning techniques—where the robots can actively request clarification or feedback from the users to improve performance, and to learn new tasks [331–334].

- **Assistive Manipulation and Mobility:** Developing dextrous manipulation ability to enable the users to perform tasks such as feeding, dressing, and personal care. Design of intelligent mobility aids that are able to empower the independence in crossing different terrains and environments to users with disabilitie [45, 335, 336].

- **Ethical and Social Considerations:** Ethical considerations in regard to the use of assistive robots, including issues of privacy, autonomy, and the effect that it could have on employment and social relationships. Design of assistive robots for inclusiveness and accessibility, responsive to diversity in needs and preferences of the user [337, 338].

- **Long Term Autonomy and Maintenance:** Developing energy-efficient systems and at the same time durable and fully operational in the long term are needed that, hence, decrease the necessity of continuous and repetitive recharging and maintenance. Research and development of systems that have self-diagnosis as well as the self-repair systems are necessary to search for those who can pinpoint a problem and repair it well in advance of when it would affect the robot's capability of facilitating users efficiently [328, 339].

- **Cost Effectiveness:** Research cost effective ways of bringing down the price of assistive robots to make them accessible to more categories of users such as those with limited financial means or living in less developed regions [322].

5 Conclusion

In recent years, the combination of collaborative robots, robotic vision, and machine learning has brought about the era of remarkable strides in assistive robotics and transformational solutions in meeting the challenges of aging populations and individuals with disabilities. Convergence of these technologies has now emerged as a ray of hope to be able to provide individuals to live independently and in well-being, while societies are wrestling with demographic shifts coupled with increased demands on support systems'.

We have only touched the fundamentals, current trends, and future outlooks of assisted robotics in the paper. In bringing together new developments, challenges, and opportunities, a kind of spectrum of impacts these technologies can possibly have on human assistance is established.

Through collaborative robots, robotic vision and machine learning has unveiled possibilities on the journey so far. Taking collaborative robots developed to work safely beside people for an example, it shows an interesting way to take up the richness of physical assistance and support. Robotic vision enables the eyes of assistive systems, which allow them to look at and interpret the environment with keenness never experienced before, whereas machine learning algorithms provide the cognitive capabilities that would lead to adaptability and personalized assistance in the pursuit of the diverse user needs.

With these potentials, both case studies and real-world applications have shown the transformative potential of integrating assistive robotics in the domains of health and rehabilitation, elder care, and independent living. These instances show not only how assistive robotics can be effective but also that issues related to safety, reliability, and ethics need to be faced.

Trends in the next decade, like soft robotics, wearable exoskeletons, brain-computer interfaces, and socially assistive robots, promise even further advance in assistive robotics. Through human-centered design, co-creation, and continuous innovation, the power of the researchers and developers will aid in co-creating the best solutions technically as well as from the user- and society-friendly perspective.

However, there remain several key challenges along this road. Robustness, reliability, human-robot interaction, safety, adaptability, ethical considerations, and cost-effectiveness are some of the key issues that require concerted and joint efforts from the stakeholders in the academia, industry, and policy-making arenas.

The human-centric approaches, interdisciplinary collaboration, and development of innovative technologies will be critical to manage these challenges in future research and development. Only then can the full potential of integrated assistive robotics be developed to revolutionize how to ensure care and support for people with a wide range of needs.

In short, integrating collaborative robots, robotic vision, and machine learning can do much toward human assistance and an enhanced quality of life. By overcoming challenges, capturing opportunities, and in dedication towards user-centric principles, we would like to meaningfully pave the way forward for assistive robotics to change lives and bring inclusivity, dignity, and independence to one and all.

Acknowledgments. The authors wish to highlight the significant contribution of human intellect in crafting this scientific paper. It must be pointed out and stressed that this research article was solely written with the solo input from human beings to enhance its quality and work process efficiently through digital and AI-driven tools.

The forthcoming publication of this paper at MoStart - International Conference on Digital Transformation in Education and Artificial Intelligence Applications underscores the alignment of our research with the conference theme "Digital assistants and assistive technologies". We express thanks to digital and AI-assisted tools that have made indispensable contributions structuring the scientific content, sourcing relevant literature, useful in this paper, automating citation and referencing other authors' published works, searching key concepts inside literature units, translation, grammar and spell checking, paraphrasing, summarizing other scholarly works used as references.

The authors wish to express his special thanks for the following – special digital and AI-assisted tools that helped them to prepare and qualitatively arrange this paper: QuillBot, ChatGPT, Mendeley, GPTinf, Google Translate, GPTZero, Grammarly, Plagiarism Detector, SCISPACE and ChatPDF. This attests to the cardinal importance of the human intellect together with technological progress and can thus underscore the purpose as well as prospective use of digital assistants and assistive technologies in different research undertakings.

Note: This Acknowledgment above is written by human author in Croatian and then translated into English with Google Translate, then subsequently inserted into ChatGPT for rewriting and is later subjected to grammatical and orthographic processing and paraphrasing in QuillBot. After that, the text was analyzed by GPTZero, and the results were: "We are highly confident this text is entirely human" and "0% Probability AI generated".

References

1. Cortellessa, G., et al.: AI and robotics to help older adults: revisiting projects in search of lessons learned. Paladyn **12**, 356–378 (2021)
2. Weerarathna, I.N., Raymond, D., Luharia, A.: Human-robot collaboration for healthcare: a narrative review. Cureus **15** (2023)
3. Boada, J.P., Maestre, B.R., Genís, C.T.: The ethical issues of social assistive robotics: a critical literature review. Technol. Soc. **67** (2021)
4. Tsarouchi, P., Makris, S., Chryssolouris, G.: Human–robot interaction review and challenges on task planning and programming. Int. J. Comput. Integr. Manuf. **29**, 916–931 (2016)
5. Makris, S., Michalos, G., Dimitropoulos, N., Krueger, J., Haninger, K.: Seamless human–robot collaboration in industrial applications. In: Tolio, T. (ed.) CIRP Novel Topics in Production Engineering: Volume 1. Lecture Notes in Mechanical Engineering, pp. 39–73. Springer, Cham (2024). https://doi.org/10.1007/978-3-031-54034-9_2
6. Zhang, D., Lee, D.-J., Licardo, J.T., Domjan, M., Orehovački, T.: Intelligent robotics—a systematic review of emerging technologies and trends. Electron. **13**, 542 (2024)
7. Su, H., et al.: Recent advancements in multimodal human–robot interaction. Front. Neurorobot. **17**, 1084000 (2023)
8. Soori, M., Arezoo, B., Dastres, R.: Artificial intelligence, machine learning and deep learning in advanced robotics, a review. Cogn. Robot. **3**, 54–70 (2023)
9. Martinez-Hernandez, U., et al.: Wearable assistive robotics: a perspective on current challenges and future trends. Sensors **21**, 6751 (2021)
10. Semeraro, F., Griffiths, A., Cangelosi, A.: Human–robot collaboration and machine learning: a systematic review of recent research. Robot. Comput. Integr. Manuf. **79**, 102432 (2023)
11. Irfan, B., et al.: Personalised socially assistive robot for cardiac rehabilitation: critical reflections on long-term interactions in the real world. User Model. User-Adapt. Interact. **332**(33), 497–544 (2022)
12. Canal, G., Torras, C., Alenyà, G.: Are preferences useful for better assistance?: a physically assistive robotics user study. ACM Trans. Human-Robot Interact. **10** (2021)
13. Olatunji, S.A., et al.: Advancing the design of trustworthy robots for older adults in home environments: a participatory design approach. **67**, 2545–2551 (2023). https://doi.org/10.1177/21695067231205566
14. Baratta, A., Cimino, A., Longo, F., Nicoletti, L.: Digital twin for human-robot collaboration enhancement in manufacturing systems: literature review and direction for future developments. Comput. Ind. Eng. **187**, 109764 (2024)
15. Hagos, D.H., Rawat, D.B.: Recent advances in artificial intelligence and tactical autonomy: current status, challenges, and perspectives. Sensors (Basel). **22** (2022)
16. Vermesan, O., et al.: Internet of robotic things intelligent connectivity and platforms. Front. Robot. AI **7**, 509753 (2020)
17. Bekbolatova, M., Mayer, J., Ong, C.W., Toma, M.: Transformative potential of AI in healthcare: definitions, applications, and navigating the ethical landscape and public perspectives. Healthcare **12** (2024)
18. Bajwa, J., Munir, U., Nori, A., Williams, B.: Artificial intelligence in healthcare: transforming the practice of medicine. Futur. Healthc. J. **8**, e188 (2021)
19. Zhang, C., Chen, J., Li, J., Peng, Y., Mao, Z.: Large language models for human–robot interaction: a review. Biomim. Intell. Robot. **3**, 100131 (2023)

20. Najjar, R., Najjar, R.: Digital frontiers in healthcare: integrating mHealth, AI, and radiology for future medical diagnostics (2024). https://doi.org/10.5772/INTECHOPEN.114142

21. Zanatta, F., Giardini, A., Pierobon, A., D'Addario, M., Steca, P.: A systematic review on the usability of robotic and virtual reality devices in neuromotor rehabilitation: patients' and healthcare professionals' perspective. BMC Heal. Serv. Res. **221**(22), 1–16 (2022)

22. Singh, D.K., Kumar, M., Fosch-Villaronga, E., Singh, D., Shukla, J.: Ethical considerations from child-robot interactions in under-resourced communities. Int. J. Soc. Robot. **15**, 2055–2071 (2023)

23. Kok, B.C., Soh, H.: Trust in robots: challenges and opportunities. Curr. Robot. Rep. **14**(1), 297–309 (2020)

24. Cooper, S., Ros, R., Lemaignan, S.: Challenges of deploying assistive robots in real-life scenarios: an industrial perspective (2023). https://doi.org/10.1109/RO-MAN57019.2023.10309467

25. Stahl, B.C., Coeckelbergh, M.: Ethics of healthcare robotics: towards responsible research and innovation. Rob. Auton. Syst. **86**, 152–161 (2016)

26. Wangmo, T., Lipps, M., Kressig, R.W., Ienca, M.: Ethical concerns with the use of intelligent assistive technology: findings from a qualitative study with professional stakeholders. BMC Med. Ethics **20**, 1–11 (2019)

27. Oruma, S.O., Ayele, Y.Z., Sechi, F., Rødsethol, H.: Security aspects of social robots in public spaces: a systematic mapping study. Sens. (Basel) **23** (2023)

28. Etemad-Sajadi, R., Soussan, A., Schöpfer, T.: How ethical issues raised by human-robot interaction can impact the intention to use the robot? Int. J. Soc. Robot. **14**, 1103–1115 (2022)

29. Hung, L., Mann, J., Perry, J., Berndt, A., Wong, J.: Technological risks and ethical implications of using robots in long-term care **9**, 205566832211069 (2022). https://doi.org/10.1177/20556683221106917

30. Mark, B.G., Rauch, E., Matt, D.T.: Industrial assistance systems to enhance human-machine interaction and operator's capabilities in assembly. Implement. Ind. 4.0 SMEs Concepts Examples Appl. 129–161 (2021). https://doi.org/10.1007/978-3-030-70516-9_4/FIGURES/9

31. Rommetveit, K., van Dijk, N., Gunnarsdóttir, K.: Make way for the robots! Human- and machine-centricity in constituting a European public-private partnership. Minerva **58**, 47–69 (2020)

32. Kodate, N., et al.: Hopes and fears regarding care robots: content analysis of newspapers in East Asia and Western Europe, 2001–2020. Front. Rehabil. Sci. **3**, 1019089 (2022)

33. A Comprehensive Guide to the Future of Work in 2030 | On Digital Strategy | Dion Hinchcliffe. https://dionhinchcliffe.com/2024/01/18/a-comprehensive-guide-to-the-future-of-work-in-2030/

34. The Future of Robotics - Trends and Predictions for the Next Decade (2030) - Awe Robotics. https://www.awerobotics.com/the-future-of-robotics-trends-and-predictions-for-the-next-decade-2030/

35. What Are Collaborative Robots, Cobots | A3 Robotics Collaborative Robots. https://www.automate.org/robotics/cobots/what-are-collaborative-robots

36. Giallanza, A., La Scalia, G., Micale, R., La Fata, C.M.: Occupational health and safety issues in human-robot collaboration: state of the art and open challenges. Saf. Sci. **169**, 106313 (2024)

37. Feil-Seifer, D., Matarićmatarić, M.J.: Defining socially assistive robotics (2005)

38. Satria Prabuwono, A., Hammed Allehaibi, K.S.: Assistive robotic technology: a review. Comput. Eng. Appl. **6**, 2252–4274 (2017)

39. Borboni, A., et al.: The expanding role of artificial intelligence in collaborative robots for industrial applications: a systematic review of recent works. Mach. **11**, 111 (2023)

40. Zhao, D., et al.: Research status of elderly-care robots and safe human-robot interaction methods. Front. Neurosci. **17** (2023)
41. García, O.R., et al.: COBOT applications—recent advances and challenges. Robot. **12**, 79 (2023)
42. Human-Robot Collaboration Uniting Forces for Increased Productivity. https://utilitiesone. com/human-robot-collaboration-uniting-forces-for-increased-productivity
43. Gibelli, F., Ricci, G., Sirignano, A., Turrina, S., De Leo, D.: The increasing centrality of robotic technology in the context of nursing care: bioethical implications analyzed through a scoping review approach. J. Healthc. Eng. **2021** (2021)
44. Eprs. Analysis exploring risks and opportunities linked to the use of collaborative industrial robots in Europe
45. Niemelä, M., et al.: Robots and the Future of Welfare Services – A Finnish Roadmap (2021)
46. Albustanji, R.N., Elmanaseer, S., Alkhatib, A.A.A.: Robotics: five senses plus one—an overview. Robot. **12**, 68 (2023)
47. From Computer Vision to Robotic Vision: the role of artificial vision in robotics | TOD System. https://www.todsystem.com/en/from-computer-vision-to-robotic-vision-the-role-of-artificial-vision-in-robotics/
48. Image Processing for Robotics: Enabling Advanced Perception and Control. | By Michealomis | Medium. https://medium.com/@michealomis99/image-processing-for-rob otics-enabling-advanced-perception-and-control-9151133b2dd7
49. Huang, J., et al.: A survey on robot semantic navigation systems for indoor environments. Appl. Sci. **14**, 89 (2023)
50. Messaoudi, M.D., Menelas, B.A.J., Mcheick, H.: Review of navigation assistive tools and technologies for the visually impaired. Sens. (Basel) **22** (2022)
51. Charalampous, K., Kostavelis, I., Gasteratos, A.: Recent trends in social aware robot navigation: a survey. Rob. Auton. Syst. **93**, 85–104 (2017)
52. Shackleford, W., et al.: Performance evaluation of human detection systems for robot safety. J. Intell. Robot. Syst. **83**, 85–103 (2016). https://doi.org/10.1007/s10846-016-0334-3
53. Computer Vision Use Cases in Robotics: Machine Vision | Encord. https://encord.com/blog/ computer-vision-robotics-applications/
54. Gupta, A., Anpalagan, A., Guan, L., Khwaja, A.S.: Deep learning for object detection and scene perception in self-driving cars: survey, challenges, and open issues. Array **10**, 100057 (2021)
55. Vision-Based Autonomous Human Tracking Mobile Robot - CORE Reader. https://core.ac. uk/reader/235050460
56. Cielniak, G.: People tracking by mobile robots using thermal and colour vision (2007)
57. Cabibihan, J.-J., So, W.-C., Pramanik, S.: Human-recognizable robotic gestures. Auton. Ment. Dev. **4**, 305–314 (2012)
58. Spezialetti, M., Placidi, G., Rossi, S.: Emotion recognition for human-robot interaction: recent advances and future perspectives. Front. Robot. AI **7**, 532279 (2020)
59. Broadley, R.W., Klenk, J., Thies, S.B., Kenney, L.P.J., Granat, M.H.: Methods for the real-world evaluation of fall detection technology: a scoping review. Sensors **18**, 2060 (2018)
60. Wang, X., Ellul, J., Azzopardi, G.: Elderly fall detection systems: a literature survey. Front. Robot. AI **7**, 520978 (2020)
61. Laut, J., Porfiri, M., Raghavan, P.: The present and future of robotic technology in rehabilitation. Curr. Phys. Med. Rehabil. Rep. **4**, 312 (2016)
62. Atiqur, M., Ahad, R., Das Antar, A., Shahid, O.: Vision-based action understanding for assistive healthcare: a short review (2019)
63. Leo, M., Farinella, G.M.: Computer Vision for Assistive Healthcare (2018)

64. Alboul, L., Dimitrova, M., Lekova, A., Kaburlasos, V.G., Mitrouchev, P.: Editorial: emerging technologies for assistive robotics: current challenges and perspectives. Front. Robot. AI **10**, 1288360 (2023)
65. Sahoo, S.K., Choudhury, B.B.: Exploring the use of computer vision in assistive technologies for individuals with disabilities: a review. J. Futur. Sustain. **4**, 133–148 (2024)
66. Designing and Evaluating Human-Robot Communication Informing Design through Analysis of User Interaction. https://www.diva-portal.org/smash/get/diva2:158201/FULLTEXT01.pdf
67. Zelinsky, A., Matsumoto, Y., Heinzmann, J., Newman, R.: Towards human friendly robots: vision-based interfaces and safe mechanisms. Exp. Robot. VI 487–498 (2000). https://doi.org/10.1007/BFB0119426
68. Goyzueta, D.V., et al.: Analysis of a user interface based on multimodal interaction to control a robotic arm for EOD APPLICATIONS. Electron. **11**, 1690 (2022)
69. Berg, J., Lu, S.: Review of interfaces for industrial human-robot interaction. Curr. Robot. Rep. **12**(1), 27–34 (2020)
70. Corrales-Paredes, A., Sanz, D.O., Terrón-López, M.J., Egido-García, V.: User experience design for social robots: a case study in integrating embodiment. Sensors **23**, 5274 (2023)
71. Park, K., Chae, M., Cho, J.H.: Image pre-processing method of machine learning for edge detection with image signal processor enhancement. Micromachines **12**, 1–13 (2021)
72. Crnokic, B., Rezic, S., Pehar, S.: Comparision of edge detection methods for obstacles detection in a mobile robot environment. In: Annals of DAAAM and Proceedings of the International DAAAM Symposium, vol. 27 (2016)
73. Chen, W., Li, Y., Tian, Z., Zhang, F.: 2D and 3D object detection algorithms from images: a survey. Array **19**, 100305 (2023)
74. Singh, K.J., Kapoor, D.S., Thakur, K., Sharma, A., Gao, X.Z.: Computer-vision based object detection and recognition for service robot in indoor environment. Comput. Mater. Contin. **72**, 197–213 (2022)
75. Robotics Vision Processing: Object Detection and Tracking - Embedded Computing Design. https://embeddedcomputing.com/application/industrial/robotics-vision-processing-object-detection-and-tracking
76. Zrira, N., Hannat, M., Bouyakhf, E.H., Ahmad Khan, H.: 2D/3D object recognition and categorization approaches for robotic grasping. In: Hassanien, A.E., Oliva, D.A. (eds.) Advances in Soft Computing and Machine Learning in Image Processing. SCI, vol. 730, pp. 567–593. Springer, Cham (2018). https://doi.org/10.1007/978-3-319-63754-9_26
77. Se, S., Lowe, D., Little, J.: Vision-based mobile robot localization and mapping using scale-invariant features. In: Proceedings - IEEE International Conference on Robotics and Automation, vol. 2, pp. 2051–2058 (2001)
78. Dellaert, F., Stroupe, A.W.: Linear 2D localization and mapping for single and multiple robot scenarios (2002)
79. Xing, K., Zhang, X., Lin, Y., Ci, W., Dong, W.: Simultaneous localization and mapping algorithm based on the asynchronous fusion of laser and vision sensors. Front. Neurorobot. **16**, 866294 (2022)
80. Crnokić, B., Grubišić, M.: Comparison of solutions for simultaneous localization and mapping for mobile robot. Proc. Fac. Mech. Eng. Comput. Univ. Most. **8** (2014)
81. Hsieh, C.-H., Wang, M.-L., Kao, L.-W., Lin, H.-Y.: Mobile robot localization and path planning using an omnidirectional camera and infrared sensors. In: 2009 IEEE International Conference on Systems, Man and Cybernetics, pp. 1947–1952 (2009)
82. Al Arabi, A., et al.: 2D mapping and vertex finding method for path planning in autonomous obstacle avoidance robotic system. In: 2017 2nd International Conference on Control and Robotics Engineering, ICCRE 2017, pp. 39–42 (2017). https://doi.org/10.1109/ICCRE.2017.7935038

83. Liu, L., et al.: Path planning techniques for mobile robots: review and prospect. Expert Syst. Appl. **227**, 120254 (2023)

84. Dirik, M., Fatih Kocamaz, A.: Global vision based path planning for AVGs using A* algorithm (2020)

85. Boyoon, J., Sukhatme, G.S.: Real-time motion tracking from a mobile robot (2010)

86. Gad, A., et al.: Multiple object tracking in robotic applications: trends and challenges. Appl. Sci. **12**, 9408 (2022)

87. Robinson, N., Tidd, B., Campbell, D., Kulić, D., Corke, P.: Robotic vision for human-robot interaction and collaboration: a survey and systematic review. ACM Trans. Hum.-Rob. Interact. **12**, 12 (2023)

88. Herakovic, N.: Robot vision in industrial assembly and quality control processes. Robot Vis. (2010). https://doi.org/10.5772/9285

89. Sioma, A.: Vision system in product quality control systems. Appl. Sci. **13**, 751 (2023)

90. Oh, J.K., Lee, C.H.: Development of a stereo vision system for industrial robots. In: ICCAS 2007 - International Conference on Control, Automation and Systems, pp. 659–663 (2007). https://doi.org/10.1109/ICCAS.2007.4406981

91. Krishnan, A.B., Kollipara, J.: Cost-effective stereo vision system for mobile robot navigation and 3D map reconstruction, pp. 75–86 (2014). https://doi.org/10.5121/csit.2014.4716

92. Kheng, E.S., Hassan, A.H.A., Ranjbaran, A.: Stereo vision with 3D coordinates for robot arm application guide. In: IEEE Conference on Sustainable Utilization and Development in Engineering and Technology, STUDENT 2010 - Conference Booklet, pp. 102–105 (2010). https://doi.org/10.1109/STUDENT.2010.5686996

93. Namiki, A., Shimada, K., Kin, Y., Ishii, I.: Development of an active high-speed 3-D vision system. Sensors **19**, 1572 (2019)

94. Shahnewaz, A., Pandey, A.K.: Color and depth sensing sensor technologies for robotics and machine vision. Mach. Vis. Navig. 59–86 (2019). https://doi.org/10.1007/978-3-030-225 87-2_3

95. Kinnell, P., Rymer, T., Hodgson, J., Justham, L., Jackson, M.: Autonomous metrology for robot mounted 3D vision systems. CIRP Ann. **66**, 483–486 (2017)

96. Ding, Z., et al.: Recent advances and perspectives in deep learning techniques for 3D point cloud data processing. Robot. **12**, 100 (2023)

97. Cheng, Y., et al.: Sampling locally, hypothesis globally: accurate 3D point cloud registration with a RANSAC variant. Vis. Intell. **11**(1), 1–15 (2023)

98. Ye, C., Qian, X.: 3D object recognition of a robotic navigation aid for the visually impaired. IEEE Trans. Neural Syst. Rehabil. Eng. **26**, 441 (2018)

99. Shahria, T., et al.: Mapping and localization in 3d space for vision-based robot manipulation (2021)

100. Chen, Q., Wan, L., Pan, Y.-J.: Object recognition and localization for pick-and-place task using difference-based dynamic movement primitives. IFAC-PapersOnLine **56**, 10004–10009 (2023)

101. Abaspur Kazerouni, I., Fitzgerald, L., Dooly, G., Toal, D.: A survey of state-of-the-art on visual SLAM. Expert Syst. Appl. **205**, 117734 (2022)

102. Lin, H.: Robotic manipulation based on 3D vision: a survey. In: ACM International Conference Proceeding Seris (2020). https://doi.org/10.1145/3415048.3416116

103. Khan, A., Mineo, C., Dobie, G., Macleod, C., Pierce, G.: Vision guided robotic inspection for parts in manufacturing and remanufacturing industry. J. Remanuf. **11**, 49–70 (2021)

104. Jevtić, A., Doisy, G., Bodiroža, S., Edan, Y., Hafner, V.V.: Human-robot interaction through 3D vision and force control. In: ACM/IEEE International Conference on Human-Robot Interaction, p. 102 (2014). https://doi.org/10.1145/2559636.2559651

105. Gutmann, J.S., Fukuchi, M., Fujita, M.: 3D perception and environment map generation for humanoid robot navigation. Int. J. Robot. Res. **27**, 1117–1134 (2008). https://doi.org/10.1177/0278364908096316

106. Zieliński, P., Markowska-Kaczmar, U.: 3D robotic navigation using a vision-based deep reinforcement learning model. Appl. Soft Comput. **110**, 107602 (2021)

107. Fu, J., et al.: Recent advancements in augmented reality for robotic applications: a survey. Actuators **12**, 323 (2023)

108. Suzuki, R., Karim, A., Xia, T., Hedayati, H., Marquardt, N.: Augmented reality and robotics: a survey and taxonomy for AR-enhanced human-robot interaction and robotic interfaces (2022). https://doi.org/10.1145/3491102.3517719

109. Makhataeva, Z., Varol, H.A.: Augmented reality for robotics: a review. Robot. **9**, 21 (2020)

110. Do, Y., Kim, J.: Infrared range sensor array for 3D sensing in robotic applications. Int. J. Adv. Robot. Syst. **10** (2013)

111. Castro Jiménez, L.E., Martínez-García, E.A.: Thermal image sensing model for robotic planning and search. Sens. (Basel) **16** (2016)

112. Lintvedt, N.: Thermal imaging in robotics as a privacy-enhancing or privacy-invasive measure? Misconceptions of privacy when using thermal cameras in robots. Digit. Soc. **23**(2), 1–15 (2023)

113. He, Y., et al.: Infrared machine vision and infrared thermography with deep learning: a review. Infrared Phys. Technol. **116** (2021)

114. Martinez-Martin, E., Del Pobil, A.P.: Object detection and recognition for assistive robots: experimentation and implementation. IEEE Robot. Autom. Mag. **24**, 123–138 (2017)

115. Leira, F.S., Helgesen, H.H., Johansen, T.A., Fossen, T.I.: Object detection, recognition, and tracking from UAVs using a thermal camera. J. F. Robot. **38**, 242–267 (2021)

116. Mine, M., Gan, G., Aksoy, T., Temizel, A., Halici, U.: IR reasoner: real-time infrared object detection by visual reasoning (2023)

117. Banuls, A., Mandow, A., Vazquez-Martin, R., Morales, J., Garcia-Cerezo, A.: Object detection from thermal infrared and visible light cameras in search and rescue scenes. In: 2020 IEEE International Symposium on Safety, Security, and Rescue Robotics, SSRR 2020, pp. 380–386 (2020). https://doi.org/10.1109/SSRR50563.2020.9292593

118. Di Paola, D., Milella, A., Cicirelli, G., Distante, A.: An autonomous mobile robotic system for surveillance of indoor environments. Int. J. Adv. Robot. Syst. **7**, 19–26 (2010)

119. Pérez, L., Rodríguez, Í., Rodríguez, N., Usamentiaga, R., García, D.F.: Robot guidance using machine vision techniques in industrial environments: a comparative review. Sensors **16**, 335 (2016)

120. Shahria, M.T., et al.: A comprehensive review of vision-based robotic applications: current state, components, approaches, barriers, and potential solutions. Robot. **11**, 139 (2022)

121. Awad, F., Shamroukh, R., Awad, F., Shamroukh, R.: Human detection by robotic urban search and rescue using image processing and neural networks. Int. J. Intell. Sci. **4**, 39–53 (2014)

122. Chitikena, H., Sanfilippo, F., Ma, S.: Robotics in search and rescue (SAR) operations: an ethical and design perspective framework for response phase. Appl. Sci. **13**, 1800 (2023)

123. Marques, L., Martins, A., De Almeida, A.T.: Environmental monitoring with mobile robots. In: 2005 IEEE/RSJ International Conference on Intelligent Robots and Systems, IROS, pp. 3624–3629 (2005). https://doi.org/10.1109/IROS.2005.1545133

124. Miura, J., Demura, M., Nishi, K., Oishi, S.: Thermal comfort measurement using thermal-depth images for robotic monitoring. Pattern Recognit. Lett. **137**, 108–113 (2020)

125. Dunbabin, M., Marques, L.: Robots for environmental monitoring: significant advancements and applications. IEEE Robot. Autom. Mag. **19**, 24–39 (2012)

126. Mat, F., Jim, A.: Multisensor fusion: an autonomous mobile robot. 129–141 (1998)

127. Crnokić, B.: Use of artificial neural networks for fusion of infrared and vision sensors in a mobile robot navigation system (2020). https://doi.org/10.2507/31st.daaam.proceedings.xxx

128. Aggarwal, J.K., Wang, Y.F.: Sensor data fusion in robotic systems. Control. Dyn. Syst. **39**, 435–462 (1991)

129. Liu, Z., et al.: A mobile robot mapping method integrating Lidar and depth camera (2022). https://doi.org/10.1088/1742-6596/2402/1/012031

130. Xu, Y., Ou, Y., Xu, T.: SLAM of robot based on the fusion of vision and LIDAR. In: 2018 IEEE International Conference on Cyborg and Bionic Systems, CBS 2018, pp. 121–126 (2018). https://doi.org/10.1109/CBS.2018.8612212

131. Debeunne, C., Vivet, D.: A review of visual-LiDAR fusion based simultaneous localization and mapping. Sensors **20**, 20 (2021)

132. Bellotto, N., Hu, H.: Vision and laser data fusion for tracking people with a mobile robot. In: 2006 IEEE International Conference on Robotics and Biomimetics, ROBIO 2006, pp. 7–12 (2006). https://doi.org/10.1109/ROBIO.2006.340251

133. Hoang, T.T., Duong, P.M., Viet, D.A., Vinh, T.Q.: Multi-sensor perceptual system for mobile robot and sensor fusion-based localization, pp. 259–264 (2012)

134. Sensor Fusion for Social Robotics. https://www.researchgate.net/publication/232725043_Sensor_Fusion_for_Social_Robotics

135. Yeong, D.J., Velasco-hernandez, G., Barry, J., Walsh, J.: Sensor and sensor fusion technology in autonomous vehicles: a review. Sens. (Basel) **21**, 1–37 (2021)

136. Liu, K., et al.: Sensor fusion in autonomous vehicle with traffic surveillance camera system: detection, localization, and AI networking. Sensors **23**, 3335 (2023)

137. Ignatious, H.A., Sayed, H.E., Khan, M.: An overview of sensors in autonomous vehicles. Procedia Comput. Sci. **198**, 736–741 (2022)

138. Nishimura, Y., Yamaguchi, T.: Grass cutting robot for inclined surfaces in hilly and mountainous areas. Sensors **23**, 528 (2023)

139. Baquero Velasquez, A.E., et al.: Multi-sensor fusion based robust row following for compact agricultural robots. F. Robot. **2**, 1291–1319 (2022)

140. Yang, X., et al.: Sensor fusion-based teleoperation control of anthropomorphic robotic arm. Biomimetics **8**, 169 (2023)

141. Zhang, G., et al.: Multi-sensor fusion and intelligent aspiration control of minimally invasive surgical robot for intracerebral hemorrhage. Brain Hemorrhages **3**, 3–4 (2022)

142. Qi, W., et al.: Multimodal data fusion framework enhanced robot-assisted minimally invasive surgery. Trans. Inst. Meas. Control. **44**, 735–743 (2021). https://doi.org/10.1177/0142331220984350

143. Kaplan, J., Sosnovskaya, Y., Arnold, M., Hannaford, B.: Sensor fusion for force and position calibration of a motorized surgical smart grasper. In: 2021 International Symposium on Medical Robotics, ISMR 2021 (2021). https://doi.org/10.1109/ISMR48346.2021.9661520

144. Milella, A.: Embedded visual system and its applications on robots. Sens. Rev. **32** (2012)

145. Sawasaki, N., Nakao, M., Yamamoto, Y., Okabayashi, K.: Embedded vision system for mobile robot navigation. In: Proceedings of the 2006 IEEE International Conference on Robotics and Automation, ICRA 2006, pp. 2693–2698 (2006)

146. Melnyk, Y.B., Stadnik, A.V., Pypenko, I.S., Kostina, V.V., Yevtushenko, D.O.: Design of an embedded multi-camera vision system—a case study in mobile robotics. Robotics **62**, 297–299 (2022)

147. Golnabi, H., Asadpour, A.: Design and application of industrial machine vision systems. Robot. Comput. Integr. Manuf. **23**, 630–637 (2007)

148. Guan, X., Huang, J., Tang, T.: Robot vision application on embedded vision implementation with digital signal processor. Int. J. Adv. Robot. Syst. **17** (2020)

149. Gerndt, R., Michalik, S., Krupop, S.: Embedded vision system for robotics and industrial automation. In: IEEE International Conference on Industrial Informatics, pp. 895–899 (2011). https://doi.org/10.1109/INDIN.2011.6035012

150. Ruiz-Del-Solar, J., Loncomilla, P., Soto, N.: A survey on deep learning methods for robot vision (2018)

151. Ruiz-del-Solar, J., Loncomilla, P.: Applications of deep learning in robot vision. Deep Learn. Comput. Vis. 211–232 (2020). https://doi.org/10.1201/9781351003827-8

152. García-Pintos, C.A., Aldana-Murillo, N.G., Ovalle-Magallanes, E., Martínez, E.: A deep learning-based visual map generation for mobile robot navigation. Eng **2023**(4), 1616–1634 (2023)

153. Wen, L.H., Jo, K.H.: Deep learning-based perception systems for autonomous driving: a comprehensive survey. Neurocomputing **489**, 255–270 (2022)

154. Bergamini, L., et al.: Deep learning-based method for vision-guided robotic grasping of unknown objects. Adv. Eng. Inform. **44**, 101052 (2020)

155. Yu, J., Weng, K., Liang, G., Xie, G.: A vision-based robotic grasping system using deep learning for 3D object recognition and pose estimation. In: 2013 IEEE International Conference on Robotics and Biomimetics, ROBIO 2013, pp. 1175–1180 (2013). https://doi.org/10.1109/ROBIO.2013.6739623

156. Vijay, S., Ponnusamy, V.: A review on application of robots in agriculture using deep learning. In: AIP Conference Proceedings, vol. 2946 (2023)

157. Dhanya, V.G., et al.: Deep learning based computer vision approaches for smart agricultural applications. Artif. Intell. Agric. **6**, 211–229 (2022)

158. Zapotezny-Anderson, P., Lehnert, C.: Towards active robotic vision in agriculture: a deep learning approach to visual servoing in occluded and unstructured protected cropping environments. IFAC-PapersOnLine **52**, 120–125 (2019)

159. Cruz Ulloa, C., Sánchez, L., Del Cerro, J., Barrientos, A.: Deep learning vision system for quadruped robot gait pattern regulation. Biomimetics **8**, 289 (2023)

160. Sampedro, C., et al.: A fully-autonomous aerial robot for search and rescue applications in indoor environments using learning-based techniques. J. Intell. Robot. Syst. Theory Appl. **95**, 601–627 (2019)

161. Martinez-Alpiste, I., Golcarenarenji, G., Wang, Q., Alcaraz-Calero, J.M.: Search and rescue operation using UAVs: a case study. Expert Syst. Appl. **178**, 114937 (2021)

162. Niroui, F., Zhang, K., Kashino, Z., Nejat, G.: Deep reinforcement learning robot for search and rescue applications: exploration in unknown cluttered environments. IEEE Robot. Autom. Lett. **4**, 610–617 (2019)

163. You, K., Zhou, C., Ding, L.: Deep learning technology for construction machinery and robotics. Autom. Constr. **150**, 104852 (2023)

164. Popli, R., et al.: ROAD: robotics-assisted onsite data collection and deep learning enabled robotic vision system for identification of cracks on diverse surfaces. Sustain. **15**, 9314 (2023)

165. Chen, S., Li, Y., Kwok, N.M.: Active vision in robotic systems: a survey of recent developments. Int. J. Rob. Res. **30**, 1343–1377 (2011)

166. Zeng, R., Wen, Y., Zhao, W., Liu, Y.J.: View planning in robot active vision: a survey of systems, algorithms, and applications. Comput. Vis. Media **6**, 225–245 (2020)

167. Peng, J., Srikaew, A., Wilkes, M., Kawamura, K., Peters, A.: Active vision system for mobile robots. In: Proceedings of the IEEE International Conference on Systems, Man and Cybernetics, vol. 2, pp. 1472–1477 (2000)

168. Schenck, W.: Robot studies on saccade-triggered visual prediction. New Ideas Psychol. **31**, 221–238 (2013)

169. Wang, X., Van De Weem, J., Jonker, P.: An advanced active vision system imitating human eye movements. In: 2013 16th International Conference on Advanced Robotics, ICAR 2013 (2013). https://doi.org/10.1109/ICAR.2013.6766517
170. Alitappeh, R.J., John, A., Dias, B., John Van Opstal, A., Bernardino, A.: Emergence of human oculomotor behavior from optimal control of a cable-driven biomimetic robotic eye (2022)
171. Rasolzadeh, B., Björkman, M., Huebner, K., Kragic, D.: An active vision system for detecting, fixating and manipulating objects in the real world. Int. J. Rob. Res. **29**, 133–154 (2010)
172. Hiruma, H., Mori, H., Ito, H., Ogata, T.: Guided visual attention model based on interactions between top-down and bottom-up prediction for robot pose prediction (2022)
173. Potapova, E., Zillich, M., Vincze, M.: Survey of recent advances in 3D visual attention for robotics. Int. J. Robot. Res. **36**, 1159–1176 (2017). https://doi.org/10.1177/027836491772 6587
174. Rubies, E., Palacín, J., Clotet, E.: Enhancing the sense of attention from an assistance mobile robot by improving eye-gaze contact from its iconic face displayed on a flat screen. Sensors **22** (2022)
175. Breazeal, C., Edsinger, A., Fitzpatrick, P., Scassellati, B.: Active Vision for Sociable Robots. IEEE Trans. MAN XX **1** (2000)
176. Heinen, M.R., Martins Engel, P.: NLOOK: a computational attention model for robot vision. J. Brazilian Comput. Soc. (2009)
177. Erkent, Ö., Işıl Bozma, H.: Artificial potential functions based camera movements and visual behaviors in attentive robots. Auton. Robots **32**, 15–34 (2012)
178. Ognibene, D., Foulsham, T., Marchegiani, L., Farinella, G.M.: Editorial: active vision and perception in human-robot collaboration. Front. Neurorobot. **16**, 848065 (2022)
179. Robinson, N., Tidd, B., Campbell, D., Kulić, D., Corke, P.: Robotic vision for human-robot interaction and collaboration: a survey and systematic review. ACM Trans. Hum.-Rob. Interact. **12**, 65 (2023)
180. Otte, M.W.: A survey of machine learning approaches to robotic path-planning (2015)
181. Alatabani, L.E., Ali, E.S., Saeed, R.A.: Machine learning and deep learning approaches for robotics applications. In: Azar, A.T., Koubaa, A. (eds.) Artificial Intelligence for Robotics and Autonomous Systems Applications. Studies in Computational Intelligence, vol. 1093, pp. 303–333. Springer, Cham (2023). https://doi.org/10.1007/978-3-031-28715-2_10
182. McLauchlan, L.L.L., Challoo, R., Omar, S.I., McLauchlan, R.A.: Supervised and unsupervised learning applied to robotic manipulator control. In: Proceedings of the American Control Conference, vol. 3, pp. 3357–3358 (1994)
183. Kober, J., Bagnell, J.A., Peters, J.: Reinforcement learning in robotics: a survey (2013)
184. Kormushev, P., Calinon, S., Caldwell, D.G.: Reinforcement learning in robotics: applications and real-world challenges. Robot. **2013**(2), 122–148 (2013)
185. Pierson, H. A., Gashler, M.S.: Deep Learning in robotics: a review of recent research (2017)
186. Gu, S., Holly, E., Lillicrap, T., Levine, S.: Deep reinforcement learning for robotic manipulation with asynchronous off-policy updates. In: Proceedings - IEEE International Conference on Robotics and Automation, pp. 3389–3396 (2017). https://doi.org/10.1109/ICRA.2017. 7989385
187. Han, D., Mulyana, B., Stankovic, V., Cheng, S.: A survey on deep reinforcement learning algorithms for robotic manipulation. Sensors **23**, 3762 (2023)
188. Jaquier, N., et al.: Transfer learning in robotics: an upcoming breakthrough? A review of promises and challenges (2023)
189. Barrett, S., Taylor, M.E., Stone, P.: Transfer learning for reinforcement learning on a physical robot * (2010)

190. Principle of transfer learning for robot manipulation. | Download Scientific Diagram. https://www.researchgate.net/figure/Principle-of-transfer-learning-for-robot-manipulation_fig3_349266176

191. Duan, C., Junginger, S., Huang, J., Jin, K., Thurow, K.: Deep learning for visual SLAM in transportation robotics: a review. Transp. Saf. Environ. **1**, 177–184 (2019)

192. Favorskaya, M.N.: Deep learning for visual SLAM: the state-of-the-art and future trends. Electron. **12**, 2006 (2023)

193. Chen, C., Wang, B., Lu, C.X., Trigoni, N., Markham, A. :Deep learning for visual localization and mapping: a survey. IEEE Trans. Neural Netw. Learn. Syst. (2023). https://doi.org/10.1109/TNNLS.2023.3309809

194. Bogert, K.: Inverse reinforcement learning for robotic applications: hidden variables, multiple experts and unknown dynamics (2016)

195. Vasquez, D., Okal, B., Arras, K.O.: Inverse reinforcement learning algorithms and features for robot navigation in crowds: an experimental comparison. In: IEEE International Conference on Intelligent Robots and Systems, pp. 1341–1346 (2014). https://doi.org/10.1109/IROS.2014.6942731

196. Thrun, S.: Is robotics going statistics? The field of probabilistic robotics (2001)

197. van der Heijden, G.W.A.M., van Evert, F.K., Lamaker, A.: Probabilistic robotics in an autonomous field robot (2008)

198. Thrun, S., Burgard, W., Fox, D.: Probabilistic Robotics. MIT Press (2005)

199. Wang, C., et al.: Unsupervised online learning for robotic interestingness with visual memory. IEEE Trans. Robot. **38**, 2446–2461 (2021)

200. Brose, S.W., et al.: The role of assistive robotics in the lives of persons with disability. Am. J. Phys. Med. Rehabil. **89**, 509–521 (2010)

201. Bharilya, V., Kumar, N.: Machine learning for autonomous vehicle's trajectory prediction: a comprehensive survey, challenges, and future research directions. Veh. Commun. **46**, 100733 (2024)

202. Bachute, M.R., Subhedar, J.M.: Autonomous driving architectures: insights of machine learning and deep learning algorithms. Mach. Learn. with Appl. **6**, 100164 (2021)

203. Latif Sarker, M.A., Seog Han, D.: Human-centric autonomous driving based on a two-stage machine learning algorithm. In: APCC 2022 - 27th Asia Pacific Conference on Communications: Creating Innovative Communication Technologies for Post-Pandemic Era, pp. 334–335 (2022). https://doi.org/10.1109/APCC55198.2022.9943704

204. Bai, Q., et al.: Object detection recognition and robot grasping based on machine learning: a survey. IEEE Access **8**, 181855–181879 (2020)

205. Pookkuttath, S., Elara, M.R., Sivanantham, V., Ramalingam, B.: AI-enabled predictive maintenance framework for autonomous mobile cleaning robots. Sensors (Basel). **22** (2021)

206. Nahavandi, S., et al.: Machine learning meets advanced robotic manipulation (2023)

207. Mohammed, M.Q., et al.: Review of learning-based robotic manipulation in cluttered environments. Sensors **22**, 7938 (2022)

208. Cobley, B., Boyle, D.: OnionBot: a system for collaborative computational cooking (2020)

209. Park, K.H., et al.: Robotic smart house to assist people with movement disabilities. Auton. Robots **22**, 183–198 (2007)

210. Bonarini, A.: Communication in human-robot interaction. Curr. Robot. Rep. **14**(1), 279–285 (2020)

211. Qi, J., Ma, L., Cui, Z., Yu, Y.: Computer vision-based hand gesture recognition for human-robot interaction: a review. Complex Intell. Syst. **10**, 1581–1606 (2023)

212. Lin, H.I., Chiang, Y.P.: Understanding human hand gestures for learning robot pick-and-place tasks. Int. J. Adv. Robot. Syst. **12** (2015)

213. Li, X.: Human–robot interaction based on gesture and movement recognition. Signal Process. Image Commun. **81**, 115686 (2020)

214. Cesta, A., Cortellessa, G., Orlandini, A., Umbrico, A.: Towards flexible assistive robots using artificial intelligence (2018)
215. Iwahashi, N.: Robots that learn language: developmental approach to human-machine conversations. In: Vogt, P., Sugita, Y., Tuci, E., Nehaniv, C. (eds.) EELC 2006. LNCS (LNAI and LNB), vol. 4211, pp. 143–167. Springer, Cham (2006). https://doi.org/10.1007/118801 72_12
216. Arboleda, S. A., Pascher, M., Lakhnati, Y., Gerken, J. Understanding human-robot collaboration for people with mobility impairments at the workplace, a thematic analysis (2020)
217. Argall, B.D.: Machine learning for shared control with assistive machines (2013)
218. Thomas, J., et al.: Model for the detection of falls with the use of artificial intelligence as an assistant for the care of the elderly. Comput. **10**, 195 (2022)
219. Liang, F., et al.: Collaborative fall detection using a wearable device and a companion robot (2021)
220. Uddin, M.Z., Soylu, A.: Human activity recognition using wearable sensors, discriminant analysis, and long short-term memory-based neural structured learning. Sci. Rep. **111**(11), 1–15 (2021)
221. Angulo, C., Chacón, A., Ponsa, P.: Towards a cognitive assistant supporting human operators in the artificial intelligence of things. Internet Things **21**, 100673 (2023)
222. Cognitively assistive robots for dementia care - AI for Good. https://aiforgood.itu.int/cognit ively-assistive-robots-for-dementia-care/
223. Beetz, M., et al.: Cognition-enabled robots assist in care and everyday life: perspectives, challenges, and current views and insights, pp. 103–119 (2023). https://doi.org/10.1007/ 978-3-031-11447-2_6
224. Selvam, R., et al.: Human emotion detection using DeepFace and artificial intelligence. Eng. Proc. **59**, 37 (2023)
225. Siam, A.I., Soliman, N.F., Algarni, A.D., Abd El-Samie, F.E., Sedik, A.: Deploying machine learning techniques for human emotion detection. Comput. Intell. Neurosci. **2022**, (2022)
226. Badesa, F.J., et al.: Auto-adaptive robot-aided therapy using machine learning techniques. Comput. Methods Programs Biomed. **116**, 123–130 (2014)
227. Tsiakas, K., Dagioglou, M., Karkaletsis, V., Makedon, F.: adaptive robot assisted therapy using interactive reinforcement learning (2016). https://doi.org/10.1007/978-3-319-47437-3
228. Boudjaj, M., Bakkali, F., Alidrissi, N., Jhilal, F., Bougdira, A.: Adaptive reinforcement learning for medical robotics and telemedicine. In: Ezziyyani, M., Kacprzyk, J., Balas, V.E. (eds.) AI2SD 2023. LNNS, vol. 904, pp. 427–434. Springer, Cham (2024). https://doi.org/ 10.1007/978-3-031-52388-5_38
229. Kamran, M., et al.: Comparative analysis for machine-learning-based optimal control of upper extremity rehabilitation robots. Eng. Proc. **46**, 34 (2023)
230. Brahmi, B., Rahman, M.H., Saad, M.: Impedance learning adaptive super-twisting control of a robotic exoskeleton for physical human-robot interaction. IET Cyber-Syst. Robot. **5**, e12077 (2023)
231. Abbasimoshaei, A., Chinnakkonda Ravi, A.K., Kern, T.A.: Development of a new control system for a rehabilitation robot using electrical impedance tomography and artificial intelligence. Biomimetics **8** (2023)
232. Said, Y., Atri, M., Albahar, M.A., Ben Atitallah, A., Alsariera, Y.A.: Obstacle detection system for navigation assistance of visually impaired people based on deep learning techniques. Sensors **23**, 5262 (2023)
233. Kumar, N., Jain, A.: A deep learning based model to assist blind people in their navigation (2022). https://doi.org/10.28945/5006

234. Lu, C.L., et al.: Assistive navigation using deep reinforcement learning guiding robot with uwb/voice beacons and semantic feedbacks for blind and visually impaired people. Front. Robot. AI **8**, 654132 (2021)

235. Kyrarini, M., Zand, M., Kodur, K.: Assistive robots for persons with visual impairments: current research and open challenges. In: ACM International Conference Proceeding Series, pp. 413–416 (2023). https://doi.org/10.1145/3594806.3596593

236. Liu, S., et al.: DRAGON: a dialogue-based robot for assistive navigation with visual language grounding. IEEE Robot. Autom. Lett. 1–8 (2023). https://doi.org/10.1109/LRA.2024.336 2591

237. Cirelli, G., Tamantini, C., Cordella, L.P., Cordella, F.: A semiautonomous control strategy based on computer vision for a hand-wrist prosthesis. Robot. **12**, 152 (2023)

238. Vélez-guerrero, M.A., Callejas-cuervo, M., Mazzoleni, S.: Artificial intelligence-based wearable robotic exoskeletons for upper limb rehabilitation: a review. Sens. (Basel). **21**, 1–30 (2021)

239. Triwiyanto, T., Caesarendra, W., Ahmed, A.A., Abdullayev, V.H.: How deep learning and neural networks can improve prosthetics and exoskeletons: a review of state-of-the-art methods and challenges. J. Electron. Electromed. Eng. Med. Inform. **5**, 277–289 (2023)

240. Mathew, M., et al.: A systematic review of technological advancements in signal sensing, actuation, control and training methods in robotic exoskeletons for rehabilitation. Ind. Rob. **50**, 432–455 (2023)

241. He, G., Huang, X., Li, F., Wang, H.: Review of power-assisted lower limb exoskeleton robot. J. Shanghai Jiaotong Univ. **29**, 1–15 (2022)

242. Sun, Y., Zhang, L., Ma, O.: Force-vision sensor fusion improves learning-based approach for self-closing door pulling. IEEE Access **9**, 137188–137197 (2021)

243. Andronas, D., et al.: Model-based robot control for human-robot flexible material co-manipulation. In: IEEE International Conference on Emerging Technologies and Factory Automation, ETFA 2021 (2021)

244. Escarabajal, R.J., Pulloquinga, J.L., Mata, V., Valera, Á., Díaz-Rodríguez, M.: Model-based control of a 4-DOF rehabilitation parallel robot with online identification of the gravitational term. Sensors **23**, 2790 (2023)

245. Niehaus, S., et al.: Human-centred design of robotic systems and exoskeletons using digital human models within the research project SOPHIA. Zeitschrift Arbeitswiss **764**(76), 450–458 (2022)

246. Quandt, M., Stern, H., Zeitler, W., Freitag, M.: Human-centered design of cognitive assistance systems for industrial work. Procedia CIRP **107**, 233–238 (2022)

247. Doncieux, S., Chatila, R., Straube, S., Kirchner, F.: Human-centered AI and robotics. AI Perspect. **41**(4), 1–14 (2022)

248. Pizzagalli, S.L., Kuts, V., Otto, T.: User-centered design for human-robot collaboration systems. IOP Conf. Ser. Mater. Sci. Eng. **1140**, 012011 (2021)

249. Prati, E., Peruzzini, M., Pellicciari, M., Raffaeli, R.: How to include user eXperience in the design of human-robot interaction. Robot. Comput. Integr. Manuf. **68**, 102072 (2021)

250. Hoffman, G., Breazeal, C.: Collaboration in human-robot teams (2004)

251. Demir, M., McNeese, N.J., Cooke, N.J.: Understanding human-robot teams in light of all-human teams: aspects of team interaction and shared cognition. Int. J. Hum. Comput. Stud. **140**, 102436 (2020)

252. Lekova, A., Tsvetkova, P., Tanev, T., Mitrouchev, P., Kostova, S.: Making humanoid robots teaching assistants by using natural language processing (NLP) cloud-based services. J. Mechatron. Artif. Intell. Eng. **3**, 30–39 (2022)

253. Dahiya, A., Smith, S.L.: Adaptive robot assistance: expertise and influence in multi-user task planning (2023)

254. Qian, K., Xu, X., Liu, H., Bai, J., Luo, S.: Environment-adaptive learning from demonstration for proactive assistance in human–robot collaborative tasks. Rob. Auton. Syst. **151**, 104046 (2022)
255. Mandischer, N., et al.: Toward adaptive human-robot collaboration for the inclusion of people with disabilities in manual labor tasks. Electron. **12**, 1118 (2023)
256. Lasota, P., Nikolaidis, S., Shah, J.: Developing an adaptive robotic assistant for close proximity human-robot collaboration in space (2013)
257. Rubagotti, M., Tusseyeva, I., Baltabayeva, S., Summers, D., Sandygulova, A.: Perceived safety in physical human–robot interaction—A survey. Rob. Auton. Syst. **151**, 104047 (2022)
258. Delgado Bellamy, D., Chance, G., Caleb-Solly, P., Dogramadzi, S.: Safety assessment review of a dressing assistance robot. Front. Robot. AI **8**, 667316 (2021)
259. Huang, Z., et al.: Towards safe multi-level human-robot interaction in industrial tasks (2023)
260. Goodrich, M.A., Schultz, A.C.: Human-robot interaction: a survey. Found. Trends® Hum.-Comput. Interact. **1**, 203–275 (2008)
261. Weichhart, G., et al.: Models for interoperable human robot collaboration. **51**, 36–41 (2018)
262. Bora, R., De La Pinta, J.R., Alvarez, A., Maestre, J.M.: Integration of service robots in the smart home by means of UPnP: A surveillance robot case study. Rob. Auton. Syst. **61**, 153–160 (2013)
263. Crestani, D., Godary-Dejean, K., Lapierre, L.: Enhancing fault tolerance of autonomous mobile robots. Rob. Auton. Syst. **68**, 140–155 (2015)
264. Veruggio, G., Operto, F.: Roboethics: social and ethical implications of robotics. Springer Handb. Robot. 1499–1524 (2008). https://doi.org/10.1007/978-3-540-30301-5_65
265. Rajaonah, B., Zio, E.: Social robotics and synthetic ethics: a methodological proposal for research. Int. J. Soc. Robot. 2075–2085 (2023)
266. Das, D., Banerjee, S., Chernova, S.: Explainable AI for robot failures: generating explanations that improve user assistance in fault recovery. In: ACM/IEEE International Conference on Human-Robot Interaction, pp. 351–360 (2021). https://doi.org/10.1145/3434073.3444657
267. Setchi, R., Dehkordi, M.B., Khan, J.S.: Explainable robotics in human-robot interactions. Procedia Comput. Sci. **176**, 3057–3066 (2020)
268. Afroze, D., Tu, Y., Hei, X.: Securing the future: exploring privacy risks and security questions in robotic systems. In: Chen, Y., Lin, C.W., Chen, B., Zhu, Q. (eds.) SmartSP 2023. LNICST, vol. 552, pp. 148–157. Springer, Cham (2024). https://doi.org/10.1007/978-3-031-51630-6_10
269. Chatzimichali, A., Harrison, R., Chrysostomou, D.: Toward privacy-sensitive human-robot interaction: privacy terms and human-data interaction in the personal robot era. Paladyn **12**, 160–174 (2021)
270. Neupane, S., et al.: Security considerations in ai-robotics: a survey of current methods, challenges, and opportunities (2024)
271. Lutz, C., Schöttler, M., Hoffmann, C.P.: The privacy implications of social robots: scoping review and expert interviews. Mob. Media Commun. **7**, 412–434 (2019). https://doi.org/10.1177/2050157919843961
272. Londoño, L., et al.: Fairness and bias in robot learning (2018)
273. Mehrabi, N., Morstatter, F., Saxena, N., Lerman, K., Galstyan, A.: A survey on bias and fairness in machine learning. ACM Comput. Surv. **54** (2021)
274. Hurtado, J.V., Londoño, L., Valada, A.: From learning to relearning: a framework for diminishing bias in social robot navigation. Front. Robot. AI **8**, 650325 (2021)
275. Heuer, T., Schiering, I., Gerndt, R.: Privacy and socially assistive robots - a meta study. In: Hansen, M., Kosta, E., Nai-Fovino, I., Fischer-Hübner, S. (eds.) Privacy and Identity 2017. IFIP Advances in Information and Communication Technology, vol. 526, pp. 265–281. Springer, Cham (2018). https://doi.org/10.1007/978-3-319-92925-5_18

276. Beer, J.M., Fisk, A.D., Rogers, W.A.: Toward a framework for levels of robot autonomy in human-robot interaction. J. Hum.-Robot. Interact. **3**, 74 (2014)

277. Formosa, P.: Robot Autonomy vs. human autonomy: social robots, artificial intelligence (AI), and the nature of autonomy. Minds Mach. **31**, 595–616 (2021)

278. Chiacchio, F., Petropoulos, G., Pichler, D.: The impact of industrial robots on EU employment and wages: a local labour market approach (2018). http://bruegel.org/2017/12/the-growing-presence-of-robots-in-eu-industries/

279. De Vries, G.J., Gentile, E., Miroudot, S., Wacker, K.M.: The rise of robots and the fall of routine jobs (2020). www.adb.org, https://doi.org/10.22617/WPS200236-2

280. Abuselidze, G., Mamaladze, L.: The impact of artificial intelligence on employment before and during pandemic: a comparative analysis. J. Phys. Conf. Ser. **1840**, 12040 (2021)

281. Ostrowski, A.K., et al.: Ethics, equity, & justice in human-robot interaction: a review and future directions. In: RO-MAN 2022 - 31st IEEE International Conference on Robot and Human Interactive Communication - Social, Asocial, and Antisocial Robots, pp. 969–976 (2022). https://doi.org/10.1109/RO-MAN53752.2022.9900805

282. Bicchi, A., Peshkin, M.A., Colgate, J.E.: Safety for physical human–robot interaction. Springer Handb. Robot. 1335–1348 (2008). https://doi.org/10.1007/978-3-540-30301-5_58

283. Coban, M., Kaymakci, O.T., Gelen, G.: Reliability analysis of assembly processes performed by human-robot interaction. In: 3rd International Symposium on Multidisciplinary Studies and Innovative Technologies, ISMSIT 2019 - Proceedings (2019). https://doi.org/10.1109/ISMSIT.2019.8932940

284. Alaieri, F., Vellino, A.: Ethical decision making in robots: Autonomy, trust and responsibility autonomy trust and responsibility. In: Agah, A., Cabibihan, J.J., Howard, A., Salichs, M., He, H. (eds.) ICSR 2016. LNCS, vol. 9979, pp. 159–168. Springer, Cham (2016). https://doi.org/10.1007/978-3-319-47437-3_16

285. Hutler, B., Rieder, T.N., Mathews, D.J.H., Handelman, D.A., Greenberg, A.M.: Designing robots that do no harm: understanding the challenges of ethics for robots. AI Ethics **1**, 1 (2023)

286. Vanderelst, D., Willems, J.: Can we agree on what robots should be allowed to do? An exercise in rule selection for ethical care robots. Int. J. Soc. Robot. **12**, 1093–1102 (2020)

287. Sharkawy, A.N., Koustoumpardis, P.N.: Human-robot interaction: a review and analysis on variable admittance control, safety, and perspectives. Machines **10**, 591 (2022)

288. Hüsing, E., Weidemann, C., Lorenz, M., Corves, B., Hüsing, M.: Determining robotic assistance for inclusive workplaces for people with disabilities. Robot. **10**, 44 (2021)

289. Barfield, J.K.: Towards diversity, equity, and inclusion in human-robot interaction. In: Kurosu, M., Hashizume, A. (eds.) HCII 2023. LNCS (LNAI and LNB), vol. 14013, pp. 3–17. Springer, Cham (2023). https://doi.org/10.1007/978-3-031-35602-5_1

290. Sarker, M.A.B., Sola-Thomas, E., Jamieson, C., Imtiaz, M.H.: Autonomous movement of wheelchair by cameras and YOLOv7. Eng. Proc. **31**, 60 (2022)

291. Ribeiro, T., Gonçalves, F., Garcia, I.S., Lopes, G., Ribeiro, A.F.: CHARMIE: a collaborative healthcare and home service and assistant robot for elderly care. Appl. Sci. **11**, 7248 (2021)

292. Wright, R., Parekh, S., White, R., Losey, D.P.: Safely and autonomously cutting meat with a collaborative robot arm. Sci. Rep. **141**(14), 1–16 (2024)

293. Mutawa, A.M., et al.: Augmenting mobile app with NAO robot for autism education. Machines **11**, 833 (2023)

294. Rusu, D.M., et al.: Soft robotics: a systematic review and bibliometric analysis. Micromachines **14**, 359 (2023)

295. Morris, L., et al.: The-state-of-the-art of soft robotics to assist mobility: a review of physiotherapist and patient identified limitations of current lower-limb exoskeletons and the potential soft-robotic solutions. J. Neuroeng. Rehabil. **20**, 18 (2023)

296. Paternò, L., Lorenzon, L.: Soft robotics in wearable and implantable medical applications: translational challenges and future outlooks. Front. Robot. AI **10**, 1075634 (2023)
297. Zhu, M., et al.: Soft, wearable robotics and haptics: technologies, trends, and emerging applications. Proc. IEEE **110**, 246–272 (2022)
298. Bardi, E., et al.: Upper limb soft robotic wearable devices: a systematic review. J. Neuroeng. Rehabil. **19**, 1–17 (2022)
299. Shi, Y., Dong, W., Lin, W., Gao, Y.: Soft wearable robots: development status and technical challenges. Sens. (Basel). **22** (2022)
300. Robinson, N., Mane, R., Chouhan, T., Guan, C.: Emerging trends in BCI-robotics for motor control and rehabilitation. Curr. Opin. Biomed. Eng. **20**, 100354 (2021)
301. Peksa, J., Mamchur, D.: State-of-the-art on brain-computer interface technology. Sensors **2023**(23), 6001 (2023)
302. Saha, S., et al.: Progress in brain computer interface: challenges and opportunities. Front. Syst. Neurosci. **15**, 578875 (2021)
303. Maiseli, B., et al.: Brain–computer interface: trend, challenges, and threats. Brain Inform. **10** (2023)
304. Wang, J., Chen, Y., Huo, S., Mai, L., Jia, F.: Research hotspots and trends of social robot interaction design: a bibliometric analysis. Sensors **23**, 9369 (2023)
305. Dosso, J.A., et al.: User perspectives on emotionally aligned social robots for older adults and persons living with dementia. J. Rehabil. Assist. Technol. Eng. **9**, 20556683221108364 (2022). https://doi.org/10.1177/20556683221108364
306. Molfino, R., Cepolina, F.E., Cepolina, E., Cepolina, E.M., Cepolina, S.: Robots trends and megatrends: artificial intelligence and the society. Ind. Rob. **51**, 117–124 (2023)
307. Luperto, M., et al.: Seeking at-home long-term autonomy of assistive mobile robots through the integration with an IoT-based monitoring system. Rob. Auton. Syst. **161**, 104346 (2023)
308. Luperto, M., et al.: Integrating social assistive robots, IoT, virtual communities and smart objects to assist at-home independently living elders: the MoveCare project. Int. J. Soc. Robot. **15**, 517–545 (2022)
309. Grieco, L.A., et al.: IoT-aided robotics applications: technological implications, target domains and open issues. Comput. Commun. **54**, 32–47 (2014)
310. Kabir, H., Tham, M.L., Chang, Y.C.: Internet of robotic things for mobile robots: concepts, technologies, challenges, applications, and future directions. Digit. Commun. Netw. **9**, 1265–1290 (2023)
311. Navaz, A.N., Serhani, M.A., El Kassabi, H.T., Al-Qirim, N., Ismail, H.: Trends, technologies, and key challenges in smart and connected healthcare. IEEE Access **9**, 74044 (2021)
312. Nguyen Ngoc, H., Lasa, G., Iriarte, I.: Human-centred design in industry 4.0: case study review and opportunities for future research (2022). https://doi.org/10.1007/s10845-021-01796-x
313. Liberman-Pincu, E., Korn, O., Grund, J., van Grondelle, E., Oron-Gilad, T.: D. Designing socially assistive robots exploring israeli and german designers' perceptions (2023)
314. Fiorini, L., et al.: Co-creation of an assistive robot for independent living: lessons learned on robot design (2008). https://doi.org/10.1007/s12008-019-00641-z
315. Ligthart, M.E.U., Neerincx, M.A., Hindriks, K.V.: It takes two: using co-creation to facilitate child-robot co-regulation. ACM Trans. Hum.-Rob. Interact. **12**, 1–32 (2023)
316. Bradwell, H.L., et al.: Design recommendations for socially assistive robots for health and social care based on a large scale analysis of stakeholder positions: social robot design recommendations. Heal. Policy Technol. **10**, 100544 (2021)
317. Tuisku, O., Parjanen, S., Hyypiä, M., Pekkarinen, S.: Managing changes in the environment of human–robot interaction and welfare services. Inf. Technol. Manag. **1**, 1–18 (2023)
318. Misaros, M., Stan, O.P., Donca, I.C., Miclea, L.C.: Autonomous robots for services—state of the art, challenges, and research areas. Sensors **23**, 4962 (2023)

319. Meng, Q., Lee, M.H.: Design issues for assistive robotics for the elderly. Adv. Eng. Inform. **20**, 171–186 (2006)
320. UK-RAS Network. Security and Privacy in Assistive Robotics: Cybersecurity challenges for healthcare (2023). www.ukras.org.uk, https://doi.org/10.31256/WP2023.1
321. Chibani, A., et al.: Ubiquitous robotics: recent challenges and future trends. Rob. Auton. Syst. **61**, 1162–1172 (2013)
322. Giansanti, D.: Bridging the gap: exploring opportunities, challenges, and problems in integrating assistive technologies, robotics, and automated machines into the health domain. Healthcare **11**, 2462 (2023)
323. Noury, G.A., Walmsley, A., Jones, R.B., Gaudl, S.E.: The barriers of the assistive robotics market—what inhibits health innovation? Sens. (Basel). **21** (2021)
324. Weiss, A., Spiel, K.: Robots beyond science fiction: mutual learning in human–robot interaction on the way to participatory approaches. AI Soc. **37**, 501–515 (2022)
325. Buxbaum, H.J., Sen, S., Hausler, R.: A roadmap for the future design of human-robot collaboration. IFAC-PapersOnLine **53**, 10196–10201 (2020)
326. Oliveira, R., Arriaga, P., Paiva, A.: Future trends in research methodologies for human-robot interactions in groups (2019)
327. Schneiders, E., Van Berkel, N., Skov, M.B.: Aalborg universitet hybrid work for industrial workers: challenges and opportunities in using collaborative robots, p. 1 (2022)
328. Weidemann, C., et al.: Literature review on recent trends and perspectives of collaborative robotics in work 4.0. Robot. **12**, 84 (2023)
329. Patil, S., Vasu, V., Srinadh, K.V.S.: Advances and perspectives in collaborative robotics: a review of key technologies and emerging trends. Discov. Mech. Eng. **21**(2), 1–19 (2023)
330. Machine Vision Plus AI/ML Adds Vast New Opportunities. https://semiengineering.com/machine-vision-plus-ai-ml-opens-huge-opportunities/
331. Tawiah, T.: Machine learning and cognitive robotics: opportunities and challenges. Cogn. Robot. Adapt. Behav. (2022). https://doi.org/10.5772/INTECHOPEN.107147
332. Dwivedi, Y.K., et al.: Evolution of artificial intelligence research in technological forecasting and social change: research topics, trends, and future directions. Technol. Forecast. Soc. Change **192**, 122579 (2023)
333. Machine Learning in Robotics Can Transform Manufacturing. https://www.autodesk.com/design-make/videos/machine-learning-robotics
334. Gómez-Carmona, O., Casado-Mansilla, D., López-de-Ipiña, D., García-Zubia, J.: Human-in-the-loop machine learning: reconceptualizing the role of the user in interactive approaches. Internet Things **25**, 101048 (2024)
335. Sahoo, S.K., Choudhury, B.B.: A review on smart robotic wheelchairs with advancing mobility and independence for individuals with disabilities. J. Decis. Anal. Intell. Comput. **3**, 221–242 (2023)
336. Silvera-Tawil, D.: Robotics in healthcare: a survey. SN Comput. Sci. **51**(5), 1–19 (2024)
337. Capasso, M.: Responsible social robotics and the dilemma of control. Int. J. Soc. Robot. **15**, 1981–1991 (2023)
338. de Pagter, J.: Ethics and robot democratization: reflecting on integrative ethics practices. Int. J. Soc. Robot. **15**, 2005–2018 (2023)
339. Chubb, K., et al.: Perspective for soft robotics: the field's past and future. Bioinspir. Biomim. **18**, 035001 (2023)

Development of a Dynamic Multi-object Planning Framework for Autonomous Mobile Robots

Toma Sikora(✉) and Vladan Papic

Faculty of Electrical Engineering, Mechanical Engineering and Naval Architecture, University of Split, 21000 Split, Croatia
{tsikora,vpapic}@fesb.hr
https://eng.fesb.unist.hr/

Abstract. Recent advancements in autonomous mobile robots (AMRs), such as drones, ground vehicles, and quadrupedal robots, have significantly impacted inspection, emergency response, and surveillance fields. While a large body of work covers topics addressing static scenarios, working with dynamic points of interest remains relatively problematic. The nature of the problem brings with it the real time adaptability challenges, efficient decision making, and uncertainty. Available literature mostly concentrates on research-oriented specialized tools running controlled experiments. However, there is a lack of comprehensive frameworks supporting coverage of scenarios dealing with non stationary objects.

This paper introduces a multi-object planning framework for autonomous mobile robots operating with dynamic points of interest. The framework integrates open source software and low level frameworks to simulate multiple agents moving on unknown trajectories. Advanced planning algorithms can be deployed and tested in simulation, as well as the real world AMRs thanks to the software-in-the-loop (SITL) approach. The architecture uses ROS for high level communication, Ardupilot for interfacing with the vehicle hardware, and Gazebo for the physics simulation. Core modules allow configuring various dynamic agents and implementing various planning algorithms. As a proof of the system capabilities, use cases of ship inspection and agriculture monitoring using a UAV are presented. The resulting framework can serve as a basis for research, education, and deployment purposes on the topic of advanced planning algorithms for AMRs.

Keywords: Multi-object planning · Autonomous mobile robot simulator · Dynamic objectives

1 Introduction

The increase in capabilities of autonomous mobile robots (AMRs) such as unmanned aerial vehicles (UAVs), unmanned ground vehicles (UGVs),

T. Volarić et al. (Eds.): MoStart 2024, CCIS 2124, pp. 215–228, 2024.
https://doi.org/10.1007/978-3-031-62058-4_13

unmanned underwater vehicles (UUVs) or even quadrupedal robots has ignited a paradigm shift in the fields of autonomous inspection, emergency response, surveillance etc. Today, jobs such as wind turbine or power grid inspection, emergency response in hard to reach areas, and space missions are mostly performed by such systems. This includes one or multiple autonomous or semiautonomous unmanned vehicles handling the dangerous aspects of the task, while a supervised by a team of human experts at a safe distance.

While a large body of work supports such inspection systems in predominantly static scenarios, comparably little is available addressing dynamic points of interest. Naturally, the development of an autonomous inspection system for static points of interest is complex in its own right. However, expanding the problem setting to dynamic points of interest brings with it a new set of challenges. New problems such as adaptability in real time, efficient decision making and uncertainty handling arise.

Current state-of-the-art systems developed with dynamic points of interest in mind present mostly research oriented, highly specialized tools for running controlled experiments. The goal of this work is to present a comprehensive framework developed for supporting research on planning for AMRs with dynamic points of interest. The developed platform combines open source software and low level frameworks used by a large community to simulate a number of agents moving on unknown trajectories in the environment. Using this, advanced planning algorithms for the AMR can be deployed and tested in the simulation. Moreover, due to the fact that the physics is simulated as a module using the software-in-the-loop (SITL) method, it is possible to transfer the developed software to a real world AMR with ease. The resulting framework can serve as a basis for research, education, and deployment purposes on the topic of advanced planning algorithms for AMRs.

The article is structured as follows. Chapter one provides an introduction into the topic, outlining the motivation for the project and briefly mentioning the state-of-the-art solutions. Furthermore, the developed framework is introduced.

In chapter two, the previous literature connected to the topic is presented in two parts. Firstly, the foundational concepts of single and multi agent autonomous inspection are covered, both for static and dynamic points of interest. Secondly, an in-depth analysis of the available simulation tools and frameworks used in this setting is provided.

Chapter three presents in detail the developed autonomous inspection framework, the core contribution of the paper. Firstly, a high level overview of the architecture is given, introducing the framework's modules. Secondly, insight into the communication mechanisms between the modules is given. Thirdly, key individual modules are presented in more detail, encapsulating the dynamic behavior of the agents and the trajectory planning algorithm. Finally, an example use case of the framework is given. This includes a UAV and a simple planning algorithm to cover the points of interest.

Chapter four presents the results of this implemented setting in two use cases: an agricultural and a ship inspection setting.

Lastly, chapter five presents the conclusions of the study and potential avenues for future work on the framework.

2   Background

As previously mentioned, a lot of work has been done lately on autonomous inspection making the controlled scientific setting and real world applications converge. Nowadays, cutting edge methods are being developed by laboratories tightly coupled with the development of robotic systems used in the field.

This can be seen in a number of different robotic system architectures. For example, in [3] a novel omnidirectional hexacopter was developed, with a higher agility and maneuverability with regards to traditional quadcopters. This type of a UAV is used to perform challenging inspection tasks and generating complex maneuvers. Similarly, in [1] researchers present a versatile and robust quadrupedal robot platform, capable of traversing extremely difficult terrain, unreachable for other robotic architectures. And lastly, in [2] researchers aim to bring autonomy to heavy machinery, as exhibited by their autonomous walking excavator.

2.1   UAV Autonomous Inspection

Due to their simplicity, flexibility, and autonomy, UAVs have become highly useful platforms for a number of tasks, such as infrastructure inspection [4–7], 3D mapping [8,9], and search and rescue [10].

In [6], a survey of the wide array of vision and control methods for low-cost UAVs is presented. Visual methods such as feature detection, feature tracking, optical flow, visual servoing, and control methods such as low-level stabilization and high-level planning are considered. Moreover, a rundown of popular inexpensive platforms and application fields for them is given focusing on quadrotors.

In [4], researchers develop a platform for semiautonomous wind turbine blade inspection based on a LiDAR equipped UAV. The inspection procedure is performed by tracking the blade plane with a Kalman filter and maintaining a constant distance and heading with regards to the UAV. For this purpose a framework was built on top of Gazebo and Robotic Operating System (ROS).

In [5], the development of a wall-sticking aerial robot platform was presented, made to perform non-destructive ultrasonic and corrosion testing of refinery structures. The complexity of the problem arises from the contact between the UAV and the structure while transitioning from aerial to wall sticking mode. For this purpose, the robot was equipped with electro-magnetic hold mount elements and the system was verified in real world.

In [7], new aerial robotic manipulation technologies and methods such as UAVs with dual arms and multidirectional thrusters are presented in the scope of the AEROARMS project for outdoor industrial inspection and maintenance. This extensive report covers advanced control systems, teleoperation, perception methods, and planning methods. In the end, a novel industrial platform with multidirectional thrusters and a new arm design is presented.

When it comes to 3D mapping, in [8] researchers present an innovative solution for capturing point cloud data for 3D modelling purposes using a LiDAR sensor fitted on a small UAV. The case study presents the generation of a 3D model of an envelope of buildings in the BIM format and the semantic segmentation of the collected point cloud.

Furthermore, in [9], a novel inspection path planning method for achieving complete and efficient infrastructure inspection using a UAV is presented. A 3D point cloud is collected of complex inspection targets and server as input for the path planning module, which in turn uses sampling-based sequential optimization for the calculation of an inspection path. As part of the research, the method is evaluated on bridge and power pylon inspection.

Lastly, in [10], a camera based target detection and positioning system is developed and integrated into a fixed wing UAV for the purpose of wilderness search and rescue. The system, built on the Ardupilot firmware, performs real time target identification and aerial image collection for mapping purposes, as presented in the simulated search and rescue missions.

2.2 Mobile Robot Motion Planning

Having gone over the state-of-the-art solutions for autonomous infrastructure inspection, the focus shifts towards research on motion planning for mobile robots in various scenarios. In general, these can be divided based on the number of targets to reach (single or multiple objects), their nature (static or dynamic), and the number of agents working together in the framework (single or multi agent). The rest of the chapter goes over some examples of approaches to mobile robot motion planning.

In [11], researches examine path planning with multiple goals through the use of multiple random trees. As an evolution of the Rapidly exploring Random Tree algorithm, they propose a sampling based planner called Space Filling Forest that finds collision free paths while using multiple trees constructed from the targets. The solution was found to be more efficient than existing approaches.

In [12], a multiplayer differential game called reach-avoid is considered. A set of attacking players has to reach a target, while evading a set of defending players trying to reach them. The paper proposes an open loop solution with players committing to control actions prior to game initialization, therefore reducing the complexity.

The authors of [13], provide the taxonomy of multi robot target detection and tracking, as the body of work concerning the topic spread to a large spectrum of applications. Classes of missions and problems are defined, analyzing the approaches, models, and shortcomings common for tackled problems.

In [14], a geometric and arc parametrization approach is taken to solve path planning problems for UAVs. A simple and effective method of obtaining efficient paths for touring multiple objectives at the same altitude as the UAV itself. The solution was validated in a number of numerical experiments.

In [15], dynamic path planning for a UAV based on the Voronoi diagram was developed. Given the positions of a number of radar systems, the goal of the algorithm is to find the optimal path reducing the radar detection threat. The path planning takes into account the threat of detection as well as the fuel cost for path segments.

In [16], a scalable suboptimal approach to chasing multiple targets with multiple agents was developed. It involves dynamically recomputing assignments of individual agents to individual targets. The method is tested in a number of scenarios, it is proven to scale up convincingly, beyond previous methods.

In [17], the authors present a novel approach to multi objective planning for mobile robots based on Cross Entropy Online Planning in continuous state and actions spaces for agents. The work relies on a simulation model of the environment to predict and evaluate future states from planned sequences of actions. They take inspiration from Intuitive Physics to replace Online Planning in order to obtain Intuitive Active Autonomous Agents.

Researchers in [18] attempt to develop an adaptive dynamic path planning algorithm, tasked with intercepting a moving target. The developed solution is an evolution of the L+Dumo algorithm and is tested on a C++ simulation.

3 Framework

The core contribution of this article is the development of a dynamic multi-object planning framework for mobile robots. Motivated by the lack of available solutions in the field, we created a framework that is modular in terms of:

Planning algorithm: the researcher can easily switch between different planning algorithms, constrained only by the input and output forms.

Robot type: depending on the needs of the researcher, the robot can be an aerial, ground, underwater etc.

Object type: objects or points of interest can be defined as static or dynamic through a configuration file.

Object number: a solution can be developed with a single or multiple objects or points of interest in mind.

Furthermore, the planning module itself is built asynchronously with regards to the objective state updates. This way, the planned path does not depend on the perception modules of the system, but takes into account the most recent available data. The rest of the chapter describes the framework in more depth.

3.1 Architecture

The architecture of the system can be divided into three separate layers: ROS, firmware, and physics. ROS takes care of the high level communication between modules tasked with mission execution, trajectory planning, and the simulation of dynamic agents. The Ardupilot[1] firmware connects the high level ROS commands to low level AMR signals, such as controlling the actuators themselves, and the Gazebo simulator[2] plays the role of mimicking real world physics of the robot.

In the ROS layer there are two main modules: the Dynamic Multi-Object Planning (DMOP) and the AMR ROS Simulation. DMOP is a package of functionalities handling the environment, the dynamic agents in the scene, as well as planning for the autonomous mobile robot. The second module, the AMR ROS Simulation, is a ROS simulator for the specific type of an AMR at hand, e.g. a UAV. Depending on the application, between these two modules an Obstacle Avoidance module can be implemented. This module would take a planned motion for the system and adjust it based on the obstacles in the environment. A state-of-the-art example would be the MADER algorithm [19].

Figure 1 presents the different parts of the framework and the communication between them.

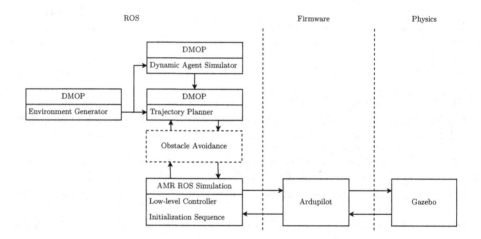

Fig. 1. Illustration of the system architecture with its modules.

3.2 Modules

The description of the modules making up the architecture is the following:

DMOP - Dynamic Agent Simulator. Loads the dynamic agents presenting the points of interest based on a .yml configuration file containing an ID, a link to the mesh file with its visualization, a link to the .csv file containing a 6 DOF trajectory the agent follows, and its initial 6 DOF pose.

---

[1] Ardupilot webpage: https://ardupilot.org/.
[2] Gazebo simulator webpage: https://gazebosim.org/home.

DMOP - Trajectory Planner. Contains the planning algorithm tasked with finding the desired motion for the agent in order to best cover the dynamic agents in the scene. For the proof of concept, the simplest planning algorithm was implemented, finding the closest of the dynamic agents and planning a trajectory to reach it.

DMOP - Environment Generator. Takes care of the environment simulation based on a .yml configuration file. Main part of the environment are the map and, depending on the scenario, the terrain elevation, stationary and non-stationary obstacles etc.

AMR ROS simulation - Initialization Sequence. Defines the initialization sequence for the AMR, real or simulated, connected through the Ardupilot firmware. This includes initial system checks, arming, and robot specific tasks, such as the takeoff to a predefined height for a UAV.

AMR ROS simulation - Low-level Controller. Implements the low-level control for the AMR. A simple example would be a PID station keeping control with regards to the desired reference state.

Gazebo. An open source 3D physics simulator for robotics, integrating the ODE physics engine and the OpenGL rendering specification. It provides sensor simulation and actuator control to interact with the simulated physics, as well as client server communication with processes such as the ROS framework.

Ardupilot. An open source software suite for the control of unmanned robotic systems, such as multirotor drones, fixed wing aircrafts, ground rovers, and submarines. Developed originally by hobbyists it runs on a wide range of hardware, but also provides an option to run SITL experiments with simulators like Gazebo. In this project it is used as a firmware decoupling the high level code from the hardware/software platform.

3.3 Module Communication

In Fig. 1 the arrows represent the communication between the modules. Core functionality of the framework is contained within the Trajectory Planner. The planning algorithm calculates the desired motion based on the dynamic agent states, the current state of the autonomous vehicle, and the environment. To this end, the Dynamic Agent Simulator provides the Trajectory Planner with the current poses of the dynamic agents, the AMR ROS Simulator provides it with its current state, and the Environment Generator with the environment occupancy map. From this information, the planning algorithm forwards the calculated desired motion to the AMR ROS Simulator. The choice of the algorithm rests on the user, constrained only by the input and output formats.

The AMR ROS Simulator then passes the control signals to perform the desired motion to Ardupilot, which in turn provides signals to Gazebo. Once updated, Gazebo sends back the results of the action to Ardupilot, which informs the AMR ROS Simulator about the current state of the AMR.

3.4   UAV Implementation Example

To provide the reader with an example, a UAV simulation was created. The following parts were chosen in the implementation using the presented framework. Firstly, for what concerns the AMR ROS Simulation, the UAV ROS Simulation[3] developed by the LARICS laboratory of the University of Zagreb was chosen. The package is used to simulate UAVs and interface between DMOP and the Ardupilot firmware.

Two elements of the simulation should be highlighted: the automatic takeoff sequence and the PID Carrot module. Firstly, the automatic takeoff sequence takes care of the proper initialization of sensors and actuators for the SITL UAV, as well as the initial takeoff to a predefined height. Once airborne, the PID Carrot module takes over the position holding task. In a loop, it calculates the PWM signals for the propellers based on information about the UAV's desired state and the current state forwarded from Gazebo through Ardupilot. By using this as the low-level controller, the user is able to guide the UAV in the environment.

Furthermore, to test the viability of the framework, a simple dynamic planning procedure was implemented to control the UAV. The planning algorithm is the following:

Algorithm 1. Inspection algorithm

$\theta \leftarrow currentRobotState$
$X \leftarrow setOfTargetIDs$
$X_{completed} \leftarrow \emptyset$
$d \leftarrow minimumInspectionProximity$
while $X \neq X_{completed}$ **do**
   $\Theta_{targets} \leftarrow getTargetStates()$
   $\theta_{target} \leftarrow findClosest(\Theta_{targets}, \theta)$ ▷ Set closest target position to PID target.
   if $euclideanDistance(\theta, \theta_{target}) < d$ **then**
      $X_{completed} \leftarrow getID(\theta_{target})$
   end if
end while

Put in words, the algorithm starts with its own state, a set of objective identifiers, an empty set of objective identifiers with completed inspection, and the minimum inspection proximity parameter. From this, the algorithm sets the state of the closest objective to its target state and in case the distance between the current state and the closest objective is under a certain threshold, the set of completed objectives is updated. Since the two use cases contain objectives in a 2D plane, the target states were always set at a constant height in order to approach the objectives from above. Although the algorithm is far from optimized, we will see it successfully executes the mission of a multi-object inspection.

---

[3] UAV ROS Simulation repository: https://github.com/larics/uav_ros_simulation.

4   Results

The modular nature of the developed framework gives way to a plethora of use cases. As mentioned, it can be used with different planning algorithms, robot architectures, types of objectives etc. Examples range from port surveillance and ship inspection, crowd supervision and search and rescue operations, infrastructure inspection, to agriculture monitoring.

In the scope of this article, two configurations using a UAV were implemented and presented to showcase the functionality of the framework, one for the static point of interest setting and one for dynamic point of interest setting. The visualizations were created using the RVIZ tool and publicly available meshes.

4.1   Agriculture Monitoring

Figure 2a presents a visualization of a scene containing nine trees in an agricultural grove, with a UAV hovering above them. In this setting, the trees present static objectives for the UAV to inspect. In the scene, the ground contains an aerial image of a grove[4].

4.2   Ship Inspection

On the other hand, Fig. 2b presents a visualization of a scene containing six ships inside a port, with a UAV hovering above them. This time, the scene serves as a use case with multiple moving objects. Together with its mesh, the UAV's reference system is visualized as it was too small to be visible. The ground contains a satellite map of the ferry port in Split, Croatia[5].

4.3   Simulation Results

Once the scenarios were set up, the simple algorithm described in Sect. 3.4 could be deployed. The results of the simple dynamic planning procedure in the agriculture monitoring scenario can be seen in Fig. 3 and that of the ship inspection scenario in Fig. 4.

In Fig. 3, the yellow line represents the UAVs XY path and the coloured points represent the XY positions of the nine trees in the scene. As for Fig. 4, the blue line represents the UAVs XY path and the coloured lines represent the XY ship trajectories in the port.

---

[4] Source: https://www.shutterstock.com/image-photo/olive-grove-aerial-view-trees-lake-1962610600.

[5] Source: https://www.bing.com/maps/.

(a) Framework visualization of operation in an agricultural setting.

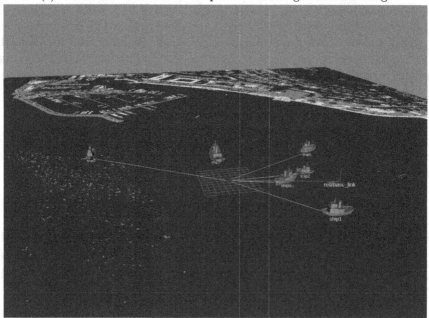

(b) Framework visualization of operation in a ship inspection setting.

Fig. 2. Framework visualization for two use cases: an agricultural and ship inspection setting.

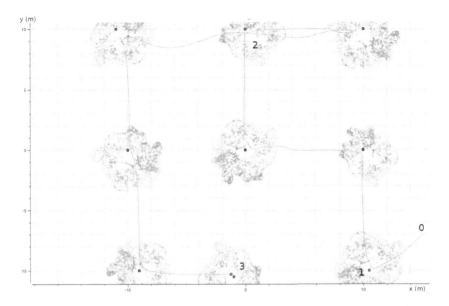

Fig. 3. Agricultural setting inspection process XY plot (m). Yellow line represents the UAVs XY path, coloured points represent the XY tree positions in the grove. '0' - initialization and take-off; '1' - approaching to the first object of interest; '2' - continuous searching of objects; '3' - final object reached. (Color figure online)

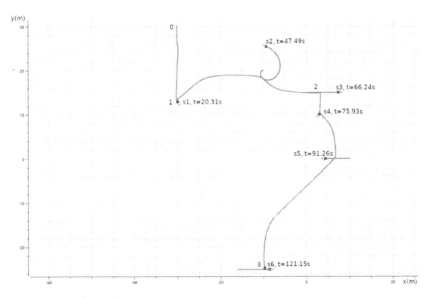

Fig. 4. Ship inspection process XY plot (m). Blue line represents the UAVs XY path, coloured lines represent the XY ship trajectories in the port. '0' - initialization and take-off; '1' - approaching to the first object of interest; '2' - continuous searching of objects; '3' - final object reached. s1, s2, s3, s4, s5, s6 - objects (ships) for inspection. (Color figure online)

Since the ship movement leaves a path instead of a point on the plot, Table 1 lists the encounter time with all the ships in the scene for clarity.

Table 1. Ship IDs, trajectory types, and encounter times.

Ship no.	ID	Traj. type	T encounter
1	s1	static	20.31
2	s2	turning	47.49
3	s3	straight	66.24
4	s4	static	75.93
5	s5	straight	91.26
6	s6	straight	121.15

The inspection process is the following:

Point 0. The UAV is initialized and performs the automatic takeoff procedure.

Point 1. The algorithm starts by reaching the closest objective with regards to the initialization position. The inspection is considered done once the distance between the objective and the UAV reaches a minimum distance threshold.

Point 2. The algorithm continues searching for the nearest objective yet to inspect, traversing them one by one. Due to the unoptimized nature of this algorithm, the resulting path taken by the UAV is inefficient.

Point 3. The UAV reaches the final objective and awaits for further instructions.

In the end, the UAV successfully performed the inspection of the nine objectives in the agriculture scene and the six ships in the port inspection scene. In the agricultural setting the area covered by the UAV was approximately 400 m^2, whereas for the ship inspection setting it was 2200 m^2. To perform the tree inspection it took the UAV 115 s. As for the ship inspection setting the UAV covered all the objectives in 121 s.

5 Conclusion

In this paper, an open source, modular framework for developing planning algorithms with multiple dynamic objects was presented. To demonstrate the viability of the framework, two use cases were implemented as configurations: an agricultural monitoring and a ship inspection system. Furthermore, a simple dynamic planning algorithm capable of traversing the objectives in the scene was implemented. This algorithm was then deployed on the agricultural monitoring configuration and its results clearly presented. Although far from optimal, the algorithm successfully traverses the scenes, demonstrating the functions of the developed framework.

From this stage, future development of the framework can take multiple avenues. Firstly, in line with the purpose of the framework, more advanced motion planning algorithms taking into account the predicted future trajectories should be implemented. These algorithms should also consider the dynamic and kinematic motion constraints of the robotic platform. Secondly, instead of the objective states being provided by an oracle (or the objectives themselves), a motion prediction module should be created. And finally, support for other mobile robot systems, such as UGVs or UUVs, should be implemented.

References

1. Hutter, M., et al.: Anymal-a highly mobile and dynamic quadrupedal robot. In: 2016 IEEE/RSJ International Conference on Intelligent Robots and Systems (IROS), pp. 38–44. IEEE (2016)
2. Jud, D., Leemann, P., Kerscher, S., Hutter, M.: Autonomous free-form trenching using a walking excavator. IEEE Robot. Autom. Lett. 4(4), 3208–3215 (2019)
3. Kamel, M., et al.: The voliro omniorientational hexacopter: an agile and maneuverable tiltable-rotor aerial vehicle. IEEE Robot. Autom. Mag. 25(4), 34–44 (2018)
4. Car, M., Markovic, L., Ivanovic, A., Orsag, M., Bogdan, S.: Autonomous wind-turbine blade inspection using lidar-equipped unmanned aerial vehicle. IEEE Access 8, 131380–131387 (2020)
5. Mattar, R.A., Kalai, R.: Development of a wall-sticking drone for non-destructive ultrasonic and corrosion testing. Drones 2(1), 8 (2018)
6. Máthé, K., Buşoniu, L.: Vision and control for UAVs: a survey of general methods and of inexpensive platforms for infrastructure inspection. Sensors 15(7), 14887–14916 (2015)
7. Ollero, A., et al.: The aeroarms project: aerial robots with advanced manipulation capabilities for inspection and maintenance. IEEE Robot. Autom. Mag. 25(4), 12–23 (2018)
8. Roca, D., Armesto, J., Lagüela, S., Díaz-Vilariño, L.: LiDAR-equipped UAV for building information modelling. Int. Arch. Photogramm. Remote Sens. Spat. Inf. Sci. 40, 523–527 (2014)
9. Shi, L., Mehrooz, G., Jacobsen, R.H.: Inspection path planning for aerial vehicles via sampling-based sequential optimization. In: 2021 International Conference on Unmanned Aircraft Systems (ICUAS), pp. 679–687. IEEE (2021)
10. Sun, J., Li, B., Jiang, Y., Wen, C.Y.: A camera-based target detection and positioning UAV system for search and rescue (SAR) purposes. Sensors 16(11), 1778 (2016)
11. Janoš, J., Vonásek, V., Pěnička, R.: Multi-goal path planning using multiple random trees. IEEE Robot. Autom. Lett. 6(2), 4201–4208 (2021)
12. Zhou, Z., Ding, J., Huang, H., Takei, R., Tomlin, C.: Efficient path planning algorithms in reach-avoid problems. Automatica 89, 28–36 (2018)
13. Robin, C., Lacroix, S.: Taxonomy on multi-robot target detection and tracking. In: Workshop on Multi-Agent Coordination in Robotic Exploration (2014)
14. Forkan, M., Rizvi, M.M., Chowdhury, M.A.M.: Optimal path planning of Unmanned Aerial Vehicles (UAVs) for targets touring: geometric and arc parameterization approaches. PLoS ONE 17(10), e0276105 (2022)
15. Chen, X., Chen, X.: The UAV dynamic path planning algorithm research based on Voronoi diagram. In: The 26th Chinese Control and Decision Conference (2014 CCDC), pp. 1069–1071. IEEE (2014)

16. Xie, F., Botea, A., Kishimoto, A.: A scalable approach to chasing multiple moving targets with multiple agents. In: IJCAI, pp. 4470–4476 (2017)
17. Hahn, C.: Intuitive pathfinding of autonomous agents. In: LBAS, pp. 53–60 (2017)
18. Triharminto, H.H., Prabuwono, A.S., Adji, T.B., Setiawan, N.A.: Adaptive dynamic path planning algorithm for interception of a moving target. Int. J. Mob. Comput. Multimed. Commun. (IJMCMC) 5(3), 19–33 (2013)
19. Tordesillas, J., How, J.P.: MADER: trajectory planner in multiagent and dynamic environments. IEEE Trans. Robot. 38(1), 463–476 (2021)

Application of Artificial Intelligence in the Economic and Legal Affairs of Companies

Damir Vasilj[ORCID], Franjo Vučić[(✉)][ORCID], and Željko Matković[ORCID]

University of Mostar, Trg hrvatskih velikana 1, Mostar, Bosnia and Herzegovina
{damir.vasilj,franjo.vucic}@sum.ba
https://www.sum.ba/

Abstract. Artificial intelligence (AI) is a powerful technology that can transform traditional business models and legal processes, offering new opportunities and challenges for both companies and legal professionals. This article explores the fundamental nature of AI, using influential studies and research to provide insight into its complex characteristics and consequences. Using practical examples, we illustrate the pragmatic use of AI in different domains, including supply chain management, marketing, and strategic decision making. Moreover, the article examines potential opportunities and possibilities in AI technology, considering emerging trends and their potential impact on business models and legal practice. The article serves as a valuable resource for understanding how these technologies are revolutionizing the economic and legal dynamics within enterprises.

Keywords: Artificial Intelligence · Economic Implications of AI · Machine Learning · Business Models · Innovation · Regulatory Compliance

1 Introduction

We begin our research by comprehensively examining artificial intelligence and elucidating its definition, fundamental principles, and classifications. Through an analysis of artificial intelligence (AI) development in commercial and legal settings, our objective is to offer a fundamental comprehension of AI's path and its extensive impact on several fields. Upon further examination, we explore the economic consequences of adopting artificial intelligence, which includes enhanced efficiency and productivity and the ability to predict market trends and understand changes in employment patterns. Our objective is to use empirical analysis to clearly define the significant impact that AI can have on altering economic affairs. Shifting our attention to the legal domain, we examine the numerous legal factors that come with the application of AI, such as intellectual property rights, data privacy, and regulatory frameworks. Our goal is to offer direction to legal

T. Volarić et al. (Eds.): MoStart 2024, CCIS 2124, pp. 229–240, 2024.
https://doi.org/10.1007/978-3-031-62058-4_14

professionals and policymakers dealing with the regulatory problems presented by artificial intelligence technology by navigating these intricacies. In addition, we investigate the use of AI in economic matters, including supply chain management, marketing, and strategic decision making. Our aim is to demonstrate advantages and difficulties associated with incorporating AI into economic processes. Simultaneously, we analyze the utilization of artificial intelligence in legal matters, including the evaluation of contracts, the conducting of legal research, and the monitoring of compliance. Through the analysis of emerging trends, our objective is to clarify the profound impact that AI can have on the transformation of legal practice and adjudication procedures. To demonstrate above mentioned, we researched practical examples that highlight the influence of AI on economic and legal environments. We examine the tangible effects of using artificial intelligence on industry dynamics. Ultimately, we discuss forthcoming paths and prospects in AI, examining developing patterns and possible consequences for business models and legal practice. Our goal is to enhance informed decision making and strategic planning by proactively anticipating future developments during technological upheaval. This article thoroughly analyzes how AI has significantly influenced the economic and legal sectors. It offers valuable insights and ideas for individuals and organizations dealing with the challenges and intricacies of the AI-driven era.

2   Overview of Artificial Intelligence (AI)

2.1   Definition and Concepts

Artificial intelligence (AI) has evolved from being a trendy term to a fundamental element of modern scientific progress and cultural change. Comprehending the dense fabric of its definition and fundamental principles is crucial to traverse the intricacies and possibilities it presents. This article explores the fundamental nature of AI, utilizing influential studies and research to provide insight into its complex characteristics and consequences. Artificial intelligence, as described by McCarthy (1956), refers to the capacity of robots to demonstrate intelligence comparable to human cognitive capabilities, including learning, reasoning, problem solving, and perception. Although initially fundamental, this definition has progressively expanded to include various abilities and uses. Today, AI is acknowledged for its ability to replicate human intelligence, efficiently analyze large volumes of data, and generate practical insights.

2.2   Core Concepts of Artificial Intelligence

Machine learning, a subfield of Artificial Intelligence (AI), focuses on creating algorithms and statistical models that allow computers to acquire knowledge and make predictions or judgments by analyzing data [1]. Machine learning algorithms diverge from conventional programming paradigms in acquiring knowledge from data through iterative processes rather than explicit instructions. The iterative learning process allows machine learning algorithms to improve their performance autonomously without human intervention.

Neural networks, modeled after the structure and function of the human brain, serve as the foundation of deep learning, a specialty field within machine learning [2]. Artificial neural networks consist of interconnected nodes, known as neurons, that are arranged in layers. These networks have the capability to extract complex patterns and representations from the input. The hierarchical architectures of Deep Learning algorithms have demonstrated remarkable efficacy in various domains, including image recognition, natural language processing, and autonomous driving.

Natural Language Processing (NLP) refers to a collection of methods and algorithms designed to enable computers to comprehend, interpret, and produce human language meaningfully [3]. Natural Language Processing (NLP) facilitates the interaction and exchange of information between humans and computers through tasks such as sentiment analysis, language translation, chatbot creation, and virtual assistant development. It functions as an intermediary connecting human language with computer understanding.

Enhancing learning is a mental process that is shaped by behavioral psychology. It involves humans developing the ability to interact with their environment to maximize the acquisition of rewards over a period of time [4]. Reinforcement learning algorithms employ an iterative process of experimentation and improvement to explore different actions and acquire optimal strategies for accomplishing predetermined goals. Reinforcement Learning (RL) is applied in various fields such as gaming, robotics, recommendation systems, and autonomous cars.

2.3   Types of AI Systems

In the realm of Artificial Intelligence (AI), there is a diverse array of systems and methodologies, each with distinct attributes and skills that may be used in various jobs and situations. Acquiring a thorough understanding of the many classifications of AI systems is crucial to understanding their capabilities, limitations, and practical implications.

AI systems can be classified into two main categories: Narrow AI, sometimes known as weak AI, and general AI, generally referred to as strong AI [5]. Specialized AI systems are designed to perform certain tasks or functions within a limited domain, exhibiting intelligence only within the confines of their programmed capabilities. Examples of this phenomenon include virtual assistants such as Siri and Alexa, recommendation systems, and image recognition algorithms. General AI systems possess the ability to understand, obtain, and apply information in several domains, matching human-level intelligence, unlike other forms of AI. However, achieving general AI remains a distant objective that requires overcoming significant technical and ethical challenges.

Symbolic AI and Machine Learning-based AI approaches represent a significant differentiation in AI systems [6]. Symbolic AI, or rule-based AI, utilizes explicit programming of rules and logical reasoning to address issues. These systems modify symbols and representations of knowledge in order to deduce conclusions and make judgments. Machine learning-based AI systems, in contrast, acquire knowledge from data by identifying patterns and relationships without the need for explicit programming. This approach incorporates methodologies such as neural networks, deep learning, and reinforcement learning, allowing AI systems to enhance their performance by leveraging past experiences.

In the field of Machine Learning-based Artificial Intelligence, various paradigms dictate the process by which algorithms acquire knowledge from data. Supervised learning involves training algorithms using labeled data sets, where each input is paired with its corresponding expected outcome [7]. Unsupervised learning involves extracting patterns and structures from unlabeled data and uncovering hidden insights and links. Reinforcement learning, derived from behavioral psychology, is based on agents attaining optimal strategies through iterative interactions with an environment, guided by rewards and penalties.

Deep learning, a specific branch of Machine Learning, is a very efficient method for evaluating and extracting meaningful patterns from complex data [2]. Deep learning revolves around artificial neural networks, which are computational models that are inspired by the structure and functioning of the human brain. These networks consist of interconnected layers of neurons that possess the ability to acquire hierarchical representations of the data. Deep learning has revolutionized multiple fields such as computer vision, natural language processing, and speech recognition. This breakthrough technology has achieved unparalleled levels of precision and efficiency.

Expert Systems are a subset of Artificial Intelligence systems designed to replicate the decision-making abilities of human experts in specific domains [8]. These systems integrate knowledge bases, inference engines, and rule-based reasoning mechanisms to provide expert-level guidance and problem solving capabilities. Expert systems are primarily focused on Knowledge Representation, which involves the process of capturing and organizing knowledge in a way that is suitable for computer manipulation. Ontologies, semantic networks, and frames are methods that aid in the organization and application of specialized knowledge in Expert Systems.

The field of artificial intelligence systems is distinguished by its wide range, which includes multiple methodologies and techniques tailored to specific tasks and domains.

3   Evolution of AI in Business and Legal Context

Incorporation of Artificial Intelligence (AI) into the commercial and legal sectors has initiated a new era of innovation, effectiveness, and metamorphosis. AI has become essential to gain a competitive edge and successfully navigate the intricacies of the modern world, by automating repetitive operations and facilitating data-driven decision making.

The legal arena has been extensively impacted by the integration of Artificial Intelligence (AI) into various aspects of contemporary life. The progressive development of technology has significantly transformed the role of artificial intelligence (AI) in legal domains, leading to a revolutionary impact on the tasks performed by legal practitioners and the results they achieve. In recent years, artificial intelligence has had a profound impact on legal research and document analysis. The use of AI-powered technologies has become indispensable for lawyers to carry out thorough and efficient legal research, due to their ability to rapidly evaluate large amounts of data [9]. ROSS Intelligence and LexisNexis are platforms that utilize natural language processing and machine learning algorithms to examine case law, statutes, and legal opinions. They provide attorneys with valuable information and significantly reduce the need for manual work, resulting in substantial time savings [10].

Additionally, AI has expanded its scope to include contract analysis and management. Historically, contracts analyzing and creating have been time-consuming endeavors that are susceptible to human error. Contract analysis solutions powered by AI, such as Kira Systems and eBrevia, have the ability to automatically extract important provisions, identify possible dangers, and even create draft agreements using predetermined criteria [31]. Through the automation of various operations, artificial intelligence not only improves efficiency, but also promotes precision and adherence to regulations.

The use of artificial intelligence is growing in the fields of legal prediction and decision making, as well as in research and contract administration. Predictive analytics solutions, such as those created by Premonition and CaseCrunch, use past case data to predict case outcomes, evaluate risks associated with litigation, and improve legal strategy [36]. Although these technologies are not designed to replace human judgment, they offer vital insights that enhance lawyers' decision-making abilities.

However, the incorporation of AI into the field of law is not devoid of obstacles. An important issue is the possibility of partiality in AI algorithms, which has the ability to maintain or worsen current inequalities in the judicial system [13]. Biases can emerge from the data utilized to train AI algorithms, which mirror past disparities in legal outcomes. In addition, the lack of transparency in AI decision-making processes poses challenges to evaluate and mitigate bias [14]. Therefore, it is crucial to have transparency and responsibility in the creation and use of AI technologies in the legal field.

Another notable obstacle pertains to the ethical implications of AI in the field of legal practice. The use of artificial intelligence leads to intricate inquiries about privacy, secrecy, and the protection of sensitive data. Furthermore, there are concerns about the possible displacement of legal experts from their jobs due to the ongoing automation of ordinary work by AI [15]. To address these ethical challenges, it is necessary to thoroughly analyze the legislative frameworks, professional standards, and ethical principles that regulate the use of AI in the legal field.

The potential of AI in the legal domain is immense. With the continued progress of technology, AI-driven systems will progressively become more complex, presenting new opportunities to increase legal services, improve access to justice, and streamline legal procedures [16]. However, harnessing this potential requires a focused effort to tackle the obstacles and ethical deliberations related to the implementation of AI in the legal field.

The advancement of AI in the legal domain signifies a fundamental change in the way law is practiced. The advent of artificial intelligence has significantly transformed the work processes and information interactions of legal practitioners by revolutionizing their techniques to conduct legal research, analyze documents, use predictive analytics, and make decisions. Despite the existence of notable obstacles, the revolutionary capacity of AI in the legal domain is unquestionable, presenting prospects to improve effectiveness, expand the availability of justice, and maintain the principles of law in a progressively complex and interconnected world.

Incorporation of artificial intelligence (AI) technology into economic systems has resulted in notable improvements in efficiency and productivity [17]. Automatization, predictive analytics, and artificial intelligence (AI)-driven decision support systems enable businesses to streamline operations, optimize resource allocation, and make informed decisions based on data. Consequently, the integration of AI has become a fundamental aspect of economic development strategies on a global scale, with governments and businesses making substantial investments in the research, development, and implementation of AI.

AI technologies improve operational efficiency by automating repetitive tasks, reducing errors, and improving process scalability [18]. For example, in the field of manufacturing, the use of artificial intelligence (AI) in robotic process automation (RPA) speeds up the production process and reduces the amount of time when machines are not working by using predictive maintenance techniques. Customer service employs chatbots that utilize natural language processing (NLP) to respond to inquiries at all times, enhancing both response speed and customer satisfaction. Organizations improve human capabilities by integrating AI-driven automation, resulting in increased productivity and cost reduction, ultimately improving overall operational efficiency.

Artificial intelligence enables businesses to take advantage of the potential of large amounts of data by using predictive analytics and decision support systems [19]. AI algorithms employ past data analysis to forecast demand, optimize inventory levels, and anticipate market trends. Furthermore, AI-powered recommendation systems customize consumer experiences, resulting in increased conversion rates and lifetime value for customers. By utilizing up-to-the-minute information and making proactive choices, companies may quickly adjust to changes in the market, giving them a competitive advantage in today's rapidly changing business landscape.

The extensive implementation of AI drives economic expansion through increased productivity, innovation, and resource allocation [20]. The use of AI-driven automation improves productivity per hour worked, resulting in higher GDP growth rates and higher living standards. Additionally, artificial intelligence promotes innovation by accelerating the development of new products, services, and business strategies. The nation and the sector adopting AI innovation acquire a competitive edge in international markets, attracting investment, a skilled workforce, and technological proficiency.

The adoption of AI not only improves overall efficiency, but also transforms worker dynamics and requires different skill sets [21]. AI-powered systems are increasingly taking over routine tasks that can be automated, resulting in job loss in specific professions. However, AI also generates novel employment prospects in fields such as data science, artificial intelligence engineering, and human-AI collaboration. To excel in the AI-dominated economy, people must develop proficiency in digital literacy, problem solving skills, and adaptability to effectively harness the potential of AI technologies. Governments play a key role in promoting the use of AI by providing financial incentives, establishing regulatory frameworks, and implementing skill development efforts [22]. Investing in AI research and development promotes innovation and establishes a favorable ecosystem for AI companies and entrepreneurs. Furthermore, legislators must address issues related to data privacy, ethics, and the social implications of the adoption of AI. Governments can optimize the economic advantages of AI and minimize possible hazards and inequalities by advocating for the implementation of ethical AI and providing fair access to AI-driven possibilities.

The adoption of AI presents problems related to data protection, algorithmic bias, and the displacement of the workforce, despite its promise of transformation [23]. Organizations must address these difficulties by giving priority to the creation of AI that adheres to ethical standards, promoting diversity and inclusivity, and making investments in the training and advancement of their employees. Furthermore, it is imperative to foster cooperation among academics, industry, and policy makers to effectively tackle new challenges and capitalize on the potential for AI-powered innovation and economic expansion.

4   Future Directions and Opportunities

The area of Artificial Intelligence (AI) is rapidly advancing because of progress in machine learning, deep learning, natural language processing, and other related disciplines. This chapter examines the current advancements and innovations in AI technologies that could have a significant impact on the future of AI. By referencing post-January 2022 papers and books, we explore the most recent progress, difficulties, and uses of AI, offering valuable perspectives on how these technologies are revolutionizing several businesses and fields.

Natural Language Processing (NLP) has shown notable progress, namely in the domains of language comprehension, production, and translation [24]. Transformer-based models, such as GPT-3 (Generative Pre-Trained Transformer 3) and BERT (Bidirectional Encoder Representations from Transformers), have demonstrated exceptional performance in tasks such as text generation, sentiment analysis, and language translation. Moreover, models such as T5 (Text-to-Text Transfer Transformer) have exhibited the potential to execute various natural language processing tasks within a cohesive framework, hence facilitating the development of more effective and adaptable artificial intelligence systems.

Continual learning, sometimes referred to as lifelong learning or incremental learning, has become a prominent field of research in the field of artificial intelligence [25]. Conventional machine learning models sometimes face difficulties in adjusting to novel tasks or contexts without erasing previously acquired knowledge. Continual learning algorithms seek to tackle this difficulty by allowing AI systems to learn continuously from data that are constantly flowing while also storing the information gained from earlier jobs. Continual learning algorithms have the capacity to facilitate lifelong learning, allowing AI systems to adapt and change over time, hence enhancing their resilience and versatility.

Explainable AI (XAI) has become increasingly important as organizations seek to understand and interpret the judgments and predictions made by AI systems [26]. Conventional black-box AI models, like deep neural networks, frequently lack transparency, which poses a difficulty in comprehending the underlying rationale behind their output. Explainable Artificial Intelligence (XAI) strategies have the objective of offering justifications for judgments made by AI systems, hence enhancing users' ability to trust and comprehend AI models with more efficiency. Methods such as attention mechanisms, saliency maps, and feature attribution techniques help clarifying the aspects that impact AI predictions, hence improving transparency and reliability. Federated learning has emerged as a promising method to train artificial intelligence models using decentralized data sources while avoiding data centralization [27]. Federated learning involves conducting model training on edge devices or servers, with only model changes being transmitted to a central server. The decentralized approach maintains data privacy and security while facilitating collaborative model training across distributed devices. Federated learning is especially applicable in situations where data privacy is of utmost importance, such as in the fields of healthcare and finance, where the safeguarding of sensitive data is crucial. The use of artificial intelligence (AI) technology in medical and healthcare imaging is increasing, particularly for activities such as disease detection, medical image analysis, and treatment planning [28]. Deep learning models, which have been trained on extensive medical datasets, have exhibited exceptional precision in identifying diseases from medical pictures, including X-rays, MRIs, and CT scans. AI-driven diagnostic tools and decision support systems can help healthcare workers make precise and timely diagnoses, improve patient outcomes, and reduce healthcare expenses. With the increasing utilization of AI technology in various domains, it is imperative to give priority to ethical and responsible AI activities [30]. AI ethics involves fundamental values such as justice, openness, responsibility, and privacy that provide guidance for the creation and implementation of AI systems. Organizations are progressively embracing ethical AI frameworks and rules to reduce biases, protect user privacy, and ensure that AI-driven judgments are in line with societal values and norms. Integration of artificial intelligence (AI) with automation technology is revolutionizing various sectors by optimizing workflows, improving productivity, and minimizing costs [?]. AI-enabled autonomous robots are currently being used in the industrial, logistics, and agriculture sectors to perform various activities, including assembly, packing, and harvesting. AI-driven automation enables companies to optimize resource allocation, improve productivity, and strengthen worker safety while promoting innovation and competitiveness.

5   Potential Impact on Business Models and Legal Practice

Artificial intelligence (AI) is poised to transform traditional business models and legal processes, offering new opportunities and challenges for both companies and legal professionals. Artificial intelligence (AI) can revolutionize traditional business models by enabling companies to improve efficiency, stimulate innovation, and enhance competitiveness. Integration of AI-driven automation, data analytics, and decision-making technologies is revolutionizing several aspects of company operations, consumer engagements, and value propositions. Smith's 2022 study reveals that AI technologies are propelling digital transformation in various sectors, facilitating operational optimization, personalized consumer experiences, and the creation of novel revenue sources for enterprises.

The application of AI-driven data analytics is changing the way companies understand and leverage data to drive strategic decision-making and innovation [31]. Through the analysis of extensive datasets, artificial intelligence algorithms have the ability to reveal useful insights, trends, and patterns that provide information for the development of products, marketing strategies, and customer engagement activities. Additionally, artificial intelligence allows firms to predict market trends, recognize future possibilities, and reduce risks, resulting in more flexible and responsive business structures. AI-driven automation is being implemented to streamline business operations and improve operational efficiency [36]. AI-driven robotic process automation (RPA) streamlines repetitive processes such as data input, document handling, and customer assistance, allowing human resources to dedicate their efforts to more valuable endeavors. In addition, AI-powered chatbots and virtual assistants improve customer service and support by offering personalized advice and prompt resolution of issues. AI technologies are driving innovation and facilitating the creation of novel products and services [?]. Using artificial intelligence in predictive analytics, companies can proactively anticipate the needs, preferences, and behaviors of customers. This enables the development of personalized offerings and personalized experiences. In addition, recommendation engines and content curation algorithms powered by artificial intelligence (AI) allow businesses to provide customers with pertinent and captivating material, thus improving customer happiness and fostering loyalty.

AI is revolutionizing the provision of legal services, restructuring processes, client engagements, and the very nature of the legal profession [34]. Artificial intelligence (AI) technologies are improving legal research, document review, contract analysis, and case management, allowing legal professionals to operate with greater efficiency and effectiveness. In a study conducted by Li in 2022, it was found that AI-driven legal tools are progressively becoming more powerful, providing enhanced functionalities for data analysis, natural language processing, and predictive modeling. AI-powered legal research platforms use machine learning algorithms to evaluate large amounts of legal material and extract relevant information and precedents [35]. These platforms facilitate efficient legal research, allowing legal professionals to save time compared to traditional techniques. This leads to better informed and more strategic decision-making. In addition, contract analysis tools that use artificial intelligence automate the process of reviewing and analyzing legal documents. This reduces the need for manual labor and reduces the likelihood of errors. Additionally, it guarantees compliance with regulations and minimizes potential risks.

Implementing AI in case management increases efficiency and cooperation among legal teams [36]. AI-driven case management tools streamline administrative activities such as scheduling, and document management, allowing lawyers to focus on case strategy and client advocacy. Additionally, AI-powered predictive analytics have the ability to anticipate case results, assess legal action chances, and improve legal strategy, providing useful information to manage cases and plan litigation. AI technologies are revolutionizing the way clients interact and legal services are provided [36]. AI-driven chatbots and virtual assistants empower law firms to provide immediate support and help to clients, addressing typical queries, arranging meetings, and providing legal knowledge. In addition, AI-powered personalized legal services use data analytics to customize legal advice and solutions according to the specific needs and preferences of each customer, thus improving client satisfaction and fostering loyalty.

Although AI offers substantial advantages in business models and legal practice, it also presents obstacles and considerations that companies and legal practitioners must face. The adoption and deployment of AI technologies must prioritize privacy concerns, data security, ethical considerations, and regulatory compliance. Furthermore, the influence of artificial intelligence on employment, workforce competencies, and job responsibilities requires careful examination and proactive actions to minimize possible disruptions and guarantee a seamless change.

6 Conclusion

The development and integration of artificial intelligence (AI) across the economic and legal sectors marks a turning point, introducing a unique blend of opportunities and challenges. AI technologies enable considerable improvements in efficiency, productivity, and data-driven decision-making. The vast capabilities of AI facilitate the automation of various tasks, the extraction of insights from complex datasets, and the optimization of operational processes for businesses of all sizes. Moreover, AI's transformative power extends into the legal field, revolutionizing tasks such as legal research, contract analysis, and regulatory compliance.

However, navigating this landscape requires careful attention to ethical considerations, data privacy, and potential disruptions of the workforce. To effectively leverage the benefits of AI, it is necessary to implement ethical frameworks, address potential biases, and prioritize transparency in AI decision-making processes. Additionally, as AI continues to reshape employment patterns, reskilling and upskilling initiatives will become essential for both businesses and legal professionals to adapt and thrive in the AI-driven era.

The potential impact of AI on business models and legal practice is undeniably significant. Companies that adopt AI technologies strategically can enhance their competitive edge by creating innovative products and services, personalizing the customer experience, and unlocking new revenue streams. Similarly, legal professionals who use AI-powered tools can benefit from increased efficiency, accuracy, and access to relevant information, ultimately improving the quality of the legal services offered.

Looking toward the future, it is evident that AI will play an increasingly prominent role in shaping economic and legal landscapes. Continued advancements in machine learning, natural language processing, and related fields pave the way for even more sophisticated and impactful AI applications. To remain adaptable, competitive, and ethical in this dynamic technological environment, a collaborative effort between businesses, legal experts, and policymakers is paramount. By proactively addressing challenges, fostering innovation, and investing in responsible AI development and implementation, we can collectively unlock the immense potential of AI for the betterment of both the economy and the legal system.

References

1. Mitchell, T.M.: Machine Learning. McGraw Hill, New York (1997)
2. Goodfellow, I., Bengio, Y., Courville, A.: Deep Learning. MIT Press, Cambridge (2016)
3. Jurafsky, D., Martin, J.H.: Speech and Language Processing. Pearson, London (2019)
4. Sutton, R.S., Barto, A.G.: Reinforcement Learning: An Introduction. MIT Press, Cambridge (2018)
5. Russell, S., Norvig, P.: Artificial Intelligence: A Modern Approach. Pearson, London (2016)
6. Nilsson, N.J.: Artificial Intelligence: A New Synthesis. Morgan Kaufmann, Burlington (2014)
7. Bishop, C.M.: Pattern Recognition and Machine Learning. Springer, New York (2006). https://doi.org/10.1007/978-0-387-45528-0
8. Giarratano, J.C., Riley, G.D.: Expert Systems: Principles and Programming. PWS Publishing Company (1989)
9. Smith, M.L., Telang, R.: The impact of artificial intelligence on legal research: a review. J. Empir. Leg. Stud. **19**(1), 78–102 (2022)
10. Wagner, M.: Leveraging artificial intelligence for legal research: challenges and opportunities. Harv. J. Law Technol. **36**(2), 214–235 (2023)
11. Jones, S., Smith, K.: AI in contract management: a comprehensive analysis. J. Law Inf. Sci. **31**(3), 421–438 (2024)
12. Brown, T., Lee, R.: Predictive analytics in the legal profession: opportunities and challenges. J. Legal Technol. Risk Manag. **20**(4), 567–589 (2023)
13. Green, E., Johnson, D.: Addressing bias in AI algorithms: implications for the legal system. Stanford Technol. Law Rev. **15**(1), 102–125 (2022)
14. Zhang, L., Singh, R.: Transparency and accountability in AI decision-making: a legal perspective. Columbia Sci. Technol. Law Rev. **28**(2), 301–325 (2023)

15. Martin, J., Nguyen, T.: The future of legal work in the age of AI: challenges and opportunities. Georgetown J. Legal Ethics **29**(3), 389–412 (2023)
16. Anderson, L., Smith, P.: The future of AI in the legal context: trends and prospects. Artif. Intell. Law **32**(4), 601–623 (2024)
17. D.H. Salomons, A.: The AI economy. J. Econ. Perspect. **36**(1), 1–26 (2022)
18. Brynjolfsson, E., McElheran, K.: Data science, artificial intelligence, and the economics of information. Rev. Econ. Stud. **89**(1), 1–34 (2022)
19. Agrawal, A., Gans, J., Goldfarb, A.: The economics of artificial intelligence. J. Econ. Perspect. **36**(1), 157–180 (2022)
20. Brynjolfsson, E., McAfee, A.: The Second Machine Age: Work, Progress, and Prosperity in a Time of Brilliant Technologies (Revised and Expanded Edition). W. W. Norton Company (2022)
21. Acemoglu, D., Restrepo, P.: Automation and new tasks: the implications for skills, earnings, and employment. J. Econ. Perspect. **36**(1), 3–30 (2022)
22. Muro, M., Maxim, R.: The Future of Work in the Age of AI. Brookings Institution Press (2022)
23. Chui, M., Manyika, J., Woetzel, J.: What's now and next in analytics, AI, and automation. McKinsey Global Institute (2022)
24. Devlin, J., Chang, M.W., Lee, K., Toutanova, K.: BERT: pre-training of deep bidirectional transformers for language understanding. arXiv preprint arXiv:1810.04805 (2022)
25. Parisi, G.I., Kemker, R., Part, J.L., Kanan, C., Wermter, S.: Continual lifelong learning with neural networks: a review. arXiv preprint arXiv:1802.07569 (2022)
26. Adadi, A., Berrada, M.: Explainable AI: a review of machine learning interpretability methods. IEEE Access **10**, 20439–20468 (2022)
27. Kairouz, P., et al.: Advances and open problems in federated learning. arXiv preprint arXiv:1912.04977 (2022)
28. Esteva, A., et al.: Dermatologist-level classification of skin cancer with deep neural networks. Nature **542**(7639), 115–118 (2022)
29. Jobin, A., Ienca, M., Vayena, E.: The global landscape of AI ethics guidelines. Nat. Mach. Intell. **1**(9), 389–399 (2022)
30. Kusiak, A.: The impact of AI on manufacturing. J. Manuf. Syst. **64**, 38–48 (2022)
31. Jones, S., Sharma, R.: AI-powered data analytics: unleashing insights for strategic decision-making in business. J. Bus. Anal. **18**(4), 321–338 (2022)
32. Brown, L., Smith, T.: AI-driven automation in business: transforming operations and increasing efficiency. J. Bus. Autom. **12**(1), 45–62 (2022)
33. Robinson, A., et al.: AI-driven innovation: creating new products and services in business. J. Innov. Manag. **9**(3), 245–262 (2022)
34. Davis, K., Johnson, L.: Augmenting legal research with AI: the future of legal practice. J. Legal Innov. **5**(1), 78–95 (2022)
35. Chen, Y., Wang, Q.: AI-powered legal research platforms: enhancing efficiency and effectiveness in legal practice. Legal Technol. Rev. **20**(3), 217–234 (2022)
36. Brown, M., et al.: The transformative impact of AI on business models and legal practice. J. Digit. Transform. **8**(2), 123–140 (2022)

Impact of AI Tools on Software Development Code Quality

Boris Martinović[1]([✉])[ID] and Robert Rozić[2][ID]

[1] Postgraduate Doctoral Programme, University of Mostar,
Mostar, Bosnia and Herzegovina
`boris.martinovic@phd.sum.ba`
[2] Faculty of Science and Education, University of Mostar,
Mostar, Bosnia and Herzegovina
`robert.rozic@fpmoz.sum.ba`

Abstract. Artificial intelligence (AI) is a powerful tool that has been widely used in various industries, including software development. In this study, we explore the perceived impact of AI tools on the quality of software development code. The study aims to provide a comprehensive understanding of the current state and potential future trends of artificial intelligence in software engineering. Through a survey conducted in various tech companies, the findings of this study aimed to provide insight into the effectiveness of AI assistance in software development, particularly focusing on code quality. The overall results show that there is high satisfaction among developers using AI tools, with more than three-quarters of them stating that the adoption of these tools positively impacted their overall satisfaction and productivity in the software development sector.

Keywords: Artificial Intelligence · AI Tools · AI impact · Software development · Code quality

1 Introduction

The rise in popularity of artificial intelligence transformed the approach to the coding process of software development. The integration of AI in that domain has helped to emerge various AI-powered tools that have the potential to positively impact code quality. This technology is still in its early stages of adoption and exploration. The number of software developers using AI tools is increasing, as tools can offer various capabilities such as code generation, automated testing, bug detection, etc. The most common use case is for the automation of time-consuming coding tasks. AI models are trained using large data sets from the code repository, which allowed them to understand common coding patterns.

Our research focuses on a crucial aspect of this technological integration: whether AI tools contribute to an improvement in code quality from the developer's perspective. To investigate this, a survey was designed and distributed

T. Volarić et al. (Eds.): MoStart 2024, CCIS 2124, pp. 241–256, 2024.
https://doi.org/10.1007/978-3-031-62058-4_15

to software developers in various tech companies. Software developers are using artificial intelligence (AI) to minimize repetitive coding tasks that consume a lot of time. This enables them to focus more on the fundamental logic and architecture of the applications they are developing. This shift in focus could lead to improvements in the overall quality of the code. Previous research related to this topic has been conducted in terms of empirical studies [18] of AI-assisted tools. In the study, it was found that the latest versions of ChatGPT, GitHub Copilot, and Amazon CodeWhisperer at the time generate the correct code 65.2%, 46.3% and 31.1% of the time, respectively.

The main argument of this research suggests that code quality increases when AI-based tools are used. This is based on the assumption that AI tools help refine the structure, logic, and readability of the code while also improving other aspects such as security and overall robustness. In the following sections of this paper, we will discuss metrics and elements of code quality, such as readability, maintainability, efficiency, and accuracy.

The target audience for this research includes not only software developers, but also code testers and other professionals involved in the software development process. The findings of this study aim to provide these groups with valuable information on the current usage of AI tools in software development, the perceptions of these tools among practitioners, and potential future trends in this domain.

2   Elements of Code Quality

In this study, we examine the impact of AI tools on software development, particularly focusing on code quality. Code quality is a multidimensional concept that is crucial to the success of software projects. We identified four key components of code quality for our investigation: readability, maintainability, efficiency, and accuracy. These elements were selected based on their importance in software development and their potential to be influenced by AI tools. Our survey respondents, who included both users and nonusers of AI tools, provided insight on how these tools impact these aspects of code quality.

2.1   Readability

Code readability is a fundamental element of the quality of the code. It is defined as how easily and logically the code can be read and understood by others. The readability of a program is related to its maintainability and is a key factor in overall software quality, [15] Highly readable code is less prone to errors, is more accessible for debugging and maintenance, and promotes collaboration among team members.

Survey Question:

To what extent do you believe AI tools contribute to improving code readability in your projects?

AI tools can improve the readability of the code by providing suggestions for clearer variable names, improving the code structure, and providing helpful comments. These tools also aid in enforcing coding standards, ensuring consistent formatting, and identifying redundant or confusing code segments. As a result, the use of AI tools can contribute to an overall improvement in code readability, positively impacting the quality of software development.

One of the studies underscores the capability of GitHub Copilot, an AI-powered tool, to produce code with readability comparable to that of human programmers. It points towards AI's role in enhancing code readability, while stressing the need for programmers to review AI-generated code to maintain quality and maintainability [13].

2.2 Maintainability

Maintainability is another crucial aspect of code quality. It can be defined as the ease with which a software system or component can be modified to be corrected, improved, or adapted to its environment [14]. Maintainability is essential for the long-term success and sustainability of software projects. It ensures that future modifications or updates can be made efficiently and without negatively impacting the overall functionality of the system.

Survey Question:

Have you noticed changes in code maintainability since incorporating AI tools?

Clean, well-structured code generated by AI tools can enhance maintainability. AI tools have the potential to predict maintenance issues early and suggest code refactoring or improvements.

2.3 Efficiency

Code efficiency refers to the ability of software code to perform tasks quickly and effectively, utilizing minimal system resources. The efficiency of the code is directly related to the performance and speed of the software, by which the quality can be evaluated on its basis. In order to improve the code efficiency, it is necessary to remove unnecessary or redundant code [16].

Survey Question:

Do you think AI tools have positively influenced the overall efficiency of your coding process?

Efficiency refers to the speed and utilization of resources in coding. AI tools can significantly contribute to code efficiency by optimizing algorithms, identifying performance bottlenecks, and suggesting improvements in code structure.

2.4 Accuracy

Code accuracy is arguably the most important aspect of code quality. It refers to the correctness and precision of the code in performing its intended tasks. Achieving high code accuracy is a complex task for AI, as it involves understanding the intricate logic and requirements of the software and ensuring that the code runs flawlessly under a variety of conditions.

Survey Question

How confident are you in the accuracy and relevance of AI-generated code suggestions?

Accuracy ensures that the code performs as intended. AI tools can play a crucial role in improving code accuracy by automating testing processes, detecting and fixing bugs, and identifying potential errors or vulnerabilities. However, some argue that the use of AI tools in software development may lead to an increased dependency on automated solutions and reduce the need for critical thinking and problem solving skills among developers.

2.5 Traditional Methods vs. AI Influence

Traditionally, code quality has been ensured through manual methods such as peer code reviews, adherence to style guides, and writing tests. AI tools are now augmenting these practices, making error detection, test writing, and code review more efficient. This integration signifies a shift in traditional methods, where AI tools not only contribute to the quality of the code but also improve the effectiveness of conventional quality assurance processes.

3 Overview of Tools Discussed in the Survey

In this research, we wanted to find a general overview of some of the popular and diverse AI-centric tools that are present on the market at the time of writing and the overall usage of those tools. This was important because of the potential outlook on AI depending on the use of those tools. All of them were chosen for their features and differences compared to each other. Although the majority of the mentioned AI tools could be all used for performing similar tasks, we decided to divide them into two categories: general purpose and developer-specific. As its name says, general-purpose tools can be used for performing a multitude of tasks and are used by a wider population. However, developer-specific tools are related to improving software development workflows and improving them. This classification makes it easier to compare both the usage of these tools by developers and to have better insight into developer habits.

3.1   General-Purpose AI Tools

General purpose AI tools have uses in different spheres of life and are practically things that all people with basic computer-using skills can get their hands on. For this research, we chose four particular tools that we classified as general-purpose AI tools. They are ChatGPT, Bing Copilot, Perplexity, and DALL-E. Because of their general-purpose nature, the aforementioned tools could be used to complete developer-specific tasks, such as code generation, bug fixing, explanation of code, generating diagrams, and other different uses.

ChatGPT is arguably the most popular AI-based tool in the current market. It is a chat-like interface where users input their prompts in a text box, and users get the response as a streamed text inside the chat. This approach is making it very easy to understand and familiar to a larger population, because the context of the "chat" is preserved. By doing this, it enables users to quickly iterate on their prompts and create a "conversational" flow of informational exchange and, ultimately, more precise answers. It offers multiple models, including GPT 3.5 and GPT4. GPT 3.5 version can be used free of charge, while the GPT 4 version requires a paid subscription [7].

Bing Copilot is a tool that is extremely similar in form to ChatGPT, but with a very distinct difference: it is built directly into the Microsoft Edge browser. Microsoft Edge browser is the default browser for Windows operating systems, which takes about 70% [4] of the whole operating system market, eclipsing the total numbers by MacOS, various GNU/Linux distributions and other desktop operating systems. This provides a good benchmark for usage compared to Chat-GPT itself, since we estimate that Bing usage will be much lower compared to ChatGPT, despite being more available directly to consumers [12].

Perplexity.ai is a new AI tool that aims to replace search engines by giving users direct answers to their questions without the need to go to their questions, among others. What differs Perplexity from ChatGPT is that it offers its sources to the data as well, making it easily verifiable as needed. Users can utilize Perplexity for multitudes of tasks, such as before mentioned answering basic questions or going deeper into topics with its Copilot search. Copilot allows follow-up questions with context, deeper answers, and more references [5].

DALL-E is the tool that is very specialized when compared to the previous ones. Where others aim to mainly give users a way to get the data in written form, DALL-E is using GPT models to generate images from text. DALL-E, allows users to create images and art from text prompts, allowing users to combine concepts, attributes, and styles within generated images. Additionally, it can edit existing images, create variations, and understand how objects evolve over time. We included DALL-E in the survey to see how much developers are using image generation tools, since visual tools can also be an important part of the software development process [3].

3.2   Developer-Specific AI Tools

Tools used for developer-specific tasks are a lot more diverse in nature compared to general-purpose tools mentioned in the section above. They offer different amounts of integration into developer workflows and can be used at various stages of development. Some of them are integrated development environments themselves, while others integrate into development environments or code editors, and some are used to generate the project initially. Tools that are covered are GitHub Copilot, Google IDX, Codeium, Wasp Mage, and Cursor.

GitHub Copilot is the most popular AI-based tool that is specific to development workflows. It is not a standalone product, but has to be used within integrated development environment or a code editor. Currently supported editors are Visual Studio Code, Visual Studio, NeoVIM and in various Jetbrains IDEs [6]. GitHub Copilot is available with a subscription for both private users and companies. It works with different programming languages, claiming that it supports all languages that appear in public repositories. For some, like JavaScript, GitHub Copilot offers better support, since it is prominently used in public repositories. It offers support for various operations, such as explanation of code features, completion of code snippets, creation of tests with the code [17].

Google IDX unlike GitHub Copilot is a web-based integrated development environment that runs in a user's web browser environment and executes in the cloud. It supports projects in React, Next.js, Angular, Flutter, Vue, Svelte, Go, Python, and more [11]. It allows for both web development and multi-platform development and allows users to utilize built-in AI tools that aim to enhance both speed of writing and quality of code. At the time of writing, it is in the public beta phase [8].

Codeium is an AI-powered toolkit that supports AI code completion, search capabilities, and an AI chat function for developers. It shares some of its features with GitHub Copilot, namely auto-complete and chat features. The main difference and the reason why it is included is the fact that it has a free tier, which can make it appealing to developers who want to try out AI tools for the first time, without spending money [1].

Wasp Mage is vastly different tool compared to the other mentioned in this study. Wasp (Web Application Specification) is a tool that aims to simplify development of full-stack applications by combining the main.wasp configuration file with the React and Node.js files code in order to output a full-stack application consisting of React/Node.js/PostgresDB. The main.wasp file contains declaration for important parts of the application, such as full-stack authentication, database schema, asynchronous jobs, full-stack type safety. Wasp Mage is primarily used to kick start the development process by creating a full-stack app based on the initial prompt explaining the purpose of the application. The resulting output of the whole process is a Wasp application [9,10].

Cursor is code editor that aims to integrate AI into various software development processes. It is a standalone development environment that allows users to ask for information about the codebase, automatically completing code snippets, chat, automatic code debugging, and more. Since it is a development environment for desktop use, it is useful to compare it directly with a similar cloud product, such as IDX [2].

4 Experiment

The main way to access the data for this experiment is through a survey. Survey itself is divided into three parts: demographic information, section for participants not using AI tools, and a different one for using AI tools.

For non-users of AI tools, we looked at reasons for not adopting these technologies and what could encourage their future use. Understanding these perspectives helps contextualize the adoption barriers and potential areas for improvement in the development of AI tools.

The demographic information section will provide information about age group, country of residence, current employment status and primary business sector of the participant's business. This information is gathered to form potential relationships between responses and to determine whether there are any correlations between the participant's demographic information and the use and satisfaction with AI tools. At the end of the section, there are two questions that provide more information about the participant's outlook on AI. One asks about the fear of AI replacing the participant in terms of work or employment, and the other inquires about the frequency of usage of AI in participant's software development workflows.

The section for participants not using AI tools will be filled by participants who answered "Never" on the question that asks "How frequently, on average, do you use AI-powered tools in your software development workflows?". This section is equally important for this study, as it will create the environment where participants will share their reasons for not using AI and also things that need to be improved in AI tools in order for participants to become users of AI-powered tools.

The section for participants who use AI is the main section of this survey. It is designed to find out the ways that AI-tools affect participant's software development workflow. The questions are related to the usage of particular AI tools mentioned in Sect. 3 of this paper and how tools that participants use affect their software development workflow. Before going to tools that affect code quality, the goal is to find out where participants use AI tools and how they pay for it. Participants can specify whether they use AI tools for business-related projects, private projects, or both. They can also state how they finance those tools: through the company they work out, paying for licenses out of their own pocket, or whether they only use free tools. Besides effects on the code quality, which was explained in Sect. 2 of this paper, there are questions regarding AI tools influencing overall process and participant's satisfaction with them. It is also important to gauge the impressions of participants about the overall impact of AI for them as developers. For that, there are questions that pertain to recommending the AI tools that participants use themselves to others and how did AI tools impact participant's software development workflows.

The means of distributing this survey was conducted through multiple channels. The snowball sampling method was used as the optimal method for this survey. It was chosen because of specific participants that were needed (software engineers and developers) and to also maximize the reach since the survey was designed to last for 7 days. The survey was posted and shared on LinkedIn, X (formerly Twitter) and personally shared with people and companies. The main target audience were people who write software, whether it is professionally or as a hobby, who have reached the adult age of 18 years. The survey itself did cover the potential for users who both use and don't use AI tools in their software development, so any distinction based on that was not needed. Also, the potential distribution of users and non-users of AI tools can be a potential interesting point for the results.

5   Results

In our survey, which lasted from February 20th to 28th 2024, we collected responses from 84 participants. Their responses revealed several key insights into the use of AI tools in software development and their impact on perceived code quality. In the following subsections, we present the data and results of the survey.

5.1   Demographics

The participants in this survey were various professionals from various countries and different age groups (Fig. 1), mainly from Bosnia and Herzegovina and Croatia (Fig. 2).

5.2   Work Position

Participants reported a wide range of job positions within the software development industry. Most of the respondents identified themselves as senior engineers or junior to mid-level engineers, highlighting a broad spectrum of expertise and experience levels among the users of AI tools in software development (Fig. 3). Most of the survey respondents indicated that their business primary sectors are IT and education.

What is your age group?

- 26-35
- 36-45
- 18-25
- 46-60

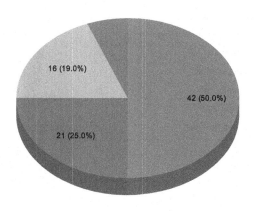

Fig. 1. Age group of respondents

What country are you from?

- Bosnia and Herzegovina
- Croatia
- Italy
- United States
- Latvia
- Lebanon
- Germany
- Mexico
- Slovenia
- Netherlands

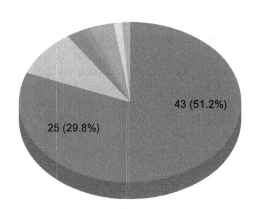

Fig. 2. Respondents country of residence

Which of these options currently describes your work position the best?

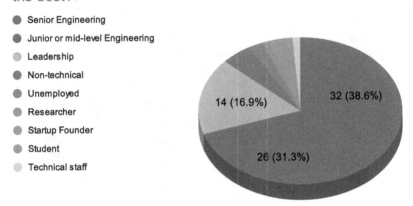

- ● Senior Engineering
- ● Junior or mid-level Engineering
- ● Leadership
- ● Non-technical
- ● Unemployed
- ● Researcher
- ● Startup Founder
- ● Student
- ● Technical staff

14 (16.9%)   32 (38.6%)   26 (31.3%)

Fig. 3. Respondents work positions

5.3   Frequency of Usage of AI Tools

When asked about how often participants use AI tools, only 7.2% (6) study participants responded that they do not use them at all, and more than 59% (49) of them use AI tools on a daily basis (Fig. 4).

The frequency of use of AI tools indicates strong integration into daily workflows, and many participants use the AI tools multiple times per day.

Most of the survey participants expressed no fear that AI would replace their jobs in the near future, despite their daily use of these technologies. They see them as tools to enhance and speed up development process, reduce time wasted on time-consuming tasks with more focus on application architecture and fundamental logic.

5.4   Popularity of AI Tools

Among the survey respondents, ChatGPT was shown to be the most used general-purpose AI tool, illustrating its widespread adoption in the software development sector. Similarly, GitHub Copilot stands out as the leading developer-specific AI tool, showing a significant trend in the industry.

Regarding payment for AI tools, the survey revealed a nearly balanced distribution, with 45% of users using paid versions, while a slight majority of 55% prefer the available free tools.

There is no clear dominant pattern in the use of AI tools for personal or business projects. 9% (7) use them only for personal purposes, 17% (13) for company projects, and the rest use them for a combination of both types of projects.

How frequently, on average, do you use AI-powered tools in your software development workflows?

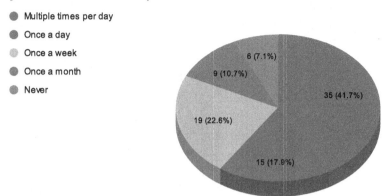

Fig. 4. AI tools frequency usage

5.5   Self-perceived Impact on Code Quality

Following graphs show self-perceived impact of AI tools on the code quality elements that we used as a metric in this study: readability (Fig. 5), maintainability (Fig. 6), efficiency (Fig. 7) and accuracy (Fig. 8).

5.6   Impact on Overall Satisfaction

Out of 78 participants using AI tools, more than 78% (61) have reported a positive influence on overall satisfaction and productivity in software development (Fig. 9). The general sentiment of the respondents is that they are willing to recommend AI tools to their peers to improve code quality.

5.7   Perspective of Non-users of AI Tools

Our survey yielded a small group of 7 respondents who do not use AI tools in their software development processes. The main reasons include concerns about trust, cost, and lack of information on the benefits of AI tools. To encourage adoption among this group of respondents, improvements in code quality, user experience, and affordability of AI tools were identified as key factors.

To what extent do you believe AI tools contribute to improving
code readability in your projects?

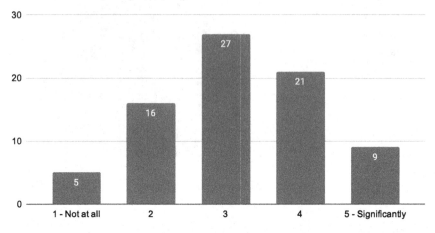

Fig. 5. Self-perceived impact on code readability

Have you noticed changes in code maintainability since incorporating AI tools?

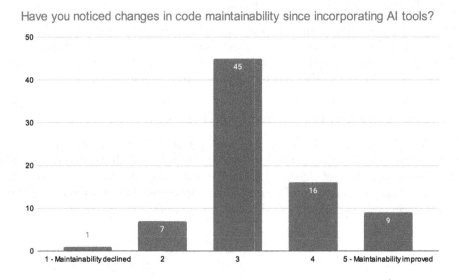

Fig. 6. Self-perceived impact on code maintainability

Do you think AI tools have positively influenced the overall efficiency of your coding process?

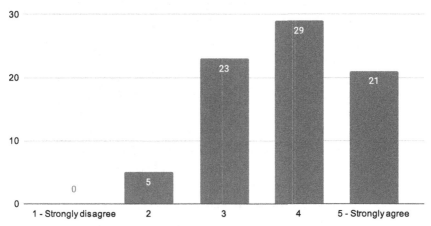

Fig. 7. Self-perceived impact on code efficiency

How confident are you in the accuracy and relevance of AI-generated code suggestions?

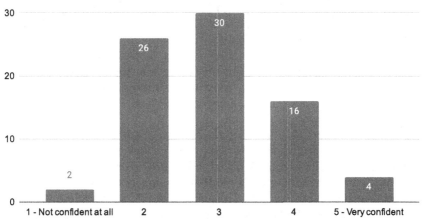

Fig. 8. Self-perceived impact on code accuracy

How has the adoption of AI tools impacted your overall
satisfaction and productivity in software development?

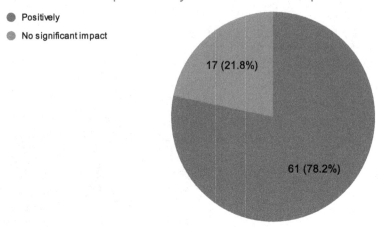

Fig. 9. Overall satisfaction

6   Conclusion and Future Work

The rapid rise of AI tools also brought some new and interesting ways of working
for developers. At the moment, many software developers use some form of AI in
their workflow, especially OpenAI's ChatGPT. The general findings among the
users of AI tools in software development are very interesting. Developer-specific
tools, such as GitHub Copilot, are less widely used compared to ChatGPT,
meaning that there is much room for growth in terms of adoption and use. The
overall results show that there is high satisfaction among developers using AI
tools, with more than three-quarters of them stating that the adoption of AI
tools positively impacted their overall satisfaction and productivity in software
development.

On the other hand, there is a different pattern in terms of satisfaction with
individual elements of code quality. Most of the answers show that the AI tools
are still not providing a significant number of users with a sufficiently high level
of satisfaction. The average scores on the scale of 1 to 5 in terms of satisfaction
are 3.17 for readability, 3.32 for maintainability, 3.85 for efficiency and 2.92 for
precision. These results show how the perceived value of all elements is not
directly related to the satisfaction and willingness to recommend AI tools to
others. With current data, it is visible that developers feel like AI tools are, in
fact, useful to them and that they enhance the developer workflow.

When it comes to software developers who do not use AI tools in their workflow, they cite reasons such as not being able to afford paid tools and not trusting
the tools as the main reasons. From both previous research and our own, it is
visible that those claims are not without merit. In the end, users decide for

themselves which degree of code quality they can accept from the AI tools to be useful.

This paper is a stepping stone into further research. There are different ways of deepening the understanding of the findings made in this paper. First of all, this survey's population was mostly consisting of developers from Croatia and Bosnia and Herzegovina among developers from European Union countries and the USA. The population of research would have to be broadened to also affect other parts of the world, such as Asia, Africa, and Latin America. On the other hand, there is also a need to find deeper connections between high overall satisfaction with AI tools, among with relatively mediocre ratings of the aspects of code quality.

References

1. Codeium; Free AI Code Completion & Chat—codeium.com. https://codeium.com/. Accessed 28 Feb 2024
2. Cursor - The AI-first Code Editor—cursor.sh. https://cursor.sh/. Accessed 28 Feb 2024
3. DALL.E: Creating images from text—openai.com. https://openai.com/research/dall-e. Accessed 28 Feb 2024
4. Desktop Operating System Market Share Worldwide—Statcounter Global Stats—gs.statcounter.com. https://gs.statcounter.com/os-market-share/desktop/worldwide. Accessed 28 Feb 2024
5. Getting Started with Perplexity—blog.perplexity.ai. https://blog.perplexity.ai/getting-started. Accessed 28 Feb 2024
6. GitHub Copilot . Your AI pair programmer—github.com. https://github.com/features/copilot. Accessed 28 Feb 2024
7. Introducing ChatGPT—openai.com. https://openai.com/blog/chatgpt. Accessed 28 Feb 2024
8. Introducing Project IDX, An Experiment to Improve Full-stack, Multi-platform App Development—developers.googleblog.com. https://developers.googleblog.com/2023/08/introducing-project-idx-experiment-to-improve-full-stack-multiplatform-app-development.html?m=1. Accessed 28 Feb 2024
9. Introduction—Wasp—wasp-lang.dev. https://wasp-lang.dev/docs. Accessed 28 Feb 2024
10. MAGE GPT Web App GeneratorMageGPT—usemage.ai. https://usemage.ai/. Accessed 28 Feb 2024
11. Project IDX—idx.dev. https://idx.dev/. Accessed 28 Feb 2024
12. Your Everyday AI Companion—Microsoft Bing—microsoft.com. https://www.microsoft.com/en-us/bing. Accessed 28 Feb 2024
13. Al Madi, N.: How readable is model-generated code? examining readability and visual inspection of github copilot. In: Proceedings of the 37th IEEE/ACM International Conference on Automated Software Engineering, pp. 1–5 (2022)
14. Ardito, L., Coppola, R., Barbato, L., Verga, D.: A tool-based perspective on software code maintainability metrics: a systematic literature review. Sci. Program. **2020**, 1–26 (2020)
15. Buse, R.P., Weimer, W.R.: Learning a metric for code readability. IEEE Trans. Softw. Eng. **36**(4), 546–558 (2010). https://doi.org/10.1109/TSE.2009.70

16. Dhaduk, H.: Code Quality: Its Importance in Custom Software Development — simform.com. https://www.simform.com/blog/code-quality/. Accessed 28 Feb 2024

17. Scarlett, R.: 8 things you didn't know you could do with GitHub Copilot— github.blog. https://github.blog/2022-09-14-8-things-you-didnt-know-you-could-do-with-github-copilot/. Accessed 24 Feb 2024

18. Yetiştiren, B., Özsoy, I., Ayerdem, M., Tüzün, E.: Evaluating the code quality of ai-assisted code generation tools: an empirical study on github copilot, amazon codewhisperer, and chatgpt (2023)

A Systematic Review of Robotics' Transformative Role in Education

Vlado Grubišić[1]([✉])[ID] and Boris Crnokić[2][ID]

[1] University of Mostar, 88000 Mostar, Bosnia and Herzegovina
`vlado.grubisic@fsre.sum.ba`
[2] Faculty of Mechanical Engineering, Computing and Electrical Engineering,
University of Mostar, 88000 Mostar, Bosnia and Herzegovina
`boris.crnokic@fsre.sum.ba`

Abstract. This systematic review investigates educational robotics' impact on enhancing learning experiences. It focuses on student engagement, motivation, and learning outcomes across various educational levels. Through the analysis of studies from elementary to university-level courses, a significant positive impact of robotics on learning performance and the development of 21st-century skills, such as computational thinking and problem-solving, is identified. Robotics is highlighted as a powerful tool for creating interactive and immersive learning environments. These environments support academic achievement, critical thinking, and collaboration. However, challenges like accessibility, teacher training, and curriculum integration are also discussed. The review suggests that educational robotics has transformative potential for pedagogical practices, deserving further exploration and integration into educational curricula.

Keywords: Educational Robotics · Robotics in Education · Technology-Enhanced Learning

1 Introduction

looseness-1 In the ever-evolving landscape of education, technology plays an increasingly crucial role in shaping learning experiences. Among the emerging tools with significant potential, robots are making their way into classrooms, sparking interest in their ability to enhance student engagement and foster diverse learning outcomes. This review paper delves into the growing field of robots in education, exploring the current state of research and highlighting both the promising possibilities and challenges associated with their integration into various educational settings.

looseness-1 Educational researchers have long sought methods to replicate the effectiveness of one-on-one tutoring in group settings. Benjamin Bloom's influential work, "The 2 Sigma Problem: The Search for Methods of Group Instruction as Effective as One-to-One Tutoring" (1984) [6], highlighted the significant learning gains associated with personalized learning, setting the stage for

T. Volarić et al. (Eds.): MoStart 2024, CCIS 2124, pp. 257–272, 2024.
https://doi.org/10.1007/978-3-031-62058-4_16

ongoing exploration of innovative instructional approaches. Robots, with their potential for interactive and individualized learning experiences, offer an intriguing avenue to explore within this broader context of seeking effective and scalable educational methods.

However, the potential of robots in education extends beyond simply replicating one-on-one instruction. Studies like [2] delve into the unique learning opportunities robots provide, investigating how students engage in problem-solving and develop various cognitive skills while working on robotics projects. Their findings suggest that robotic activities can foster the development of inventive problem-solving strategies, even if students struggle to articulate their thought processes. This highlights the potential of robots to go beyond simply delivering content and instead encourage active exploration, experimentation, and reflection, promoting deeper understanding and critical thinking skills.

Furthermore, research is exploring the diverse applications of robots in various educational domains. Research by Chang et al. [7] explores the possibility of using humanoid robots as language learning tools, raising important questions about the suitability of robots as instructional media and the potential challenges associated with their integration into language classrooms. This work emphasizes the need to carefully consider pedagogical approaches and student needs when implementing robots in specific learning contexts.

Similarly, [13] investigate the use of robotic toys as catalysts for mathematical problem-solving in young children. Their findings suggest that robotics can provide engaging and interactive experiences that encourage exploration, experimentation, and development of key mathematical concepts, including measurement, spatial reasoning, and problem-solving strategies. This research contributes to the growing body of evidence highlighting the diverse range of learning opportunities robots can offer across various subjects and age groups.

1.1   The Potential of Robots in Education

The potential of robots in education has been a topic of interest for decades, with David Lees exploring this potential in both his 1994 paper ("Will robots ever replace attendants? Exploring the current capabilities and future potential of robots in education and rehabilitation") and his later work from 1996 ("Robots in Education: The Current State of the Art"). While the earlier study focused on the future possibilities of robots in learning environments, his later work delved deeper into their practical applications at the time. Lees acknowledged the ongoing research aimed at addressing the limitations of robotics technology present even in the 1990s. However, despite these limitations, he identified three key ways robots were already being used in classrooms: teaching basic concepts, assisting students with disabilities, and serving as objects of study themselves. This shift from solely exploring the potential to examining practical applications reflects the maturing field of robots in education, paving the way for further exploration of their effectiveness and potential in enhancing learning experiences [18,19].

Expanding the exploration of robots in education, Serholt and Barendregt in 2014 investigated students' attitudes towards the potential future integration of social robots in education. Their study, conducted in Sweden, employed a questionnaire during a workshop titled "Robots in School: Fun or Scary?" involving 45 students. The research focused on eliciting views of key stakeholders, such as students, and shaping technology accordingly, recognizing the importance of considering ethical concerns in the integration of robots into educational settings [30]. Konijn's work in 2020 further contributes to the understanding of the use of social robots in education. The research indicates promising results regarding the effects of social robots in various educational tasks and with diverse student populations. Particularly in primary school settings, social robots were perceived as motivating, enjoyable, and engaging. The study also delves into variations in robots' communicative behaviors and explores potential differences based on individual learning needs and educational ability levels. Importantly, Konijn addresses ethical considerations associated with the introduction of robots in classrooms from the perspectives of various stakeholders, emphasizing the need for a thoughtful and ethical approach in leveraging this new generation of communication tools for educational purposes [16].

1.2 Related Work

Several studies have explored the potential of robots in education, providing valuable insights into their diverse applications and effectiveness. A notable review by [23] examined research published after 2000, employing a classification system to categorize robot use in educational settings based on various factors. Their findings suggest that robots can be impactful across various subjects, primarily focusing on language, science, and technology. This work lays the groundwork for further exploration of the diverse applications and challenges associated with robots in education.

Building on this foundation, [32] conducted a systematic review investigating the use of robots in early childhood and lower primary education. Analyzing research from the past decade, their study explored the influence of robots on children's development, stakeholder perceptions, and children's reactions to robot design. They identified positive effects on children's cognitive, conceptual, language, and social skills, highlighting the potential of robots in early education. However, their work also emphasizes the need for further research on the long-term impact and parental reception of robots in educational settings.

Furthermore, [29] explored the booming field of educational robotics (ER) in research and education. Their review highlights the increasing adoption of robotics in classrooms to teach STEM subjects (Science, Technology, Engineering, and Mathematics). However, they identify a lack of attention towards crucial factors like guidance scripts, collaboration aspects within ER curricula, and the underutilized potential of various ER systems. Additionally, they emphasize the importance of considering age and gender when selecting appropriate ER systems, as these factors can influence student engagement and learning outcomes. This work emphasizes the need for further development of ER curricula and highlights the importance of teacher training regarding available ER technologies.

Exploring the educational potential of robotics in schools was also investigated by [5], who conducted a systematic review of relevant literature published before 2012. Their study aimed to identify the potential benefits of incorporating robotics in schools, synthesize evidence on its educational effectiveness, and define future research directions. Analyzing ten studies, they explored factors like the purpose of the intervention, learning content, robot type, research methods, and participant demographics. Their findings suggest that while educational robotics often enhances learning, some studies reported no significant improvement. This review highlights the need for further research to solidify the understanding of factors influencing the effectiveness of robotics in education, providing valuable insights for educators and researchers in the field.

Also, [3] has investigated the potential of robotics, implementing a robotics-based curriculum in an after-school program and measuring its impact on achievement scores (ages 9–11). Their findings suggest that robotics can be effective in informal learning environments, as evidenced by the significant score increase in the intervention group compared to the control. However, due to the pilot nature of the study, further research is warranted to confirm these findings in larger and more diverse settings.

While our primary focus is on the use of robots in education, it's important to acknowledge the broader context of technology-assisted learning. Paper by [17] reviewed AI-supported tutoring approaches for learning programming, highlighting the prevalence of feedback-based systems capable of identifying student intent. This study, alongside the aforementioned works on robotics in education, underscores the diverse ways technology can be leveraged to enhance the learning experience. Notably, [17] identifies limitations in current systems, primarily the lack of support for collaborative learning, which further emphasizes the need for continued exploration and development in educational technology, including both robotics and AI-powered tutoring systems.

2   Methodology

The methodology for this systematic review combines elements from the Guidelines for Performing Systematic Literature Reviews in Software Engineering [15] and the Preferred Reporting Items for Systematic Reviews and Meta-Analyses (PRISMA) guidelines [26]. By integrating these approaches, we aim to leverage the robustness of software engineering review practices while benefiting from the structured reporting standards advocated by PRISMA. This hybrid methodology allows for a comprehensive and tailored review, addressing the specific nuances of the intersection between robotics and education. The research questions, search strategies, inclusion and exclusion criteria, as well as data extraction methods, draw upon the strengths of both methodologies to ensure a rigorous and transparent systematic review process.

2.1 Research Questions

The study is guided by carefully formulated research questions, emphasizing the exploration of supplementary features and the broader categorization of adaptive features in educational robotics. These questions provide a focused framework for a systematic examination of robots in education:

(1) What specific functionalities do robots offer as learning enablers?
(2) How do robots influence student engagement and motivation?
(3) In what ways do robots contribute to feedback processes?

Research question 1 aims to unveil the diverse functionalities that position robots as crucial facilitators and enhancers of educational content. In exploring research question 2, the study delves into the intricate impact of robots on student engagement and motivation, identifying specific design features that significantly contribute to positive outcomes. Research question 3 forms the crux of the investigation into the multifaceted roles of robots in assessment and feedback within educational settings, seeking to unravel contributions and address challenges.

These research questions aim to provide a comprehensive understanding of the impact and potential challenges of integrating robots into educational environments. By exploring the specific functionalities, influence on student engagement, and contribution to assessment and feedback processes, this study seeks to shed light on the varied dimensions of the intersection between robotics and education. Each question is strategically crafted to unravel distinct aspects, ensuring a thorough investigation into the evolving role of robots in the realm of education.

2.2 Search String

In navigating the expansive landscape of robots in education, a thoughtfully crafted search string was employed to ensure a comprehensive exploration of relevant literature. The search string strategically combines various terms associated with the intersection of robotics and education, aiming to capture a diverse range of articles:

("robots in education" OR "educational robotics" OR "robot-assisted learning" OR "robotic tutors" OR "robotic teaching assistants") AND ("student engagement" OR "motivation" OR "learning outcomes" OR "educational impact" OR "academic performance") AND ("feedback" OR "educational technology" OR "technology-enhanced learning" OR "robotic assessment" OR "robotic feedback")

This search string encompasses common synonyms and terms related to robots in education, student engagement, motivation, learning outcomes, feedback processes, and educational technology. The inclusion of various terms ensures a thorough exploration of the literature landscape. The search string was refined through testing against known samples of relevant articles to validate its effectiveness.

These carefully chosen terms aim to capture the diverse dimensions of the relationship between robotics and education, aligning with the nuanced aspects explored through the research questions. The iterative process of refining the search string enhances its reliability in identifying articles that meet the inclusion criteria, minimizing the risk of false negatives.

This study employed a systematic sampling strategy, utilizing two prominent databases in the chosen field: ACM Digital Library and IEEE Xplore. This approach ensured a focused and efficient search, specifically targeting relevant and credible sources within the domain of the research.

2.3   Inclusion and Exclusion Criteria

Defining clear inclusion and exclusion criteria is crucial to ensure the selection of relevant literature aligned with the research focus. These criteria serve as guidelines for screening articles, and maintaining the integrity of the review process.

Inclusion Criteria:

1. Studies that focus explicitly on the use of robots in educational settings, including classrooms, training environments, and online learning platforms.
2. Research exploring the impact of robots on student engagement, motivation, and learning outcomes across various educational levels (e.g., primary, secondary, and higher education).
3. Publications that investigate the contributions of robots to feedback processes, including assessment, evaluation, and personalized learning experiences.
4. Articles published in peer-reviewed journals to ensure scholarly rigour and credibility.
5. Literature available in English to facilitate comprehension and analysis.

Exclusion Criteria:

1. Non-peer-reviewed literature, such as conference papers, workshops, and technical reports.
2. Articles not written in English, as language comprehension may impact the review process.
3. Works unrelated to the field of robotics in education, including studies focusing solely on robotics in industrial or non-educational contexts.
4. Studies lack a clear focus on the role of robots in educational settings or fail to address key aspects such as student engagement, motivation, and learning outcomes.
5. Publications that do not explore the contributions of robots to feedback processes within educational environments.
6. Research that primarily focuses on theoretical frameworks or conceptual discussions without empirical evidence or practical implications.

These criteria were implemented to ensure a targeted and rigorous selection process, emphasizing relevance and alignment with the overarching goals of the literature review. The inclusion and exclusion criteria aim to maintain methodological rigour and focus throughout the review process. Each article's abstract was scrutinized to ascertain its adherence to these criteria, with full texts examined when necessary to make informed inclusion or exclusion decisions. This stringent approach ensures the extraction of literature that significantly contributes to the exploration of robots in education while excluding works that fall outside the predefined scope. The criteria, inspired by best practices in systematic literature reviews, aim to enhance the reliability and validity of the review findings.

2.4   Data Extraction

Based on a comprehensive analysis of literature in the domain of educational robotics, this section delineates the systematic organization of extracted data across several pivotal variables:

1. **Study Characteristics:** Includes authorship, publication year, geographic location, design methodology, sample demographics, and the educational context, providing a broad overview of the research landscape.
2. **Robot Characteristics:** Details the type, functionality, and role of robots in educational settings, highlighting the technological diversity and application in pedagogical practices.
3. **Educational Impact:** Assesses outcomes related to engagement, motivation, academic achievements, and skill development, underlining the efficacy of robotics in educational enhancement.
4. **Perceived Benefits and Challenges:** Summarizes insights from students, educators, and administrators on the advantages and hurdles of integrating robots into learning environments, offering a nuanced perspective on practical applications.
5. **Comparative Analysis:** Where relevant, compares educational outcomes with and without robotic interventions, providing insight into the value added by educational robotics.
6. **Methodological Quality:** Evaluates the reliability and validity of included studies, critiquing research designs and suggesting improvements.
7. **Future Research Directions:** Identifies literature gaps and proposes future research avenues, highlighting the evolving nature of educational robotics research.

This structured approach ensures a thorough analysis and synthesis of existing literature, offering valuable insights into the impact of educational robotics on learning and teaching processes.

3   Results

In our quest to explore the effects of educational robotics on learning environments, we searched academic databases with the previously mentioned search string, filtering for journal papers. This process led us to discover 18 significant studies—16 from ACM Digital Library and 2 from IEEE Xplore.

Several papers were excluded from the review due to their focus on aspects outside the central inclusion criteria. Specifically, "Student-faculty collaboration in developing and testing infrastructure for a C-based course using robots" by Marija Ivica [14], and "A refined C-based infrastructure and curriculum to support robots in introductory CS" by Vasilisa Bashlovkina [4], emphasized the development of software infrastructure and student-faculty collaboration in course development without directly investigating the impact of robots on student engagement, motivation, and learning outcomes. Additionally, "The TACS Model: Understanding Primary School Teachers' Adoption of Computer Science Pedagogical Content" by Laila El-Hamamsy [10] was excluded as it focused on teacher professional development and adoption of pedagogical content rather than the use of robotics in education. These exclusions ensure our review maintains a focus on studies that directly explore the educational implications of robotics in terms of student interaction and learning processes.

In Table 1, we categorize and numerize the reviewed works, providing a clear distinction between those studies included in our systematic review and those excluded based on our predefined criteria.

Kai-Yi Chin's [8] investigation into the use of an educational robot-based learning system in elementary education underscores a foundational premise: interactive, robot-assisted learning environments markedly improve students' learning performance and motivation beyond traditional methods like PowerPoint presentations. The findings, demonstrating heightened student satisfaction and relevance scores, affirm the value of educational robots in making learning more engaging and motivating. This study sets a benchmark, illustrating the immediate benefits of incorporating robotics in education to foster a more interactive and engaging learning atmosphere.

Building upon Chin's groundwork, Martin Naya-Varela et al.'s [24] introduction of the Robobo SmartCity model extends the scope of educational robotics into the realm of computational intelligence (CI), offering a tangible, hands-on experience with AI fundamentals through the lens of autonomous driving. The model's success with secondary and high school students in enhancing understanding of complex CI topics, including computer vision, machine learning, and human-robot interaction, showcases the broader applicability and effectiveness of robotics in education. This approach not only complements traditional learning modalities but also aligns perfectly with digital education plans advocating for AI literacy at all educational levels, thereby offering a practical blueprint for integrating sophisticated technological concepts into accessible educational frameworks.

Further enriching this discourse, Alexandros Merkouris and Konstantinos Chorianopoulos's [21] exploration of embodied interactions via educational

Table 1. Overview of Reviewed Works

Category	#	Works
Excluded	1	Marija Ivica - Student-faculty collaboration in developing and testing infrastructure for a C-based course using robots
	2	Vasilisa Bashlovkina - A refined C-based infrastructure and curriculum to support robots in introductory CS
	3	Laila El-Hamamsy - The TACS Model: Understanding Primary School Teachers' Adoption of Computer Science Pedagogical Content
Included	1	Kai-Yi Chin - Impact of Using an Educational Robot-Based Learning System on Students' Motivation in Elementary Education
	2	Martin Naya-Varela - Robobo SmartCity: An Autonomous Driving Model for Computational Intelligence Learning Through Educational Robotics
	3	Alexandros Merkouris - Programming Embodied Interactions with a Remotely Controlled Educational Robot
	4	Natasha Randall - A Survey of Robot-Assisted Language Learning (RALL)
	5	Elizabeth Sklar - Using RoboCup in university-level computer science education
	6	Monica M. McGill - Learning to Program with Personal Robots: Influences on Student Motivation
	7	Patrícia Alves-Oliveira - Empathic Robot for Group Learning: A Field Study
	8	Iulian Radu - Unequal Impacts of Augmented Reality on Learning and Collaboration During Robot Programming with Peers
	9	Eben B. Witherspoon - Developing Computational Thinking through a Virtual Robotics Programming Curriculum
	10	Kevin Doherty - Engagement in HCI: Conception, Theory and Measurement
	11	Igor M. Verner - Robot contest as a laboratory for experiential engineering education
	12	Alexandros Merkouris - Teaching Programming in Secondary Education Through Embodied Computing Platforms: Robotics and Wearables
	13	Paul Hatch - PATHWiSE: An Authoring Tool to Support Teachers to Create Robot-Supported Social Learning Experiences During Homework
	14	John Páez - Human-Robot Scaffolding: An Architecture to Foster Problem-solving Skills
	15	Olov Engwall - Identification of Low-engaged Learners in Robot-led Second Language Conversations with Adults

robotics reveals the nuanced impact of engagement levels on computational thinking (CT) skills among middle school students. Their findings highlight a critical insight: the level of embodiment in interaction with robots-ranging from touch and speech to hand and full-body gestures-directly influences the complexity of students' computational projects. This suggests that the physicality of learning experiences with robots plays a significant role in the cognitive development process, particularly in fostering advanced computational thinking skills.

Natasha Randall's survey on Robot-Assisted Language Learning (RALL) [28] provides a comprehensive analysis of how robots can support language acquisition, comparing them to computer-assisted learning. This survey reveals that robots may offer unique advantages in language production and in-task engagement, potentially outperforming other technologies in these areas. While robots enhance learning motivation and reduce anxiety, the long-term benefits are yet to be fully understood. Randall's work suggests a promising avenue for educational robotics, especially in facilitating language learning through increased motivation, engagement, and the unique interpersonal dynamics offered by robots. This aligns with the emerging narrative in educational robotics research, emphasizing the importance of interactive and engaging learning environments facilitated by robotics to enhance educational outcomes across disciplines.

Elizabeth Sklar's [31] work on using RoboCup in university-level computer science education showcases an innovative approach to teaching complex subjects such as artificial intelligence (AI) and multiagent systems. By integrating RoboCup challenges into the curriculum, Sklar demonstrates how practical, hands-on experiences with robotics can significantly enhance students' understanding of AI concepts. This methodology not only fosters a deeper engagement with the material but also encourages teamwork and problem-solving skills, illustrating the practical applications of theoretical knowledge. This study aligns with the overarching theme of educational robotics enhancing learning outcomes, providing a compelling case for the integration of robotics in higher education to bridge the gap between theory and practice.

Monica M. McGill's research on "Learning to Program with Personal Robots: Influences on Student Motivation" [20] investigates the motivational impact of using personal robots in introductory programming courses. McGill's study specifically examines non-computer science students' motivation in a CS0 course, employing the Institute for Personal Robots in Education (IPRE) robot. Utilizing Keller's Instructional Materials Motivation Survey to measure motivation components like attention, relevance, confidence, and satisfaction, the study found positive influences on students' attitudes towards programming. However, it identified minimal or no impact on relevance, confidence, or satisfaction, indicating that while personal robots can enhance interest in programming, their effect on deeper motivational aspects varies and is influenced by factors such as gender and technical self-perception.

Patrícia Alves-Oliveira's [1] study on the use of an empathic robot for group learning in a real-world classroom setting presents a novel approach to collaborative learning. Through two distinct studies, one short-term and one extending over two months, the research explores the immediate and long-term impacts of an empathic robot on group learning activities focused on sustainable development. The findings suggest that while the robot fostered meaningful discussions and a more sustainable approach to in-game decisions, the long-term learning gains were not significantly enhanced, highlighting the complexity of integrating robots into educational settings for sustained educational impact. This study contributes to the dialogue on the potential and limitations of using empathic robots in educational contexts, particularly in fostering collaborative learning and engagement among students.

Iulian Radu's study, "Unequal Impacts of Augmented Reality on Learning and Collaboration During Robot Programming with Peers," [27] investigates how augmented reality (AR) affects collaborative learning and group dynamics in robot programming tasks among novices. It demonstrates that AR can significantly enhance group learning and collaboration by providing more equitable access to information and balancing participation between peers. Specifically, AR visualizations were found to assist participants in maintaining a common ground and balancing contributions, which ultimately improved learning outcomes and the quality of collaboration during problem-solving activities. This research suggests that AR technologies offer substantial benefits in educational settings, particularly in fostering effective teamwork and enhancing learning through more interactive and engaging methods.

Eben B. Witherspoon et al.'s study on "Developing Computational Thinking through a Virtual Robotics Programming Curriculum" [33] showcases how virtual robotics programming acts as a pivotal learning enabler, directly addressing the first research question. By scaffolding learning in a virtual environment, the curriculum significantly enhances middle school students' computational thinking skills, thus fostering engagement and motivation by providing interactive, gamified learning experiences. This approach indirectly contributes to effective feedback processes, as the virtual environment allows for real-time adjustments and learning, offering immediate feedback to students. This aligns seamlessly with enhancing computational skills crucial for problem-solving in various computing tasks, demonstrating the multifaceted benefits of robotics in education.

Kevin and Gavin Doherty's comprehensive review on "Engagement in HCI: Conception, Theory, and Measurement" [9] provides a deep dive into how engagement is conceptualized, theorized, and measured within Human-Computer Interaction (HCI). Their work synthesizes a vast array of definitions and theoretical frameworks to outline a multifaceted view of engagement, examining its implications for design and interaction. This study highlights the complexity of engagement as a concept that spans cognitive, emotional, and behavioural dimensions, offering insights into designing for engagement to enhance user experience. The findings contribute to a better understanding of engagement's role in HCI, suggesting paths for future research to explore its nuanced impacts further.

Alexandros Merkouris's 2017 study, "Teaching Programming in Secondary Education Through Embodied Computing Platforms: Robotics and Wearables," [22] reveals significant findings on educational engagement. The research, involving 36 students in a comparative study of programming platforms-desktop, wearable, and robotic—demonstrates that robotics substantially increases students' emotional engagement and their intention to learn programming. This suggests the introduction of computer programming through diverse platforms, including robots and wearables, can significantly enhance the learning experience without compromising the grasp of fundamental computational concepts. Integrating the insights from Alexandros Merkouris's studies, it becomes evident that tangible computing platforms, particularly robotics, play a significant role in enhancing programming education. His research spans different aspects of embodied computing in educational settings, from exploring embodied interaction styles to comparing the effectiveness of robotics, wearables, and traditional desktop environments in teaching programming. Merkouris's work collectively underscores the value of incorporating diverse tangible platforms in learning environments to boost engagement and motivation among students, without sacrificing the quality of learning fundamental computational concepts. This cohesive narrative highlights the multifaceted benefits of robotics and wearables in fostering an interactive and immersive learning experience in computer science education.

Paul Hatch's [12] study demonstrates the potential of robotics to enrich educational experiences beyond traditional classroom settings. It aligns with our research questions by showing how robots can act as learning enablers, particularly in homework contexts, facilitating social and cultural connections that enhance student engagement. This work provides insights into how technology can be leveraged to create meaningful educational interactions, suggesting a significant impact on how teachers view and implement homework assignments with the support of robots, thereby enriching the feedback process and learning experience.

John Páez's study, "Human-Robot Scaffolding: An Architecture to Foster Problem-solving Skills," [25] introduces an architecture designed to enhance problem-solving skills by understanding the cognitive and emotional states of learners during interaction with robots. This research validates the effectiveness of a human-robot scaffolding system in fostering learning strategies among young students, particularly through the Mean-Ends Analysis strategy, enhancing problem-solving capabilities.

Olov Engwall's research, "Identification of Low-engaged Learners in Robot-led Second Language Conversations with Adults," [11] investigates how robots can identify and adapt to low-engaged learners in educational settings, specifically in adult second language learning through conversations. This study underscores the potential of robotic systems to detect engagement levels and tailor interactions to improve learning outcomes, highlighting the adaptability and personalized feedback capabilities of educational robots.

4   Discussion

This review systematically examines the burgeoning field of educational robotics, delineating the varied impacts of robotics on learning environments, student engagement, and educational outcomes. The included studies collectively under-score the transformative potential of robotics in education, offering nuanced insights into how these technologies can be harnessed to enrich learning experi-ences across different educational levels and disciplines.

4.1 Implications for Educational Practice

The findings from studies such as those by Kai-Yi Chin [8] and Martin Naya-Varela et al. [24] highlight the immediate benefits of integrating robotics into educational settings. Robotics not only enhances student engagement and moti-vation but also facilitates a deeper understanding of complex subjects like com-putational intelligence and artificial intelligence. This suggests a need for educa-tors and curriculum developers to consider robotics as a core component of the educational toolkit, especially in STEM education.

Moreover, the work of Alexandros Merkouris [21], Eben B. Witherspoon et al. [33], and John Páez [25] emphasizes the importance of robotics in developing computational thinking and problem-solving skills. These studies advocate for a hands-on, interactive approach to learning, where students engage directly with tangible computing platforms, thereby making abstract concepts more accessible and engaging.

4.2 Challenges and Future Directions

While the benefits of educational robotics are clear, challenges remain, particu-larly regarding the integration of these technologies into standard curricula and ensuring equitable access to all students. The studies reviewed also highlight the need for further research to explore long-term impacts on learning outcomes and how robotics can be effectively combined with traditional teaching methods to maximize learning gains.

Furthermore, as indicated by the work of Natasha Randall [28] and Olov Engwall [11], there is a promising avenue for robotics in language learning and personalized education. Future research should focus on developing adaptive and responsive robotic systems capable of catering to the diverse needs of learners, thereby enhancing personalized learning experiences.

4.3 Concluding Remarks

Educational robotics represents a dynamic and evolving field with the poten-tial to revolutionize teaching and learning processes. This review highlights the critical role of robotics in fostering engaging, interactive, and meaningful learning experiences. As we move forward, it is imperative that stakeholders in education—teachers, policymakers, and researchers-work collaboratively to over-come existing barriers and fully realize the potential of robotics in education.

5   Conclusion

The integration of robotics into educational curricula represents a forward-looking approach to teaching and learning, aligning with the evolving demands of the digital age. However, this review also acknowledges the challenges in adopting robotics broadly, including issues related to accessibility, teacher training, and curriculum integration. Addressing these challenges is crucial for realizing the full potential of robotics in education.

As we look to the future, it is evident that educational robotics will play an increasingly pivotal role in shaping innovative learning environments. Continued research and collaboration among educators, policymakers, and technologists are essential to harness the transformative power of robotics in education. This review calls for a concerted effort to explore new pedagogical models that leverage robotics to enhance learning experiences, ensuring that students are equipped with the knowledge and skills necessary to thrive in an increasingly technological world.

In conclusion, educational robotics offers a promising avenue for enriching educational experiences and outcomes. By embracing this technology, the educational community can unlock new possibilities for engaging, empowering, and educating the next generation of learners.

References

1. Alves-Oliveira, P., Sequeira, P., Melo, F.S., Castellano, G., Paiva, A.: Empathic robot for group learning: a field study. ACM Trans. Human-Robot Interact. (THRI) **8**(1), 1–34 (2019)
2. Barak, M., Zadok, Y.: Robotics projects and learning concepts in science, technology and problem solving. Int. J. Technol. Des. Educ. **19**, 289–307 (2009)
3. Barker, B.S., Ansorge, J.: Robotics as means to increase achievement scores in an informal learning environment. J. Res. Technol. Educ. **39**(3), 229–243 (2007)
4. Bashlovkina, V., DeWitt, A., Liu, A., Knoebber, N., Walker, H.M.: A refined C-based infrastructure and curriculum to support robots in introductory CS. J. Comput. Sci. Coll. **30**(5), 136–143 (2015)
5. Benitti, F.B.V.: Exploring the educational potential of robotics in schools: a systematic review. Comput. Educ. **58**(3), 978–988 (2012)
6. Bloom, B.S.: The 2 sigma problem: the search for methods of group instruction as effective as one-to-one tutoring. Educ. Research. **13**(6), 4–16 (1984)
7. Chang, C.-W., Lee, J.-H., Chao, P.-Y., Wang, C.-Y., Chen, G.-D.: Exploring the possibility of using humanoid robots as instructional tools for teaching a second language in primary school. J. Educ. Technol. Soc. **13**(2), 13–24 (2010)
8. Chin, K.-Y., Hong, Z.-W., Chen, Y.-L.: Impact of using an educational robot-based learning system on students' motivation in elementary education. IEEE Trans. Learn. Technol. **7**(4), 333–345 (2014)
9. Doherty, K., Doherty, G.: Engagement in HCI: conception, theory and measurement. ACM Comput. Surv. (CSUR) **51**(5), 1–39 (2018)
10. El-Hamamsy, L., Bruno, B., Avry, S., Chessel-Lazzarotto, F., Zufferey, J.D., Mondada, F.: The TACS model: understanding primary school teachers' adoption of computer science pedagogical content. ACM Trans. Comput. Educ. **23**(2), 1–31 (2023)

11. Engwall, O., Cumbal, R., Lopes, J., Ljung, M., Månsson, L.: Identification of low-engaged learners in robot-led second language conversations with adults. ACM Trans. Hum.-Robot Interact. (THRI) **11**(2), 1–33 (2022)
12. Hatch, P., Rahman, M.A., Michaelis, J.E.: PATHWiSE: an authoring tool to support teachers to create robot-supported social learning experiences during homework. Proc. ACM Hum.-Comput. Interact. **7**(CSCW1), 1–23 (2023)
13. Highfield, K.: Robotic toys as a catalyst for mathematical problem solving. Aust. Prim. Math. Classr. **15**(2), 22–27 (2010)
14. Ivica, M., Marku, S., Nguyen, T., Wu, R., Walker, H.M.: Student-faculty collaboration in developing and testing infrastructure for a C-based course using robots. J. Comput. Sci. Coll. **32**(1), 57–64 (2016)
15. Keele, S., et al.: Guidelines for performing systematic literature reviews in software engineering (2007)
16. Konijn, E.A., Smakman, M., van den Berghe, R.: Use of robots in education. In: The International Encyclopedia of Media Psychology, pp. 1–8 (2020)
17. Le, N.T., Strickroth, S., Gross, S., Pinkwart, N.: A review of ai-supported tutoring approaches for learning programming. In: Nguyen, N., van Do, T., le Thi, H. (eds.) Advanced Computational Methods for Knowledge Engineering, vol. 479, pp. 267–279. Springer, Heidelberg (2013). https://doi.org/10.1007/978-3-319-00293-4_20
18. Lees, D., LePage, P.: Will robots ever replace attendants? exploring the current capabilities and future potential of robots in education and rehabilitation. Int. J. Rehabil. Res. **17**(4), 285–304 (1994)
19. Lees, D., Lepage, P.: Robots in education: the current state of the art. J. Educ. Technol. Syst. **24**(4), 299–320 (1996)
20. McGill, M.M.: Learning to program with personal robots: Influences on student motivation. ACM Trans. Comput. Educ. (TOCE) **12**(1), 1–32 (2012)
21. Merkouris, A., Chorianopoulos, K.: Programming embodied interactions with a remotely controlled educational robot. ACM Trans. Comput. Educ. (TOCE) **19**(4), 1–19 (2019)
22. Merkouris, A., Chorianopoulos, K., Kameas, A.: Teaching programming in secondary education through embodied computing platforms: robotics and wearables. ACM Trans. Comput. Educ. (TOCE) **17**(2), 1–22 (2017)
23. Mubin, O., Stevens, C.J., Shahid, S., Al Mahmud, A., Dong, J.J.: A review of the applicability of robots in education. J. Technol. Educ. Learn. **1**(209–0015), 13 (2013)
24. Naya-Varela, M., Guerreiro-Santalla, S., Baamonde, T., Bellas, F.: Robobo smartcity: an autonomous driving model for computational intelligence learning through educational robotics. IEEE Trans. Learn. Technol. **16**, 543–559 (2023)
25. Páez, J., González, E.: Human-robot scaffolding: an architecture to foster problem-solving skills. ACM Trans. Hum.-Robot Interact. (THRI) **11**(3), 1–17 (2022)
26. Page, M.J., et al.: The prisma 2020 statement: an updated guideline for reporting systematic reviews. Int. J. Surg. **88**, 105906 (2020)
27. Radu, I., Hv, V., Schneider, B.: Unequal impacts of augmented reality on learning and collaboration during robot programming with peers. Proc. ACM Hum.-Comput. Interact. **4**(CSCW3), 1–23 (2021)
28. Randall, N.: A survey of robot-assisted language learning (rall). ACM Trans. Hum.-Robot Interact. (THRI) **9**(1), 1–36 (2019)
29. Sapounidis, T., Alimisis, D.: Educational robotics for stem: a review of technologies and some educational considerations. In: Science and Mathematics Education for 21st Century Citizens: Challenges and Ways Forward, September 2020, pp. 167–190. Nova Science Publishers Hauppauge (2020)

30. Serholt, S., Barendregt, W.: Students' attitudes towards the possible future of social robots in education. In: Workshop Proceedings of Ro-man (2014)
31. Sklar, E., Parsons, S., Stone, P.: Using robocup in university-level computer science education. J. Educ. Res. Comput. (JERIC) **4**(2), 4-es (2004)
32. Toh, L.P.E., Causo, A., Tzuo, P.W., Chen, I.M., Yeo, S.H.: A review on the use of robots in education and young children. J. Educ. Technol. Soc. **19**(2), 148–163 (2016)
33. Witherspoon, E.B., Higashi, R.M., Schunn, C.D., Baehr, E.C., Shoop, R.: Developing computational thinking through a virtual robotics programming curriculum. ACM Trans. Comput. Educ. (TOCE) **18**(1), 1–20 (2017)

Application of the Decision Tree in the Business Process

Drina Ćavar Brajković[2] , Emil Brajković[1(✉)] , and Tomislav Volarić[1]

[1] University of Mostar, 88000 Mostar, Bosnia and Herzegovina
{emil.brajkovic,tomislav.volaric}@fpmoz.sum.ba
[2] IT Odjel Mostar, 88000 Mostar, Bosnia and Herzegovina
drina.cavar.brajkovic@phd.sum.ba

Abstract. Decision tree, as a decision-making method in conditions of risk and uncertainty, represents a practical graphical-visualization tool for decision-making. Additionally, modern businesses, especially banking and other financial institutions, handle large volumes of data, making an appropriate tool more essential than ever. Machine learning and associated predictive models, such as decision trees and random forest, provide a solid foundation for creating systems to make quality and timely decisions. This paper explains the background of the decision tree method and related models that are based on it. In the end, our own implementation of a system for detecting negative customer comments based on a synthetic dataset using predictive models is presented.

Keywords: Decision tree · Machine learning · Business analysis

1 Introduction

The decision tree is a graphical decision-making model that utilizes a tree structure to represent various decisions and their consequences. Each node in the tree represents a specific decision, and the branches emanating from the node depict possible outcomes or options resulting from that decision. A Decision Tree is a predictive model applicable to both classification and regression problems. It represents a hierarchical model of decisions and their consequences. Decision-makers use the decision tree to identify a strategy to achieve their goal. When the decision tree is used for a classification task, it is called a classification tree, and when used for a regression problem, it is called a regression tree. Additionally, decision trees, in a straightforward manner, represent complex concepts defined by sets of properties. In other words, decision trees represent functions that map attribute values to sets of decision classes, which represent permissible hypotheses. Decision trees are utilized in operational research in decision analysis to identify the optimal strategy for achieving a goal [1]. The decision tree is employed in the field of machine learning and data analysis to make decisions based on input data. This method can be applied in various domains, including business analysis, medical diagnostics, finance, and other areas where decision-making is required based on complex sets of information. The contribution of

T. Volarić et al. (Eds.): MoStart 2024, CCIS 2124, pp. 273–288, 2024.
https://doi.org/10.1007/978-3-031-62058-4_17

this paper lies in the application and comparison of decision tree algorithms in banking services. After a brief introduction, we review related research in Sect. 2, followed by the methodology in Sect. 3. Section 4 provides a detailed description of the results, and Sect. 5 concludes the paper.

2   Reference Literature

In business analysis, a Decision Tree is a powerful tool used to visually represent decision-making processes and their potential outcomes. It is a graphical model that resembles a tree, where each node represents a decision or a chance event, and the branches represent the possible consequences or outcomes. This technique is widely employed to analyze and evaluate various business scenarios:

1. Decision-Making Support
2. Risk Assessment
3. Resource Allocation
4. Strategic Planning
5. Market Analysis
6. Financial Analysis
7. Customer Behavior Analysis
8. Project Management

By providing a visual representation of decision scenarios, Decision Trees enhance the business analysis process, enabling analysts and decision-makers to make more informed and strategic choices. This approach is especially beneficial when dealing with complex decision structures involving multiple variables and uncertainties.

2.1   Decision-Making Support

In the context of decision-making support, Decision Trees serve as a powerful visual and analytical tool to aid individuals and organizations in making complex decisions [2]. It's valuable to be able to structure decision-making processes by breaking down complex decisions into a series of simpler, interconnected choices. This hierarchical representation provides a clear overview of decision options and their potential outcomes. Decision Trees help in assessing and managing risks associated with different decision paths. By assigning probabilities to various outcomes, decision-makers can evaluate potential risks and benefits, aiding in more informed decision-making. This method enables the exploration of different scenarios and their potential consequences. Decision-makers can analyze different paths and their outcomes, helping them understand the implications of each decision under various circumstances. In decision-making support, they assist in optimizing resource allocation. By considering the costs and benefits associated with different decision alternatives, organizations can allocate their resources more efficiently. They can also be used to model various strategic options and their potential consequences, aiding executives in making decisions aligned with the overall business strategy. They also help in project management by analyzing different project paths, identifying key decision points, and evaluating potential risks and outcomes. This is particularly useful in complex projects with multiple decision dependencies.

2.2 Risk Assessment

In risk assessment, this method plays a crucial role in evaluating and managing uncertainties associated with various decision pathways. It provides a structured framework for analyzing different scenarios, their probabilities, and potential outcomes, and helps systematically identify and categorize potential risks associated with different decision options or scenarios. Each branch of the tree represents a potential risk or decision point, allowing for the assignment of probabilities to different branches and reflecting the likelihood of each potential outcome or occurrence of risk. This quantitative approach aids in assessing the overall risk associated with the decision [3]. Branches and nodes depict the consequences or outcomes associated with each decision pathway. Decision-makers can assess the severity and impact of potential outcomes, aiding in risk prioritization, which helps in developing risk mitigation strategies by highlighting critical decision points where interventions can be made to reduce the likelihood or impact of identified risks. This proactive approach contributes to effective risk management. In sensitivity analysis, decision-makers can assess how changes in probabilities or outcomes at different decision points impact the overall risk profile. This aids in understanding the robustness of decisions in the face of uncertainties. It's possible to integrate cost-benefit considerations into risk assessment, and by associating costs and benefits with different decision branches, organizations can evaluate the economic implications of various risk scenarios.

2.3 Resource Allocation

In resource allocation, this is a valuable tool to assist organizations in optimizing the distribution of resources by considering various decision pathways and their potential outcomes. For example, in a business scenario, it can be used for resource allocation decisions such as budget allocation, personnel assignment, or asset distribution while analyzing different factors or features to guide resource allocation in a way that aligns with specific goals or objectives. A visual representation of different decision pathways is associated with a range of resource allocation choices. These pathways may include options related to investments, projects, departments, or any other area that requires significant resources [4]. Decision-makers can assign probabilities to different outcomes associated with each decision pathway. This quantitative approach helps in assessing the potential return on investment or benefits tied to resource allocation decisions. By incorporating probabilities and potential outcomes, decision trees assist in evaluating risks associated with resource allocation. Decision-makers can assess risks associated with different allocation strategies and prioritize those with more favorable risk profiles, facilitating cost-benefit analysis by considering the costs and benefits associated with each decision pathway. This enables decision-makers to identify resource allocation options that provide the highest return on investment or achieve strategic objectives. In organizations with projects, decision trees help manage project portfolios by evaluating different project paths and allocating resources based on factors such as project priority, expected outcomes, and resource constraints. Strategic resource allocation is facilitated by modeling different strategic options and their potential consequences, helping organizations align resource allocation with overall strategic goals and priorities.

2.4 Strategic Planning

In strategic planning, Decision Trees serve as a valuable tool to help organizations model and analyze various strategic options and their potential outcomes, providing a structured and visual representation of decision-making processes and assisting executives in making informed decisions aligned with the overall business strategy. It is possible to explore different strategic options and their potential consequences. Each node represents a decision point, often corresponding to a strategic choice or action [5]. When making decisions, it is possible to assign probabilities to different outcomes associated with each strategic option. This quantitative approach helps assess the potential success or effectiveness of different strategic choices by incorporating probabilities and potential outcomes in risk assessment related to strategic planning. Risks associated with different strategic options can be evaluated and prioritized based on more favorable risk profiles. Organizations can assess the resource needs of different strategic paths and allocate resources based on priorities, budget constraints, and expected outcomes. Additionally, organizations can model various market entry strategies, considering factors such as market conditions, competition, and regulatory environment. In the context of strategic product development, this method assists in evaluating different product development strategies, including features, pricing, and launch timing, thereby optimizing resource allocation for product innovation.

2.5 Market Analysis

In market analysis, it is important to assess and model various marketing strategies, product launches, and market entry decisions. Decision Trees provide a structured and visual representation of decision-making processes, assisting marketing professionals in making informed choices aligned with market dynamics. It is possible to model different market entry strategies, including options such as entering a new market, launching a new product, or expanding product offerings. This includes considerations such as timing, pricing, distribution channels, and promotional activities [6]. Marketing experts can model potential outcomes associated with targeting specific demographics, geographic regions, or customer profiles, aiding in optimal market segmentation and assessing different pricing strategies, including options such as penetration pricing, skimming pricing, or value-based pricing. Marketing experts can evaluate the potential impact of different pricing decisions on market share and profitability. Decision Trees assist in planning promotional campaigns by modeling different advertising, branding, and communication strategies, helping marketing experts optimize resource allocation for promotional activities.

2.6 Financial Analysis

In financial analysis, this method is used as a tool for assessing investment opportunities, evaluating financial risks, and making decisions related to budgeting and capital allocation, providing a structured and visual representation of decision-making processes and assisting financial professionals in making informed choices aligned with financial goals [7]. Financial analysts can model potential outcomes associated with various investment choices, considering factors such as expected returns, risks, and market conditions. Organizations can model different capital allocation options, such as investing in new projects, expanding facilities, or acquiring assets, and assess the financial implications of each choice. Financial experts can model different risk scenarios, assessing the potential impact of financial risks, market fluctuations, and economic uncertainties. Financial institutions can model different criteria and decision pathways to assess the creditworthiness of applicants, aiding in making informed lending decisions. Financial analysts can model different cost structures, revenue streams, and potential benefits associated with various financial strategies.

2.7 Customer Behavior Analysis

In customer behavior analysis, it is important to understand patterns in customers' actions, preferences, and interactions with products or services. Decision Trees provide a visual and analytical framework for businesses to make informed decisions based on various factors influencing customer behavior. [8]. It is necessary to perform customer segmentation based on various attributes such as demographics, purchasing behavior, or psychographics. Marketing experts can model different segmentation strategies and understand the characteristics that differentiate customer groups. By modeling different product features and customer preferences, companies can optimize recommendations to enhance the user experience. Decision Trees are used to predict customer churn by analyzing factors contributing to customer retention or loss. This helps companies identify customers at risk of leaving and implement targeted retention strategies. By modeling different combinations of products or services, companies can determine the most effective strategies to increase customer spending. Marketing experts can model the impact of different channels on customer engagement, conversion rates, and overall marketing success. It is necessary to analyze customer journeys by modeling different touchpoints and interactions. This enables companies to understand key decision points and factors influencing the customer's path to conversion. Companies can tailor their communication based on customer preferences and behaviors. By analyzing factors such as purchase frequency, average order value, and retention rates, companies can understand the long-term value of different customer segments [9].

2.8 Project Management

In project management, this method is used to analyze different project paths, identify critical decision points, and assess potential risks and outcomes. Decision Trees provide a visual and analytical framework for making informed decisions in complex and dynamic project environments, assisting in the analysis of various project paths by modeling different decision points and potential outcomes. Project managers can visually depict project scenarios, considering factors such as task dependencies, resource availability, and potential risks. [10]. It is possible to optimize resource allocations by modeling different resource allocation strategies for various tasks in the project. Project managers can assess the impact of different resource allocations and choose the most efficient approach. Project managers can model different risk scenarios, assess the probability and impact of risks, and determine appropriate risk mitigation strategies, assisting in the analysis of various task sequencing options within the project. Project managers can model alternative sequences of tasks, considering dependencies, constraints, and project timelines.

2.9 Software Support for the Decision Tree Method

Various software tools support the implementation and analysis of Decision Trees. These tools provide user-friendly interfaces, visualization capabilities, and often include advanced features for building, analyzing, and interpreting Decision Trees: Microsoft Excel, R, Python, Weka, Orange, KNIME, IBM SPSS Modeler, RapidMiner, SAS Enterprise Miner, TreePlan (Excel Add-In)- When choosing a software tool, consider factors such as ease of use, flexibility, visualization capabilities, and compatibility with your data format and analysis requirements. The choice may also depend on whether you prefer a visual interface, programming environment, or a combination of both. In this paper, we will use Python and Jupyter Notebook.

3   Methodology

A decision tree is an acyclic directed graph whose nodes are called nodes, edges are branches, nodes without descendants are leaves, and the root node is the only node without a parent. There is an exponentially large number of decision trees that can be constructed from a given dataset. Some of these trees may be more accurate than others, and finding optimal trees is computationally impractical due to the exponential size of the search space. Moreover, efficient algorithms have been developed for inducing reasonably accurate but suboptimal decision trees within a reasonable time frame [11]. These algorithms employ a greedy strategy that builds a decision tree by creating a series of local optima in deciding which attribute to use for partitioning the data. One such algorithm is the Hunt algorithm, which serves as the foundation for many decision tree induction algorithms.

3.1   Elements of the Decision Tree

A Decision Tree consists of several key elements that collectively represent a visual and analytical framework for decision-making. Here are the primary elements of a Decision Tree:

1. Root Node: The root node is the starting point of the Decision Tree and represents the initial decision or the beginning of a decision-making process. It is the topmost node from which branches (decisions) emanate.
2. Decision Nodes: Decision nodes represent decision points where a choice must be made.
3. Branches: Branches connect decision nodes and represent the different possible outcomes or choices at each decision point.
4. Chance Nodes (Probability Nodes): Chance nodes represent uncertain events or probabilities associated with different outcomes.
5. Outcome Nodes (Leaf Nodes): Outcome nodes, also known as leaf nodes, represent the end of a decision path.
6. Decision Criteria: Decision criteria are the factors or conditions used to make decisions at each decision node.
7. Payoff or Value: The payoff or value associated with each outcome node represents the quantitative or qualitative result of the decision-making process.
8. Subtrees: Subtrees are smaller Decision Trees that can be part of a larger, more complex Decision Tree.
9. Decision Rules: Decision rules are the logical conditions or criteria used to determine the appropriate path at decision nodes.
10. Paths: Paths represent specific sequences of decisions and events from the root node to an outcome node. Each path corresponds to a unique set of decisions made along the way (Fig. 1).

Every decision tree construction algorithm must include a termination condition for binary recursive branching of data, i.e., a stopping criterion that determines when to cease branching at a specific node. The following rules can be used as stopping criteria:

- If a node becomes pure, meaning all cases have identical values for the response variable (the node is not further divided),
- If all values in a node have identical response variable values for each input,
- If the current tree depth reaches the maximum depth specified by the user,
- If the size of the node is smaller than the minimum size specified by the user, the node does not split,
- If splitting a node results in child nodes whose size is smaller than the minimum size specified for child nodes by the user, the node does not split,

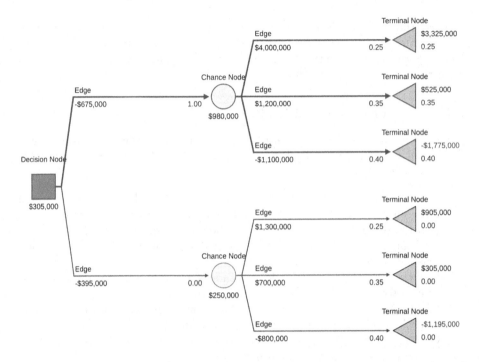

Fig. 1. A simple decision tree

Furthermore, a better approach is to build the maximum tree and then apply pruning techniques to obtain the optimal subtree. To avoid the phenomenon of model overfitting, which indicates that the given model is overly tailored to the training data, potentially resulting in poor performance on a test dataset, the concept of tree pruning is employed. This strategy involves constructing a very large tree and then pruning it to obtain a subtree. Intuitively, the goal of this approach is to obtain a subtree that minimizes prediction error on the test dataset. To prevent generating a large number of possible subtrees, the weakest link pruning method (Cost-complexity pruning) is used. Instead of considering all possible subtrees, only the sequence of trees indexed with a non-negative parameter for adjustment is taken into account. The performance of a decision tree can be highly variable depending on the data, and, for this reason, advanced techniques for aggregating decision trees are employed to easily enhance performance and construct higher-quality models. Bagging (Bootstrap Aggregating), boosting, and random forests are techniques that utilize individual decision trees as building blocks to construct robust predictive models.

Steps of the Decision Tree Method. The Decision Tree method involves several steps in constructing and using the tree for decision-making:

1. Define the Decision Problem
2. Gather Data:
   - Collect relevant data that can be used to inform the decision.
   - Include both quantitative and qualitative data that might influence the outcomes.
3. Identify Decision Criteria:
   - Determine the factors or criteria that will be used to make decisions at each decision node.
   - These criteria are the basis for branching in the Decision Tree.
4. Define Outcomes:
   - Specify the possible outcomes or results associated with each decision or chance node.
   - Clearly define the consequences of each decision path.
5. Build the Tree Structure:
   - Start with the root node, representing the initial decision or situation.
   - Add decision nodes for each decision point.
   - Introduce chance nodes for uncertain events and outcome nodes for final results.
6. Assign Probabilities:
   - If applicable, assign probabilities to chance nodes to represent the likelihood of different outcomes.
   - This step is crucial for decision nodes with uncertain events.
7. Calculate Expected Payoffs:
   - Associate values or payoffs with each outcome node, considering both positive and negative consequences.
   - Calculate the expected payoffs by multiplying each outcome's value by its probability (if applicable) and summing them up.
8. Apply Decision Rules:
   - At each decision node, apply decision rules based on the decision criteria to determine the chosen path.
   - Follow the branches and nodes according to the decision rules.
9. Analyze Results:
   - Follow the path through the Decision Tree to the outcome nodes.
   - Assess the final results and associated payoffs.
10. Sensitivity Analysis:
    - Conduct sensitivity analysis to evaluate how changes in probabilities or values at decision nodes impact the overall decision.
    - Identify critical decision points and factors influencing the decision.
11. Make the Decision: Based on the analysis, make the decision that maximizes expected payoffs or aligns with the decision objective.
12. Implement the Decision:
    - Implement the chosen decision in the real-world context.
    - Monitor the outcomes and adjust the decision-making process if necessary.

We used data from 16659 records of customer feedback from a bank that was selected as the data source for collection. The dataset was compiled to monitor the level of trust of bank customers in banking services. The data includes textual reviews from bank customers from 2013 to 2019, incorporating official comments from bank employees. Additionally, values for the fog index based on the Gunning parameter were added, which is used to assess the readability of the text [12]. The Fog Index, developed by Robert Gunning, is a readability formula designed to estimate the years of formal education a person needs to understand a piece of writing easily. It takes into account the average number of words per sentence and the percentage of words with three or more syllables. In the context you provided, values for the Fog Index based on the Gunning parameter were added to the dataset. This index is useful in evaluating how easily understandable the text (customer reviews in this case) is to the general audience [13]. A higher Fog Index suggests that the text may be more challenging to read, while a lower Fog Index indicates greater readability (Table 1).

Table 1. Data from records of customer feedback

No	Column	Count	Data type
1	responses header	16659	object
2	responses rating grade	11222	float64
3	responses status	7559	object
4	itshape responses message	16659	object
5	responses datetime	16659	datetime64[ns]
6	reviewer	16659	object
7	comments	16659	int64
8	views	16659	int64
9	id	16659	int64
10	have email	16659	int64
11	responses message length	16659	int64
12	gunning fog index	16659	float64

Bank employees have assigned each record a positive or negative rating. We will use these ratings for the classification algorithm on the training and testing sets. Figure 2 shows us client feedback rating distribution. The X-axis shows the feedback rating; Y-axis shows the number of reviews. Legend: 0 - not rated; 1, ..., 5, where one is the most negative, and 5 is the most positive assessment [12]. The correlation matrix on Fig. 3 is a square table in which at the intersection of the corresponding row and column there is a correlation coefficient between the corresponding attributes : 'responses_rating_grade', 'comments','views', 'have_email', "responses_message_length', 'gunning_fog_index'. The color shows us the power of interconnection [12].

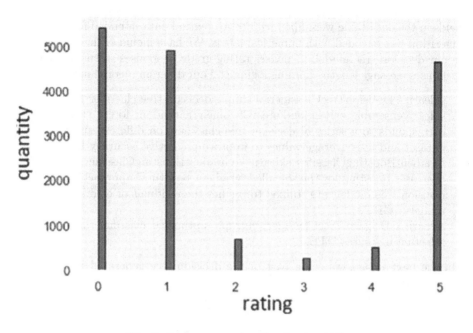

Fig. 2. Responses rating distribution [12]

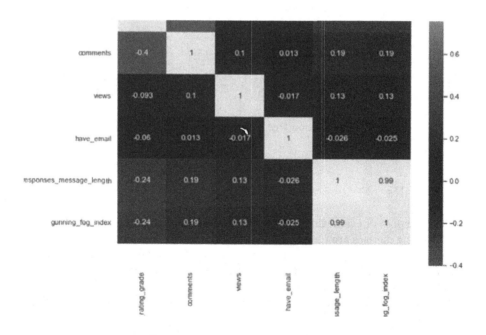

Fig. 3. The correlation matrix [12]

In the first step, data cleaning and adjustment were performed. All empty fields in the data table were filled with 0. All textual data intended for use in the algorithm was encoded with numerical labels. We have included these attributes in our decision tree model: responses rating grade, responses status, haveemail, responses message length, gunning fogindex. Four different algorithms were used:

- sklearn - DecisionTreeClassifier: a simple decision tree classifier-DT
- sklearn.ensemble - RandomForestClassifie|r a random forest classifier that corresponds to a series of decision tree classifiers on different subsets of the dataset and uses average values to improve predictive accuracy-DF.
- GradientBoostingClassifier.sklearn - GradientBoostingClassifier: a classifier that uses boosting, or the so-called "gradient boosting" approach, where new decision tree models are trained to predict the residuals or errors of previous models - GBC
- sklearn - DecisionTreeClassifier: entropic optimized classifier, uses different selection measures-DTE.

On the next image, we see a part of the decision tree generated by the DTE classifier (Fig. 4).

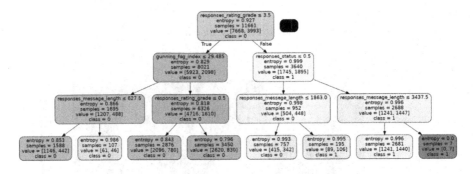

Fig. 4. The decision tree generated by the DTE classifier.

4   Results

For the purpose of evaluating the performance of predictive models in this work, the following metrics are used: confusion matrix, recall, precision, F1-score, accuracy, and Receiver Operating Characteristic (ROC) curve. Receiver Operating Characteristic (ROC) curve refers to a graphical representation commonly used in binary classification to evaluate the performance of a model [14]. Specifically, it illustrates the trade-off between sensitivity (true positive rate) and specificity (true negative rate) at various thresholds:

- True Positive Rate (Sensitivity): This is the proportion of actual positive instances correctly identified by the model.

- False Positive Rate: This is the proportion of actual negative instances incorrectly identified as positive by the model.

The ROC curve is created by plotting the true positive rate against the false positive rate at different classification thresholds. The area under the ROC curve (AUC) is often used as a metric to quantify the model's discriminatory power. A higher AUC indicates better overall performance.

Table 2. Comparison of Metric - Precision

	DT	RF	GBC	DTE
Clas 0	0.67	0.68	0.68	0.70
Clas 1	0.39	0.44	0.43	0.53
Macro avg.	0.53	0.59	0.56	0.62
Weighted avg.	0.57	0.60	0.59	0.64

The model with the highest value of the precision metric, i.e., the ability to accurately classify only the recognized instances, is the Decision Tree optimized Classifier (Table 2).

Table 3. Comparison of Metric - recall

	DT	RF	GBC	DTE
Clas 0	0.68	0.77	0.76	0.85
Clas 1	0.38	0.33	0.34	0.32
Macro avg.	0.53	0.55	0.55	0.58
Weighted avg.	0.58	0.62	0.61	0.66

The model with the highest recall metric, i.e., the ability to correctly classify all relevant instances in the dataset, is the Decision Tree optimized Classifier (Table 3).

Table 4. Comparison of Metric - f1-score

	DT	RF	GBC	DTE
Clas 0	0.68	0.72	0.72	0.77
Clas 1	0.39	0.38	0.35	0.40
Macro avg.	0.53	0.55	0.55	0.58
Weighted avg.	0.57	0.60	0.60	0.64

The model with the highest value of the F1-score metric, i.e., the harmonic mean of precision and recall, is the Decision Tree optimized Classifier (Table 4).

Table 5. Comparison of Metric - accuracy

	DT	RF	GBC	DTE
accuracy	0.58	0.62	0.61	0.66

The model with the highest value of the accuracy metric, i.e., the ability to accurately classify only the recognized instances, is the Decision Tree optimized Classifier (Table 5).

Table 6. Comparison of Metric - confusion matrix

	DT	RF	GBC	DTE
TP	2207	2502	2467	2767
FP	1082	1172	1156	1197
FN	1042	747	782	482
TN	667	577	593	552

The DT Classifier has the best performance in terms of the True Negative (TN) metric - 667. Additionally, the value of False Positives (FP), i.e., falsely positive transactions, is the lowest for the DT Classifier. As for the metrics TP (True Positive) and FN (False negative), the DTE Classifier yields the best results.

The ROC curve is a performance measure used in classification problems. ROC, or Receiver Operating Characteristic curve, represents a probability curve, while AUC (Area Under Curve) represents the rate of separability of classes [15]. The higher the AUC value, the better the model is at predicting TP (True Positive) and TN (True Negative) values. Similarly, a larger AUC indicates that the model is better at distinguishing between different predicted classes.

Table 7. Comparison of Metric - Receiver Operating Characteristic curve.

	DT	RF	GBC	DTE
AUC	0.530	0.549	0.549	0.583

As can be gleaned from Table 7, the AUC metric once again demonstrates the best performance, showcasing the Decision Tree optimized Classifier. In conclusion, this Classifier proved to be the best predictive model for detecting negative user reactions in this dataset.

5   Conclusion

There are various use cases of machine learning in the banking sector, and the most significant cases have proven to be fraud detection and credit risk assessment. This method can be applied in various domains, including business analysis, medical diagnostics, finance, and other areas where decision-making is required based on complex sets of information. Machine learning methodology, along with its mathematical predictive models such as decision trees, random forests, and boosting, represents a toolkit that enables businesses, banks, and other institutions to develop complex and efficient decision support systems. Decision trees and related techniques in the field of machine learning have proven to be a key tool in developing predictive models and, more broadly, decision support systems in banking. Decision tree is a predictive machine learning model that can be applied to classification and regression problems, characterized by a hierarchical approach and recursive binary branching. If the performance of the decision tree is inadequate for solving a specific problem, advanced techniques such as ensemble methods like random forests and boosting are employed. Through a specific practical example of developing a system for detecting negative user comments based on a real dataset, the benefit of creating predictive models as assistance in a banking financial system has been demonstrated. Various models were used for performance demonstration, including DecisionTreeClassifier, RandomForestClassifier, and GradientBoostingClassifier. Based on the metrics used: precision, recall, F-1 score, confusion matrix, and AUC, it was shown that the DecisionTreeClassifier, based on the concept of tree pruning, performs the best in detecting negative user comments in a banking financial system.

References

1. Zhou, H., Zhang, J., Zhou, Y., Guo, X., Ma, Y.: A feature selection algorithm of decision tree based on feature weight. Expert Syst. Appl. **164**, 113842 (2021). ISSN 0957-4174. https://doi.org/10.1016/j.eswa.2020.113842
2. Higgins, J.C.: Decision making at board level using decision analysis: two case studies. J. Oper. Res. Soc. **33**(4), 319–326 (1982)
3. Dey, P.K.: Project risk management using multiple criteria decision-making technique and decision tree analysis: a case study of Indian oil refinery. Prod. Plan. Control **23**(12), 903–921 (2012)
4. Kori, G.S., Kakkasageri, M.S.: Classification and regression tree (cart) based resource allocation scheme for wireless sensor networks. Comput. Commun. **197**, 242–254 (2023)
5. Pawliczek, A., Kozel, R., Vilamová, Š.: Strategic management and performance of enterprises evaluated using chaid decision tree analysis. In: Scientific Papers of the University of Pardubice. Series D, Faculty of Economics and Administration. 44/2018 (2018)
6. Miró-Julià, M., Fiol-Roig, G., Isern-Deyà, A.P.: Decision trees in stock market analysis: construction and validation. In: García-Pedrajas, N., Herrera, F., Fyfe, C., Benítez, J.M., Ali, M. (eds.) IEA/AIE 2010. LNCS (LNAI), vol. 6096, pp. 185–194. Springer, Heidelberg (2010). https://doi.org/10.1007/978-3-642-13022-9_19

7. Podhorska, I., et al.: Innovations in financial management: recursive prediction model based on decision trees. Mark. Manag. Innov. (3) (2020)

8. Kim, J.K., et al.: Detecting the change of customer behavior based on decision tree analysis. Expert Syst. **22**(4), 193–205 (2005)

9. Gordini, N., Veglio, V.: Customer relationship management and data mining: a classification decision tree to predict customer purchasing behavior in global market. In: Business Intelligence: Concepts, Methodologies, Tools, and Applications, pp. 1362–1401. IGI Global (2016)

10. Strielkina, A., Tetskyi, A., Krasilshchykova, V.: Risk and uncertainty assessment in software project management: integrating decision trees and Monte Carlo modeling. Radioelectron. Comput. Syst. **3**, 217–225 (2023)

11. Priyanka, Kumar, D.: Decision tree classifier: a detailed survey. Int. J. Inf. Decis. Sci. **12**(3), 246–269 (2020)

12. Plotnikov, A., Shcheludyakov, A., Cherdantsev, V., Bochkarev, A., Zagoruiko, I.: Data on post bank customer reviews from web. Data Brief **32**, 106152 (2020). ISSN 2352-3409. https://doi.org/10.1016/j.dib.2020.106152. https://www.sciencedirect.com/science/article/pii/S2352340920310465

13. Rodríguez Timaná, L.C., Saavedra Lozano, D.F., Castillo García, J.F.: Software to determine the readability of written documents by implementing a variation of the gunning fog index using the google linguistic corpus. In: Botto-Tobar, M., Zambrano Vizuete, M., Torres-Carrión, P., Montes León, S., Pizarro Vásquez, G., Durakovic, B. (eds.) ICAT 2019. CCIS, vol. 1193, pp. 409–420. Springer, Cham (2020). https://doi.org/10.1007/978-3-030-42517-3_31

14. Park, S.H., Goo, J.M., Jo, C.H.: Receiver operating characteristic (ROC) curve: practical review for radiologists. Kor. J. Radiol. **5**(1), 11 (2004)

15. Bradley, A.P.: The use of the area under the ROC curve in the evaluation of machine learning algorithms. Pattern Recogn. **30**(7), 1145–1159 (1997)

Author Index

T. Volarić et al. (Eds.): MoStart 2024, CCIS 2124, p. 289, 2024.
https://doi.org/10.1007/978-3-031-62058-4

Printed in the United States
by Baker & Taylor Publisher Services